P9-DOE-803

BY JUDD APATOW

Sicker in the Head: More Conversations About Life and Comedy

It's Garry Shandling's Book

Sick in the Head: Conversations About Life and Comedy

I Found This Funny

SICKER
IN THE
HEAD

SICKER IN THE HEAD

More Conversations About Life and Comedy

JUDD APATOW

RANDOM HOUSE  NEW YORK

Published in the United States by Random House, an imprint
and division of Penguin Random House LLC, New York.

Random House and the House colophon are registered trademarks
of Penguin Random House LLC.

LIBRARY OF CONGRESS CATALOGING-IN-PUBLICATION DATA
Names: Apatow, Judd, author.
Title: Sicker in the head: more conversations about life and comedy / Judd Apatow.
Description: First edition. | New York: Random House, [2022]
Identifiers: LCCN 2021048092 (print) | LCCN 2021048093 (ebook) |
ISBN 9780525509417 (hardcover; acid-free paper) | ISBN 9780525509431 (ebook)
Subjects: LCSH: Comedians—United States—Interviews. | Stand-up comedy—United
States. | Television actors and actresses—United States—Interviews. | Motion picture
actors and actresses—United States—Interviews. | LCGFT: Interviews.
Classification: LCC PN1969.C65 A64 2022 (print) | LCC PN1969.C65 (ebook) |
DDC 792.7/60922—dc23/eng/20211221
LC record available at https://lccn.loc.gov/2021048092
LC ebook record available at https://lccn.loc.gov/2021048093

Printed in the United States of America on acid-free paper

randomhousebooks.com

2 4 6 8 9 7 5 3 1

ScoutAutomatedPrintCode

First Edition

Dedicated to all the people who make us laugh,
whether they get paid for it or not.

And to Iris, Maude, and Leslie.

CONTENTS

INTRODUCTION

I started this book before the pandemic. I did a few interviews—Mort Sahl, Whitney Cummings, Nathan Fielder, Gary Gulman—but I wasn't exactly putting a ton of time into it. Then the pandemic hit and I realized that most of the people I wanted to speak with were stuck at home with nothing to do, too. It's hard to say no to an interview when it is clear you are available. We all were available—for everything.

So, I began making calls and lining up conversations. And as we talked, a weird thing happened: Many of these conversations became way more personal and honest than they otherwise might have been, because we were in this vulnerable, raw space together. It's hard to hold back in an interview when you have been pondering your life (and death) for the past few months—when not overeating, drinking, or watching streaming programming you don't even like.

Finishing this project was challenging. There were so many people I wanted to speak to, and I knew that as soon as the world calmed down it would become much harder to get access to them. As things opened up again, I was forced to give up my quest for Pete Townshend and Meghan Markle. Maybe for the next book. (Or the next pandemic?)

It's hard to write the intro to this book because I still feel so in between. I am not who I was before the pandemic began and yet I am not sure who I am now. I am, frankly, existentially confused. What meaning does my life have? What is the point of all of the work I have done? Why am I so disinterested and interested at the same time? How come I have become so close to my cats? Why do I keep getting more cats? Maybe the conversations in this book will shed some light on these questions.

Other than my love for my family, the one consistent observation I have had, during all of this madness, is that I needed to laugh. I needed the insights of comic minds. I also was told by a lot of people that my work had given them brief, happy breaks from all we are experiencing, which was nice. I spent months getting those same breaks with *Ted Lasso, Schitt's Creek, Jackass,* and anything by Maria Bamford.

I have always seen comedy as a lifeline—which is why I've been interviewing comedians about why they do what they do since I was fifteen years old. Without comedy, I don't know how I would survive. When the pandemic was at full force, I grabbed my family and made a really silly movie. I didn't know what else to do. Is that healthy? Is it denial? Is it medicine? Is it sick? I am not sure. But now I know that when the world seems to be collapsing my reaction is to make a movie about a group of people having a meltdown during a pandemic as they attempt to make a movie about flying dinosaurs. The process of making that film with my family got me through. It gave me purpose: to be ridiculous. Isn't it all ridiculous? It also got me out of the house and into a community of people with the same goal—to make people smile. When the shit hits the fan that is all I have to offer. I may not know how to turn the gas off when the building is on fire, but I might be able to make you piss your pants. That's got to be worth something?

I am still struggling. I don't feel right. But maybe if things get back to normal, and maybe after I do another book and make a few more ridiculous movies, I will feel right again. And the world will have some more weird stuff to read and some more stupid shit to watch with the shades closed as the world teeters outside.

SICKER
IN THE
HEAD

AMBER RUFFIN

December 2020

Judd: I am amazed at how strong so much of the political work that people like you and the other writers at *Late Night with Seth Meyers* are doing. I'm astounded that people can take things that are so horrifying and find a way to turn it into something that has joy and entertainment in it. The country has always been a disaster, but it's hit another level these last few years. How has it been for you to develop this skill of political comedy at a time like this?

Amber: I'm always pressing right up against it. I think to myself, *Can I talk about all of this stuff?* And you're right, the ugly stuff has always been there. But I feel like I'm slowly revealing it, little by little. Plus, they'll let me talk about all kinds of shit now. There are no rules.

Judd: It's really changed, the idea that you were allowed to say that things are fucked, right?

Amber: You can't complain too much, no matter how true it is, or else you're a bad guy. So you have to choose what you swallow and what you call out. Luckily, I'm in comedy so no one cares if you say something provocative. But for some normal lady in an office to be like, "I'm not Black Linda. I'm Linda"? And people go, "Yeah, it was shitty of me to say that"?

Judd: I often think about the journey comedians go on, before they fully mature and come into their own. First, you have years of just figuring out how to get up onstage and not be terrified. Then, slowly, you get older and you realize what you want to talk about, now that you have the skills to talk about it. It takes a long time to get comfortable enough and to be strong enough to then move into what matters to you, whether it's politics and social issues or not. Did you have an arc like that, or did you talk about these things from day one?

Amber: When I did the Second City Mainstage, we did all kinds of political stuff. We were performing for a young, liberal audience, and they loved it. But you can't do that with your regular improv show because you don't necessarily know the audience or the people you're improvising with. So, I certainly didn't start out making any provocative political points right off the bat. I also did Boom Chicago for years. Are you familiar with it?

Judd: Jason Sudeikis started there.

Amber: Jason Sudeikis, Seth Meyers, Jordan Peele, Kay Cannon . . . And actually, Boom Chicago is located in Amsterdam. There's no Boom Chicago in Chicago. But they audition you in Chicago, L.A., New York, and so on. Once you're picked, you go to Amsterdam, and you have four corporate shows a week. I hosted the International Paper Awards, for instance. And there are a number of game shows that are based in Holland, so when they have an idea and they want to shoot a pilot, they go to Boom Chicago, and they pick us.

Judd: How long did you go for? I was recently talking to someone who did that for a year or two.

Amber: Almost everyone was there for two years.

Judd: That's so long. Do you get better at what you do in that environment?

Amber: You become untouchable when it comes to writing, but it's a lot of short-form comedy. That's not everyone's favorite form, but that's all you need, fundamentally. All I need to do is be able to come up with a punch line under pressure; that's all any comedy is. So, once you are doing nine, ten, eleven shows a week over there, you are sharpened by the audience. One time, I was performing for three hundred Italian sailors, and English was their third language. I realized if I could get them to laugh, then I can do anything. An experience like that knocks the fear right out.

Judd: On some level, it's all terrifying, even when you're performing with other people. I remember I had to give out an award with Maya Rudolph at the *Critics Choice Awards.* And there were about seven thousand people in the crowd in L.A., at the Nokia Theatre. As we were walking up the stairs to the stage to do our bit, I had never seen anyone look more confident than Maya Rudolph. I'm shitting a brick, thinking, *Damn I hope this thing works.*

Amber: I think you have to have failed really loud, really big quite a few times. And it has to sting really bad. You have to lose some sleep over how bad it went. And that kind of failure can only happen to you a couple of times before you say to yourself, *No more.*

Judd: Or till you start laughing. I remember Norm Macdonald used to enjoy the bomb. You'd see it in his eyes when it was happening. He just lit up. Did you study improv in college?

Amber: I never went to college. I don't know how I could have ever gotten into college with my grades and lack of money. I also figured out that a lot of college was children talking instead of the teacher. There is no way I could have lasted there for one minute. Also, our drama teacher in high school would say, "People from now on are going to try to teach you how to do theater, but you can't learn unless you do it."

Judd: That's kind of arrogant of the teacher. He sort of told you guys, "I just taught you everything that you could ever learn about this."

Amber: He was cocky, and right. You're created by the audience.

Judd: What kind of improv group were you a part of in Omaha?

Amber: It was the best little group of friends rehearsing and doing shows downtown together. We just did long-form improv. Everyone who came to see one of those shows is a saint. It was so bad. So bad.

Judd: Did you think you would ever get anywhere else?

Amber: Never. Firstly, everyone was white. But also, I just thought, *When I get to perform at a tiny theater downtown, it'll be the best.* And I was right. Every time, it was a delight. I loved those people so much. We put on beautiful shows. But what did stick with me was when we would do a show that someone in that group wrote, I would always ask, "How did you do that?" and they would always say, "I sat down and I wrote it." That was interesting to me, but I also didn't think that it was actually possible.

Judd: What was your day job when you were doing that at night?

Amber: I was having people sign things downtown. I had a clipboard, and people would sign forms and stuff. I was selling them things, but out on the street.

Judd: That's a form of improv. That's confrontational. You learn self-esteem right there, talking to strangers. When did you first make enough money from comedy that [it] allowed you to quit the day job?

Amber: Never. I'm still doing it. Would you buy a magazine? It was after I auditioned for Boom Chicago.

Judd: And then you went to Amsterdam for two years. Did you join Second City when you came back?

Amber: I had just finished up my second year in Amsterdam and had grown tired of it. So, I called Second City on the telephone and I asked, "Will you give me a job?" They said yes, and they moved me to Denver to do a Second City show there for a year. Then I went back to Chicago and did [Second City] Mainstage for two years, and then I went back to Boom Chicago for another three years.

Judd: So, you did a total of five years in Amsterdam. At the end of the last year, was there a moment where you thought, *I've been here long enough*?

Amber: I did think, *Maybe I can have a career here*. I was happy with the thought of living in Amsterdam forever. But I was very aware that, eventually, I was going to be an old Black lady—and I've never seen an old Black lady do improv. So, I got married to a Dutch guy and then moved to Los Angeles to make it as an actress.

Judd: And how did that go?

Amber: Horribly. It was truly terrible. I hate auditioning. I'm bad at it.

Judd: Kevin Hart would always say, "I'm just trying to make this casting person laugh so they remember me for something at some point. This audition is just for me to show you I'm talented, I don't even care if I don't get the part." But I know so few people who could emotionally pull that off. It is a soul-crushing experience, because you also think to yourself, *I could do hundreds of these and never work the rest of my life*.

Amber: Absolutely.

Judd: Did you have to bail on L.A., or did you get something that kept you there for a little bit?

Amber: While I was in L.A., I was a part of a theater called Sacred Fools Theater. We all just wrote stuff and put it up all the time.

That gave me life. It was a really nice thing to hold on to. Then I got the call to audition for *SNL*. But I didn't get it, and I felt like I could have died. I don't really know what this says about me, but I thought for sure I was going to get the job. I was so certain, which is so unlike me.

Judd: Did you feel like you had a good audition?

Amber: Yeah, it was great. But I went up just as Leslie Jones was finishing. And as I'm coming in, people are *still* laughing. She's yards and yards away, she's done with her audition, and people are still laughing.

Judd: That'll hurt your confidence, just stepping into the energy of that room. But you still had a good audition.

Amber: I had a good audition. Four of us got to stay and watch the show and talk to everyone so they can see if you're crazy or not. And the other three women—Sasheer Zamata, Leslie Jones, and LaKendra Tookes—all got hired.

Judd: How soon after that audition did Seth call you about his show?

Amber: Three days after I heard about *SNL*, Seth called me and asked, "Will you do my show?" We knew each other previously, too. He would come to Boom Chicago every year and would see me up there. So, he knew who I was, and I knew who he was.

Judd: How do you look at the *SNL* audition in retrospect? Do you go, *Oh, that's a missed opportunity*?

Amber: Not so much, because at *Late Night*, everyone is very kind and supportive. I'm not going to say that they coddle you, but they do a little bit.

Judd: Seth's a special type of leader. I've heard people talk about him as the best head writer ever at *SNL*. His people felt supported and encouraged. He specifically creates an environment where people do their best work.

Amber: And that's all he wants. Some managers think it's important for you to show up on time and format your scripts a specific way, or else. It's important that you never make a mistake and always have your this and your that. But for Seth, you get the sense that all he wants is our best work, and that however he's going to get it—if you have to be ten minutes late to work every day—he doesn't care. And if a script isn't perfect, he doesn't care—the script department will help fix it. Seth is just like, "Get me my laughs." And I like that.

Judd: It's a different environment also because you're featuring yourself. Your ideas are not watered down; you're able to come up with things for yourself, such as characters and sketches. It doesn't sound like you're at war with the other writers, competing to get stuff on the air. That kind of competition can crush people.

Amber: I don't know that I would have been up for the challenge. I think they might have been able to shout me down. And I would have easily been like, "Yeah, yeah, let me write for you. You want something?" I think I could have become that person. It's scary to think.

Judd: Now you're doing your own show. How do you split your time between writing your own show and writing for Seth?

Amber: I'm always writing as much as possible. Sometimes what I write goes into the Seth pile, and sometimes it goes into the Ruffin pile. I would love to be the kind of person who says, *I specifically think of this for this show, and bada boom!* But my process looks more like, *Which of these ideas make it to the end of the sketch? Okay, those are the ideas that are good to go. Which one of these should I hand in to Seth, and which one should I keep?* I do it like that.

Judd: You started your show without a live audience. You're completely exposed because there's no support of an audience or the feedback of their laughter. But instead, it looks like you're creating this intimate connection with the audience at home, *I have no tricks. It's me and you, right here.* How did that feel to launch? What was your personal take on how to even approach a challenge like this?

Amber: *The Amber Ruffin Show* started after months and months of quarantine. We had already been doing shows from home, so I had already done bits from my couch. Once we started, and we got to shoot from the studio, I thought, *I love this. I'm not on my couch anymore.* I never missed the audience, even though I was looking at two hundred empty seats. It doesn't feel weird. Performing in front of an audience feels like a million years ago. And comics always say, "Oh, you miss the laughs." But you know what? I don't miss the silence. No one talks about that, about what it feels like to do a joke and it just doesn't land. I know I'm going to get wrecked when the audience comes back in there. I'll be standing out on the edge of a punch line to nothing. It's going to be horrible.

Judd: You must write differently when you know you don't have to worry if a joke bombs, because as long as you believe in the joke, it doesn't matter, right? I wonder what it'll feel like for everybody when showbiz returns. Will people be better? Will it be richer in some way?

Amber: Everything is getting so weird. We have built this whole show in quarantine thus far. If we ever get the chance to do it in front of an audience, will they be like, *We don't like this. You already sang a song, what are you doing?* Who knows how people are going to react? I'm also scared that when we get an audience, I'm just going to be hamming it up and go way off script because I'm just feeling the vibe. That's entirely possible, too. Who knows? I just know it's going to be a mess.

Judd: Did you feel like you learned something from the lack of a crowd? When you were doing the bits about racism and police brutality, it seemed like it would have felt different with a crowd. Maybe you would have felt the need to be funny, but the lack of crowd may have allowed it to be exactly what it was.

Amber: It was certainly an exercise in learning that we don't always have to go up there and tell a bunch of jokes. Sometimes, you can just be honest. You don't have to say something you wrote, rewrote, and then rewrote again. You can just say your true feelings. I kind of already knew that that was true, but I just didn't know it was true to that extent.

Judd: People had such a strong reaction to your stories about everyday racism and your interactions with the police.

Amber: I've worked here for six years, going on seven. And over that time, I've maybe received four pieces of fan mail. When I got back to the office after doing that show, there was a huge stack of cards from white people who said, "I cannot believe this, I cannot believe that this happened to you. This really makes me take a hard look at what the world is like for other people. It makes me look back at my life and remember all the times where I believed the police instead of the people." People just really understood it. They took what I said, and they wrung all the truth out of it. I couldn't believe it.

Judd: What is your process when you're working on a bit like that, where it's funny, but it's also about this really urgent, weighty issue?

Amber: When George Floyd's murder happened, I immediately wrote a sketch and turned it in. Less than twenty-four hours later, the whole country shifted, and I realized that I couldn't do that sketch anymore. I thought, *Let me write a rant, instead. A real mean rant where I stick it to everybody.* But by the time I'd written that rant, everything else changed again. The whole thing felt crazy. And while there was a national outcry, there were some people who were saying that police brutality just wasn't that big, or widespread, of a problem. There were some people saying that George Floyd's death was one isolated incident, and that just made me feel crazy. So, then I pitched to the showrunners that I tell a story, just a real story from my own life. And they said okay. I recorded it, they played it at the top of the show—which I didn't expect—and it was ultimately well received. Afterward, I went to my colleagues and said, "Hey, how many of these do you want to do? I have a million of these stories."

Judd: That experience is a great example of how comedy can be hugely impactful. But there has also always been that element of comedy that's just plain stupid—a break from the ugliness of the real world. When Trump lost the election, for example, I wondered if some people in comedy thought, *Thank God. I just want to do some fart jokes for a year or two.* Your show is very much focused on the news, and I think we're still going to be deeply polarized going forward. Has this experience changed your thoughts about the purpose of comedy?

Amber: My goal with my show is always to de-gaslight a nation. That's always the first goal. Wait, sorry, that's always the *second* goal. My *first* goal is to get them sweet, sweet laughs. Second goal is de-gaslight a nation. But comedy is just telling the truth. Eventually we'll get to a point in our society where we're going to be able to say, "This horrible thing happened, but this is how I feel about it. And this is a part of our history. Let's fix it." But to get to your question, I also think comedy is whatever people want it to be. I'm sure there's someone out there right now farting into a microphone, and their friends love it. That's fine, too. I don't think comedy has to just be commentary about what's happening in the world. Not everybody has to do that. Not everybody has time for it. Not everybody feels like doing it. But we can't all just be one thing. I need to be able to watch a dinosaur slam-dunk a basketball. And I need to be able to watch someone satirize what is happening. I've got to have all of it. And even though

Trump lost the election, I don't think we're going to go back to the way things were before he came into the office: You can't unring this bell. We know too much now, as a society. Everyone feels like it's not enough to just not be racist. We've got to be antiracist. And my hope is that, going forward, when people see racist shit, they'll call it out for what it is, and that will just be a regular part of our reality.

Judd: People are wrong to think of entertainment and show business as unilaterally progressive. You're the first Black woman with a political comedy talk show, and it's 2020. Historically, talk shows almost never had female writers—even some of our favorite people took forever to hire a woman on the writing staff.

Amber: There was Whoopi Goldberg and Wanda Sykes and Robin Thede. Other shows had Black female writers, like *Chappelle's Show*. But in terms of network TV, then yes, it's true that I was the first Black woman writer with a show.

Judd: We're now seeing a sea change when it comes to representation both onscreen and throughout the business, where everyone's like, "We can't do this anymore, we can't just hire white men." It feels very real right now, and it feels as though it will stick.

Amber: Yes, and also, the word is out about how good Black women are at the job, no matter what that job is. The only true stereotype about Black women is how Black women will say, "Well, no one's doing it, so I guess I'll do it." Once you put that lady in your office, no matter what your office is, if you treat her right, she is going to do your job and her job. And I think people are slowly realizing that. So, I agree with you that this shift in representation, this shift in hiring practices, might just stick around, because once you create a safe space for Black people at your job, which a lot of television shows are capable of doing now, then you see Black people excel. It really is electrifying.

Judd: So many comedians are sensitive to being criticized when they're awful. They'll defend themselves by saying, "Oh, I'm just working that premise out." Obviously we all believe in freedom of speech, but it seems like comedians in particular don't want to be criticized when they say things that are wrong or hurtful. They can be the most thin-skinned people in the world in that regard. In this moment, you do feel the division in the comedy world. There are the free-speechers who are like, "Leave me alone. I'm allowed to make mistakes." And then there are other people who want to be sure that comedians are tuning in to these cultural shifts, where we're trying to figure out what hurts people and what makes people feel seen.

Amber: I haven't had to make a public apology yet, but I think I can imagine what that would look like. I think if I said something that hurt a bunch of people's feelings, I would hate it, because that's not my goal. That is severely off-brand for me. I'm trying to give everybody a hug, and I don't want to hurt people's feelings—unless they're racist, of course. I do believe that you do not have to be nice to people who do not value you as a human being. When someone treats you like shit, raise your hand and say something. We have to shake off that conditioning that taught us that we can't do anything about mistreatment. I can't act like you're a nice person if you don't care if my workplace is safe, if you don't care if I can't breathe because a police officer is using excessive force. I want people to think about what it must do to minorities to be told that they are second-class citizens by their president and then to be expected to look at his supporters in the face and smile. That is not good for you, and you don't have to be part of it.

BOWEN YANG

June 2021

Judd: I want to talk about *Las Culturistas*, the podcast you're doing with Matt Rogers. How did you two meet?

Bowen: Matt and I met in college. We were both in the closet at NYU, which was just such a funny place to be in the closet, especially circa 2008. I was in the improv group, and he was in the sketch group, and we were both just obsessed with comedy. Recent alums of note from NYU at that point were, like, Donald Glover and D.C. Pierson, and we were just like, "This is the future." And we put in the work early on and just started to write. My awful snobbery with people who are working in comedy is *This can't be your plan B.*

Judd: Sometimes I go to a comedy club and see all these hilarious people onstage, and I wonder if they've ever sat down and written a sketch or a screenplay. Or taken the effort to ask themselves, *What else can I do with my talent and ideas?*

Bowen: I think I heard the legend that you told Bill Hader, maybe during his second season of *SNL*, that he had to start putting the wheels in motion then, so that things will bear fruit further down the line.

Judd: Absolutely. And I did it *with* Bill, where he worked on a screenplay for us and with some writers from *SNL*, and we just never cracked it. That screenplay was never made. But we did write a lot together. He said that he was writing like seven screenplays over the course of his time at *SNL*, of which none were made. But that was all his rehearsal for *Barry*. He was learning what to do. You have to write, because nobody will be able to write the thing for you that you probably should be doing. It's daunting to figure out, *How does this character or persona work in a full story, in a full movie?* That has been the challenge for some *SNL* people: It's about figuring out who you are *separate* from your characters. Once you get past that initial challenge, there's still the precariousness of the movie business, where you could commit the time to get a movie going, and you still don't know if someone will want to make it happen.

Bowen: All of that runs counter to the *SNL* process, where there's such an efficiency with how things are made. Nothing gets made like that anymore except for summer stock theater. I'm getting a little *too* used to this. But even now I'm realizing, *Oh the credits don't transfer from SNL, because none of it is made like this.* And also, the performance style is you're pitching to the rafters and you're screaming and you're reading off a cue card. That's not how it works anywhere else.

Judd: It must be an interesting moment for you. When I first started, I felt unrepresented in Hollywood. It was like, *Why can't the goofy, unattractive person ever be the lead?* So, in my work over the years, I tried to prove that that was possible, because the non-cool guy as the lead wasn't available in the culture when I was young. Now our culture has evolved to where people are trying to correct for the fact that performers of color and LGBTQ+ performers have been criminally underrepresented. What does this moment feel like for you?

Bowen: I think, for a long time, Asian people would be used as an existential punch line. Now what's happening is that, on a collective scale, everyone's kind of getting on the same page—we're catching up to some baseline understanding about what the material realities are for Asians in the business. And I don't know where that's going yet; I have no foresight into what it will be like. This is all kind of a new thing, and I'm trying not to erase and destroy what people like Margaret Cho have accomplished, or what Alec Mapa has done as a queer Asian comedian. All the groundwork has been laid out by that generation; I'm just benefiting from coming in at the right time. That's basically how I feel about being at *SNL*, too. It's like, *Oh I lucked out so, so, so deeply.*

Judd: Do you feel like you have a responsibility to use your position?

Bowen: I approach every week at *SNL* without a care for how something will be received on a social level. The week after the Atlanta shooting in March, I called the one other Asian writer on the show. We got on the phone and were just in a terrible mood, because everything around that story was so bleak. But we asked each other, "How do we want to approach this? Do we address it at all? Do we take a hard left and just not even think about that, and do something that has nothing to do with what happened?" By Saturday, the end result of those conversations was this kind of strident rallying cry, a "Weekend Update" piece that wasn't particularly funny, but it did bring levity to the situation in whatever way it could. And I had such a weird hangover the next week about it being received well. People were very kind about it, but I was like, *I don't know, I don't want this to be my role at the show.*

Judd: You didn't want to be like Jon Stewart after 9/11 every week.

Bowen: Even for just one week. Jon Stewart shouldn't even be in that position, you know?

Judd: The people who are doing political comedy these days have to be the commentators on tragedy and the worst of humanity. It's such a strange thing that's happened in comedy, and people are brilliant at it. But I know what you mean. I can't even imagine being in their shoes, thinking, *This shooting just happened, let me try out this piece.*

Bowen: Well, the thought was *I don't have all the answers,* that I shouldn't even be doing this. Afterward, I really couldn't make sense of how I felt about it. Then, two weeks later, I did another "Weekend Update" piece where I was the iceberg who sank the *Titanic,* and that was just purely me doing my job. It was me co-writing this piece with one of the head writers, Anna Drezen, and creating a fun moment of pure absurdity. Yet the social and political comedy is something that you have to do, especially at a show like *SNL,* and especially now where there's a dearth of Asian people who have this big of a platform. So, I don't bemoan it. It's just an interesting thing to think about.

Judd: You came to America as a kid, and you didn't speak English that well because you were still learning the language, but you obviously had a sense of humor. Did you realize at some point, *That's my thing, I'll be the funny person*? Because that's how I felt as a kid. I was terrible at sports, I didn't think I was as attractive as the people around me—*I guess making people laugh is my thing, because no one else is trying to do it.* Was it similar for you?

Bowen: It was exactly like you're describing it, where I realized, *Humor can be my thing.* I would come into school on Mondays and ask everyone, "Did you guys watch *SNL* or *MADtv* from Saturday?" And some people would be like, "Yeah." Most kids would be like, "No, what are you talking about? My parents don't let me watch that yet." I had these immigrant parents who had no idea what the programming was. So, beyond it being my identity where I was funny and goofy, there was also this extra layer on top where it'll be my thing to nerd out on comedy, too, which at that age just meant watching *SNL* every week. That became the keystone for my identity early on, and then I built concentric circles from there.

Judd: As you were watching *SNL* as a kid, did you ever look at the cast and think, *I'm going to be on there someday*?

Bowen: I have to be very honest with myself and say I never specifically said the words, "I will be on *SNL* someday." But I did have this feeling that it would work out somehow.

Judd: If you have that confidence and drive, then you also know that you need to be ahead of the curve. You know you need to work harder than everybody to realize that dream.

Bowen: Totally. My little secret pet peeve now is the people who are getting into comedy as a fallback. People who were musical theater majors who didn't want to audition and didn't want to do Broadway because that is a whole crazy world of its own. There are those sorts of people who go, *Well, I'll just do comedy instead.* And I'm like, "Uh, it doesn't work like that." I put forward this crazy purity test for those people, where I was like, "No, *you* didn't write down who the writers were on this one episode of *The Office* as it was airing." I just got so snobbish about that, and I need to unlearn that now, because I can't put those gates up for other people who want to get into it through their own means, through their own journey.

Judd: When you went to college, was it your family's dream that you would go into comedy?

Bowen: No.

Judd: Did your parents see this career as an option for you at all, even if they didn't love it for you at first? You did premed for a bit. Did you eventually open up to them and say, "I'd rather do stand-up"?

Bowen: My parents could tell that I took comedy seriously even when I was in high school. It was a very big thing for me as a fifteen-year-old to be a part of this short-form improv group in high school. I thought it was the best thing in the world. I would go downtown every week on Mondays, perform with a bunch of thirty-year-olds, and think, *This is the thing that I enjoy the most.* And my parents could tell I was enjoying it too much. And they had tried to be like—

Judd: "Don't have joy."

Bowen: Not even that. I had expressed many times before that I wanted to be an actor someday. And my parents were like, "Well, Bowen, that's really hard, because there aren't a lot of Asian ones, and that world is full of rejection." They weren't even being domineering; they were just being protective. It was their version of loving me. But when it came time for me to decide on a college, I would visit these campuses and ask them, "Can you tell me about your sketch team here?" That's essentially what I based my whole college decision on, and I ended up at NYU. I knew all of the people's names in the improv group by the April *before* I matriculated. And then I was just obsessed. Everyone around me knew this is what I wanted to do. But I had to take cover behind the premed thing—and it's so ironic that I was such a jerk about being a purist in terms of pursuing comedy, because my backup plan was medicine.

Judd: You just want to yell at all the other people who are being distracted.

Bowen: My distraction was academics. The thing that got me out of bed every morning was the excitement of seeing everyone in my troupe later that day, and that we would run sets, and do this and that. That improv group was my life.

Judd: Did it make your grades better or worse?

Bowen: Worse, oh worse.

Judd: You would have been a terrible, distracted doctor. When did you stop doing premed?

Bowen: I graduated with my degree, and I had my applications in for medical school. And I was taking my MCAT for the second time, and there was the short-answer portion. When I got to that, I remembered the Steve Carell interview where he said that he was thinking of applying to law school after things weren't working out for him acting-wise or comedy-wise, but then he got to the essay portion of the LSAT, and he realized then that he couldn't do it. He couldn't follow through on this law school thing. And then, at that moment, I had this out-of-body experience, thinking about Steve Carell, and zoomed back down to me, and it was just like, *Oh, this is what's happening to me right now. I can't do this.* I voided my score, left the testing center, and called my parents. I was like, "I don't think I can go to med school. I'll figure out how to stay in the city and live in the city and work in the city and make money, but med school isn't going to happen." And they were very confused. To their credit, they gave me a shot to figure it out within two years.

Judd: That's a big biopic moment, walking out of the testing center in protest. Isn't it funny that you have to take it that far, till your entire mind and body break down in the middle of the test. Why do you think your parents gave you a chance to figure things out after that?

Bowen: *The Big Sick* was the first time that we watched a movie that helped my parents understand what I was doing, because all the scenes where he's doing stand-up, I'm like, "That's what I'm trying to do, Mom and Dad." And they were like, "That's interesting," and that was a little proof of concept for them. So, I do my best to not retroactively make my parents out to be people who never rooted for me or who counted on me to fail.

Judd: Did they find you funny, though?

Bowen: No, there's just a big cultural difference between being funny at school with a bunch of kids who speak English and then going home to your parents, who grew up in Communist China. Humor can be culturally specific, and I wasn't nimble enough to pivot between those two worlds. So, I would come home [and] just be this shy, boring kid.

Judd: When was the moment when you would say, "Come to the improv show"?

Bowen: It was in high school, and I don't know if it helped or hurt my case. Because they went, and they didn't get it. They were like, "What is this? We don't understand." Then, at one point during college, they came to see one of my sketch shows at [University of California, Berkeley], and they were like, "We didn't like that. That's not for us."

Judd: They were just honest.

Bowen: They just said, "What are you doing?" And to be fair, I would have rated it as, like, a "six" of a show. It wasn't until Matt and I did this quick little bit on Fallon. My mom went into work the next day, and her coworkers were like, "Oh my God, aren't you so proud of Bowen for being on TV last night?" It took other people to mirror it to her that her son was doing well. Then she was like, "Okay, maybe this will work out."

Judd: For me, my dream to get into comedy wasn't questioned. My family was like, "Yeah, go to that as a career." Even though I had no confidence in anything else in life, I had a delusional confidence in that.

Bowen: I love that for comedy. Either your dream to pursue it is challenged or it's reinforced and supported. Either way, we both end up in the same place where we love comedy. I always love telling people my whole story with my parents and how they have come around only recently. But I also don't think the environment you were raised in, and how comedy figured into it, really makes a difference. If you love it, you love it, and you pursue it. And it has to be a sustained, lifelong thing. You can't have a cursory engagement with it later on in life.

Judd: Your story is so interesting because now you come across as a very bold performer and a very confident performer, but you fought against a lot of judgment. That's the hardest part: to be doubted or to feel a lack of engagement from your parental figures when you're still in your formative years.

Bowen: Sure, and I'm still working through this in therapy, where I don't know how much of it had to do with what it meant to just be a gay kid in the early aughts. All the queer people I know are, in some way, a little damaged from just the process of understanding themselves to be queer. There's this bell hooks quote about how it's not queerness in terms of who I have sex with or what gender I am. It's queerness in terms of living in a world where things are hostile toward you. And I think that's it. I think it transcends my weird little relationship with my parents.

Judd: Is it now possible to feel close and happy and celebrate this with them?

Bowen: For sure. Definitely. My mom came to the show on Mother's Day, and we just all paraded out our moms. And then we got lunch with my dad the next day, and their whole thing to impart on me was like, "You're able to do this, but you should realize and remember that this is very lucky, very fortuitous." I was like "Yeah, of course." And then, ironically enough, Lorne [Michaels] said the same thing to me at that dinner: to just enjoy and appreciate the moment.

Judd: When you're doing something that's working on *SNL*, do you feel how good it is in the moment? Or are you so focused that you don't get the enjoyment till afterward?

Bowen: The only time that's happened has been with the iceberg bit. I knew at the time, and I was like, *I'm having so much fun.* And:

Thank God the audience is on board. Because every other time I've done something on the show, it's only been thinking ahead to: *How are people going to respond? How do I look? Are they going to use this on my reel when I die?* So, that's been the only time. And I don't mean to reduce it down to a mindfulness thing, but it's something where you just feel your feet, you feel the weight of yourself, where you are, and that is enough to bring you to the moment. Right now, I'm tired, but I'm still recouping from just how exhausting the last season was. But I am really grateful to have done it. I keep wanting to frame things as luck.

Judd: What season is this as a performer on the show?

Bowen: I've just finished my second season as a performer. And I had written one season prior to that.

Judd: The show has also never been as multicultural as it is now, and it looks like it's going to keep moving in that direction. That makes it very exciting to watch.

Bowen: I keep thinking about *SNL* as this monolithic thing, but then I remember that it aired in a completely different cultural environment when [Adam] Sandler and [David] Spade and Chris Rock and [Chris] Farley were on. I can't believe that is the same container as what it is now. Or *SNL* in the mid-aughts, when it was [Andy] Samberg and [Bill] Hader and [Kristen] Wiig. Even that feels like a completely different show, too. So often, you're only thinking of the show's highlight reel, where it's just the best stuff, which gives the illusion that it's always at a certain quality level. But really, *SNL* has always been this weird little petri dish of ideas, and it's just stood on the counter in the lab for all these decades. I love the fact that I don't have that much in common with Michael Che in terms of our backgrounds and our approaches to writing and what we've seen in the comedy world thus far. We came from completely different poles. But now he and I have some common ground as far as working at the show goes. We had this really nice moment at the finale, where he brought everyone to his apartment at, like, four A.M., and he and I just had a nice little heart-to-heart. And I couldn't believe it. I would never have expected to get this from Michael Che, of all people. Yet, there he was, with this, like, *sageness* that I never would have thought that I could have access to.

Judd: This was in appreciation of the show and your work for the year?

Bowen: Just for each other, in the way that we both look to each other, like, *Hey, I'm so glad that we experienced this pressure cooker of a show together.*

CAMERON CROWE

September 2020

Judd: What is that line in *Almost Famous*, like, "You are home?"

Cameron: That was improv. A Judd-Apatow-at-the-side-of-the-camera move.

Judd: When were you shooting that movie?

Cameron: Ninety-nine.

Judd: I'm shooting *Freaks and Geeks* at the same time, and I was very aware that you were making a movie that I was so desperate to see. Because your movies before then, *Fast Times at Ridgemont High* and *Say Anything . . .*, taught me how to express my experience of being young in a movie.

Cameron: Do you remember *Over the Edge*, with Matt Dillon? It's like the forgotten cousin. It's pre–John Hughes, and it's about being young from a young person's point of view, and it goes to a crazy place. That's what taught me how to capture being young in a movie. I was like, *Oh, wow, you can do this.* And that gave us *Fast Times.* But the studio always said, "You're never going to have a movie that will work and be seen by an audience if it's just for kids." It needs to be *American Graffiti*; then you'll get the audience. We were told that you need the Ray Walston crowd for it to be a hit. But *Over the Edge* was like somebody bled to make that movie, and Matt Dillon is amazing in it.

Judd: I paid close attention, especially to *Say Anything*. For some reason, it was that and the kid who works at the movie theater in *Fast Times*. What was that character's name?

Cameron: The Rat?

Judd: I really recognized the sweetness of that kid at the movie theater dreaming of being with the pretty girl or the cool girl and going, *Am I allowed in this universe to believe I can be loved by her?*

Cameron: When the Rat leaves Jennifer Jason Leigh and does not follow up and kiss her and stay there, as he's walking down the walkway, having fucked up, half of the audience feels bad for him and half of them wants to throw shit at the screen because he was a wimp.

Judd: On *Freaks and Geeks*, we always talked about cocky nerds. You're a nerd, and everyone can beat the shit out of you, and you're not an athlete, but on some level you think, *I'm better than them.* I'm always amused by the parallels of our high school experience in terms of loving something—music for you, comedy for me—and going, *I need to connect to it.* Not just, *I'm gonna listen to the records*, but *I'm gonna go fucking talk to Gregg Allman.* I did that, but it might have been Steve Allen or Jerry Seinfeld. What do you think it is that made us take that leap?

Cameron: My mom would say that we had magic boots on, that our fervor for this thing that moved us so much pushed us out the door to find the people behind it and complete the fan experience and interview them. We needed to learn about, as a young writer not looking to be a character or an adversary, but a frontline emotional reporter, this feeling that we love so much. That's how it felt for me. I just wanted to get closer to the flame. And I was always worried that somebody was going to be a dick and say, "What are you doing here?" That only happened once. Mostly people were just really grateful for the worshipful interest.

Judd: I remember walking in to interview Jerry Seinfeld in 1983 or '84. His apartment had nothing on the walls, no books in the bookshelves—he was just there to write his jokes. And he looked at me when I walked in like, *I can't believe I have to do this with this child.* But, ultimately, he felt my love for the craft and what he did, and he started enjoying it and letting me know how it worked. It's funny that even in rock and roll, which you think would be more intimidating than nerdy comedians, they sense your knowledge and your affection for it.

Cameron: The Allman Brothers [Band] experiences, the first time I went on the road . . . I couldn't believe that all these people were talking to me. There had been a *Rolling Stone* reporter named Grover Lewis who went on the road with the Allman Brothers Band and did a hit piece on Duane and Gregg—basically called them crackers. That band was really wounded by that and did not want to talk to *Rolling Stone,* but for some reason, Dickey Betts let me in, and then Gregg started talking to me. But the night before I left, Gregg freaked out and wanted all the tapes back. *This kid could be from the FBI and be here to bust us.* So, that really is the scene in *Almost Famous,* where I'm in the airport and I run into my sister, who I haven't seen in a while, and she's like, "What are you doing here? You're a wreck." That moment for me was like, *I have no magic boots. I am a fool. Everything I've ever thought of myself and everything that anybody ever said to me at school that was brutal and vicious is true. And it's over.* I went home a failure, and it was photographer Neal Preston who went on the tour and got my tapes back from Gregg. I never called *Rolling Stone,* because they would have fired me for even having had that happen, much less not having written about it yet. So, I owe everything to them getting those tapes back from Gregg, because

I would have never had another shot at *Rolling Stone*. It would have been over. I probably would have been a poor, untalented lawyer, because my heart would have been with music.

Judd: Who was your first mentor? Was it Lester Bangs? Who was the first person that actually walked you through it?

Cameron: There were a number of them. Ben Fong-Torres was one. Bill Maguire, the editor of the San Diego *Door*. He was pretty hilarious. Robert Hilburn was another person that gave me an assignment but said, "You're on a road here where you could be the victim of publicists. Be careful." But Lester was so charismatic and such a big figure that you got a physical buzz around him. You knew that whether it was part performance or charisma or passion or whatever, this was a full-blooded dude that you wanted to be like, so he was probably the most all-purpose mentor. Until Jim Brooks.

Judd: Do you remember any of the things he told you about the actual writing?

Cameron: He said, "Hey, man, sometimes I stay up all night. I just drink a little cough syrup, and I just write." This little underground paper in San Diego, they had this black cabinet, which was files and articles and promotional things that had been sent to them. I was looking through it, because they let me hang out in their communal office, and I found this big fucking wad of stuff that was in a file. I started looking at it, and it was all reviews by Lester Bangs. Unsolicited, just shit that he had written in those hallowed nights where he was just writing to write. He'd write them on the back of promotional bios, eight-by-tens of Bruce Lee and shit—on anything that's nearby. None of them were published. He would delete going backward and just writing xxxxx over the sentence he had just written, so it was all in a rush, and I read those things and it was like, *This is the shit. This is like a guy opening up his veins. Not doing it for any agenda except to get it out of his system and put it in the mail and send it to this little newspaper.* You got to love writing to do this. You got to love it. And nobody can say, "No, this is not the right job for you." Nobody can say that, because you turned on the spigot out of pure love, and it's coming out of you now. That was the biggest lesson of Lester.

Judd: I always say, "It's so weird that you get paid to make movies and make comedy," because there's no scenario [in which] I *wouldn't* do it. It just happens to be something that there's a marketplace for. You could love something, like playing the spoons, and you never make any money, but you got to play the spoons. I always felt that way in my gut. *This is the thing that I'm supposed to do.* I thought that on some level from the time I was nine or ten years old. I was fascinated by these people, but also fascinated by rock and roll and jazz. My grandfather Bobby Shad produced the first Janis Joplin record.

Cameron: I love that story.

Judd: They just talked about it all the time, "Janis was the best," but also, "Janis fucked it all up," "She died from drugs, don't do drugs." So, it was both the thing that inspired me, like, *My grandfather was a hustler who found Janis Joplin,* and at the same time, this thing that was scary, like, *Oh, you can die from this.* They also loved comedy; they would go see Lenny Bruce. There were a lot of records around, but for them, it was mainly jazz and blues, which I didn't understand as a little kid. I understood the Beatles. I was born in '67, so I didn't have any sense of the world existing without the Beatles. When I think about how popular they must have been when I was three, it must have just been everything. It just programs your mind. I was reading—you were talking about Joni Mitchell as being someone that represented that to you in a lot of ways: *This is the kind of person that I am just completely hypnotized by.*

Cameron: I remember one of the first times we got to bring rock into the house was—my mom liked Dick Cavett, you know, because he was an intellectual. So, we would watch Dick Cavett, and he had an amazing show that he did on the night of Woodstock. It was just supposed to be Joni Mitchell, but some of the Grateful Dead, and Jefferson Airplane, and Crosby, and all these people showed up. But I was mesmerized by Joni, who wasn't high and was keyed into Cavett and the jokes that Cavett had that were three levels above your head. Joni was right there and gorgeous; and then she plays "Both Sides Now" or "Cactus Tree," and you're like, *Oh my God, she plays guitar like that, too.* So, that was my Beatles, in a lot of ways.

Judd: When you first started writing about music, you were thirteen or fourteen. Where were you in the hierarchy of school? I know you were a smart kid who skipped grades, but were you considered someone that people got a kick out of—or were you a forgotten kid?

Cameron: They say you look back and you always make yourself out to be more of a loner than you really were, but I was alone. Or, I had one friend. I was younger than everybody else, a mascot at best, and ridiculed often. Music was the thing where I just felt like, *This is a club that I belong to,* in my head. Maybe that's the quest to go and start doing interviews. *Could I really be in this club somehow because I was drawn to it?* There was one day where I brought *Randy Newman Live,* David Bowie's *Hunky Dory,* and maybe Joni Mitchell's *Blue* to my English class, and I played pieces of those records for everybody. And the teacher was like, "Yes, that's good music." I remember walking around the campus with the *Hunky Dory* cover under my arm, and I felt cool, like I finally felt like I had something that was my own. I'm never gonna be a jock. I totally will never be a surfer in San Diego—that was the hierarchy. So, music gave me a card to punch in my head that there was a place to belong, if only when the lights are out and you're listening to *Hunky Dory.*

Judd: That's how I felt about comedy, which no one else was interested in. I thought, *Oh, I have a thing. I don't know what's happening with my popularity level or the fact that I don't get great grades, but I* *think this is my ticket out.* It meant a lot to me, like a secret mission that was going to pay off. Then I moved to L.A., and I met all these other people—it was like the Judd of every high school in America had moved to L.A. "Oh, so you *all* know every sketch from Monty Python?" Suddenly, we're here and we're gonna try to take it to the next place and see if we can really do this.

Cameron: Would you do the routines?

Judd: Senior year of high school, in May, I started going to open mics, but I was very scared to admit I wanted to do it. I knew it was gonna be painful. It was to get up and go, *Okay, now I have to prepare to be really bad and be humiliated for a couple of years.* But I was ready, and I knew it was going to happen, and it did happen. The first interview I ever did was with Mookie Wilson from the New York Mets, in seventh or eighth grade. My grandfather told me he met someone who worked for the Mets, like the vice president, so my friend and I knocked on the door of the Mets offices at Shea Stadium and said, "My grandfather knows this guy." He let me in and gave me an autographed ball and bat, and later I just called him or sent him a letter and said, "Can I interview Mookie Wilson?" They set it up, and that's the first time I realized, *Oh, you can meet people.*

Cameron: Now, what if they [had] said, "Fuck off, you little kid"? Would it have wounded you? Or would you have just kept going?

Judd: I think I would have kept going. I think I was crazy. I knew that my grandfather had just decided to be in music. He would pay money out of his own pocket to jazz musicians, record them, have the records manufactured himself, and then go to record stores and say, "Hey, you want a hundred twenty of these Charlie Parkers?" and on some level, I think I realized, *Oh, that's how you make it in the world.* I'm not gonna climb the ladder; I'm gonna do something weird and flip it on its side. It's wild, because I would put myself in situations with people that I really admired, but also not sure how I could keep up. How was it for you being very young and being in rooms with people like Bob Dylan and having to talk in a way where you could get his respect?

Cameron: Oh wow, that's really a good question. They were so kind of open-door Mookie Wilson-ish in the beginning. So, I would take little steps out into being relaxed. I remember the Allman Brothers [Band was] in the Continental Hyatt House, and they're all sitting around in this room, and they're playing "Come On in My Kitchen," and the roadies are pulling up a guitar and playing a little something and, man, it's like Macon, Georgia, and you can almost feel Duane in the room. There's a guitar next to me, and I couldn't play, but I held it and kind of acted like I could play. Gregg Allman took one look at me and then looked away, and one of the roadies saw the one look—he just gently eased the guitar out of my hands, like, *You're in heaven, and it's all beautiful, and you just can't play this anymore.* And that was me going like, *Okay. I have some guardrails.* But they made me feel so good about it. It was like, *It's not really your thing.* And I just went, "Okay." I remember that feeling so clearly right now, and my feeling was: *If I love the music, they're gonna know it, and I will belong.* It stays with me to this day. Scorsese has that thing that if you meet a hero that you had when you were seventeen, you'll always be nervous. So, I'm still kind of nervous around Neil Young or somebody like that because, *Oh, that's a poster in my room.* Living molecules are almost too much.

Judd: They're not easy characters, Neil Young and Dylan. They're not the easiest people in the world to talk to.

Cameron: No, but they sense authenticity. Pete Townshend was a true hero of mine, and I loved his rock writing. I still think he's the best rock journalist. He covered rock for *Rolling Stone.* So, when I met him, I felt like, *This guy knows my world because he's a rock journalist, too.* And he made me feel that way. That was the first amazing interview that I ever got to do. What was your first epic, they-spent-four-hours-with-me-and-I-asked-everything interview?

Judd: That's the funny part, I don't think they're good interviews. They're very—I didn't know much about comedy the way I thought that I did. There were people who were nice to me, who answered very simple questions deeply. They were very helpful to me because I would ask basic questions: "How long does it take to get good?" "How do you get stage time?"

Cameron: But these are great questions. I tried to interview some comics in the day. I went backstage and tried to interview Franklin Ajaye. He was fucking dark. He went on a thing to me like, "You expect me to be funny, don't you? Everybody expects me to be funny. The cop pulls me over and expects me to be funny. You know what? I'm not funny. Okay?" I'm like, *Argh! Take me back to the musicians.* He was great, but he was honest, and I can't say that the comedians that I've read and interviewed after didn't have a piece of that. I got scared by the comics a little bit. George Carlin was nice to me.

Judd: You're writing profiles about these musicians, and there's an enormous amount of heartbreak and death and struggle—all the things of life. You're a very young person, and these people are dealing with grief and their addictions. How are you even able to process it? When you're interviewing a band like the Allman Brothers, and their brother just died, what was your level of comprehension of what you were dealing with?

Cameron: That question makes me emotional. I have to think about it. I think you're right, because seeing what happened on the road with the Allman Brothers [Band] was heartbreaking. There was all of that in the air, all of it—death was hanging there and the loss of their leader; it was all fresh. Life had given them some strange lightning-strikes-twice moments, like Pearl Jam many years later. But Dickey Betts moves up, Gregg becomes more of a leader—suddenly the band is bigger than ever. That was an intense life experience. But really, as you asked me that, I go back to the living room, because my mom was a counselor as well as a teacher. I would come home from, like, interviewing the Eagles, who [had] just put out "Take It Easy" or something, and I was so high from having met these guys, and Glenn Frey was the coolest guy in the world. And I found a way back home, because they didn't drive, and I walked in, and there were all these students from my mom's college crowded around her, and my dad was trying to comfort her. Something bad had happened. There had been a political movement and somebody had tried to force her out of her job at the college, and she was crying. And the young people were comforting her. That night really was the yin and yang: You can have this incredible high two miles away at the Concourse, but at the same time, they have ganged up on your mom, and she's weeping in your living room. And this is all part of the human experience. It's the roller coaster, you've got to love that roller coaster. That's everything. The biggest gift is to be able to put that in a movie where people go to that place together, and sadness becomes laughter, and laughter becomes sadness. All that stuff is the best.

Judd: If you're interviewing Neil Young and he's talking about all these losses in his life, and they're talking about how they're dealing with it and their spirituality, were you picking up on that?

Cameron: Absolutely. There had been a death in my family, but I was kind of too young to process it. I really keep going back to this Allman Brothers tour. It's not too long of a story, but I loved that song "Brandy," by Looking Glass. They were playing this club, the 21 Club in San Diego, so I interviewed them in their bus. Then Elliot Lurie, the lead singer of Looking Glass, was like, "Come, now let's go in the club." The bouncer at the door stopped me and said, "You're too young." And Elliot Lurie said, "He's a reporter," and now the owner of the club comes in and says, "Okay, mention my club a lot, whatever you write, and I will put you in this dressing room. You can't leave the dressing room, but you'll be in the club, and Looking Glass can come back into the room after. But you don't leave that dressing room." And I was like, "Okay," so I'm in this dressing room, and I'm hearing the muffled show that's starting, and the door opens and in walks Jim Croce, and he sees me with a tape recorder and a bunch of questions, and he goes, "My first interview; this is fantastic." I wasn't even that big of a Jim Croce fan, but I just interviewed him on the spot. He was fantastic. And then I interviewed Gram Parsons right after that. The point of all this is I'm on the road with the Allman Brothers, with Neal Preston. We're waiting for Gregg to call, because it's two in the afternoon and we're waiting to interview him, and over the radio comes this announcement that Jim Croce has died in this plane crash with the dude that he was with, who was also really great (his accompanist, Maury Muehleisen). Then the guy said on the radio, "This is a terrible thing, because we've already lost Gram Parsons." And I remember sitting in the Hyatt House lobby with Neal, just going like, *Two people that I knew and kind of bonded with are dead.* And these are the first dead people I've ever known. It was a huge thing, because it all felt a little bit fantasy-like, and I was able to be empathetic toward everything, but there's a body count in this job, and people die, and it just really rocked me, so when Neil Young talks about Danny Whitten dying, and Ronnie Van Zant dies later, this is all stuff that really was emotional. I always wanted to write about loss, because loss is the other side of the giddy highs of the music, and loss is probably part of the reason why the giddy highs can feel so powerful, because it all fits together. Suddenly, you're such a far way away from high school where people laughed at you for not having enough pubic hair yet. And if I can capture how this feels, I could be a writer.

Judd: Your transition to filmmaking—was it because you wrote the book of *Fast Times at Ridgemont High* and you stumbled in that direction? Or was there an intention to make it into a movie? I know as a kid I didn't watch movies thinking I would direct or write movies.

Cameron: Me, neither.

Judd: It feels like journalism and the type of profile writing you were doing was good preparation for understanding the human condition in a way that naturally sets you up if you're now inventing a scene.

Cameron: Transcribing those interviews, really, to this day, is probably the best thing that could have ever happened for my screenwriting. Just to feel how people talked. You become aware that people are inelegant speakers a lot of the time, and that's the beauty of the way they speak. They do say "like," they do say "um," they do fall apart in the middle of a sentence and find another way to say things—and that's the way real life sounds. That helped me want to try out screenwriting. When Art Linson was like, "You're the cheapest person available to write your own screenplay. Why don't you do it?" that was really helpful. Then that happened later, when everybody turned down directing *Say Anything* . . . Jim Brooks was so cool. He was like, "Buddy, you have one more on your list, and if they say no, you're up." I was like, "I don't know anything about blocking or any of that stuff," and he was like, "You just need to learn to change your socks several times a day. You'll feel a lot better on the set." Later, of course, I realized he was being very generous and inviting, and it was a little more than that. Mostly we loved Mike Nichols movies in our house, so there was a part of me that thought, *Well, you know, maybe I can do that as the director*, but it was never a dream or anything. I just loved movies and music and the idea of putting music in a movie, like Mike Nichols had done. And that's never changed.

Judd: When you were writing the *Fast Times* book, you went to high school? How many months did you do it for?

Cameron: Two semesters. Pretty loose second semester.

Judd: But you had this idea to go back to school and write about high school in the early eighties. What year was it that you did that?

Cameron: Nineteen seventy-nine was the research year and—fuck, man. It's really weird to think that that was the seventies, but life is the best writer. You just can't top it. Like, Jeff Spicoli was a real guy. All those characters in *Fast Times* were real people. There's a little bit of compositing going on, but they're real people. I'd been really doing a lot of clandestine reporting, and the realization was *They're all trying so hard to be adults at younger and younger ages, because they have this lifestyle that needs to be supported.* So, they're like forty-year-old parents. It's like, *How do I supply? How do I buy the shit that I need? I need to work.* They're all stressing about their jobs, which was a change from when I was in high school a few years earlier. There was one day where a kid came into a journalism class in this big puffy jacket, and he said, "I've decided that Ronald Reagan is the future." And I was like, "What?" This is the death of liberalism. This is the death of so much. Ronald Reagan has infiltrated the English journalism class. And nobody argued the point, and I realized, *This is the future.* This quest to support their lifestyle is changing their politics; it's going to change the future. That was what I wanted the book to be: the changing of the guard, where they're trading their adolescence now for a position in the big capitalistic train. They want to get on that train already at fifteen and sixteen. That was really just journalism. I couldn't make that up, the stuff that went on that year. But that became the movie of *Fast Times.*

Judd: How old were you?

Cameron: Twenty-two. I went for four months. The end of the school year, I think I had two classes a week. I had never had a senior year. My sister was very popular in school, so I knew these things existed, like prom and grad night at Disneyland. So, it was a way to go do all that.

Judd: But on some level, did you feel like a narc? Were you having real relationships with friends where you felt there was some sort of *Donnie Brasco*–type betrayal?

Cameron: I told a few of them by the end of the year, one in particular. But I didn't feel like I was narc'ing as much as kind of catching something that hadn't been written about. Because there were times in doing these [music] stories for *Rolling Stone* where I would go in the [concert arena] parking lot and interview fans. The stories from the fans were better than Rod Stewart's stories—just how they got their tickets and how it's so great. So, to me, it was like I got to tell their story now.

Judd: Which is more like *your* story. It's almost like the path to talking about yourself. Which you then actually did, in *Almost Famous.* In my movies—and I learned this from Garry Shandling, where he was taking a version of himself and fictionalizing huge hunks of it—I've worked with people who take their history and try to capture the spirit of it, and it's so hard to do. *Freaks and Geeks* isn't real, but to Paul Feig, it captures his family. And he doesn't even have a sister in real life. It's a soup of true and made-up stuff trying to capture the essence of something.

Cameron: I love this whole conversation because it's reminding me how there's a spiritual center to what you do, and that's why it resonates. Shooting *Almost Famous* in San Diego did give us one little leg up on having a spiritual center, because we shot in all the places where that stuff happened: the sports arena, the radio station where I met Lester Bangs, the street where we talked . . . There was a mojo that was still operating, if we could catch it. But when I saw the four-hour version of it, I thought it was a complete disaster. I showed it to my mom, and I said, "I don't know what to do," and she said, "If you just calm down, there's a great movie in here."

Judd: I'm fascinated by your mom, in that she resisted music and then, at some point, she got it. What was she thinking when she didn't get it?

Cameron: She thought it was a hand being slipped into the pockets of American youth, using sex and drugs to get your money and lower the intellectual standards of a generation. And she was kind of right. Her thing about adolescence as a marketing tool was very real. Though she loved *The Graduate*, she thought [the song] "Mrs. Robinson" was snidely antireligious and Jesus-referencing. So, she was weaponized about that, and she didn't want it in the house. I could never buy tickets to a show, but I thought if I won the tickets on the radio, she would have to deal with the fact that they're free and [that] I did something enterprising to get them. So she went to see Elvis Presley with me. They said to call in at a certain time and get tickets to an amazing show. I was hoping it was Creedence Clearwater or something. Then I won a ticket to go see Derek and the Dominos a week later, so I made a deal with her: "Let's go see Elvis together, and let's go see Eric Clapton, and we'll decide together what's authentic and what's not about this music." So, we go to see Elvis, and he was high as shit.

Judd: What year?

Cameron: It was 1970, and it was a forty-two-minute show that was mostly selling scarves during the set. It was so ridiculous. The blue-haired ladies were going nuts, and [my mother] was very somber about it. She's like, "That's not my generation. I like Mike Nichols. I like Dick Cavett. This is BS." Then we went to see Eric Clapton, and there was a riot going on in this big glass window behind him as he played, dope everywhere. A guy offers my mom cocaine in the audience, and we left, and she said, "You're right, your music is better." So, it was a Derek and the Dominos show at the UC [San Diego] gym.

Judd: What's it like having a mom that was such a force like that and such a character? My mom was a real character, too, but I can't say it was all for good.

Cameron: My dad watched her like Cary Grant watches Katharine Hepburn. She's a big character. That's another thing about movies. There are big characters in life, and celebrating the big characters is the greatest. I think she'd had sadness in her life and wanted to process it. The knocks can become a gift, and she turned her life into finding the light in the dark. I haven't really talked about this, but her thing was I had to do the play of *Almost Famous*. I would say to her, "I don't know how to do this. I have really great people that I'm working with, but I think we got lucky on the movie, and I think this is going to the well one too many times. Plus, we're talking about putting this on at the Old Globe Theatre, across from where we live. What is worse than failing in your hometown? I don't want to do this." She said, "You got to do it. You are creating the negativity. Stop it. You've got to do this, and you'll love what you do." And she died unexpectedly two days before the first paying audience came to see the play.

Judd: Did she get to see a dress rehearsal?

Cameron: She saw a tape and dug it. I have one picture of her watching it. She and I can be really tough on my stuff. The play was good. She was right. I'm really glad we did it. If Broadway never opens up, and we never have any more life to the play, I still walk away with probably the best experience I ever had right across from where I grew up, in the theater where we used to go see Shakespeare. Joni Mitchell came on the first premiere night, down from L.A. with her girlfriends, to watch it. I was terrified. *Blue*'s "River" is in the play, so I'm like, *Oh my God. This is more stress.* She comes out of it, and she goes, "Better than the movie." And in many ways, she's right.

Judd: When you revisit that material as an older person, do your instincts change in terms of how you adapt it and discuss the older characters in the play?

Cameron: Maybe that's why the mother character really stands out in the play—because when you revisit it, you're the older character now.

Judd: Who was the person with *Fast Times* that was the mentor and helped you get that script right?

Cameron: Art Linson. He was also the guy that saw the short that Amy [Heckerling] did, "Getting It Over With," and said, "She's raw and real and authentic and she's a woman, and she knows how this feels from the other point of view on some of these relationships." Amy came in and knocked it out of the park and was all with my mom. I love that we've talked so much about my mom. My mom always used to say, "You should be so happy that Amy Heckerling directed *Fast Times at Ridgemont High*, because if you [had] directed it, you would have turned it into an art film. It's funny when they smell the Xerox papers. That's funny."

Judd: Then the other mentor you had, who was also a mentor for me—James L. Brooks. I got to work on the cartoon *The Critic*. You had to pitch him the story ideas. Mike Reiss and Al Jean ran the show, but he was a presence and at the tables and giving notes, and I got to watch how he ran a show. I also remember, when I was around the Gracie offices, that they had a little library, and there were some papers stuck in there that I pulled out, and it was their notes on *Say Anything*.

Cameron: Whoa!

Judd: What was your experience like with Jim?

Cameron: I think about Jim every day I write. Jim is just so pure. Nobody was going to care as much as Jim, and nobody was gonna care as much when a cut didn't work. You'd be in a dark room, and he'd be watching a cut, and you would just hear these yellow legal tablets. The anger or the frustration that he would never show you, because he's too classy, comes out in the sound of the yellow legal tablets whipping over from page to page. You'd be looking at each other like, *Okay, we're gonna have some notes after this.* But generally, he had the most amazing ideas. He was saying stuff like, "What if Jerry Maguire had a religious father and Jerry tithed his money?" It turned into a monologue about "My dad spent his whole life with one comfortable chair." And you leave the office after two hours of talk like this, and you're fucking high. You want to write all night, and you want to capture what that comfortable chair could be. I don't know that I've ever gotten that or seen that in anybody else. I think you're like that. I see it in the way Billy Wilder would talk about how he dealt with [screenwriter] I. A. L. Diamond. I don't see it a lot.

Judd: You've said that *Jerry Maguire* started just from a photo of an agent with a young athlete.

Cameron: It was a picture that Jim showed me at lunch. We were just trying to figure out if there's another movie we could do, and he was like, "What is that relationship?" Then I went off and wrote a whole thing and didn't do as much research as I should have and gave him a big, thick draft of stuff. Jim took a weekend, and I met with him, and he said, "Well, I've never seen so much story with no plot." I think about that all the time. "Let's not go down too many story roads; there needs to be a plot."

Judd: What was the moment where you realize what the essence of that movie was?

Cameron: It's interesting. We made the movie *Singles*, and the whole grunge scene exploded in the time after we shot the movie and before we were out. The studio hung on to it for a long time, not knowing how to sell it. Then the grunge thing happened, and they figured out how to sell it. "Let's call it *Come as You Are*, and we're good"— which didn't work out, mercifully. The people in Seattle, some of my friends—not Eddie and not the Pearl Jam guys, but—some of the people really turned their noses up at that movie. I felt some ridicule in some places and the feeling that I'd capitalized on the scene or something. But the oddest people supported that movie, and it surprised me. I was so taken with the idea that when you really hit a wall, the people that come to help you are very rarely the people you expect to be there. And that's *Jerry Maguire.* I knew what that movie was about when our conversations became about expressing that kind of abandonment that I'd felt in Seattle and turning that into a story of the redemption of the sports agent that makes it with the woman in the office that he never even knew. And the player that was the last on the list of the people that he was pleased to support. Those two people come together to put him on the path, and I just thought, *That's what the movie's about.*

Judd: When my mom died, I was in the middle of writing *Funny People,* and I was trying to write about how, when my mom thought she was going to die, she was much saner than when she thought she was going to live. And every time she thought the medicine was working, she became neurotic and materialistic and kind of crazy. When they said, "You have no shot," she became so cool and real and grounded and right there. So, that's what it was. I never talked about it at the time, but it was trying to express this thing I was watching my mom go through. Can you learn the lessons from your near-death experience, or not? I was quietly in so much pain, I didn't know how to process it. You go into a trance and you just turn it into the next piece of work. Like *Jerry Maguire.* You would never think *Jerry Maguire* is related to *Singles.* Now, let's talk about when you visited the set of *Knocked Up* with Tom Cruise.

Cameron: That was an amazing day. I was stuck on some ideas, I think it was the whole Marvin Gaye movie that I wanted to do, and it had been taking forever. He just said, "Look, man, you got to get out of your house. I want to take you to Judd Apatow's movie set. It's just two minutes away, and you're gonna see something that's happening. It's gonna fire you up." And he took me over to the set, and it fired me up. It was like the guys from *Say Anything . . .*, like [John] Cusack and his gang, if they'd moved on to another movie.

Judd: I remember Leslie [Mann] was about to shoot something, and I had to go to Leslie like, "Tom Cruise is here. He's watching. And Cameron Crowe's watching, too." Because Leslie read for you for *Jerry Maguire* and got really down to the end, and she didn't get the part. And the letter you wrote telling her that she didn't get the part gave her so much confidence. It was such a kind, thoughtful letter. That movie is really about just trying to be a better version of yourself. That's something that I find that I always want to have these movies be about.

Cameron: It's always the best type of theme, right? We want to tell stories that make people want to take the risk to love better or connect more, to take a risk to improve somehow. Do you have whole drafts where you were just getting something out emotionally, and it's like, *I'm never gonna make that movie, but I wrote it, and I have it, and it represents this time in my life*?

Judd: I don't write a lot of extra stuff. I just obsess until it's somewhat makeable and maybe not in a good way, either. I think it's related to working in television. If we have to shoot an episode next week, and we're going to write it this week and give it to Garry [Shandling] on Sunday and then do the table read Monday, at a certain point, my head thinks, *The train is unstoppable.* Do you notice a common theme when you look back at all of your work? For me, people say, "You do a lot of coming-of-age stories." Recently, I keep thinking every story is a coming-of-age story.

Cameron: I like coming-of-age stories. And I definitely like the embattled optimist. I keep getting drawn to aspects of that. If your heart's in the right place, you have the shot at a sequence that can make you feel like all the oxygen in the world is just inside you right now. I go to the Billy Wilder thing, of "If you do your job right, they might talk about your movie for fifteen minutes after they see it." That's the most you can ever hope for.

DAVID LETTERMAN

November 2020

Judd: How are you doing? I think the last time I saw you was at that USO show with Joe Biden. We were all excited to meet Barack Obama, and we didn't know we should be as excited about meeting Joe Biden.

David: I remember meeting Joe Biden at *The Regis Philbin Show.* I was with there with my friend and colleague Mary Barclay, who's from Pennsylvania. And in the dressing room was Vice President Biden, just seated by himself, and he got up, and I said, "Hello," and I introduced myself, and then he and Mary had a lovely conversation about being from Pennsylvania. And that's really all you want.

Judd: I remember when I was doing the documentary about Garry Shandling, he guest-hosted for Regis and interviewed Trump. Then he wrote about it in his diaries at the time, that it scared him how empty [Trump] was—and this was before Trump was in politics. Shandling was like, "I'd never met a person like this. It was like looking into a black hole."

David: I, like everyone else, have grown fatigued trying to understand what it is. Because this is not what I knew of him when he was on the show maybe two dozen times.

Judd: You had a lot of politicians on your show over the years. Who were the politicians, from the earliest part of the talk show, that you remember being on?

David: We probably had Ed Koch on. But it's so different, at least for me and people doing what I did back then—how much we paid attention to politics then compared to what people are doing now. It was different. Politics was like knowing a lot about European soccer. We sort of knew about it, but then, suddenly, you realize later, *Oh my God, this is something to be taken seriously.*

Judd: Now, every other night, you see hosts dealing with some massive tragedy or a school shooting. What you had to deal with on 9/11, it didn't seem like it happened a lot on the show in that era.

David: That's right. And thank goodness, because I don't think, at that point, I would have had the energy to do it justice. You can talk about it for a month, talk about it for six weeks, but to have to address it night after night after night for over four years—that takes great resources, great durability, and real presence of mind. And the guys who are doing it, the women who are doing it—good for them. They're doing a good job, but I was tapped out by then.

Judd: Now you're doing your show on Netflix, *My Next Guest Needs No Introduction.* I was watching your Kim Kardashian interview last night, and I thought that her telling the story of getting robbed is one of the most riveting things I've ever seen on television. How does it feel to be in a different format? When you were doing interviews on your old shows, did you wish you could just have a real talk with your guests and not feel pressure to be amusing for five minutes?

David: It used to be we'd do four minutes in the first segment and then three minutes in the second segment, and then it's goodbye. But this way, you get to follow your curiosity and the terrain of the conversation. I just thought Kim was fantastic. I got to know a little bit about her when we talked to Kanye for the show, and I realized that I was under the wrong impression about who she was. So, I felt good about correcting that for myself. I think, in the beginning, people were saying, "Good Lord, why are you talking to Kim Kardashian?" I felt like I had to be defensive about it. Then I talked to her, and I realized, *No, no, no, this is a woman of substance. Someone who knows what she's up to, who is up to quite a lot, and who is making her mark other than just being on her TV show.*

Judd: When you were at the end of the CBS show, you would talk about not wanting to attempt to do what everyone else was doing in terms of viral videos and Instagram jokes. Does it feel like you've figured out how to do it in your own way?

David: Well, I just kind of fell into it. I didn't want to be part of conventional television. I had done that and did it too long. This seemed different enough, but also within—excuse the expression—my skill set. So, this seemed about right.

Judd: When you're picking the guests for your show, what do you find you're drawn to in people as subjects of a long-form interview?

David: I always look for the front door; I look for a way for me to get in. The most recent version of this is Lizzo. She had been on our show once, and that's the extent of what I knew of her. And she was nice enough to let us come to her home. This was right after the pandemic had really started to get everyone's attention. She and I just started talking, and she was telling me about a birthday party she'd had, and what she was eating and drinking at her birthday party, and she referenced something in the pharmaceutical world that I have no knowledge of. So, I thought, *Great, I want to know everything about this.* And that was our in. She was satisfying my curiosity of something that I'm too inexperienced and ignorant to understand. I felt like, *Well, this is what you would do with a friend.* So, that's what I'm always looking for, and then everything else that you know about that person, or don't know about that person, is much easier to access.

Judd: I don't know if you've ever seen Gary Gulman—we did a stand-up special with him about depression, where he talked about it for an hour.

David: I know the psychiatrist featured in that offering.

Judd: Do you? Yeah, he's very good.

David: And I said to him, "Wait a minute, I thought that we had a deal here. You're only supposed to treat one depressed comedian at a time."

Judd: What is the common trait there? I produced two stand-up specials about depression. It seems to be a very common thing that we all go through at some point. I don't know if comedians are just more open about it. You've talked about how you didn't even know that's what was happening.

David: I knew something had gone haywire. And I wonder if people are talking about it more, not just because comedians are talking about it, but because it doesn't seem to have the stigma that it used to. But I didn't know what was happening to me until a psychiatrist said, "Oh here's what this is. This is depression." And I always thought depression was, *Oh jeez, the Reds got beat last night. My day is ruined.* But you don't know it's a real sinkhole. And when you understand it, you have a greater awareness for the trap that it can be, because it's not just *Go out and run around the block, you'll feel better.*

Judd: It was interesting when Bruce Springsteen started talking about it. We've all been watching him do these huge shows for decades, and then he finally said, "I didn't want to get off the stage." The moment he leaves, he's bummed out. He's said the only place he wasn't depressed was while doing a show.

David: That's him self-medicating. And you know, good for him and good for everybody else who really benefited from that. Millions of people around the world get the benefit of that, but who knew the guy was suffering? I experienced a much smaller version of the self-medicating dynamic. It started for me in high school, when the only time I felt any self-worth at all was when I started taking a public speaking course. I couldn't do algebra. I couldn't do history. I couldn't do chemistry. I couldn't do anything. But public speaking, jeez, it was the first time I didn't feel like the dumb kid in my class. I thought, *All you have to do is find out where this will take you in life, and it will help support you. It will support your impression of yourself*—which was, and still is, dented.

Judd: You started out doing the weather and having a local broadcasting career. Was it in your mind that, at some point, it would turn into a career in stand-up?

David: No, I originally just thought, *I gotta find out how you can get on radio.* That was my original thought. And then I got very lucky, and a friend of mine's brother hired me to work at a TV station when I was in college. That's when everything changed for me. I was afraid of being in front of people, so the camera or the microphone is ideal. There were stand-up comedians I would see that just made me laugh silly. But I did not think, *Oh, that's what I'm gonna do.* I always thought if I can just get to a fifty-thousand watt, clear-channel, middle of the road radio station, I can live a happy life.

Judd: And then you did that?

David: I got to do radio, I got to the television, I got to do weather, I got to do news, I got to do public service shows, I got to do announcing, I got to do commercials. And after a while, you realize, *I'm tired of this.* Then I became aware of *You know what? Maybe I could just get out of here and try something else.*

Judd: Was there someone you saw as a model? Someone who had pulled it off where you thought, *I'm gonna move to L.A. and try to do this path*?

David: It's like a kid who gets a look at Joe DiMaggio and says, "You know what? I think I can do that." But I used to watch Johnny Carson, Steve Allen, and I thought, *Wait a minute. These guys are broadcasting, but they're also really, really funny. Let me just see if that can be done.* But the whole thing from that moment, my sophomore year in high school to the first time I hosted *The Tonight Show*—it's just luck; it just worked. I can't understand the good fortune, and the only reasonable explanation is the people around me, who helped me and encouraged me and opened doors for me that I did not feel deserving of, but certainly took great advantage of.

Judd: What do you think formed your point of view or your sense of humor, because you showed up with your take, even from the first. It wasn't very long from the moment you got to the Comedy Store until you were hosting *The Tonight Show*, like a ridiculously brief amount of time. Did you have a sense of what you were doing? What you felt was funny about yourself?

David: Well, there's two things. When I got to California, I was twenty-eight, and I had hosted a show called *Clover Power*. It was with kids, and they'd have their pet goat on, or they'd show me how they made a pie. So, the skill is no different: A kid brings on a goat. Is there something funny to say about the goat? Great. You do *The Tonight Show*, and on comes an actor or actress—is there something funny to say? Especially if the actor or actress has a goat. Whoa, that's pay dirt. I think it was more the broadcasting experience that made me suitable as a possibility for hosting *The Tonight Show*.

Judd: There's also a delusion of youth. I always think about when I lived with Adam Sandler, when he went and did your show for the first time, when he was a kid. I think all of us had this lunatic belief that it was all going to happen. There's something about being young: You're just so stupid. You must have had some of that, to think, *I can host* The Tonight Show.

David: For me, the awareness that you just described took place almost the minute I crossed from Arizona into California. I thought, *At least geographically, I know I'm in the right place. I think I got a shot at this.* It's interesting that these other people shared that.

Judd: So, when you get to L.A., your crew of guys was, like, Witherspoon and Dreesen and George Wallace?

David: Pretty good group: George Wallace, John Witherspoon, Tom Dreesen, George Miller, Jeff Altman, Johnny Dark, Jay Leno, Elayne Boosler. And then, a year later, Robin Williams arrived. Paul Mooney was also in that group. I know I'm overlooking people that will come to me. But we thought we were pretty good, and we thought, *Oh, these are the golden years.*

Judd: Were you writing for Jimmie Walker just to pay your bills?

David: I left Indiana with five thousand dollars. But Jimmie Walker was so kind to me, and he hired me and Elayne and Jay Leno and Byron Allen. And every Sunday, we would go over to Jimmie's house and pitch him jokes. I got a hundred bucks a week for that. Then, when I would emcee at the Comedy Store, I would get twenty bucks. So, unlike the typical story for people of that era, I had a little bit of cash flow.

Judd: What was your impression of the scene at the time?

David: We always made fun of guys who did impressions, and we always made fun of guys who closed their set with a song. We liked guys like Tim Thomerson, who could come in and do his thing, and the walls would collapse in on themselves from people laughing so hard.

And then you had the guy that came out and was, "Here's Jimmy Stewart doing a medley of Beatles songs." That's impressions and music. *What? Get off!* We felt like you had to stand by your material—and no gimmicks.

Judd: What was it like in that era, when someone like Richard Pryor or Robin Williams comes in, and it's just another level? Is it inspiring? Or does it make everyone want to quit comedy?

David: In the beginning, lineup for Tuesday night or Wednesday night or whatever would be set. There'd be two shows. You'd call, then you'd find out, *Did I get a time?* Yes. You're eight-fifteen, first show Wednesday. So, you fell prey to the idea that there was an order to this. But all of that went out the window when a guy like Steve Landesberg would show up. A guy like Gabe Kaplan would show up, or Freddie Prinze would show up. And then the eight-fifteen meant nothing. What that really meant was *eleven*-fifteen, maybe—because these guys would get up and do an hour, and why not? It was great for business. But there was nothing like Richard Pryor. He was like the Manhattan Project. It was an explosion. It really didn't matter what Richard was doing. He suddenly decided that he was working on a new album, and I don't know the chronology of which album was which, but this was an album he was going to work out at the Comedy Store. And he came in two or three nights a week. People got wind of this, and so the place was packed, and Richard would come onstage and—I mean, just when he was in the room, you could feel it. Even as he walked onstage, and you saw him silhouetted in the darkness, it was hard to describe. And then he would get onstage and—oh my God. Because he was the God of comedy of his day, and to be looking at him, and then to hear him—it was delightful. Delightful and the kind of electricity you only feel every now and then.

Judd: And you're seeing how he writes, because you're seeing the set come together.

David: And whatever he's doing, you don't care. Because he could be up there tying his shoes. And then [after his set,] people would leave, because they thought, *I've been to the top of the mountain. I've seen everything you could want in comedy. Let's go home.*

Judd: I remember when Robin Williams used to come into the Improv when I was hosting. You really felt like you had to shut the show down afterward. You couldn't even do a show. It kind of sucked the energy out on their exit. I remember Sandler had a good set following Robin, as an unknown comic, and I thought, *Oh, Sandler's gonna make it.* He took that energy and somehow found a way to keep it going.

David: I remember George Miller and I used to stand in the back of the Comedy Store when Robin was onstage. You know, comics are the best of friends and also hate each other. Like, *What do you mean he's going to be on* The Dinah Shore Show? *Why am I not on* Dinah? But we're all in the same battle. But Robin Williams comes in, and George and I actually discussed whether the arrival of Robin Williams meant that we were going to have to leave show business.

Judd: I stopped doing stand-up when Jim Carrey hit. I used to open for Jim Carrey on the road. I was doing some writing for him, and I thought, *I'm not even in the same business as him.*

David: There are many people that caused me to feel that way about myself. But as it turns out, there is room for a wide variety of things, and if you're funny—really, that's all that counts.

Judd: When you were trying to get on *The Tonight Show*, and you'd been rejected a couple of times, were you feeling it was the right path? Was that becoming a more specific goal?

David: That's all I wanted. That's all anybody wanted. You either wanted to get a situation comedy like a Gabe Kaplan, like Freddie Prinze, or you wanted to host a talk show. I felt like the single purpose was for me to be there. I had gone on the road. I got so comfortable working at the Comedy Store, that I could do it easily and loved it. But what you learn quickly is you have to be comfortable everywhere you go. And I was not comfortable everywhere I went. So, when I would go on the road, I would bomb, and that's when I knew I have to just concentrate on getting on *The Tonight Show*, because I'm never going to be these guys. Leno is probably on the road right now, in the middle of three or four shows somewhere. A lot of guys, a lot of women, thrived on it. I couldn't do that. So, I knew that I had to sharpen my focus to get on *The Tonight Show*.

Judd: Did you feel like—[from the perspective of] this era, where you don't have the pressure of the show—that how you're perceiving the world has shifted? I've only hosted a talk show once. For two days before Corden took over, I guest-hosted when they would let anybody do it just to fill some days. And the thing I noticed about it that was panic-inducing was when you interview someone, the second they sat down, there was a clock over their shoulder counting down the amount of time you had with them. It made your heart race, the need to have this not be awful. What does it feel like to be in that creative flow, but also panic, for so long? And then have it go away?

David: Having it go away—it took me about a year to realize that the moving sidewalk had stopped. So, that was a huge adjustment, as with anybody who does something all their life and then does not do it. A huge adjustment. At least about a year. But what you're discussing there—I always felt that if the guest was not entertaining, not interesting, not funny, then it's my responsibility to fix it. Then the other thing, the pressure of the clock: I got to a point where I just ignored that. I just let it go. For the last ten years of the show, they'd be editing almost up to the time that the show had to be sent out to network. And we'd be eighteen to twenty minutes over. It's a hugely inconsiderate thing for me to have done. But at the time, I just didn't care. I had things I wanted to talk about.

Judd: You've said that you felt like you hosted your show for ten years too long. How do you categorize all the decades you've worked?

David: I don't know the exact time line; I just picked ten years because had I left ten years earlier than I did, I still would have been on the air for twenty years or so. And in those ten years, I think it would have been nice to experience a different kind of stimulation in my life. Because, in the day, it was Leno and myself going head to head—preoccupied with *They had so-and-so. We've got to get so-and-so. He's killing me in the ratings. What are we going to do?* I kept thinking, *I'm going to get better, I'm going to get better.* So, that was the motivation for staying on so long. But sadly, the motivation for staying on so long was not commensurate with the desire to go to work and make the thing better. I just got lazier and lazier.

Judd: It certainly is one of the few jobs that people really see as a lifetime gig when they take it.

David: I think that model was set by Johnny Carson. Prior to that, Jack Paar only did it for four or five years. Steve Allen only did it for two or three years. Rick Dees only did it for a week and a half. But that's the idea. I think if you got somebody like Kimmel, or Colbert, or Jimmy Fallon, or Seth Meyers, and when the show's successful, it's just a license to print money. They're pretty inexpensive to produce, because everything is right there—the host, the theater. And it's fun, to be sure. I don't know, maybe it's just something to say, maybe it's just hollow rhetoric, but I do wish I had more time to examine other things.

Judd: When I look at periods of my career, or a movie I've made, sometimes I feel like I lost my mind and created something almost in a fever dream. Where I don't even know how it happened. Is there a part of the show that feels that way for you?

David: It comes right back around to the discussion of depression and self-medicating. If it's Monday and the show was great, I'd feel great about myself. Then Tuesday, if the show sucked, I'd start to slip. And then if Wednesday, it sucked again, I would slip a little deeper. And then Thursday, if the show was better, then I'd feel human again. So, for me, I think the real reason I stayed so long was selfishness, because I was using that as a prescription to make myself feel worthwhile. I was using the show to try and prove myself to myself.

Judd: When you were first starting on the morning show, did you have a sense that you were about to dismantle talk shows? Was there a philosophy to what you were doing?

David: I wouldn't say a philosophy. From my standpoint, I thought, *I am the guy television has been waiting for. Wait till I get there. I'll straighten it out.* Six weeks later, when we were packing up the office, I realized, *Well, there's something else I was wrong about.*

Judd: Morning television wasn't that interesting, at that time, especially at ten-thirty in the morning.

David: We did a thing with one of the writers. That building—there's a roof garden about halfway up. You can gaze out on the city and still see up at the main tower of 30 Rock. There's a ledge that is about four feet above the next level on the roof. We had Rich Hall as the writer, and the premise was he was up there taking a nap, sleeping on the ledge. Now, from the camera's point of view, you're looking at the horizon. You don't know that just below that ledge is another level and four feet of grass. So, I'm at the desk and I say, "Rich, Rich, you got to come back to the—" And he rolls over, and it looks like he's now rolled down ten floors to Sixth Avenue. And the person from NBC in charge of the show comes up to me during the commercial, and she says, "People are gonna think he's dead." I said, "Yeah, I know. That's the joke." And she says, "We can't have people thinking we've killed somebody on television. Put him in the audience. Let people know he's still alive." That's when I knew we didn't have much more time there, and it was canceled like a month or six weeks later.

Judd: I did a sketch show with Ben Stiller for Fox. We did thirteen episodes, and they only aired twelve. It was a similarly ridiculous time slot, and I think we had the exact same experience as you, where six months later, we won the Emmy for best comedy writing. And then, suddenly, it was considered a cool thing. Did it help when you guys won the Emmy for the morning show? Or were you already going to do *The Tonight Show*?

David: No, it was a year of darkness, because I had no plan. Nobody had any plans for me, because the first show had tanked. I think Brandon Tartikoff saved us because he realized that maybe it was the time slot that was part of the problem, and so he gave me a shot at night.

Judd: You're a father now. How old is your son?

David: He's seventeen, a junior in high school. How old are your kids?

Judd: I have a daughter who is a senior in high school, and my other daughter is twenty-two. And I feel like I am an inverted version of you. You waited till you were wise. I did it by accident really young, when I had no clue what to do. We were in a wide-eyed panic. That's why we made movies about it: because we were not emotionally or mentally prepared to do it.

David: That's interesting because, irrespective of age, I'm not sure anyone is ready to be a parent.

Judd: What's your son into?

David: He's not into his father. Doesn't like being seen in public with me, because he doesn't like it when I engage with people. And I'm so desperate now for an audience that it's usually me engaging with strangers. He doesn't like that.

Judd: Does he have any sense of what you've done? I mean, my kids care so little.

David: I told this story before. When I said to Harry, "I'm quitting, I'm retiring. I won't be at work every day. My life is changing; our lives will change." And he kind of nodded and said, "Will I still be able to watch the Cartoon Network?" I said, "I think so. Let me check."

Judd: And since leaving, what has been the best part of not working that busy schedule?

David: It used to be really fatiguing, the fact of doing it every day. Now when I do something, I think, *Wow, this would be great if I could do something like this once a month.* You still get the little jolt, and the hope of self-esteem, but you're not in the makeup chair every day—which, by the way, was my favorite part.

Judd: Do you have other things you're looking to do? Are you developing other projects in addition to the Netflix show, or is that enough for you right now?

David: I have a lot of things that I would like to do that I'm afraid to tell people. Like when I left Indiana, I didn't tell people what I wanted to do. I said, "I want to be a writer." That's part of what I wanted to do. And now I have a half-dozen ideas that I would like to try, but I'm afraid that people will look at me and laugh, so I haven't verbalized them, and I haven't made a move. So, I'm doing things that people come to me with, which is great. I've been very lucky. People have been very nice to me. But I have things I want to do that I'm afraid to mention. I mean, they're all legal.

Judd: Isn't it weird that we still can be that insecure? After doing so much.

David: Yeah, well, I—see, I find it hard to believe that you might be that insecure, but I'm guessing you're finding it hard to believe that *I* might be that insecure.

Judd: The thing I like about comedy is any success does not do anything to support the next project. Every single joke is an experiment that may fail terribly, which I think is kind of great. I don't mean to embarrass you, but I just want to say that for all of us in comedy, so many people, their dream was to get on [your] show or to get your approval. It's probably hard for you to understand how many people are doing great, and great work, because they loved you and what you did, and you kind of gave them an opportunity. And the impact is massive. There are so many people who wanted to be funny and go into this business because of you.

David: Thank you. Let me just add what I think you're maybe too timid to get to, which is the fact that, without me, there would *be* no comedy.

Judd: Exactly.

ED TEMPLETON

June 2018

Judd: I was working on a movie, and I met with Warren Zevon to talk about scoring it and I told him, "I'm waiting to get notes from the studio." He said, "I don't understand," and I said, "I have to wait to see if they want me to make any changes." And he said, "Why would you change anything?" I felt so shamed by him and his artistic integrity. How important is that independence for you?

Ed: I feel like filmmaking is super collaborative overall, and everything I do is coming from a dictatorial standpoint. With Toy Machine, I am the only person who makes decisions for the skate company, for the paintings I make—whatever I do. It's total control, and if someone came and said, "You should change this," I would be like, "What? What are you talking about?"

Judd: Do you ever look for feedback on your stuff?

Ed: I do, because I think it helps to have someone you trust say something constructive. How much do you have to listen to those notes from the studio?

Judd: The funny thing is you could be resistant to notes and be wrong. I've had movies where people say, "Maybe you should do this, maybe you should shorten [that]," and I'll have a very strong reaction and think, *No, this is what it is.* And then, ten years later, you go, *I could have cut eight minutes out of that.* But it took me ten years to figure out what the eight minutes would be. Sometimes that's the hard part: When do you listen to people?

Ed: For sure. When I edit an art book or photo book, for instance, I get to a certain point and then I usually put it away for a few days. And I come back, and I do in my head what is called a "harsh edit": I look at it as if I'm someone who hates me, someone out there who thinks, *This guy is just an asshole, I hate everything he does.* I look at it from that angle, and it really helps, because I'll look at a photo with a more critical eye. You usually have to edit down pages anyway, so that helps you make it airtight and forces you to have really strong images in the final cut. I think it takes a certain kind of person that can work in two minds like that. I've talked to friends who can't get on that other side and [who] look at themselves critically in that way. I think it's helpful, and you ultimately have to end up going with your gut.

Judd: When people ask you what you do, what do you tell them?

Ed: It's a little easier now, because I feel like I just closed a chapter on pro skateboarding. It used to be the case where I would be on a plane, and there would be a guy next to me, and he'd ask, "What do you do?" And I have to assess the guy first to decide what I want to tell him. I could either say I'm a businessman or pro skateboarder or artist or something like that. And I decide which answer would be easier to get through this conversation I don't want to have with that guy on a plane. But I still don't know what to say. I don't like the word *artist* that much. Especially coming from my world, where we're always giving each other crap about everything, leading with "I'm an artist" just feels weird.

Judd: I think that I struggle with that word sometimes. If you talk about film or writing and you talk about it as your art, as it comes out of your mouth you want to punch yourself in the face. But then, if you take a beat, it is exactly what you're doing, and why should it be shameful that you need to express yourself?

Ed: It sounds weird, but that's the only language that's there to describe what you're doing. So that's what you have to do. But the minute you start talking about your work . . .

Judd: You're a dick.

Ed: You sound like a pretentious ass.

Judd: Did you grow up here in Huntington Beach?

Ed: Yes, I've been in Orange County my whole life. Born in Garden Grove, right over there, by Disneyland. We moved around a bit before settling in Huntington Beach. I take pride in having white trash credentials, because I technically lived in a trailer park at one point.

Judd: How long did you live in a trailer park for?

Ed: It wasn't that long. It's kind of a crazy story. When I was around eight years old, my dad ran off with our babysitter. He was in his forties, and he left our family for this girl, and I think she just used him to get to a ride to Colorado, where she hooked up with her real boyfriend.

Judd: Oh no.

Ed: He just bailed out on us. I did badly in school after that, after the divorce and a broken home. But that's how I found skateboarding.

Judd: How so?

Ed: Well, all the kids I was hanging out with when I started skateboarding were from broken homes. I started realizing this—like, every single one of us has some weird, bad family story. You just end up not being the kind of kid who fits in playing basketball or on teams, and so you go out and be a nerd in the parking lot by yourself. And that's what attracted me to skateboarding.

Judd: My parents got divorced and it was my mom who ultimately ended up moving out, which never happens. The dad always leaves. I think that trying to process that kind of personal history, that kind of early abandonment, pushed me to become creative.

Ed: For me, it never became a thing where I'm driven because of this bad thing that happened. I could never trace anything that I did to some inner pain. That story of him leaving—it was a good thing. That's how I saw it. Five years into skateboarding I think I looked back and went, *I wouldn't be doing any of this if he stayed.*

Judd: You don't think you would have ever skateboarded?

Ed: My mom couldn't control me like my dad could, so when he left, I just ran rampant. I just did what I wanted, and she couldn't really do that much about it. I knew I wasn't doing bad things; I was just skateboarding. I've never gotten into drugs or anything like that. So, as much as she'd be freaking out if I broke curfews, I was always like, *I'll just deal with whatever she's gonna yell at me about because I know I'm just out skateboarding.*

Judd: I got into comedy because I wanted answers. I had that same thing, where my parents weren't that strict, and I was always rambling around.

Ed: My grandparents were essentially my father and mother figures, since my mom also had like a little bit of brain damage when she was younger. She's totally fine and raised two kids and knows right from wrong, but her mentality is simple. I was basically raising myself at some point. Discipline and stuff like that came from my grandparents. If I did something bad, I'd have to go stay at their house, which was great, because they cooked great food and had all this knowledge. I think being semi-raised by that older generation helped me a lot.

Judd: What did they do?

Ed: My grandfather was in graphic design, but my creativity definitely came from my grandmother. She was always doing arts and crafts with us, took us to museums, so I had that exposure of looking at art. I would watch my grandmother sit there and look at a Modigliani painting at LACMA [the Los Angeles County Museum of Art] or something for five minutes and then discuss it. Like, *Okay, that's what we do. A guy paints this thing, and we look at it and we talk about it. That's cool.*

Judd: What did your grandfather think of your skateboarding?

Ed: He couldn't fathom skateboarding. My grandfather was always super straitlaced, like, *I don't cuss, I'm religious, I'm Republican*—all that stuff. After Pearl Harbor, he signed up and went straight into the navy. To his credit, he loved us unconditionally, and he basically did support my skateboarding, even if he didn't understand it, didn't think it was worth anything, and thought I was wasting my time like someone from that generation would. But he still let me do it and kind of supported it.

Judd: How old were you when you first started making money from skateboarding?

Ed: I was eighteen when I brought the first check home, like, *I'm a pro skater now, here's three thousand dollars I made this month as a pro.*

Judd: That's a lot of money.

Ed: I was making around three to eight grand a month right off the bat. But I always felt guilty about that success and that I had all this culture and skateboarding and all this stuff that made me happy, whereas my brother was just doing nothing. He was, like, a construction guy, and I had weird guilt about him that would bring me to tears thinking about how he got the short end of the stick.

Judd: Is he happy?

Ed: I think I eventually realized that I can't be sad, because he's not sad. For him, coming home from a hard day of work and opening a beer and watching the Packers game is all he needs, that's it. For me, that would be torture; I need so much more. I have so much more I want to do than that. But that's him, and he's fine with it.

Judd: That sounds like survivor's guilt.

Ed: It's exactly that. I feel like I got the good end. We both had the same grandparents helping us and everything, and somehow I came out where I am. But, then, maybe it's conceited to think that I'm so great. I just felt like I came out on top for what was offered to me.

Judd: I think it'd be better for everyone if they all expressed themselves through art, culture, through making things, but a lot of people just don't want to, because they couldn't care less and they're happy as can be. There are people who, all day long, are thinking, *How can I help the people in Syria?* Or, *How can I design this shoe to help you run faster?* They are certainly not writing jokes.

Ed: Here's one way to look at it for me. As a photographer, you're walking around, you're making a reading of somebody based on their looks. I sometimes realize that I have so much crap in my head that maybe these other people don't have, and I'm reading into stuff way more than they are. For instance, I'm trying to read whether this guy is going to kill me if I try to shoot his photo. I once saw this girl with a mohawk hanging out with this other kid who has all this skinhead gear on. They were smoking and hanging on this corner, and they started kissing, and I was just like, *Dude, this is such an incredible photo. I'm just gonna go up and start shooting this.* But back in my childhood, you would not go up to that guy. He would kill you. In '85, if you went up and tried to talk to a skinhead, you were going to get beaten up. That's how it was down here in Huntington at least. But that doesn't mean anything anymore.

Judd: Now they'll say, "Can you take a selfie on my phone while you're doing it?"

Ed: Exactly, I had to gather up all this bravery to go up to them, when their reaction was just like, "Oh cool." And I go, what am I thinking? This is a new generation. They all want to be famous. They love the attention. That's why they have a mohawk: because they want to be seen. So, it helps you realize, *I have all this baggage that hinders me sometimes.* The things that I'm thinking about and my assumptions about people—I feel like I'm relearning that every day out shooting.

Judd: When you started skateboarding, was the skateboarding scene pretty new?

Ed: I started in '85, so it had been going on for a while. I always thought I came in kind of late, because it was the late seventies when skateboarding started becoming its own thing, where it wasn't just a thing that surfers did to pass the time when the waves were flat. By '85, when I started, there was a big spike. Tony Hawk and Steve Caballero—these were the hot guys. And I think I was just one of the thousands of kids that got caught up in skateboarding in that time period.

Judd: So, Tony Hawk is in the generation before you, by just a couple of years?

Ed: I mean, at the time, when you're young and you're watching him, you're like, *He's super old. He's an adult compared to me.* But now I'm looking at it like, *Oh, Tony Hawk's only four or five years older than me, at the most.*

Judd: What about that movie *Dogtown and Z-Boys*? Was that a couple of years before you?

Ed: That's documenting the sixties. Craig Stecyk is the guy who was a big inspiration to me, and he still is. He does art and everything now, but he's the first person to contextualize skateboarding and see it as an art form, which I don't think the people doing it even thought. This guy was smart enough to see, *Whoa, what's happening here is incredible. This is a super weird, separate subculture that no one knows about. And I'm gonna shoot photos of it and share that with people.*

Judd: And what years was he doing that?

Ed: I think he wrote a famous article about it in the seventies. It's the piece that everyone points to as the real beginning of skate culture.

Judd: What were your intentions when you started skating? Was there a moment where it's like, *There's the potential for it to be more than just fucking around.* What was that transition for you?

Ed: Do you know the actor Jason Lee? He's been a pro skateboarder his whole life, and we both grew up together in Huntington. We skated together, and our healthy competition is what pushed each of us, I think. We loved each other, but we also kind of hated each other. We skated every day, but if he learned something new, then I had to learn it, and vice versa. It was a healthy competition that made us both get better, and we both started separating from the rest of the pack. And it's also all chance, too, because—lo and behold, we happened to live in Southern California, where skateboarding was huge. So, if you were any good, the chances that you were getting seen were just insanely high. If I had been this good in Texas, no one would have ever known.

Judd: What do you mean, "getting seen"?

Ed: There'd be, like, a trade show, and all the skateboarding companies would get together, and we would go out there. We wanted to be seen by these bigwigs, so we were like, "Let's go where we know all these industry guys are walking in and out, and we're gonna skate out in front and destroy it." And that's what happened. Steve Rocco, this guy who ended up starting one of the biggest companies in the late eighties, early nineties, saw Jason Lee skating out in front of a trade show and basically sponsored him on the spot.

Judd: That's crazy. You're just a kid, and there's this thing you're doing for fun, and then you're like, "Let's show off in front of the building here," and someone says, "Hey, I'll pay for all your stuff."

Ed: Yeah, basically. It starts with free boards, and then a sponsorship deal.

Judd: Did you ever have a vision of skateboarding as a way to make a living?

Ed: No, never. Cash was never a part of it. It was just about living that life. Had I never been sponsored, I think that everything would have been the same, almost. Skateboarding lets you not grow up, which has been amazing. I've been doing basically the same thing I've been doing since I was fourteen, and I've never stopped, so that's super fortunate.

Judd: At the same time, you're beginning to do art.

Ed: I started skating in 1985, and by 1990, I was pro, and I started painting in 1990.

Judd: When did you start photography?

Ed: I think the moment where I decided *I really need to shoot here* was in '94. That's when it hit me, that I had been living this super-charmed life, where you get paid to cruise around the world skating in front of people. That is insane. And the culture that I was a part of was insane, because I happened to be the only one who wasn't doing drugs and stuff, so I was the sober guy amongst a bunch of hard-partying kids.

Judd: Did art replace partying?

Ed: I don't know. I just never tried it.

Judd: That takes balls when everyone around you, in your subculture, is high all the time.

Ed: That was part of it. I had a little nugget of self-confidence, even in those early days, when all my friends were passing the joint around, like, "Hey don't you want to smoke?" and I just said, "If I'm not gonna be your friend because of this, then fuck you guys." And they didn't care.

Judd: My mom gave me five bucks to never smoke when I was in fifth grade, and for some reason I wanted to honor that for a long time.

Ed: I remember seeing my dad drunk all the time and smoking weed all the time. And there were a couple of moments when both my mom and my dad would pass out, and I'd be sitting there unable to wake them up. It was just me and my brother sitting in the house, like, "What do we do?" So, by the time I got into skateboarding, I was like, *I don't want to be part of that whole party scene.*

Judd: Another example of rebelling in a healthy way.

Ed: Exactly. I just wanted to get stuff done. Four years into that scene is when I realized I have something here to document. I sometimes try to explain it like, what if Robert Plant was a documentary photographer and could document those crazy stories you hear about Led Zeppelin on tour? I kind of have that situation here, where I can document this scene.

Judd: Did you have any influences for that style of documentary photography?

Ed: There was this photographer named Nan Goldin. And Larry Clark put out *Teenage Lust*, a book that documented his junkie loser scene in Tulsa, Oklahoma. I saw that book, and I realized, *I have my own world here. I'm going to shoot this world like these guys did theirs.* I started taking it super seriously and started carrying a camera everywhere and just documenting everything.

Judd: When did you first have somebody show interest in showing your work? Did it become art for you, or something that could also pay your bills?

Ed: As much as I want to say that I dug my way into this position with hard work, being a famous skateboarder helped a lot. None of the galleries I worked with knew I was a skateboarder—they all worked with me because of the work, which I'm happy about. But for ten years, I used my skateboard money to fund my art career. I was making money doing one thing, so I was able to do this other thing.

Judd: There are a lot of skateboarders who are into art. What do you think that connection is? I was talking to Spike Jonze about it, and he said filmmaking is like skateboarding because you're always trying to invent tricks. The whole point of skateboarding is to be inventive. That's why, when he started filmmaking, he thought, *I need to reinvent the wheel every time and come up with a way to shoot that no one's done before.*

Ed: That's a good way to see it. When I started, I was instantly put in this world of creative people. Then, as a sponsored skater, I'm suddenly around all these photographers who have to shoot me for magazines. Every day, I was going out and skateboarding with a dude who had a camera, and I would ask him, "How does that work? Tell me about exposure and stuff." So, I feel like the whole endeavor was creative and do-it-yourself, because the whole attitude at the time was *No one's going give you a shot at the Whiskey a Go Go, so you might* *as well just rent a warehouse and make your own show.* As kids doing art stuff, no one's going to put you in *Artforum.* Instead, somebody's going to make a zine, make a bunch of copies at Kinko's and give them out for free.

Judd: That seems different from comedy, or from people who want to be onstage and perform, where there's creativity and entrepreneurship, but also egomania to it. There's a sense of, *I want to be Eddie Murphy,* or *I want to be Bill Murray. Millions of people are going to pay attention to me and like me.* What you're describing feels very different, because it is art for art's sake. It's not like you thought this was going to take off.

Ed: Yes, but there's an ego part of it, for sure. As much as I try to suppress it and be humble, you just know that it's there, it's part of you. I want to have books out. I want to put stuff out there. And there is an ego to that. I look at an artist like David Hockney and go, *I want that giant studio. I want that acclaim even when I'm that old. I want to look back and say I inspired all these people.* You have to have a goal. I don't try and hide that fact.

Judd: When you look at all of your work, is there a consistent idea that runs through everything?

Ed: I always wanted to have a take, to have a point. And it changes, of course—it's never a fixed thing. My book *Deformer* is about how you get deformed into the person you are from all the stuff that happens to you, whether it's your crappy family life or whatever. That's the deformer that makes you who you are. And as a photographer, what I'm showing you is what I look at. As much as I say I'm just documenting life as it is, I'm hoping that, as the viewer, you get into my body and go, *Okay, this is how he sees the world.*

Judd: You got hurt this year. Is this the first year in a while that you haven't been able to skateboard?

Ed: I can still skate, but three years ago, when I broke my leg, I slowed down a lot. I had to decide whether or not I was going to try and come back to the pro level, and if I did want to do that, I would have to have one of these plates taken out, and the doctor was like, "I'd rather have you leave it in." So, he was saying retirement. I was just like, *As long as I can skate, I'm fine.* I just didn't want to stop skating.

Judd: That's a long run though. It's a Nolan Ryan–type of skating career.

Ed: I was lucky. The kids nowadays are higher, faster, and stronger than we were, but their careers are shorter 'cause they're jumping down crazy high heights, and they get hurt a lot. I'm lucky to have had this really long skate career and have stayed relatively healthy. I mean, I broke my neck and I broke my leg real bad. But relatively, I've been lucky.

Judd: The people that you started skating with, where are they now?

Ed: Well, Jason Lee went on to acting. He had that personality type that was going to succeed, whatever he did. Spike is also another person who went on to bigger fame once he left the skateboarding scene.

Judd: Mike Mills.

Ed: Mike Mills. He wasn't in my skate scene, but he was a skater.

Judd: I thought that movie was great, the *Beautiful Losers* documentary.

Ed: It's funny. I feel like a lot of us have tried to distance ourselves from that. I think that trying to make us sound like an artistic movement is weird. The Cubists were like, *We have a manifesto. We're all going to paint this way.* But with the Beautiful Losers—everyone's all over the place. I shot photos, I do paintings. And my art or style has nothing to do with Clare Rojas or Barry McGee. The only connection is that we all come from some kind of alternative subculture, whether it's the world of surfing, skating, or graffiti. That's the connection.

Judd: It's the complete wrong word to describe all of you, because everyone's doing really well, and there's no loser aspect to that, but it's kind of catchy for your show. And then people call you that for the rest of your life.

Ed: Yeah, we're the Beautiful Losers, like Freaks and Geeks.

GARY GULMAN

January 2020

Judd: You're on the tour following the special, so now you have the crowd that watched and appreciated the special. What does that feel like? Are they coming for pain that you're not providing, or are they so psyched that you're happy?

Gary: I wonder. There are people who meet me in line after the show, and they're in tears. You and I have been aware of depression for many years, and people have been open and abundant in our world, so, when I first started working on this, I thought maybe I'd missed the wave, that *This is something that everybody is familiar with, and I won't be saying anything new.* To the contrary: Everyone is relieved that I want to tell them. I wasn't the first person to bring this up. I could sense this from Richard Lewis in the eighties.

Judd: But Richard Lewis never really told us.

Gary: He wasn't explicit about his diagnosis, and he wasn't clear on his treatment, so maybe that was my adjustment or addition to it. Who knows how many people it reached, but all the people who are coming to my show have either seen it or knew somebody who it affected. The people who are in tears after the show—they've been so thankful for it. I don't know what to say except that it was a pleasure.

I mean, I've been rewarded for it to such an extraordinary degree. By the time I started writing it, the hard part was really over. The living—that's the brave part. When people say, "You are so brave"—the bravery was getting out of bed and walking my dogs. That was really hard. Talking about it to audiences who were complimentary and appreciative—that's been easy; that's been so rewarding.

Judd: When you're in the throes of depression, does it almost feel like you're another person?

Gary: It lies so beautifully. I've never been addicted to a drug, but people always say the addiction lies to you and tells you anything to get you into the position where you'll feed the drug habit or the alcohol habit. Depression is the same thing. It's telling you you're talentless, and then you don't want to get onstage, because *What have I got to say that's worthwhile?*

Judd: What else is it telling you other than that you're talentless? What is your depression saying?

Gary: That this is who I am, this is not a disease. *This is who you are, and you have made so many mistakes over the years that you'll never come out from under. You're a bad person, you're a really bad person, and if anybody knew who you really were, they would be horrified, and you wouldn't have a friend in the world, because you are petty and you are jealous and you're undisciplined and you're weak and lazy and—*

Judd: So, it's a *critical* voice?

Gary: It's so critical.

Judd: Because, when I was depressed, I just cried a lot. I didn't think I was a bad person. I felt like I had switched gears somehow and felt weak and shaky. I remember I went to a psych pharmacologist. My therapist said, "You have to go see this person. He will decide what drugs you should be on, or if you should be on drugs." And he just says, "How you doing?" and I just started crying so hard.

Gary: That's triggering, I felt the same way when people asked me. I remember going to see this pharmacist—he was behind the counter—and he said, "How you doing, big guy?" And I put my head on his shoulder and I wept. He said, "All right, come into the office," and we talked. Obviously, it wasn't a CVS. It can be as simple as *How are you doing?* I was always on the verge of tears, and that was another reason why I couldn't go out and do shows. There was one night where I rushed to the end of my set because I was about to break down in tears. While reciting the set, I was also thinking, *After this is over, I'm going to have to go home and be with myself.*

Judd: I remember when I was at the therapist, I was crying before I even got into how I was feeling. I just felt like crying instantly. Even when you're depressed, there is a solid part of your mind that's going, *Wow, you're really depressed right now,* and is observing it. So, as I'm crying to this guy uncontrollably, harder than I've cried to almost any person in my life, there's another part of my mind that goes, *I think you're going to get the medication.*

Gary: That is hilarious. I've been trying for years to make crying funny. Because it's one of those things where, if the six-day crying jag could be a bit, then I've gotten something out of it.

Judd: One of the magical things about being a comedian is when bad things happen you think, *I can use this in an act,* and it's not purely bad.

Gary: There's revenge and redemption over these tragedies if you can get a joke out of it.

Judd: What other reactions did you get from the comedy community about the special?

Gary: The thing that I couldn't get over was how people who I didn't think were even aware of me were telling me how happy they were for me. That was so nice. We learn over the years how to discount compliments, because some of the hyperbole is so ridiculous. We have to figure out from the people we work with what their compliment sounds like. Sometimes people damn you with faint praise. I had a friend who, no matter how well I did on a show, would say, "You looked great."

Judd: Whose appreciation meant the most to you?

Gary: David Letterman said really great things. He really liked it. And Amy Schumer wrote something nice, and her sister wrote something in a similarly thoughtful manner that wasn't the typical, "We loved it!" Everybody loves everything out here, but they said things. Then—so many messages from people in the mental health community. That was really moving. Doctors and professors, psychologists, social workers . . .

Judd: What did they say is the benefit of having done it? When they thank you for doing it, what are they thanking you for?

Gary: One thing a lot of them say is, "I'm going to show it to my clients," or, "I'm going to show it to my students." The other thing is that they said it reduces the stigma. It's been so hard to get people to go into the hospital or use ECT or medicine. There's so many people who are reluctant to even try medication for short term. Even people in my world, who've seen what it's done with me, and they're still reluctant. The other thing with comedians is they say they're afraid to lose their edge, their comedy, their sharpness. If that were the case, then you can just stop using the medication, but I found that I wrote maybe five, ten minutes during the two and a half years I was sick. Since then, I wrote *The Great Depresh* and I'm touring with it—ninety minutes to an hour and forty-five, depending on the audience.

Judd: That is the lie of all drugs and alcohol and medication. When you feel good, you generally write better. I've never written anything fantastic in a terrible mood.

Gary: I'm critical when I'm feeling well, but the criticism when I'm not feeling well is paralyzing.

Judd: I went on Prozac for six months, and my therapist said, "It's to even you out so you can go to therapy, start absorbing those lessons, and then, when you go off of it, maybe you'll be in a new place." And it turned out to be that way. That was the one time I had clear depression, which was uncontrollable. I had very bad panic attacks. I started getting them because I would take on these jobs punching up scripts, and in my head I thought, *If this movie is bad, it's only my fault.* I put this ridiculous amount of pressure on myself. So, I'd be rewriting *Happy Gilmore,* and I'm with all my friends, and we're all having fun, but I'm having this irrational thought: *I can take them all down if I don't make this scene historically great.* When I started having the panic attacks, I didn't know what they were. Just my temperature is rising, my heart is pounding, I'm claustrophobic, I'm melting down, but I've never heard of a panic attack. I'm a kid. So, I just think I've gone insane. I had them for a while before I finally spoke to a therapist, who said, "Oh, that's just a panic attack. Here's what you do . . ."

Gary: "Just."

Judd: The secret was you don't try not to have a panic attack, because that makes it worse. You don't run away from it. You allow yourself to feel it, and you remind yourself that everything will be fine, that nothing's going to happen. When you try to stop it, it's like taking a mirror and smashing it on the ground and stamping on the bits and creating a thousand mirrors.

Gary: That's a great analogy.

Judd: I think when you're young, you don't know what this is, you don't know how to take care of yourself, and you don't know who to speak to.

Gary: You don't understand that not everybody feels this way.

Judd: That's what the special does. It sends a message to everyone that you didn't get as a [young] person: that tons of people have this. It's not as big a deal as you think it is.

Gary: Jerry West the basketball star talked about having depression, and Bruce Springsteen said he had depression, and it made me feel better because I thought, *If I had their lives, I would be happy and wake up every day in a great mood.* While I don't think I'm anybody's Springsteen, it made other comedians think, *Oh. Being at his level is not the answer.* That was a great thing in *Funny People,* which I re-watched after the special, because you called me the next day, telling me, "It's normal for you to feel hungover and guilty about not feeling on top of the world after this special airs. Your adrenaline has been squirting constantly for three weeks and now it's over."

Judd: It's normal to get depressed after success, because you realize that it doesn't really make you happy in your core.

Gary: That was the *Funny People* message as well: that all this stardom wasn't the answer. It was the people, the misfits—that's the answer.

Judd: I needed a seventy-million-dollar budget to make the movie, but now people can say it in a podcast for free. My version of *The Great Depresh* was *Funny People.* I want to express it to other people, but it's a message to myself.

Gary: I feel the same way with *The Great Depresh.* So many times, I think to myself that I got more out of it than the audience. Because I would forget the lesson every single time. The lesson was always to do the thirty things every day—or however many it is to feel good—and not chase some achievement and not get wrapped up in an outside external project that was supposed to make me happy and didn't.

Judd: Now that you have some distance from the special, what do you think is the main idea that you wanted to tell people or yourself?

Gary: I think maybe two or three things. One: You're not alone. A lot of us are feeling this way; they just haven't told you. My therapist had told me fifteen years before, "If you tell everybody everything, they'll have nothing on you. You don't have to be so private. You don't have to keep all your flaws to yourself. It'll strengthen your relationships; people won't run away." That taught me you're not alone. And as soon as you say, "You're not alone," other people are saying, "Oh, I felt alone." Then, two: That there was hope, that it ends, that there's treatment, a lot of options for coming out of it, and that it's worth it. It's worth it. The line I really thought came off as too schmaltzy was "I'm so glad I stuck around for this," but it was true. I wanted to kill myself. I thought about it. I had plans. I had garages, I had things to jump off of. And thank God, I stuck around. Did you ever read "An Occurrence at Owl Creek Bridge"? Sometimes it feels like that—that I'm living all this [while] falling from the gallows. I'm pinching myself all the time, because I'm thinking they're showing me what I missed out on by killing myself at the worst of it.

Judd: And how close do you think you got?

Gary: Well.

Judd: Or, is there a comfort in just thinking it through?

Gary: There was the time in L.A. that I stood in my windowsill, but then, luckily, I pictured myself halfway down, thinking, *I regret this,* because I had read a *New Yorker* article about people—or just the entire San Francisco's Golden Gate Bridge.

Judd: There's a documentary about that.

Gary: Oh, really?

Judd: About all the people who tried to kill themselves.

Gary: Yes. Every person who survived said that they regretted it almost immediately after they started falling. Have I told you the comedy condo story? In Denver, at the Comedy Works, there's a great comedy condo. We've all stayed at the ones that are shitholes, but this one is actually really nice. It's in a luxury building, and it had a kitchen with that butcher block of knives. I pulled out the biggest one, held it to my wrist, and luckily thought, *There's a person who's going to have to clean this up on Monday and hates cleaning up after comedians who are alive, and this is going to ruin their life.* That was how I rationalized my way out of that. And then I had all kinds of pill things. And then there was the night I put a plastic bag over my head. It doesn't work. I think you need another person with the plastic bag technique.

Judd: Is that because of the depth of the place you're going to or how long you had been depressed?

Gary: For how long I had been sick and that there didn't seem to be any coming out. My depression also told me, *Even if you were to turn your life around at this point, what's the point?* I tell everyone who will listen that there's no "too late to have made it." There's no point where you're like, "Oh, I was too old; I can't enjoy it."

Judd: Throughout this, you were married, or you were [still] dating your wife, Sade?

Gary: I was living with Sade since 2015.

Judd: It's also clearly a chemical meltdown, because you're having it at a moment when you're also in love and supported by someone. So, the cloud isn't about the circumstances of life.

Gary: I think it's a chemical disorder, because there have been moments in my life where I was in such a worse position. I had been engaged in 2008 to a woman who was into conspiracy theories. The stock market was crashing, and she convinced me to take my retirement fund and buy a house upstate in New York, a farmhouse on a farm, because the economy was going to fall apart, and we needed to live off the land. Six months in, she got bored and less interested in me, moved out, and I was stuck with a farmhouse in the middle of the woods. My closest neighbor was a mile away. Most people just had it as a summer place. There was really nobody around, and I became best friends with my dog groomer. To this day, we're close friends. She would say, "Do you want to go to yoga today?" and then we would go to an AA meeting. I'm not sober, I don't drink, but I would go to those meetings, and those were my people. I had no money, I had this mortgage, and I was having to drive two hours to go in and do spots.

Judd: For thirty dollars?

Gary: Yes. I was losing money hand over fist, and I was much happier than I was coming off a special, making a living, having a Midtown apartment for four thousand dollars a month and a woman who loved me and was doing everything in her power to save me. So, yeah.

Judd: When I was a kid, my parents got divorced, and it was really ugly. I wish my parents [had] sent me to a therapist. I wish I'd learned some mental health skills and understood what was going on. It took until my mid-twenties to begin to start to understand it, and my most recent therapist is saying things I have never heard before that are life-changing, and I'm fifty-two.

Gary: Like what types of things?

Judd: He talks a lot about evolution and fight-or-flight responses. Cavemen were trying not to get eaten by predators, so your memory is programmed to remember bad things. If there's a bear in a cave that you walk into, you'll remember never to walk in that cave, because that's where you saw the bear, but if something good happens to you, you're not programmed to remember it unless something highly emotional happens around it. As a result, your mind is filled with more bad things than good things, because the bad things served your safety. But now we're in modern life, and things aren't bad, but your brain is still seeking to protect you by scaring the shit out of you. He also says that, to your brain, the safest place you could be is in bed in your apartment. It's not just you. That's how we've evolved. What's the safest thing I can do for you? Make sure you're not around where the bears are. And it does make perfect sense, this inclination to be negative. You're really going against your mind if you're the crazy positive person. If you want to be, it has to be a practice. You have to rewire your brain.

Gary: But can you rewire it?

Judd: You can't if you don't know that. It took until I was fifty-two years old to realize that when I'm hypervigilant and when I'm looking for trouble for no reason, it has nothing to do with me. Maybe a hundred of those happen a day. Like, *I'm going to make you fight with your wife about leaving early to the airport because we got to get there even though there's no reason to get there early.* The lack of control is terrifying. I always connected that to my parents' divorce, but I think it's well beyond that. The idea that if I'm very organized and I keep my shit together and I'm successful, life won't collapse around me, but that makes you argue with someone if they're going to make you late for the airport because you've raised the stakes.

Gary: A lot of philosophers and psychologists will say you have no control ever, and to them it's very freeing. To me—it makes me want more control.

Judd: But is there peace in letting go? The only mystical experience I've ever had—I was on my way to promote *Funny People* in Australia. I thought the movie was going to be a big hit. It wasn't. It was very expensive, and it got reasonably good reviews, but at the box office, it didn't do as well as it needed for how expensive it was. And I really had put so much of my heart into it. My mom died the year before, and I hadn't dealt with it in a healthy way. I dealt with it by making a movie about it. And I must have been very stressed out. On the plane, I heard a voice—the only time that had ever happened to me in my life—and it just said, *Surrender.* It wasn't even a concept that I knew a lot about at the time. It wasn't like I was reading a lot of self-help books using that word. But it felt like God. And I [had] never had an experience like that before. It was a couple of minutes on a plane where I really understood what the word *surrender* meant.

Gary: It was a voice or a thought?

Judd: Well, it was beyond a voice and beyond thought. It was just in me, a message.

Gary: And you were awake?

Judd: I'm awake, and it's not coming off thinking about the subject. It just hit me like a truck. Powerfully, physically—just *Surrender. Stop trying. Just let it all go. Let everything go.* And of course I ignored it.

Gary: How did that change your trip to Australia?

Judd: I did have a good trip, and I think it was very helpful to me for a long time. I certainly haven't thought enough about it. But it was the only religious experience I've ever had, whatever that means.

Gary: I think that all along the way on this special and everything since, I've had to divorce myself from the results and reset the expectations. The healthiest thing was that once I had something that people were reacting to in the live show, I said, *As long as you're making these live shows, people feel less alone, feel a little bit better, feel understood, whether HBO passes or whether HBO puts it on and people don't like it, you still helped a lot of people.* I just pray to God, had it not been well received, that I would have gotten through the way I got through the last quote-unquote *failure.*

Judd: Because, in your head, you didn't like the last special, and it started a spinout. Would you have had the spinout anyway if it wasn't a failure?

Gary: Exactly. It made me reckon with how I viewed myself since five or six years old: *If I'm great at something, then I'll feel good about myself.* And also: *I'm not a real man. I'm not aggressive.* I read an article by Peggy Orenstein in *The Atlantic*—she had covered girls for twenty-five years as a reporter, and now she wanted to write a book about boys—and I really expected to find out that Millennial boys were in touch with their emotions and could cry and were able to express traditionally feminine ideas and thoughts. But this woman, in her reporting, found that guys still equate manhood with being aggressive and dominant and that silence was the key to being a man and that crying was humiliating. I thought, *Wow, I had no idea that it's still going on.*

Judd: But that also can be partially evolutionary. It could have something to do with thousands of years of men thinking, *This is the way I'm supposed to behave, this is my role, I fight the bear.* You can't cry while fighting the bear. I like blaming everything on evolution.

Gary: When I was reading *Feeling Good,* which is sort of the bible of cognitive behavioral therapy, the fight-or-flight panic reaction is in the first chapter. And the cortisol is poison.

Judd: I was reading this morning that when your cortisol and adrenaline kick in, your brain goes into a fog, and it has trouble making choices. It delays the amount of time it takes for you to figure things out. So, the moment when you're in a panic is a moment when you're less clear than you normally are, and you're more reactive, so you're more likely to make the wrong decision if you're in a panic. That explains every horror movie.

Gary: That makes perfect sense. But the viewer has a different perspective, because they're thinking clearly, because they're not in danger; they're in a movie theater. It's taken me all these repetitions to figure out, *This is where your brain goes.* On Wednesday, I listened to a set that I did because I didn't want to repeat the jokes, and I was like, *Oh, I'm terrible. I am a terrible comedian.* And then I went over my notes, put together a setlist for the Wednesday night show, and before the show started, I was anxious, and I thought, *This is where they find me out.* But I was able to step outside of that, like another narrator saying, *This is just what you do. You're anxious because you haven't been onstage in three or four days, and you just listened to a set, and everyone listens to a set and hates it.*

Judd: I don't listen to the sets. My fear of losing material for the ages isn't enough to get me to listen to it. That's why Adam Driver doesn't watch his movies. He feels like it will make him self-conscious, that he has to be so committed and put himself out there that if he increases the critical voice in his head by watching all of his movies and being hard on himself, he won't do as good a job on the next one. Bill Hader was like that. But then he created his own show and directed it and had no choice but to pay attention to what he does, and I think it really benefited him. But there are a lot of people that never watch their own movies.

Gary: The adjustment I made with this project was I trusted Mike Birbiglia and you to tell me if it was terrible. I just have to accept that it's good enough for them, so it has to be good enough for me. Because when I watch myself, I can see every flaw, everything that I can change, so I just have to trust some people whose taste I believe in.

Judd: Sometimes when I watch myself, I'll think, *Look at that guy acting all cocky. Shut the fuck up.*

Gary: That's exactly what I say to myself. *Who do you think you are? What a fucking phony.*

Judd: Even when it's going well, you hate that guy: *Oh, look at you, having a good time. Shut up. Go home.* For me, the negative voice just always said, *Don't be a comedian.* Even when I have a good set, sometimes I feel it creep in. I did a set the other night, and the show went well, and I had a good set and enjoyed talking to everybody, and then I drive home—it's about a thirty-minute drive—and after just ten minutes, the voice just goes, *What did you say to everybody? What were you talking about in the greenroom? Was that set okay? It wasn't that good. I think Tom Papa killed way harder than you.* It's very hard to let that voice go or distract myself to not engage it. Because, for me, it really wants me to stop. It really says, *You should not be doing this. It's embarrassing. It's embarrassing that you want to do this.* I have to constantly remind myself why I do it, how it makes me feel, that maybe some people get a kick out of it, but that voice wants me to not get up again. It's still a pretty loud voice. When you go to a club, and there's comedians around, do you start trying to tune in to *Do people here think I know how to do this?*

Gary: I mean, that's the thing. It's good for us, though, I think, because we don't want to be the comedian who we roll our eyes at. The guy who doesn't know that he's dated. When somebody in their thirties or younger tells me that they enjoyed themselves, I'm like, *Okay, I've got another four or five years to rock this.* If I can just keep watching the younger people in the show. I take Emmy Blotnick on the road with me, and then Dina Hashem and this other woman who I've seen at the Comedy Cellar a few times, named Brittany Carney. Then there are guys older than me, like Eddie Pepitone, and I think, *All right, if I can be embraced by Eddie or Todd Glass . . .*

Judd: I think one of the hard things about being a comedian is you meet so many other comedians and you want all of them to like you.

Gary: No matter what the style is.

Judd: No matter who they are, no matter their personalities, you want every single one of them to like you, respect you, and have a warm relationship with you, and it's statistically impossible to not have five or ten percent of those people hate you just based on your personality. I noticed, when I was doing stand-up these last few years, that I'm meeting a lot of people and I'm getting a little neurotic. Suddenly, I'm in the clubs a couple nights a week. I'm meeting hundreds of people, and that's a lot of people to wonder if they respect you, why they don't return your text quickly. If you're a neurotic person, it's a lot to tap your neurosis into.

Gary: It's unenviable going in after you haven't been onstage in twenty years, in a position where if you're not immediately up to speed with the other comedians, people are like, *Why is this guy getting back into it?* That is not easy. I used to think if you didn't do it for twenty years, even five years, you would never be able to pick it up again. I think it was helpful seeing you, because I was planning on giving it up for six months, and part of me was like, *You may never get it back. You'll lose your spot in line.* But you made the right choice because you could have killed at mainstream clubs, the small improvs, but to go to Largo and the Comedy Cellar is going off the high-dive board.

Judd: I didn't know what I was walking into. The Cellar—everyone is such a killer there. Everyone is a beast, but you just get used to walking in there, and they say, "You're following Ray Romano tonight," or, "You're following Jim Norton tonight." "You're following Amy Schumer." I can see how it would be hard to do, year after year after year: to generate more material, feel engaged, to not feel repetitive to yourself.

Gary: That was part of my breakdown. I didn't have new stuff to go out with, and so I stopped going out, and what I didn't realize was that part of what was keeping me sane was getting out of the house once a day to be with a bunch of people who I could be myself with.

Judd: It does make you happy to just go there. I found that it's put me in a much better mood. Even making a movie this year, which I really enjoy, I wind up in an editing room for six months, but I feel like my mood has been much worse the last six months. With a set, the stakes are lower, but the joy is higher.

Gary: The feedback is instant.

Judd: There is something of value when you make a movie in that it can touch people for a long time, but in terms of your own endorphins, just trying out a bunch of stupid jokes—the amount of chemical joy I got out of it was so high. I never want to feel like my self-esteem comes from getting approval, but I also feel like it reminds me what I do, what my contribution is, so it's nice to be around people. It's not just that I want to be applauded; it's more like, *Oh, you've seen the stuff, it's meant something to you,* and then, when I go back to work writing something, it helps that I did a Q-and-A somewhere, and people reminded me that they remember some movie or something connected with them. It's easy for that to drift away, especially in a world where there's so much content. You think, *There's five hundred TV series right now. What is the point of being five hundred and one?*

Gary: Well, because five hundred and one could be *Freaks and Geeks.*

Judd: That's why you have to leave the house to remind yourself.

Gary: The first time we ever met was in a general [meeting], and I didn't have any ideas, and we just sat there, and I asked you questions about *Freaks and Geeks,* and you said that you had a cancellation and said, "Let's get everything in that we wanted to get in." You made it seem like, out of necessity, you made it so good.

Judd: It is true. There was some panic that there isn't going to be another eighteen of these, so *What were we going to do in season three? Should we do it now?* I was in the therapist's the other day, and the therapist is talking about my movies. He's very aware of what I made. Sometimes he references it. So, he says, "Judd, you know you basically do the same thing every single time. You have somebody, and he's an insecure guy, and it's a coming-of-age story, and he has to learn how to become a man, and so, bad things happen, and he gets his ass kicked a little bit, and then, at the end, he has to come through for someone and be a man, right? That's what you do, right?" It was so tossed off, not meant to disrespect, but completely accurate. And I thought, *I'm so transparent*. I thought I['d] tricked people into thinking all these movies were different, and it did make me realize, *Yeah, I guess all these movies aren't what I consciously thought they were a lot of the time*. I'm aware that they are coming-of-age stories, but he described them as learning how to be a man, which I never thought any of my movies were about. He's relating it to *Funny People* and *This Is 40*, and in a way, *Trainwreck* is about being an adult.

Gary: And *Knocked Up*.

Judd: It's funny, and it made me think about how there are certain things that you have trouble with as a person, and in your heart you talk about it over and over and over again. And it's hard to be an adult. It's hard to be a man. The world challenges you. Can you get your shit together and evolve and learn the lesson you need to learn? Then I noticed something that was at the end of almost every movie I've ever made and every TV show, almost down to the episode: I tend to write an ending where one character selflessly is present for the other character, who desperately needs it. It's everywhere. You can name anything. What is the end of *This Is 40*? It's Paul [Rudd] and Leslie [Mann] watching Ryan Adams together. We know she probably doesn't like his taste in music, and she's just trying to support him and show him she loves him. At the end of *Knocked Up*,

Seth [Rogen's Ben] reads the baby book, and he drives [Katherine Heigl's character, Alison] home from the hospital.

Gary: That's a man.

Judd: And in *Funny People,* Adam [Sandler] writes jokes for Seth. The big star drops all his bullshit and is present for Seth. It's always a selfless, giving gesture. So, then I thought, *I must want that so bad: Every time I write anything, that's what it is.* What is the end of *Freaks and Geeks*? It's the prettiest girl in school dancing with the nerd, and then Lindsay Weir dancing with the mentally challenged kid. It's a double. And I thought, *I must try to force everyone I deal with to do that ending.* It must be a mantra. Can you be selfless? Can you be giving?

Gary: But you also have turned that into your life. The other side is the secret that it actually feels really good. I wonder if that's part of the evolution. It feels good to be selfless. I read this Twain quote that if you want to cheer yourself up, cheer somebody else up. And it works, man. I'm having a tough day, so I email the *Conan* guy somebody's video. I try to get him on *Conan,* and he gets on *Conan.* It's more exciting for me than the last time *I* did it. It just feels great. Because I remember what it was like to get my first TV spot. You change the way you view yourself as a comedian, and so did your family, which is huge. Also, I've read everything Philip Roth has written, everything Kurt Vonnegut has written, saw every Judd Apatow movie, every Woody Allen movie, every Albert Brooks movie. They all work in the same themes and ideas. You read one Kurt Vonnegut book, it's not the same book, but it's the same types of people, the same relationships, the same exchanges, the same morals. Woody has become so problematic, I can't watch his shit anymore, but he was pretty much telling the same story every time.

Judd: Even when you think you're making different things you're making the same thing. When you were a kid, when did you first notice stand-up comedy or think to yourself, *There's a world where I could attempt that?*

Gary: Well, my brother had a job at the movie theater, and who knows how many nights a week he worked, but he would watch the movies. There were two movies over the few years that he worked there that he pretty much memorized: *Blazing Saddles* and *Young Frankenstein*, and he could do them word for word. He would come home and have the entire family in stitches, so I knew I loved to laugh. I knew I loved comedy and jokes, and then David Brenner was on either *Mike Douglas* or *Merv Griffin*, and I fell in love with this form. Bill on *Freaks and Geeks* sitting in front of the TV table watching Garry Shandling on *Dinah Shore*: That was my childhood. My mother would yell, "Comedian on!" I'd be in the other room or outside, and I'd come running in. I would memorize their jokes and get laughs in class. To those kids, anything Bill Murray said was automatically funny, and you can get laughs repeating it at school. In first grade, I remember the teacher said, "What is a chick?" And [one] kid said, "A baby chicken," and then, without raising my hand, I say, "Or a girl." And she laughed, and everyone in the class laughed, and I was hooked. The dopamine—I'm sure that was coursing through my feelings. It happened over this past Christmas. I was with Sade's family, and there were older relatives, Southern Black relatives, and they were telling stories, and I was laughing, and then I said something, and everybody laughed, and I was like, *Oh man, I'm having the time of my life. This is fantastic.* It wasn't in front of a real audience, but I had an audience, and I was in seventh heaven. And a lot of people say, "Gulman can't play the Black rooms."

Judd: Where were you doing it when you started? Massachusetts?

Gary: Boston. Nick's Comedy Stop in Boston. The emcee of my first open mic was Billy Martin, who writes for Bill Maher, and after my set, he said, "That was wonderful," and I was like, *Oh he thinks I'm wonderful!* So, I just kept doing it. I had a very fortunate experience, but you look back on your early stuff, and you're like, *Oh my gosh, where did I have the delusion to think that I would ever be good at this?* I remember when I did this state abbreviations joke, and people were very positive, and then Patton Oswalt wrote this glowing appreciation of it on Facebook, and I thought, *All right, you can't get out of bed, you hate yourself, and you think you're talentless. But this man, who you idolize, thinks you're funny. That is something.* And it helped a little bit, it really did.

Judd: When I have a project and people send me nice emails or tweet something nice, I will screenshot it and put it in a file I call "Self-Esteem Support."

Gary: I do that now. It's a rainy-day file. It's so helpful. I remember Nikki Glaser said that I was her favorite comic. I added it to a list. It was called "Don't Forget," and it said, "You're Nikki Glaser's favorite comedian." I feel like it's important that people who I think are funny think that I'm funny.

Judd: Those moments and compliments can power you for years.

Gary: Now that I realize it, I try to do that. I'm not phony about it, but whenever I get the opportunity, I want to keep the young people, or the people who aren't getting the recognition they deserve, going.

Judd: I remember Paul Feig got a letter from Steven Spielberg saying he liked *Freaks and Geeks*. And the letter's beautiful. I'm so jealous; I wanted that letter so bad. So, I wrote Spielberg a funny letter just to get a response, and I thought it would trigger a praise letter, and at some point I spoke to his assistant, and she said, "I read the letter. I don't think Spielberg will get these jokes." So, he didn't even read it; she just stopped it because she knew it would be ineffective. Then, years later, when *Knocked Up* came out, I get a call like, "Steven Spielberg trying to reach you on the phone."

Gary: Holy shit.

Judd: So, I refused to take the call, and I communicated that I wasn't available, but it'd be great if he wanted to send me a note. And he did! He sent me a note and said "I feel like *Knocked Up* is this generation's *American Graffiti*." That's the one that gets me through some of the rough spots. But it took years of manipulation to get it.

Gary: You handled it perfectly. You knew what you wanted, and you made it happen.

Judd: I hate that there are emails now. Only Tom Hanks will still type a letter on a typewriter.

Gary: But you can print those out and frame them.

GAYLE KING

May 2020

Judd: I want to ask you about the work you've done at *O Magazine*, because I am a self-help freak. What is your relationship with that world?

Gayle: When the magazine started twenty years ago, Oprah's mission was to do a personal growth guide that met women where they were, rather than telling them how they can get thin thighs in thirty days, so that they feel good about themselves and not try to be somebody they're not. That's where we started, and I'm proud to say we're still there, to this day. That's still a core mission that resonates today, because I feel like there are a lot of us wounded people walking around the planet, searching, trying to figure it out, trying to heal ourselves and heal each other.

Judd: It's also a weird world now, because social media has exposed us to everybody's point of view. A lot of people act out their emotional issues on social media channels, and many of them don't really think anybody's reading it.

Gayle: We read it and take it all in, too. You get a hundred good compliments, but then there's that one negative one from someone who you don't even know, whose opinion you shouldn't even care about.

The thing is, you can say stuff on social media with no accountability, and that's not a good thing.

Judd: All the social media algorithms reward our worst instincts. If you like one type of conspiratorial video on YouTube, the algorithm will take you to something even meaner, because that's how they think they're keeping people's attention. In a way, they're training you to watch the worst of us.

Gayle: We are rewarded for bad behavior in general. Look at the shows that are doing well now. On all these different franchises, you're rewarded for being your worst possible self. I'm no Pollyanna, but that stuff about doing unto others as you would have them do unto you, treat people the way you want to be treated—that stuff is real, and we need to figure out a way to get back to that without sounding outdated or out of touch.

Judd: Do you feel like everything you've done your whole life has prepared you for this moment, where people are looking to you at a time of crisis for information and emotional support?

Gayle: Listen, I majored in psychology. I wasn't going to do what I'm doing now—I was going to be a child psychologist. Or I was going to be a lawyer, because I love listening to people's problems and giving unsolicited advice. I love that and still do. But when I was in college, I got a job at a TV station and just became hooked on television news. You don't even realize you're learning stuff when you're learning it. You go from one job to the next, and it's not like you're saying, *Now I'm going to learn this. And now I'm going to learn that.*

Judd: How do you prepare for your interviews, especially when you're going to be talking to someone unpredictable or under a lot of scrutiny?

Gayle: Talk about being prepared—that came into play for me for the R. Kelly interview, when he just went batshit crazy in the middle of it. That was the first interview he did after that documentary, and he was saying it wasn't true, that everybody was lying. He really wanted to go on air and tell what he says was *his* truth. At the interview, he went from zero to one hundred and ten, just like that. Had that happened to me earlier in my career, I would have been afraid, but I had had enough experience and enough preparation. I'd watched his past interviews and noticed that when he gets upset and mad, he leaves, and I'm just sitting there with my papers, thinking, *I'm not done.* I know if I made a movement to stop him or tried to calm him down, he would have stormed off. So, I just sat down. I looked at him, looked at the chair, looked at him, looked at the chair. I let him know, *I'm not going anywhere, whatever you're doing, I'm not going anywhere.* And I think he saw that. He sat back down. And I was sort of shocked at that, because I was sure he was going to leave. But he also really wanted to tell his story, as he saw it. When that interview was over, he thanked me for allowing people to see his passion and his pain. He actually thought it went well. So, are you prepared for that? No. But I rule my life by intention, too. I believe any question can be asked, I just think that there's a time and a place to ask it. I never want to do a "gotcha" interview. I never want to humiliate anybody or put anybody on the spot. That said, there are times that you have to ask difficult and uncomfortable questions.

Judd: There's also such a long history of people like R. Kelly, who were terribly abused in their childhoods, and then, for whatever reasons, they hurt other people.

Gayle: Hurt people hurt people. But I also think, at some point, you have to take responsibility for your actions. Like, I know you're hurt. Your childhood was messed up. But that was then, this is now, and you have to take responsibility for your actions.

Judd: You came up in the *Anchorman*-like world of late seventies–era American journalism. A world ruled by the male chauvinist pig and where sexual harassment was pervasive in office spaces. How was that for you as a young person jumping into the business?

Gayle: There was a time where a camera guy said something very inappropriate, something like, "I'd like to take you in the car and lick you all over." I was twenty-three, and I didn't know what to say. Now you know what to say, but back then, even though I knew it was wrong and out of line, I just sort of ignored it. But I haven't had any stories where I felt like I was compromised by someone in a powerful position. Knock on wood.

Judd: You've been at the epicenter of this all as a journalist, it seems to keep intersecting with your life.

Gayle: It really does. I've struggled with some parts of the MeToo movement. I think [the] MeToo movement is important, but I also think that, if we're not careful, it could possibly backfire on women, and I'm concerned about that. You can't paint everybody with the same brush. For me, I'm more inclined to believe the woman, but just because she makes the accusation, it doesn't mean that a guy has to be totally destroyed without investigating what it is. I think we have to be careful with that.

Judd: It's especially complex when race enters into the discussion. I have a friend who was abused by Bill Cosby, so I was always very vocal about the fact that I thought he was guilty, and people would get very upset about it, because he knocked down walls in Hollywood for other Black performers. But at the same time, he's a violent criminal.

Gayle: Both things can be true. That's the thing. It's not an either-or; in some of these cases, both things can be true.

Judd: People don't know what to do with that, because they want a person to be a symbol so badly, and you can't say, "This legacy is great, but he's also the worst guy ever."

Gayle: In the Black community, there are so few symbols for us to look up to. So, if a Black person does something bad, I'm like, *Oh, God, oh, no.* I don't know of any white person in America who goes, *Oh, no, they're white. Oh no.*

Judd: We do that to Jews, like Harvey Weinstein. We ask, *Why did it have to be another Jew?* I think we all have some elements of that in our own communities, where we're like, *Can't we have a nice guy?* When you first got interested in journalism, what was your goal? Because it seems like you start anchoring pretty quickly.

Gayle: I just love breaking news. I remember when I was in a newsroom and there was a breaking news story, and I would see these people running around to get the news on, and I'd just go, *Whoa.* I've been hooked ever since. I do think—I think it's an honorable profession. And we're not a very big club. It may seem like it, but we're not a big club, so I take it very, very seriously. It's gotten so out of whack now, where people are so siloed, and you have extreme points of view over here and extreme perspectives over there. I try to give you the straight facts and let you sort it out for yourself. But we're also human beings, with a point of view; we're not robots sitting there.

Judd: What do people think the politics of your show is? Are you getting people from the left and the right?

Gayle: I don't think people think we're either far left or far right. I think that they think we pretty much give you the facts. Though, the Trump administration doesn't really like anybody in the mainstream media, so we're all painted with that brush.

Judd: There are so few places left that feel like the Walter Cronkite–type of show, but it's what you do every morning. It feels like there are a decent number of Fox viewers watching you.

Gayle: I've heard that. I've heard people say, "I don't like your station, but I like you." Do I say, "Thank you"?

Judd: Do you find the current climate engaging and fun as a journalist, or is there a part of you that wishes you were in one of those mellow periods of American history, so you could cover lighter fare?

Gayle: I feel like I did that already. I like having a front-row seat to whatever's happening, whatever that is, but this pandemic has struck me in a different way because of the uncertainty of it all. When you had Katrina, when you had 9/11, when you have a mass shooting, when there is a disaster normally, you know how it's going to play out. There's a beginning, where we're all going to rally together to fix it, and then we're going to go back to where things were. But this is such a moving target, because there's so much the experts don't know. That's what's so scary about it. I'm in New York, my son and daughter are in L.A., Oprah's in California. I don't know when I'll be able to see the people I care about the most.

Judd: Being a part of that messaging that you and Oprah are sending to people about spirituality and how they should treat other people—how has that affected you in this moment?

Gayle: I do think people are open to it. It's not woo-woo, and it's not complicated. For example, I think meditation is way more popular now than ever before. People are trying to figure out a way to center themselves, and you hear anecdotally about people reaching out more than they ever have to family and friends. People are craving connection. And it puts into perspective what really matters. You can have these great jobs that make a lot of money and big, wonderful houses and all that good stuff, but at the end of the day, you have people who are dying alone in the hospital.

Judd: Of the experts you've had on—because I know you've interacted with them personally—who are the ones you connect with the most?

Gayle: I really encourage you to talk to Bishop T. D. Jakes. He is amazing. It's not all religion; he just has such good common sense. Maya Angelou was a big touchstone in terms of really helping me navigate different things. I really miss her now, because she was always so wise. I can remember calling her about something. I go, "They said *da da da da da* . . ." And she goes, "Stop it. Just say thank you." I go, "What do I say thank you about?" She said, "Whining is so unbecoming. It lets them know there's a victim in the neighborhood. So, just say thank you." And she would always say, "People may not remember what you said or what you did, but they will always remember how you made them feel." That's also very true. I miss her voice.

Judd: These philosophies help me, because they force you to live in the present. Long-term thinking is rough when everything's uncertain, but it's helpful to say to myself, *Today I'm talking to Gayle, and then I'm going to have a burrito*. Like, we're all on the verge of smoking pot with our children at this point. All walls are about to come down just to get through all this.

Gayle: I know. I have never smoked pot, and Oprah has, and she goes, "We've got to have Gayle smoke pot." I just never have. I got drunk in high school, at the Christian Youth Leadership Conference, off of cheap keg beer, and I was one of the leaders. It made me so friggin' sick that, to this day, I don't drink. I remember, at the University of Maryland, sitting in a circle, and they would pass the marijuana cigarette around, although Oprah has said just the fact that I call it a "marijuana cigarette" is a problem.

Judd: What were your parents like? What was it like where you grew up?

Gayle: I grew up in Turkey from first grade to sixth grade. My dad was an electronic engineer for the government, and my mom was a stay-at-home mom. I had a very idyllic childhood. We'd go on vacation to Paris and Rome and Greece. I thought that's how everybody lived; I thought everybody traveled all the time. I was the oldest of four girls, but I always wanted a brother. My dad had diplomatic status in Turkey, and some people say my dad was in the CIA. I never thought that, but I am sort of curious now. They said a Black man in the sixties in Ankara had to have been in the CIA. He did have a room that we were not allowed to go into.

Judd: Oh boy.

Gayle: But it was because he was a ham operator, and it was his hobby. So, in the middle of the night, it'd go, *Didi didi di.* He died when I was a freshman in college, and I was executor of the estate. I was going through his things, and I found a card that said, "Scott King," which was his name, "Access to the White House, East Gate," or something. So, it lends itself to that theory, but I've had no proof of that whatsoever. I was always told he was an electronic engineer.

Judd: And did you ever consider using your journalistic skills to find out if he was in the CIA?

Gayle: I've asked a couple of people. And people always say, "I'll get back to you," and nobody does. I did ask my mom, and she said, "No, that's just not true." Then somebody said, "Well, maybe your mom didn't know."

Judd: You know what I think? I think your mom knew—she wasn't supposed to, but he told her anyway. And then your mom was good at keeping the secret.

Gayle: They said it wasn't uncommon sometimes for the spouse not to know. He did travel a lot. So, I don't know.

Judd: What is it like having access, in your personal life, to tons of fascinating people?

Gayle: It's so interesting, because you have perceptions of people, and then you meet them, and you go, *Wow, you really are just like a lot of people.* More people know their names, but they have the same insecurities, the same issues, which is why it's so refreshing when you meet somebody who you've admired and they turn out to be really terrific people. Like Tom and Rita. You meet them, and they are exactly who they appear. And then, sometimes, you meet someone else, and you think, *Gosh, they're really insecure.* I'm not saying it's all smoke and mirrors, but I find that just because somebody is famous doesn't mean they have their shit together.

Judd: No, and a lot of them are amazing precisely *because* they don't have their shit together. Who have you met that had a personal impact on you or that you always wanted to meet?

Gayle: I was in awe of Nelson Mandela. Meeting him was definitely a highlight, because I couldn't understand how someone could go through what he went through and not be bitter. Even behind closed doors, he was not bitter. Now I have a question for you, Judd. Would you agree with me that a sense of humor is a sign of intelligence? Because I think you have to be intelligent in order to be funny.

Judd: Yes, I think most comedians are trying to make sense of the universe. And comedy is their way of expressing their search.

Gayle: I like Dave Chappelle very much. I groveled to him for two years to come on my show.

Judd: Did you get him?

Gayle: Yes. He did an interview, and it was so good. I wanted Dave Chappelle and Bruce Springsteen, because I love Bruce Springsteen's music. I love country music. I just love music, period, all different kinds. And I would keep asking and asking, because Bruce doesn't need to do an interview, ever, about anything. He doesn't. And he finally agreed for his thing on *Western Stars*, which is very good. I wanted Dave, and I wanted Bruce. Now it'd be nice to talk to the Queen. But she's not doing interviews with anyone.

Judd: So, that's the person you have left on your list? The Queen?

Gayle: I like the Queen. I like Harry and Meghan. I think we have a different kind of pope now; I'm curious about him. And I'm fascinated, too, by Kim Jong-un, like, *What makes him tick, really?* I love pop culture. I love politics. That's why this job is so perfect for me, because you really get to do anything and talk to anyone. What other job do you get to do that in?

GEORGE SHAPIRO

June 2018

Judd: Let me just ask about Jerry for a minute, because you've had such a long, fruitful relationship with him. How did you guys meet?

George: It's a very simple story. At the original room at the Comedy Store, there was a young guy who worked for us at the office, named Jim Canchola—he was the one who spotted Jerry first. He said, "You have to see this guy Jerry Seinfeld." So, I went to see him, and then I brought [talent agent] Howard West, my partner, and we both loved him. He was so smart. When we first saw him, he would stand behind the microphone and wouldn't move three inches either way. Now he's sixty-three years old, and he's flying across the stage.

Judd: What year was that?

George: That was July fifth, 1980.

Judd: What's interesting is he wasn't a regular at the Comedy Store, right? He didn't spend much time there.

George: When he started out, he was there, and then there was this conflict with [Comedy Store co-owner] Mitzi Shore. Jerry believed there should be no boundaries with comedy, but Mitzi wanted people to just work at the Comedy Store and not at other places—not at the Ice House, and especially not at the Improv. It's so funny, because Garry Shandling was on one of Jerry's *Comedians in Cars Getting Coffee* episodes, and at the last minute, they decided to stop off at the Comedy Store, because they [had] both worked there at the same time. They walk around, and they're looking at all the pictures of the comedians that are up there. There's a great picture of Garry Shandling, and then Garry's looking around and asks, "Where's your picture, Jerry?" And they couldn't find it, because Mitzi probably took it down.

Judd: I remember, when I started working at the Improv in the late eighties, Jerry hadn't done a lot of acting work. He had been on the TV show *Benson*, and he got fired.

George: He was fired off of *Benson*, and they didn't tell him. He was like a messenger boy for them, and then he would write jokes for *Benson*. He did three episodes and went to the table read, and they sat around the table, and someone came over and said, "Excuse me, you know you're not in the show anymore?"

Judd: Did he get upset?

George: He was kind of stunned, but luckily for Jerry, and the great gift of stand-up comedy, he went right on the road. He went right to Tempe, Arizona, at the Improv. He killed.

Judd: At the time, all the comedians really looked up to Jerry and knew he was as great as you could be, but there was still a feeling that *This is all Jerry does*. He's not an actor, and there was zero expectation that he was going to be anything but one of the great stand-ups. He felt like the least likely guy to do what he went on to do. It didn't feel like he was chasing that; he was all about the stage.

George: Jerry was just emerging, getting a little publicity. He got this little article in *People* magazine, and then he was playing for the first time in New York City, at the Town Hall, his first theater. He only played clubs before that. Brandon Tartikoff was the president of NBC at the time, and I used to send Brandon tapes of Jerry, just to keep him up to date. Even though he was on NBC a lot, Brandon didn't see all the *Tonight Shows* and *Letterman Shows* that Jerry did. So, I sent him this simple little letter that said, "Dear Brandon, Jerry Seinfeld is appearing at the Town Hall in New York doing his first theater date, and I predict that he will have a television series on NBC very soon." No one came to see him, but it triggered a meeting, and Brandon said, "If there's anything you can think of that you'd like to do, like a talk show or a variety show, you tell me." So, Jerry responded with "All I ever wanted was a meeting like this." Then, three days later, he was doing stand-up in New York, at Catch a Rising Star, and Larry David was on the bill with him. So, Larry told him, "You know, NBC's interested in you." They were walking around to the supermarkets, ending up in a coffee shop, and Larry was saying, "This should be the show. Two comedians talking to each other." Then they decided that one of them should not be a comedian, and the George Costanza character should be a civilian type. So, they pitched it, and I always say, if there's a stand-up comedian involved in the project, let *him* do the pitch. Not the producer, not the writer, because people are going to laugh, and even if they don't love the format, they're going to know they felt good and laughed, and you'll have a much better chance of getting a deal. That's what happened when Jerry pitched it.

Judd: What's interesting about that is one might say that Larry David was failing at that moment in his career. He had been a cast member and a writer on the TV show *Fridays*, and it was canceled after two years. And he wasn't even successful as a stand-up. He didn't go on the *Tonight Show* or *Letterman* or almost any show as a stand-up. He didn't do things that would have signaled that he had the credibility to run the TV show with Jerry. It's a famous example of a show that didn't take off for years. It just kept surviving and took off in the third season.

George: The ratings were very low. In fact, the pilot got very bad reactions from the NBC research team. We all have the report framed in our bathrooms, Jerry and Larry and me. It says in bold print: **Pilot performance weak.** Audience didn't care about three guys going to a Laundromat and doing laundry, and people resented Jerry's stand-up routine being interrupted by the story line. Jerry's stand-up is why the show survived. He did stand-up at the beginning, middle, and end. So, I got the call from Brandon Tartikoff saying that it's not on the schedule; the comedy department passed on it. Then we spoke to [NBC executive] Rick Ludwin and asked, "Can we do something with the other department?" And Rick said he has two one-hour specials that he didn't order yet. He gave us an offer for four half-hour specials. It didn't do that well in the ratings, and we waited like a year, and then they ordered thirteen more. So, in two years, we did only eighteen episodes.

Judd: How did it take off?

George: This is exactly what happened: They were struggling from 1989 to '93. It was getting killed by *Home Improvement* and *Jake and the Fatman.* I always had nightmares of their fat ass burying us. During the summer reruns of 1993, the network put *Seinfeld* behind *Cheers*, and by the end of that summer, *Seinfeld* was out-rating *Cheers* in the last season, and then they got the nine o'clock time slot. Then it ended up number one with seventy-five million viewers at the last episode. And a record on top of it.

Judd: It sounds like you need somebody like Rick Ludwin to champion you.

George: He was a champion. He's the hero of *Seinfeld*, without a doubt. It never would have been on. They supported it when the ratings were very, very low. When they got the time slot, Larry David said, "I don't want those people. I don't need those people to watch the show."

Judd: Larry was always a guy who was willing to walk away. When they would give notes, Larry was like, "I'm done, I quit." Isn't that essential to making great TV?

George: After doing the first four episodes, NBC gave us this note saying they would like Jerry to marry Julia Louis-Dreyfus (Elaine Benes). After they said that, we had a meeting in the parking lot—me, Jerry, Howard West, and Larry. And Larry—who, as you pointed out, wasn't successful as a stand-up comic. He wasn't successful as a writer at the time. He said, "I'm finished. I won't do it that way. It's not the balance we want. It's not the show we want." Because, then, Kramer and George would be superfluous. They'd be dropping in and out as neighbors instead of being an essential part of the show, and that's the show. It's about four friends in New York City. That's the artist Larry is. He said, "That's all I'm going to do, because I don't think I have more than four shows in me anyway." That's a quote from Larry David, "I don't think I have more than four shows in me anyway."

Judd: How were they as showrunners, Larry and Jerry? Because it's so much work, and back then, they were still doing twenty-two episodes [a season].

George: They're dedicated because of their stand-up background. They're dedicated to every word count and every single script. They sat opposite each other at Radford Studios, and they rewrote every script, every word. They acted it out; then they rewrote it. The minute they wrapped rehearsal, Jerry would go right back to the office, sit with Larry, and write everything. They were just so dedicated to the show. They didn't think about being tired.

Judd: You've worked with some very bold and experimental people who also had giant successes. People like Seinfeld, Andy Kaufman, and the Smothers Brothers were only similar to one another in terms of how different they were from everyone else.

George: They were true to who they were. The Smothers Brothers had incredible pressure politically, and they kept doing the show. In fact, CBS was really interfering and wanted to take the editing part of the show from them—that's after the third season. I got a telegram picking up the Smothers for the fourth year, and I got the contract . . . and then Tommy stole the tapes. CBS said, "They violated the contract, and we're canceling the show." They canceled the show after three years.

Judd: You were their agent before they had the TV show—or did you join up with them later?

George: The funny thing is I was working on *The Steve Allen Show* in, like, '61, which brought me from New York to L.A. That's when I first saw the Smothers Brothers.

Judd: I remember when Steve Allen had Lenny Bruce on. Did you ever go see Bruce in those days?

George: When I was a kid, at William Morris, he used to play at this place called the Den, in the Duane Hotel in Manhattan. I used to see Lenny Bruce, and Nichols and May. I was in the mailroom at the time, when Lenny Bruce just got started, and I'll never forget it. He was so funny then, and that was before he got into the politics and the fighting for the rights and the Constitution. He was one of my great heroes.

Judd: What did people think was happening with him at that time? Was he edgy?

George: He was edgy, but he was just funny. He just had great, funny material, like George Carlin. I worked with George Carlin, and in fact, I got George Carlin's first speaking role as an actor, as Marlo Thomas's agent on *That Girl.*

Judd: Would you see Woody Allen in the Village in those days?

George: Woody I knew from way back, from his work with Sid Caesar. I used to book him when he was doing stand-up.

Judd: What was the booking job?

George: I was a variety television agent, so I was always with the comedians when they did personal appearances. Woody Allen did the Greek Theatre. There's no comedian I have ever met in my life more nervous than Woody Allen. You meet in person, and before he goes on, he's bouncing off the walls and the ceiling. He was so nervous, but that energy went right on the stage. And he was hilarious. He was a very, very funny stand-up.

Judd: You were in the mailroom, and then you were booking mainly comics and variety acts?

George: You're like a floating secretary when you're in the mailroom, so, when an agent's secretary or assistant is out, you fill in. You could work, and also it gives you a good overview of what you want to do, because I worked in the personal appearance department, a theater department, television, motion pictures, literary—once, I floated into [talent manager] Colonel [Tom] Parker's office. He would say, "George, it's eleven-thirty. How much money did we make so far?" He had a fifty-fifty deal with Elvis, as his manager.

Judd: Did you meet Elvis in those days?

George: I met Elvis. Elvis was the first person in my life to call me "sir." I was twenty-four years old; he was like twenty-two years old, and it was at *The Ed Sullivan Show.* I was with him because I was with William Morris, helping out, and I said, "Elvis, the press is ready for you now." He goes, "Yes, sir. I'll be right there, sir." So, I said, "You're the first person to ever call me 'sir.'" I'll never forget that. In the Bronx, we don't use "sir" or "ma'am," like you do in Mississippi.

Judd: Was that the first time he did *Ed Sullivan*?

George: Yeah, and that's my connection with him. That's a chapter of the book I'm not writing: "Elvis Presley Called Me 'Sir.'"

Judd: Did you work with Buddy Hackett?

George: When I first started in the mailroom, I had this one assignment on a Sunday, for a variety show called *The Patrice Munsel Show*, and I booked Buddy Hackett on the show. He goes into his dressing room, and I'm with him, and he says, "There's no telephone in my dressing room. I'm not going to do the show unless I have a telephone." So, I rush to AT&T, I'm calling to get someone down, saying it's an emergency. Meanwhile, Buddy says he's going to go for a walk, and he says to me, "If that phone isn't there . . ." And I figure that's the end of my career. I'm a very, very young junior agent. And then he comes in, the phone's been set up, and he gets a dial tone, and he rips the phone out of the wall. So, I didn't like him then, and I had another confrontation with him, and I was going to hit him in the head with a cue stick. We were shooting pool. I hated him so much. And then I booked an act that one of my clients did, at the Sahara, and he coheadlined with Buddy Hackett. Buddy was so funny that night. I could not help but laugh my ass off. I fell off the chair laughing even though I hated him.

Judd: I remember, there was a stand-up comedy competition at the Improv, and he was a judge. At the end, he went onstage and was supposed to read the ballots of the different judges and say who the winner was. Instead, he tore up all the ballots and said, "I don't think any of you guys are funny."

George: That's a perfect reflection of him.

Judd: Tell me about the Smothers Brothers. How did that show get set up, and what was the evolution of it from being a variety show to being a very political show?

George: They were just an innocent act: "Mom always liked you best" kind of comedy. They sang great, and they were very good musicians, and they were doing a lot of guest appearances. They were clients of William Morris. Phil Weltman, who was the head of our television department, was their agent. They were in a terrible time slot, but the public sort of gravitated to them and the ratings were pretty good. They were picked up, and they ended up a top-five show. They had great guest stars on, like Johnny Cash and Glen Campbell. Then they started doing political stuff, especially around the Vietnam War, which they were very opposed to. But they were always funny, and that's why the public gravitated toward them.

Judd: How did the network signal to them that they weren't happy with how much politics they were doing?

George: They had meetings with them, but they did what they had to do. They just continued doing it, but also, in the second and third year, the show was a top-ten show. Then, toward the end of the third year, it fell off, to number forty. I have a feeling if it was still in the top five, the network wouldn't have canceled it. They were such a great staff. They had Steve Martin and Rob Reiner and Bob Einstein as young writers on the show. It was a tremendous, classic comedy show.

Judd: Was there a real sense of urgency around the war where the Smothers Brothers said *This is worth losing the show over*?

George: They never said that. They just did their job. It's what they had to do, like when Larry David said, "I'm not going to do *Seinfeld*." The Smothers Brothers at least had an act that they traveled all over the world with, on tour.

Judd: The fact that you had the instinct to be supportive of their creative vision above everything else goes against what you assume about most agents. Is that why you became a manager?

George: I wanted to work with fewer people. Bernie Brillstein was my hero, because he blazed the trail for anyone who wanted to work as a manager. I worked with him at William Morris; he was a little ahead of me. I used to deliver mail for him, and he had an office with all these pictures in it. He had pictures of Kirk Douglas and Frank Sinatra and Sammy Davis, Jr., and Anne Bancroft and Sophia Loren—and so I came back to the mailroom with my first delivery on my first day and said, "Bernie Brillstein has to be the biggest agent in the world. He has all these people." And they said, "No. He left the mailroom three months ago. He's in publicity. He sends the pictures out." That's how naïve I was. Anyway, Bernie was my hero, because he left, and he signed Jim Henson right away, and Lorne Michaels and [John] Belushi and [Dan] Aykroyd and Gilda Radner, and he started producing movies. In fact, he gave me my first opportunity to produce a movie, about a fat guy on a beach who feels out of place. It was called *Summer Rental,* with John Candy, and it was based on Bernie's life, as he felt out of place as a fat guy on the beach. Like him, I wanted to get involved in producing and managing. When you're an agent, you're handling two hundred fifty to three hundred people, so there's a good percentage of assholes within that group, and that was also part of the reason why I left.

Judd: Did you find a common trait with the people who were a pain in the ass that explained why they were a pain in the ass?

George: It was part of their personality, I think.

Judd: Okay, what about someone you like? What do you love about Jerry Seinfeld as a person?

George: He's just a joy to be with. He knows how to have fun. I have this part of my brain that, even though I'm quite old, has sort of stuck from when I was eight, nine, ten years old, and he has that, too. Going to a ball game with him is just an absolute joy. We talk about everything besides the hot dogs, and he always has two hot dogs and ice cream.

Judd: Where did you first connect with Mel Brooks and Carl Reiner?

George: I first connected with Carl when I was twelve years old. Carl was a corporal in the U.S. Army, about twenty-one years old, and my aunt Estelle was dating him. Then they got engaged, and she brought Carl over to meet the family, and I was all excited, because I was a kid, and I didn't have any relatives in the army. It was World War Two, and you were a hero if you had a relative in the army. So, I was very excited my aunt was going to marry a soldier. And I was so excited about seeing him, I just leaped on his back. And Carl—you know how sweet he is, right? Instead of throwing me down, or throwing me on the couch, he gave me a piggyback ride. He jumped up and down like a little horsey. And that's how I first met him.

Judd: Were you tracking the rise of Carl as a kid?

George: Yes. After the army, he did this great Broadway show called *Call Me Mister*—I think Buddy Hackett was in it—and he was funny, and I said, *Wow, is he talented.*

Judd: Is that when you decided you wanted to find a way to work in show business?

George: Well, not really. Did you ever hear of a place called Tamiment, in the Pocono Mountains? It was like a resort, and I was there as a lifeguard, with my friend Howard and a couple of other Bronx boys. They had a playhouse that did weekly musical revues. Neil Simon and Danny Simon were the head writers. A very young, unknown Herb Ross was the choreographer; Barbara Cook was an ingénue and became a major singer there. They had all these brilliant young performers, and they put them in revues every week. That's when I really got connected to show business. You should see Herb

Ross creating these dance numbers, and then these agents came up for the weekend, and they'd have dinner. I'd give them a rowboat and a canoe. They'd hang out with these beautiful singers and dancers. I said, "This is your job?" So, when I got out of the army, that's why I looked into show business, and I brought Howard [West] in after I got a job with William Morris.

Judd: How did you know Howard?

George: I've known Howard since we were eight years old. I met him in P.S. 80, in the Bronx. He was the new kid who came to the neighborhood, and I saw him sitting alone on the stoop, and I said, "Come on and play basketball with us." Later on, I got him the job at William Morris, and we both worked there. I left first, and then I asked him to join me as a manager and producer.

Judd: Who were the first clients you had as managers?

George: We had [producer/actor] Dick Clair and [writer/producer/actress] Jenna McMahon, who worked for Carol Burnett. They created *Mama's Family*, *Facts of Life*, and a few other shows. Andy Kaufman was an early one. We had Carl [Reiner], and it was great having him as a client. We had a young comedian called Lonnie Shorr, from North Carolina. He worked a lot with Glen Campbell and did *The Johnny Cash Show.* And [director/screenwriter/producer] Bill Persky and [screenwriter/producer] Sam Denoff—I got them a job on *The Dick Van Dyke Show* and then they created *That Girl*, and they did a lot of other great specials with Dick Van Dyke and Mary Tyler Moore.

Judd: Who were your favorite stand-up clients who didn't become megastars?

George: I loved Elayne Boosler. We produced a special with Elayne, and she was just so smart. I also love—and he's still working around now—Suli McCullough.

Judd: Did you first see Andy at the Improv?

George: My connection with Andy Kaufman initially was via Carl Reiner. He was in New York, working at Catch a Rising Star and the Improv, and he called me. Carl said, "George, you have to get on a plane and fly to New York and see Andy Kaufman. I never saw anyone so original." And Carl has total audio recall. He did his whole act [for me]. He did everything but sing like Elvis. But he did the whole thing, imitating President Carter, "Hello, I'm President Carter. President of the United States, thank you very much." It was so funny. Coincidentally, Budd Friedman called me later that same day. He said he's flying in Andy Kaufman: "You should take a look at him." I said, "I want him already, just from what Carl told me." And then I saw him at the Improv here. If you're a manager, Judd, and you see Andy Kaufman onstage, what would you think? Would you have any hesitation?

Judd: Well, you think, *What do I do with this? Where does this go?*

George: Exactly. So, my question was, *Is he sane?* Because he was so crazy onstage. I said, *I have to have lunch with him,* and then he was a real person who loved his grandma. He used to fly to New York and stop off in Florida to see Grandma Lily—so, I liked him. But I loved his work. Totally loved his work.

Judd: Did he think of it more as performance art?

George: Oh, absolutely. He said, "I'm not a comedian, I'm a performer." You hit it right on the head.

Judd: Because he's trying to create moments. He's not really thinking about laugh count.

George: I tell this incredible story. Andy Kaufman had a bombing routine where he would purposely bomb. What comedian is going to do that? People are going to walk out of the comedy club. So, I had to negotiate with him. I said, "Andy, maybe fifty-five seconds, a minute, five at the most." We had a negotiation for how short the bombing routine has to be. It came down to one minute, thirty-eight seconds.

Judd: Did he ever talk about long-term career goals?

George: No, he just was satisfying his heart as a performer. He was very good musically. Conga drums; he sang really well. He was a terrific performer. That's why, when Jim Carrey—who was already a star, because he did *Ace Ventura*—wanted to play Andy so much in *Man on the Moon*, he did an audition tape for me.

Judd: I'm the person who videotaped it.

George: Oh my God. You're responsible for [his] getting the movie. You should get nominated for a Golden Globe Award.

Judd: I'm more responsible for just hitting Record on his video camera, but I was there with him.

George: That's amazing. Andy Kaufman died in 1984. The Long Beach Museum of Art had this great tribute to Andy, after he died, and Jim came running over to me after the presentation, and he said, "I love Andy Kaufman." And this was in '84, and like nine years before we talked about doing a movie about his life. I knew what a great impressionist Jim was, and a good actor. I said, "Jim, my wish would be for you to play Andy Kaufman if we do a biopic on Andy Kaufman." And it happened. I just loved that.

Judd: And now there's a documentary of Jim and Andy, which is about how Jim stayed in character the entire time. It's a beautiful documentary.

George: I saw that. I just can't tell you how emotional I was about it. I was laughing and crying, especially over how revealing it was about Jim. He wanted to lose Jim Carrey, is what he said. He said he lost himself completely in Andy Kaufman. Do you know the cast and crew never met Jim Carrey in that movie? He was Andy Kaufman when he was off-camera, the whole time. It was absolutely amazing.

Judd: How was that for you to experience that?

George: It was one of the best four months of my life, because I was with Andy again. Andy was back. He just nailed it. He got everything.

Judd: And his family would spend time with Jim as Andy.

George: Yeah. They all came in. We recreated Carnegie Hall in the Los Angeles Theatre, and Stanley Kaufman, his father, was walking down while Jim was onstage doing the conga drums and just singing. And the tears just streamed down his face. He saw Andy; he saw his son onstage. That's why the whole thing was a huge, emotional roller-coaster ride.

Judd: People really felt very close to Andy as a person. But I think it's hard for people on the outside to understand what he was like when not performing. What was it about Andy?

George: He was a regular guy who was very excited about his art. He turned down *Taxi* originally. I had to talk him into it, because he wanted to just create material. If you're doing a sitcom, it takes away from writing original material and doing it. I said, "This could enhance the whole level of your career." You're talking about doing great theater dates, Carnegie Hall. Getting a salary from them could allow you to do what you want to do production-wise. So, he thinks about it, and he says, "I'll do fourteen episodes, but they have to book Tony Clifton"—one of Andy's characters—"for four. Then I'll do it, otherwise they can forget it." So, I said okay and made this deal. I had to negotiate that Andy got much more money than Tony, because Tony wasn't well known. I also said, "They have to have separate dressing rooms, business affairs, and separate parking places, and Andy has to meditate twenty minutes in the morning and twenty minutes in the afternoon." But we worked out the deal.

Judd: Can you tell me a little bit of what happened once *Taxi* comes out?

George: It's a big hit. High ratings. Andy is a smash, and it's time for Tony Clifton to do it, and so, they write in this really good character, Danny DeVito's kid brother, who is a ne'er-do-well gambler and drinker. So, Tony Clifton comes down, and he rents a Winnebago bigger than Judd Hirsch's. A *big* trailer. He has two hookers with him, a blonde and a brunette. Then, when it comes down to the reading, he says, "I brought my friends with me. Is that okay?" So, he has one girl on each knee, and he's reading the script. He says, "Okay, okay, bullshit, bullshit, bullshit, my line, bullshit, bullshit, bullshit, bullshit, my line." He reads the script, and he goes back to his trailer with the hookers.

Judd: Were the other actors upset that he's doing this?

George: They're upset. They're impatient with him. He goes back to his trailer, drinks Jack Daniel's. Andy doesn't drink at all, ever. [Writer] Ed Weinberger calls me on, like, Thursday. He says, "It's not working out with Tony. First of all, he's not a good actor. He comes late. He's not reliable. We just want to fire him." I said, "Well, a part of his contract is that Andy has an out clause if you fire Tony." And already the show took off like a hit with Latka as an important character. They said, "Please, talk to him." I said, "I'll talk to him, but it's his call." So, I talked to Andy—and [as Latka, he] has [to wear] all this makeup—and he says, "Let them fire me." I think it was a little burdensome for him with all the makeup, to do it.

Judd: Was he enjoying that the show was a hit at all?

George: He loved that the show was a hit and that he got great reviews as Latka. But it still wasn't in his heart. He was much more interested in doing his own creativity. So, he said, "I'll let them fire me only if they do it on run-through day, with the network and all the people from Paramount." It was a hot show. All the people came down, the executives and the assistants. The place was full with ABC executives, and then they fire him. First, he comes down, and he gives gifts to everybody, and then they fire him, and he says, "What are you talking about? You can't fire me. Where's Mr. Shapiro? George Shapiro? I have a contract." So, he was resisting them. I brought a tape recorder, I recorded this, and that was in the movie [*Jim and Andy*]. I gave it to [producer/director/writer] Scott Alexander and [screenwriter] Larry Karaszewski. So, anyway, Judd Hirsch is getting pissed off; everyone's pissed off. And then we get Security. "I'm not going to let any of you guys see me in Las Vegas," [Andy] tells the whole cast. And Security's dragging him off. A photographer for the *Los Angeles Times* was taking pictures when they were throwing him off. I told Andy I'd meet him at a restaurant right around the corner from Paramount. He comes out—he had the makeup off—and he said, "George, this is the greatest day of my life. This is the theater of the street. This is what I love more than anything." And that's him.

Judd: He also loved wrestling.

George: He did. He set up all that stuff with Jerry Lawler. I wasn't involved with that, except I was in Memphis when he did the Mid-South Coliseum, and he got the piledriver [move performed on him], and he was in the hospital for three days. There's probably some news footage of me with Andy, comforting him. In the hospital, I was holding Andy's hand, but I knew he was faking it. He had an injury when he was a teenager, which resulted in a little bit of tightness of the vertebrae in his neck, so it *looked* like that could have happened [in the ring that evening]. So, he stayed in the hospital for three days when he didn't have to. He wasn't hurt. And then he got out, and he did that Letterman show, and Jerry Lawler slapped him out of his seat while Andy had his neck brace on. He and Lawler—they staged that also. Smacking him off the screen—everything was staged. And then, when we were shooting *Man on the Moon*, Jim

Carrey didn't get along with Jerry Lawler. Jim Carrey as *himself* didn't get along, and they pushed each other, and Lawler threw him down, and he was hurt. And he went to L.A. Hospital. Twelve years later, I'm holding *Jim Carrey's* hand in the hospital.

Judd: The movie [*Man on the Moon*] goes to a very emotional place when Andy gets sick. That must have been a horrible time.

George: I was with Andy when they gave him the diagnosis. It was in December 1983.

Judd: You were at the doctor's office with him?

George: I was. When they came out, I was sitting with Andy. And they said, "You have lung cancer. You have large-cell carcinoma," which is kind of a rapidly growing cancer. So, the first thing Andy said was "Listen, George, why don't you call David Letterman and the show. I'll do the show like late December, or January, and David could ask me, 'What did you get for Christmas, Andy?' and I can say, 'I got cancer.'" That was his first thought after he was given that diagnosis.

Judd: Where did he go from there?

George: Then he was sick, and I got him a job hosting this Cyndi Lauper special that he presented. That was the last thing he did. And like in the movie, he went to India for this [psychic surgery] guy. He always had the feeling that he was going to be okay. He was thinking optimistically. Then he went out very quickly at Cedars, and I was there, and Robin Williams came over. Robin visited him a couple of times. Robin was very loving—they were very loving toward each other. They had a really great relationship. It was very sad at the end. He was thirty-five years old.

Judd: That was '84, and I was sixteen. When he passed, and Belushi passed, it was hard for a young comedy fan. I finally just want to ask, since you've worked with so many of the greats with these long careers, what is the secret to all these guys staying funny?

George: Well, look at Mel Brooks. Two and a half months in Newcastle breaking in *Young Frankenstein* [the musical], and it got rave reviews. He's ninety-one and a half. And look at Norman Lear. He's ninety-five and a half, and he's working on [the] *One Day at a Time* [reboot]. If it's in your DNA and you're funny, you don't stop.

HANNAH GADSBY

September 2020

Judd: Have you been enjoying your fame? Or the opposite?

Hannah: I think that fame and celebrity add trauma. They have traumatic episodes. And I think it's difficult to process, because the trauma doesn't read *as* trauma, so you don't protect yourself from it, like when you're in a car accident, and afterward you're like, *Fuck, I need to wear a neck brace for a bit.* You can say after that accident, "I'm not comfortable in cars," and the world around you goes, "Yeah, I can see that." Whereas, it seems like nothing is bad with the type of success that leads to celebrity. But I think that's incorrect. In the beginning stages of success, you have to navigate quite a large amount of trauma, because everything around your life changes. It doesn't change for the worse, but it changes in such a huge and impactful way that nothing about your life is the same anymore. And that is tantamount to trauma. You look at all these badly behaved boys, and women also; it's looked at as *This is what being creative is.*

Judd: What's funny about you mentioning this is I've been seeing a new therapist for the last year or two. He sees a lot of creative people. And he sees the common issues that these people have, which is what you're talking about: No one has any compassion for you when you're successful. No one has any compassion for the amount of hatred you have to deal with, in addition to the love, and people don't have any compassion for the amount of stress creative people are under to do their work.

Hannah: I don't think everyone on earth should feel compassion for you because you're in a position of privilege, but I think knowing that what you're going through requires some actual navigation and requires actual maturity—that's important. I experienced a little bit of success, and I would have changed my life quite dramatically, very quickly, but I was already old and tired. The kind of hate that I got, the ratio was the same—I just got more of it. I was doing festivals, and with every good review came a pummeling, and with every bad review came a pile-on. When real success hits, then more people are interested in us, but the ratio of hate stays the same.

Judd: I was interested in your bit about this in your Netflix special *Douglas*, where you talk about how you like to snack on the hatred because it helps strengthen your immunity to it. We all have to decide what we're going to do in a world where we have so much access to everyone else's opinion of our work. I remember back when we made *The Cable Guy*, on the way to the premiere, someone handed me two faxes, and they were the reviews from *Newsweek* and *Time* magazine. They both were the worst reviews you could imagine, and the night was destroyed. Back then, there were maybe ten or fifteen reviewers in the country whom you looked to in order to determine if critics liked what you did. You had no sense of the public at all. You would not get any feedback other than box-office sales, and maybe a letter here and there. But today, millions of people have a way to get to you through social media, and the internet forces us all to decide, *Do we want to read anything?* It sounds like you do read some of them.

Hannah: I keep my finger on the pulse. I think that's important when you're creating something for public consumption. Otherwise, I'm apt to just fall into a void, and then what I create would have less relevance to anybody else on earth. I think of it as a conversation, where there's a push and pull. You can't please everyone. My new line on that is, *You can't be everyone's cup of tea. That's just a glass of water.*

Judd: But some people aren't content with simply not drinking the tea; they also want to knock the cup out of your hands.

Hannah: Their anger is fascinating. And I think most women who have a public-facing persona understand hatred. People just hate you; it's kind of incredible. It's not always so clear-cut or obvious, but there is an element that, as a woman or anyone who's different, really—it just makes people angry.

Judd: What do you think that is? I've noticed it when working with Lena Dunham, and I've also seen it with Pete Davidson. People seem deeply offended by him telling them how he feels. I wonder what that is?

Hannah: I think your two examples, Lena and Pete—they have a distinct lack of boundaries. It's very clear in their work and the way they think. People don't like it when other people don't have boundaries. But when you have a huge amount of influence, it becomes a two-way street. When people are online, they also respond to that with a distinct lack of boundaries. I have incredibly strong boundaries, so when I talk about these things, I do understand that I have "mind blindness," as they say. But that cuts both ways; so, I feel fine about it. There was a time when I would just be trying to understand what was wrong with me.

Judd: What did you learn about yourself by going from a normal working comedy person to having an enormous amount of attention and success and criticism?

Hannah: That's where I first understood just how profoundly incognizant I am to praise, but I actually think that's a good thing. I often think about the amount of adulation that was surrounding me at the time—imagine if that was something I was actively seeking? I understand, in theory, how addictive or intoxicating that would feel, but for me, it just felt unsafe, and that is because I have autism and I have trauma, so I was just scrambling for the nearest safe space, which for me was creating a new work. Creating for me is a way of providing safety, and I chose to write a new stand-up special even though, honestly, I could have done anything.

Judd: How was writing that special different from your earlier experience doing stand-up, when you weren't as well-known?

Hannah: People were just like, "Please, let me help you make the next thing you want to make." For me, that was too unsafe, because I didn't understand how that industry works. I've been doing stand-up for a long time, so I understood how to construct a show and tour a show. So, even though things changed—like the amount of people that came to see my shows and the expectations around it—the core of it was the same. There was a little level of safety to that, but that's a relational thing. And that's autism. I don't have autism when I'm on my own. The cracks appear as soon as you're trying to relate to the world. That is really what's difficult about this interconnected world that we live in: It's a really difficult space for people on the spectrum to navigate *because* everything is connected. When someone who's neurotypical feels overwhelmed by the fact that everyone has access to them, then that is especially toxic for someone on the spectrum. Because the ability to retreat, which is something that's incredibly important, is diminished.

Judd: When I was young, and I went off after school, my parents didn't even know where I was. I talked to two people most of the time; sometimes we'd visit two other people. We didn't have any awareness of who was having fun or who wasn't having fun, and we didn't feel judged by anybody. I think that the whole world doesn't know what to make of our interconnectedness. It feels like young people are really depressed and anxious from it.

Hannah: I don't think we're biologically equipped to be in the world we've created.

Judd: Did it change how you thought about why you were interested in comedy in the first place?

Hannah: No, that was always fairly obvious to me. I'd be stumbling and bumbling my way around the world and failing, but then I could reimagine my life and create something out of it. Hindsight was always my gift. But I'd fail in the moment. I wasn't an active participant in life. I watched people. I was always watching what was going on around me, and so, I would see things that other people wouldn't. Before I ever did stand-up, I would do this kind of observation at a gathering. If you were to look at me from the outside, you would say she's just a lump in the corner, but you don't understand what's happening in my mind. That's what's wrong with a lot of depictions of people on the spectrum, in literature and film and television: Those characters and those stories are being written largely by people who are witnessing autism and not experiencing it.

Judd: I produced a special for Gary Gulman where he talked about his depression. He had just stopped doing stand-up for a couple years and moved back in with his mother and really had a hard time coming out of it. But we would get tens of thousands of messages from people who felt so much better hearing a story of hope and of how he climbed out of it.

Hannah: I once did a show where I talked about coming off of antidepressants. This is before I was diagnosed correctly. It's interesting how many people come out and say that they identify with that, and I feel like that's why it's incredibly important to talk openly about it. But there is a flip side to that. People have very, very strong opinions about medication, and the amount of people who have told me that autism is dietary is wild. Or the people who told me I'm too fat to be autistic.

Judd: Were you on antidepressants before people knew you had autism? Was it a misdiagnosis?

Hannah: It's a comorbid situation, but what I have is periods of being *overwhelmed,* we'll call it. A lot of times with autism, you will have a meltdown when you have trouble regulating situations. But meltdowns were not tolerated in someone like me. I was the youngest of five in my family, and a girl—you don't get to act up. So, I learned a coping mechanism where I just shut down as a way of stopping the input.

Judd: Did you feel misunderstood by your family during your childhood?

Hannah: Well, they also understand me better than most. I make sense to them; I've never been any different. In fact, I haven't changed much since I was five. I talk more, that's it. I think it's more what girls are allowed to get away with, behavior-wise. I'd withdraw, and I like habit and routine and quiet, but you learn pretty quickly that these aren't okay. It happens to boys and girls, but I think because girls are pressured to be more social, it happens for girls a little bit more. That's why girls are often diagnosed later. It's called *masking.*

Judd: Did you often feel like you had to ignore your own need to withdraw?

Hannah: Yes. I would look at the behavior I was supposed to do, and even though it feels painful and unsafe, I'd do it anyway, because it's what is expected. I was okay at it, because I grew up in a small town where there wasn't much change, and I understood my place in my family structure. But as soon as there was a small amount of change, I'd flip out.

Judd: It seems odd to then be drawn to the world of comedy, which is all about change. There's so much traveling and working with different people in different spaces.

Hannah: I don't know how I got into comedy, to be really honest. Everything around comedy is incredibly painful for me. But being onstage makes perfect sense to me.

Judd: When did you have an awareness that comedy was something that someone could do for a living?

Hannah: It was quite late in life. I was in my late twenties, and my life was a wreck. I just couldn't get my shit together. I entered a national competition run by the Melbourne International Comedy Festival. I remember going, *This just seems very much like a thing I can do.* Now, to be fair, I'd said that about a lot of things and I failed miserably, so there was no expectation that I would be good at this. It's just like, *This is a thing I could do.*

Judd: Did you study it as a kid the way you studied other things? Were you interested in stand-up comedians at all?

Hannah: I was not obsessed in the comedians themselves, but I'm very obsessed with mimicry. And a little-known fact about me is that I memorized Bill Cosby—obviously, long before his abusive behavior was brought to light.

Judd: We all did; that's the hard part.

Hannah: I had no real concept of Bill Cosby as a person. We had *The Cosby Show*, but we weren't allowed to watch it. It was on too late for me, I think. We just had a cassette tape of his comedy, and I would memorize it. But I didn't think about that in terms of like, *This is something I could do*, because it just wasn't in my wheelhouse. We didn't have any live theater where I was growing up—we didn't even have a cinema. Show business was not a thing.

Judd: You were planting trees. Is that what you were doing around that time?

Hannah: I say that I was a farm laborer, but in reality, I was an itinerant farmworker. I was basically working with ex-cons and international tourists and students who got trapped on a visa, and it basically meant indentured labor, and that's pretty much it. That was where I was working, and no one could quite work out where I belonged, because I was not on parole, but was also from around there.

Judd: Did you have a sense that life wasn't really working out? Were you depressed?

Hannah: The thing about that industry is, you don't earn enough to live. You're trapped as soon as you enter into it. It's a really horrific cycle. I'd be surprised to find out if the food on your plate is ethically produced. When I worked there, I was stuck planting trees. You get paid like four cents a seedling, and it's baking hot. You got a tray of seedlings, which would basically add up to around three dollars, and when you finish planting that tray, you call out. Then someone comes over and fills you up again. But sometimes you could be left waiting, because the guys who were supposed to fill you up don't like you. And I have autism. Often, I found that it took a while for people to like me. Eventually, I'd get there. But you know, I'm a weird presence. So, I would earn ten dollars a day.

Judd: Did that motivate you to really work hard on those jokes?

Hannah: I wasn't doing comedy at that stage. I was essentially homeless living in Australia in a tent, with no options.

Judd: How did you finally escape?

Hannah: I had an accident on the job. I got hurt pretty badly and had to get this really significant surgery. Then I went to Adelaide, where I lived with my sister for a few years, and it was during that time that I started doing comedy. For an older woman to start doing comedy like that, and start living the lifestyle of a comic—but it was still better than planting trees. I think the fact that my life was so dismal meant that I could navigate the dismal world that is being a working comic.

Judd: And it put gas in your tank to just hang in there.

Hannah: I couldn't have done it without my family. I lived relatively rent-free for the first six years. I lived above my brother's fruit-and-vegetable shop, and then my sister let me live with her for a few years, until I got back onto my feet.

Judd: Was it strange to be embraced in such a big way after a long struggle and after everything that you've been through?

Hannah: This is the absence of confidence. If the world shat on you that much, you don't have confidence, but that also means you don't have anything to lose. When I stood onstage for the first time, I wasn't thinking, *Gee, I hope these people like me.* I'm standing up there, and I assume they hate me. And that's fine. It's kind of easier.

Judd: What happened when you realized that a fair amount of them really liked you?

Hannah: Every time I was onstage, I was able to control the room. I was very good at that. I think I sat in a weird place for people, where I was unnerving enough but also not threatening. That's a perfect place to be in comedy: enough tension, but not enough to generate hostility.

Judd: In *Nanette*, you talked about how, on some level, that didn't feel like a truthful place to stand.

Hannah: I think that's the only place to stand when you're first starting out. What became really difficult for me onstage was navigating what people expected of me and what I wanted to say—what I needed to say. It's exciting when you're starting out, where you're working and creating. Then I think there comes a time when it plateaus and people expect a certain thing from you, but that's a flattening out of who you are and how you could possibly grow. I don't think *Nanette* could have been a show I could have produced had I experienced success before *Nanette*.

Judd: I do think that your success with *Nanette*, though, proves that your theory was wrong. Because the audience ultimately did want you to go deeper.

Hannah: That was the one thing I agree with my critics—like, no, it shouldn't have worked. It wasn't meant to work. It was meant to be a bomb. But that's not what happened. So, we have to go with that evidence.

Judd: Do you think that its success says anything about the role of comedy in the world we live in now?

Hannah: That has everything to do with the kind of world we're living in now, where everyone is hyperconnected. People don't need comedians to show them how to be funny. Anytime you want to laugh, you can laugh. You can just watch cats doing dumb things on YouTube. Laughter is accessible at any point. So, the job of the comedian has to evolve.

Judd: And you have to find your audience. I think there's something about our interconnectedness today that makes a lot of people feel like they're supposed to cross over to everybody. But it really is about finding the people who enjoy the way you express yourself.

Hannah: Part of that has to do with how weird people are when they don't like something. Why do people get angry when they don't like something? Ultimately, they need to do some work on themselves. If a comedian makes me angry, I look at what it was about their joke that made me angry, and it's like, *Oh it's because they're amplifying toxic behavior and ideas.* But I can pinpoint why that makes me angry.

But the people who hated me, who I made angry—they were angry at a small number of things, and none of them makes sense. They're angry that I'm a woman. They're angry that I'm fat. They're angry that I'm Australian. They're angry that I don't like being raped.

Judd: Do you feel like we're experiencing a positive time of change? Are we just realizing how bad a pretty high percentage of people are, or are we just hearing the screams of the world as it slowly changes for the better?

Hannah: It could be both. We have a fairly blasé attitude toward history, where we look back and go, *These things change.* What's never actually spoken about is the devastation that is wrought with change. Colonialism is a good case in point. Oh, we "discovered" the world. But actually people were decimated, cultures were decimated. I think that history repeats itself because we don't learn properly from history, and that has everything to do with the fact that we only listen to the history that's written by the winners. They're hardly going to be self-reflective, like, "Well we could have done that better. We could have killed less people." Right now there's a lot of really intense energy floating, and that can only lead either to creativity or to destruction. History shows that it leads to both. We're living in a time where it's going to be an incredibly creatively intense moment, but also probably a very destructive moment. I honestly think that the only antidote to this moment is to create.

Judd: All we have is our choice of what to put into the world. We can make a choice to make the world a better place or take advantage of it and be toxic in some way and make it worse.

Hannah: There's also the option of doing nothing, and I don't think we really embrace that enough. I think sometimes people talk when they shouldn't. There's an eloquence and a grace in not talking sometimes.

Judd: What were you going to do before the pandemic started?

Hannah: I had some writing to do, so I've been able to do that.

Judd: Is it hard to write with so much chaos in the world, or can you block it out?

Hannah: I block it out. I have good boundaries in my head on those things. I lived in chaos my whole life, the whole world has always been chaos to me. The poverty cycle's always upset me. The fact that we don't value the mental well-being of the larger population, to the profit of a small amount of people, has always upset me. This feels like just the logical conclusion to that. The most annoying thing about it is people realizing this reality for the first time and then writing op-eds as if it's only just begun. That's excruciating. I get nauseous about the amount of white people suddenly having a reckoning about race. It's sort of like watching rich celebrities suffer through a lockdown.

Judd: I love that, in *Douglas*, you really allowed yourself to get very angry over some of those issues. It also seemed like you genuinely enjoyed that set.

Hannah: With *Nanette*, I had to reinvestigate what I wanted to do onstage. And I didn't enjoy performing *Nanette*, for obvious reasons. It wasn't joyful, but I didn't want people to then think that comedy has to be not joyful. It was incredibly important for me to put out a piece of work that was joy in process. I very much wrote a show that I wanted to perform. It's important for me not to be a one-note comedian—not because I didn't want to be seen as a one-note comedian, but because obviously people looked at me, and they're like, *Oh, is this what comedy is now?* No, comedy is whatever you need it to be.

Judd: Have you found that you've been able to stay creative during the pandemic?

Hannah: I've written a little screenplay, and who knows what or if anything will happen. But I've been able to be quite creative because I hate to work around people. I literally cannot socialize, and that's heaven for me. I was going to have to go to L.A. three times this year, and I don't hate L.A., but it exhausts me—the process of meetings and understanding who I'm talking to and how to navigate it all. I know that I don't always come across very well. And I haven't had to do that.

Judd: You talk about this in your comedy, like the example of being in school and not understanding your teacher's lesson about the box and the prepositions [being related to the box].

Hannah: I'm gonna give you a scoop: My whole life has been filled with things like that. That box conversation—and figuring out what preposition to use in relation to the box—happened to me as an adult last year. I was confused, because language is always confusing me. But I applied the box story to a different childhood experience that was essentially the same. I tried to tell it onstage as it happened, and people didn't laugh. They didn't find it funny, because they're just like, *What are you? Are you stupid?* I've had people use the R-word on me—grown adult people who should know better than to use that language. And this is post-*Nanette*, post-diagnosis, and having people still say things like that to me makes me very afraid. So, I learned very quickly onstage that I had to be a child in order for that material to work. I've still got a lot of work to do to try and make people understand the reality of autism. Despite the fact that I don't connect well with others, all I've ever done is strive to do that, and I think that's what's at the heart of why I found success in what I do. It's so profoundly isolating to be on the spectrum, and be unable to communicate, and to be misinterpreted. So, the goal of trying to connect is what I think is the good part. It's the act of creating, and the act of creating for me is to try and find the link between what's happening inside of me and to share it to the world.

Judd: You said that when you started working on *Nanette,* you assumed that you would not get the reaction that you ultimately got. How do you look at how people ultimately responded?

Hannah: The people who responded to it were not the people I wrote it for. I didn't know they existed. I was talking to my audience that I'd built up slowly over ten years, by doing the comedy circuit in Australia and a little bit in the UK—that's who I was talking to. So, it's not something I can honestly answer.

Judd: You mentioned to me once before that in the earliest stages of trying to do comedy, that some crowds really had a hard time as you were figuring things out.

Hannah: I was heckled violently, usually by men. Fair enough—it's a lot for men to take in the room. It was in the early days and in the smaller rooms when I got heckled, but I was also on fire, and I knew what I was saying and why I was saying it. So, I just tore them a new asshole, which is gratifying for the women who were also in those particular rooms. I had a lot of women and queer folk come up to me after those shows and just go, "I've never seen a man just be obliterated by a woman like that." That's not how comedy should be, but in those moments, it felt violent when people would heckle, when I would just say, "Well, I've been raped," and a man would go, "Good." That's violence. What kind of person does that?

Judd: I think the comedy world has been dealing with so many issues. I think Hollywood in general is just very thin-skinned about this reckoning. They want to be seen as progressive, but in a lot of ways, they're not at all. This is a city that's never treated women well.

Hannah: But also, having said that, women enter that infrastructure, and they behave badly, too. I think the power dynamic is gendered, but it doesn't have to be. Power dynamics will play out no matter what, but I don't think that means that everyone involved is a monster. I believe that sort of culture is corrosive and it's viral. I think good people do bad things because they're infected with bad culture. And I don't know how to solve it. That's why I've run away to live in the country.

Judd: What does it feel like being away from the United States, watching it from a distance? Because everyone here fantasizes about leaving.

Hannah: America's vulnerable; now's not the time to pile on. Now's the time to actually investigate and amplify and really think critically about what's great about America, what was always potentially great about America, and get on that horse, because that's the only thing you can do. What's wrong with America is evident. So, now you've got to get on the other side of the seesaw and really love your country. And I hate saying that. Like, it's not the greatest; no one's the greatest. But it's all right. What's great about America is its warts. People fix themselves, cultures fix themselves, but I think it needs some buoyancy; it needs some support. When you're on the left, what's really easy to do is pinpoint what's wrong—that's the natural habitat of those on the left. So, it's a really interesting moment, not to match fire with fire, but go, "This is what's right. And this is what we're going to focus on." I think it's a different skill set.

HASAN MINHAJ

November 2020

Judd: I remember, back in 2016, you and I were performing at the seventy-fifth anniversary of the USO. It was such a star-studded event—Joe and Jill Biden were there, Barack and Michelle Obama, David Letterman, Jon Stewart—but what I remember most about that night are two things. One was that Letterman had to hang out with us. We were all waiting in line to meet the president and take a picture with him, and Letterman had to wait in line, too—he didn't get any star treatment and was stuck talking to us and our parents for hours. I remember your parents chatting him up a bit. The other thing I remember is that you had one of the best stand-up sets I've ever seen in my life. You killed so hard. It was one of the most special sets I'd ever seen, and then, at dinner afterward, you said to me, "My parents have never seen me do stand-up in person till tonight."

Hasan: At that point, I'd been doing stand-up comedy for maybe fourteen years. But my parents had never seen me perform live, so I felt like I had to bring it. My parents always knew that I was very smart and capable, but they didn't think that stand-up comedy was much of an art form. They were a little bit bummed that I was channeling my potential into something you use to just tell jokes to drunks in basements. And I remember thinking, on the night of the USO show, *The* *people that are on this bill, the people who Mom and Dad are going to see, are the epitome of the American dream.* You have the president, you have the First Lady, you have the vice president. You have David Letterman, and he and Johnny Carson were both icons for my dad when he immigrated to the States in 1982. You have Jon Stewart, who represents a level of class and sophistication that is so much bigger than just basement jokes. And so, that night, I wanted to show them that stand-up is a very respected art form that even the president and the First Lady find valuable, too. It's so crazy that you felt that, because I thought I was the only one that was feeling that in the moment. I just felt like I had so much to prove to my parents.

Judd: What I found most fascinating was that you waited so long for the perfect opportunity. You didn't ask them to come see you on some night where you sold out the Punch Line in San Francisco, or something like that.

Hasan: That wasn't going to cut it. For my parents, they had to see one of those gigs where somebody, or an institution that they respect, found value in the art form. So, that was really big for them, to see the USO show. Michelle Obama spoke before we all started our sets, and that carried a lot of weight. And it was held at Andrews Air Force Base, and my mom had worked with the VA for many years, so she knows the significance of that.

Judd: Kumail Nanjiani has a story where his parents had never seen him do stand-up in person, and he was looking at the comments on Amazon for the DVD of his stand-up special, and he realizes that one of the positive comments was written by his mother. Did your parents start going to more of your shows after the USO show?

Hasan: After the USO show, my parents started coming to more events and shows with me. They visited the set of *Patriot Act* for Netflix, and it really blew their mind. I remember they were sitting in my office, and my assistant came in, and they said, "Hey, do you want some coffee?" And I was like, "Yeah, I'd love a black coffee. Mom, Dad, what would you like?" My dad asked for a coffee and my mom asked for tea, and when my assistant left to go get our drinks, I saw my mom look a little bit perplexed. And I said, "What is it, Mom?" And she was like, "I cannot believe a white person goes and gets you coffee." It was just a small gesture, meaning, *My son is clearly doing something of value where somebody is serving him.* I think people don't understand that my parents are both children of the Partition between India and [Pakistan], when Indians were able to break away from the British Empire after almost three centuries. So, for my parents to see that, on some level, that had some meaning to them.

Judd: It's so interesting that even after many years in America, that type of image is still so impactful to them.

Hasan: All the old images and textbooks that my parents read and got to see as children growing up showed that Indians served the British. There'd be these photos of these Indian people all dressed up, and then they're bringing tea or coffee. I mean, my assistant is from Long Island. She has no connection to any of this history. She was just getting us coffee, you know? But for my parents, that was just a surreal thing for them to witness.

Judd: When did the connection happen for you, where you became interested in comedy? Were you interested in it at all in your younger years?

Hasan: I didn't know it was a thing. I remember the cold open of every episode of *Seinfeld*, where it's Jerry in front of that brick background, and he would be all, "What's the deal with laundry?" and all that sort of stuff. That's what I thought stand-up comedy was, and I was always like, *Get rid of that, just get to the show.* I was a speech and debate kid. With impromptu debate, you'd be given a prompt, and it could be on any topic. An example of a prompt would be like, "The town of Fremont is deciding whether or not the municipality should have free internet for everybody. However, the city residents would have to pay higher taxes for the service." So, let's say I'd be debating for free internet for everybody, while another kid would debate against that. And we would have twenty or thirty minutes to come up with our argument. What I started doing in speech and debate is I would have these opening statements that would just totally break the fourth wall. Like, "I know that we're talking about free internet in the city of Fremont. But why are we in a gymnasium with the leaky roof? Can we start with the roof?"

Judd: You were inventing comedy. Which is amazing: Having not seen it, you already had the instinct of a club comedian.

Hasan: The instinct to just say, "Hey, can we just address what's happening here?" I didn't realize that that is a foundational principle in stand-up. No matter where you are, whether you're doing a wedding or bar mitzvah, or the [White House] Correspondents' [Association] Dinner, you have to acknowledge you're in a weird-ass Hilton ballroom eating lukewarm salmon. I would always get ten to fifteen points higher in debate whenever I did that kind of technique, and in the comments, the judges would always be like, "Great reference to the leaky roof!"—even if it didn't have anything to do with my argument.

Judd: When did you start realizing that stand-up comedy was a thing?

Hasan: I was in college, and a classmate at the time had downloaded Chris Rock's *Never Scared*. I remember, in the special, he's wearing a maroon suit, and he's talking about religion, the war in Iraq, relationships, President Bush—all these no-nos that you're not supposed to talk about. I remember watching him and being like, *That's just funny speech and debate. You're doing forensics but being funny about it.* After that, me and my friend went on a download spree, and I downloaded the great Greg Giraldo, may he rest in peace. And Giraldo, ironically enough, was a law school student. He was actually a practicing attorney and then transitioned into stand-up. But if you listen to his bits, he was such a great argument/take guy. Then I discovered *The Daily Show* and all those sorts of things, and I realized this thing speaks to me in that way, as a former debate kid. Having a take, having a perspective, having an argument and using this as a medium to talk about things that you're not allowed to talk about—it opened up the floodgates.

Judd: Did you go out to see live comedy shows after that?

Hasan: I would drive to San Francisco from UC Davis, and I got to see these comedians that no one really knew about at the time: Ali Wong or Arj Barker or [W.] Kamau Bell or Moshe Kasher or Brent Weinbach. All these comedians were doing these weird, cool, innovative things. Ali was this short, crass Asian girl, and Kamau was this very political Black dude. And Arj was this cerebral, one-liner, half-Indian guy. And I was like, *They see the world the way I see the world,* and I immediately found my kinship and brotherhood in that.

Judd: Did you keep all this as a secret from your parents?

Hasan: I would just tell them I was at the library.

Judd: How many years till you told them that you're actually doing stand-up?

Hasan: My fifth year at UC Davis, I was driving to the San Francisco Punch Line. It was raining, and I was driving on the [Yolo] Causeway when my car hydroplaned, and I hit the median. Luckily, I wasn't hurt, but I had to call somebody to pick me up. I had gotten all the way to Vallejo, which is halfway between Davis and Sacramento, and I remember I called home, my mom picked up, and I said, "Will you pick me up?" And she said, "Where are you?" I said, "Vallejo," and she knew that I was sneaking out to go to comedy. So she said, "I'm going to give the phone to your father." My dad picked up the phone, and he said, "Where are you?" And I said, "Vallejo," and he said, "I don't know which library is in Vallejo." It was a very quiet car ride home. That was the beginning of some very tough conversations for about eight or nine years.

Judd: What were you studying at the time?

Hasan: I was prelaw. I had taken my LSAT, and it was my senior year of college, but I think my dad could tell that I wasn't committed to academics and that I wasn't going to do the traditional job thing. I think he felt powerless, too, because he didn't really know how to coach this skill set, or how to navigate this very specific world. I could only imagine if my wife had to help our daughter navigate the comedy club community. I wouldn't wish that on her. It's such a unique beast.

Judd: I had the opposite type of launch, which was that my family loved show business. And they were like, "Don't get a real job."

Hasan: I was in my mid-twenties, and I had just rejected my law school acceptance. I remember my mom saying, "You're my only son, and I love you so much, but you're not Tom Cruise. I don't know what you're going to do here. I'm just worried about you. You have so much potential, and it's just such a shame if you're going to put it into this." What I've tried to show them is that I think America is at its best when people have new ideas, they innovate, they come up with new, creative ways to express themselves in the world. Oftentimes, it is the immigrants—the Italians, the Jews, the Asian Americans, the Indian Americans—that have come from other places in the world to imprint their DNA into the fabric of American society. What I've tried to show them over the past five to eight years is that I'm basically taking their DNA, that immigrant hustle, and imprinting it into what America does best.

Judd: Does success in America mean stability, or is it about doing something that has an impact in some way?

Hasan: I think those moments are starting to happen. There are two buckets: There's stuff that's just objectively funny, and then there's stuff that's meaningful, and sometimes comedy can be both of those things. And by the way, I love both buckets. *Talladega Nights* is just a hilariously funny movie, and then there's *The Big Sick,* which is both funny and meaningful. My parents are starting to see, *Oh, there is cultural gravitas to what Hasan is doing.* It is moving the needle in some way.

Judd: I feel like there's a journey that so many comedians go through. You start out with an instinct to be funny—sometimes it's driven by rage and resentment—and then, slowly, you realize that it's actually about personal self-discovery. I used to just want to be silly. I never really thought, as a kid and as a young man, that it was anything more than that. Only by working with people like Kumail and with Pete Davidson, people who share their stories, have I seen that comedy has such a huge impact on other people. While rewatching your stand-up special, I saw how the crowd was so rapturous, but how they also felt seen, represented. As a Jewish comedian, everyone's fucking Jewish. I grew up just bathing in my point of view. But when we made *The Big Sick,* Kumail was like, "I can't believe we're making this movie."

Hasan: There's a scene in that movie where his dad basically says, "So, you don't believe in Allah." And Kumail basically says, "I know you believe in this stuff, but I don't know if it has value for me." There's part of me where I'm like, *Man, this is a very dangerous conversation.* This is relegated to the living room or very private WhatsApp groups—you don't put this on a public stage. The fact that you captured that, people feel seen.

Judd: I think a lot of Americans are only beginning to understand what life is like for other people. I always thought I was aware, but I didn't understand any of this until spending five years in a room with Kumail and learning what his experience in America was like.

Hasan: I understand that. As artists, we're empaths, we have very vulnerable, raw nerves. We like to pick up on those vibrations and those emotions that we then make into our art form. But for a lot of folks, they're just like, *If I were to think about what other people have had to endure, if I were to actually think about that, it would be too much. It would be too horrifying, it would be crippling.* So, I can sometimes understand where they're coming from when people are like, "I just don't want to watch the news, because it's just too much for me to take."

Judd: These days, I find myself watching a lot of James Baldwin. There's so much material—so many interviews, so many moments where he's just, like, on a local station in Florida debating the sheriff, or in that documentary with Dick Gregory.

Hasan: Can you explain how profound Dick Gregory was to the history of comedy?

Judd: I think you can only look at Dick Gregory through the lens of a moment where that type of comedian simply did not exist. He's almost like an alien who was dropped into the sixties, when comedy was just waking up, and where there are only one or two other people who are thoughtful about it. Then, suddenly, you have this very intelligent, sharp, erudite thinker who is like James Baldwin, but he's funnier than you.

Hasan: Roy Wood, Jr., once explained the value of Dick Gregory to me, and it almost brought me to tears. He said, "I don't know if this is true, but I have been told that Dick Gregory was one of the first Black performers that was allowed to perform inside of the White House without dancing." Roy said it's very powerful to know that a Black man could stand in the White House and keep both of his feet placed on the ground and speak to the president. His wits and his words were respected enough that he could keep both of his heels on the floor and still talk. That story means a lot to me.

Judd: Unfortunately, that's how our country has always worked: You need to fall in love with the gay couple on *Modern Family* in order to realize that you're okay with gay marriage. You need to fall in love with Michael Jackson and Michael Jordan, or to idolize Beyoncé, in order to see through all that racist bullshit. And I think that's what you're going through as well, in a post–9/11 world, where most people in this country haven't met anybody who's Muslim.

Hasan: This is the thing where I feel a deep sense of sadness. When we talk about anti-Semitism or Islamophobia or anti-LGBTQ rhetoric or racism: Why do you have to become a superhero for people to be like, *Hey, you know what? Jewish people are pretty talented.* What makes me sad about my skill set is that it is something I cannot pass on to my children. I've been able to accomplish a lot, and very powerful people have been able to see my humanity despite my religion, but can my son or daughter also carry that? If they walk into a room and people don't know they're my son or daughter, will people be like, *Hey, are you a terrorist?* If you're not Eddie Murphy, if you're not LeBron James, if you're just a regular person—can humanity and empathy still translate? That has been my biggest frustration. I've seen the limitation of celebrity and jokes because it's only a commodity that other famous people can share.

Judd: You hope what's happening now is just the death screams of these outdated ideas. It may take a few decades, but the hope is that they're dying away.

Hasan: Do you really feel like it's the death scream? Because, to me, say what you will, Trump still got seventy million people to opt in. Sam Harris has a really interesting podcast, and he was like, "To be a progressive person, you must feel a sense of shame." You must feel a shame at the history of the country, the way we treated Black people through slavery and Jim Crow, the way we treated indigenous people, and a sense of shame in regards to current inequalities that exist economically, socially, and in terms of gender and sexuality. What Trump represents is the exact opposite: shamelessness. I still remember it clicked for me when I was listening to him. He goes, "I'm not going to shame you about your sexual habits. I'm on my third marriage. I have sex with porn stars. I'm not going to shame you about language. I said, 'I'll grab someone by the pussy' on tape. I'm not going to shame you for being white. I am white." So, Trump is shamelessness. He is all gluttony and sex and cheeseburgers. And I think there is a group of people who just feel like, *Don't make me feel bad for who I am. I can try to help you, but don't shame me into helping you.* And I think, perhaps, the progressive left has taken that too far. We cannot use shame as a tactic of inspiration. When I've tried to communicate with Asian American voters in Florida, Georgia, Michigan—instead of using words like *privilege*, I'll use *fair*. And whenever you work with the local crew in New York, a lot of those Long Island guys and gals—they come from a heavily conservative base. The episodes that we did on student loan debt, specifically, and when I testified before Congress on the issue, our security guards, our cameramen, our camera operators, were like, "Man, thank you for doing that episode, because it is unfair what is happening to us. The fact that we have to take these shitty loans for our children to go to school." And I realized the idea of fairness is what speaks to everybody. I've tried to break it down into these fundamental principles that, hopefully, will chip away at the horrible by-products of racism in this country.

Judd: You're not going to be doing your show [*Patriot Act*] anymore. Were you hoping to do more seasons, or were you burnt out?

Hasan: I was getting tired. It's funny. We were five episodes short of where I wanted to be. I wanted to end on Election Day. That was my homage to the Patriot Act, which was such a seminal piece of legislation from when I was in high school. I called the show *Patriot Act* to flip that notion on its head: This is *my* Patriot Act. We ended a few episodes short, but I feel like you and I are both in the same bucket, where we both made these cult classics that ended a little too soon. I'm super happy with what we did with the show, and I can't wait to explore storytelling in a different way and in a way that's a little less didactic. That's the one thing that I love about the medium that you've flourished in. When you tell Pete [Davidson]'s story or Amy [Schumer]'s story or Kumail's story, you're not looking at camera one and telling people how to feel. You're allowing them to come into a world and then empathize with them.

Judd: I interviewed Jon right before he stopped doing *The Daily Show*, and I knew he was going to quit. I could just tell by how he was talking, how tired he sounded, and also the guilt over how the show took so much time away from his family and his life for seventeen years. It takes a lot mentally to stay in the headspace of politics, because you're talking about pain a lot.

Hasan: It's rage. After a while, how many school shootings can you cover? It's just tragic. And so, Jon said—and I love this—it becomes impotent rage. I was at *The Daily Show* when we covered the first "I can't breathe" choking incident. And then for it to be six years later, covering George Floyd—you're just like, *It's too much.*

Judd: I don't think people understand the magic trick of modern political satire, how brilliant everybody is. I watch these shows, and I always think the same thing: *I don't know how you get even the opening monologue done in a day.* On the other hand, there is something disposable about it. Like, your stand-up special will live much longer than *Patriot Act.*

Hasan: There's something very ephemeral about it. There's no doubt that when you hit that nerve, that day, it is a high. You feel a great sense of accomplishment. But at the same time, it goes away just as fast, in the sense that you have to move on to the next story, the next take, and the next villain of the day that you're attacking or approaching.

Judd: So, now you're acting on *The Morning Show.* Is that the direction that you're looking to go in? Narrative storytelling on television or in movies?

Hasan: I want to try to think about the big ideas or the big questions that I have. I'll give you an example of a question that I wrote down after journaling one morning. I was reflecting on the feeling I have in regard to the year 2020, and if I could sum it up in one word, it's *disillusionment.* I think we all collectively feel a deep disillusionment with the debate over science, the efficacy of masks or no masks, should we open the country back up . . . And I wrote this sentence, at the end of my journal entry. I said, "How can I remain happy in a world that I fundamentally do not understand?" And I think that question cannot be answered through an episode of the *Patriot Act.* Those are the big questions that I love thinking about. And what I loved about *The Morning Show,* when I got the call about it, if you watch season one, it's answering the big questions in regard to power dynamics in the workplace. Obviously, through Steve Carell's character, they explore the unequivocally wrong position of having sex with people in the office if you're in a position of power. But then there's the other part of season one that explores the gray area of people dating, the power dynamic of people saying, "I want to date somebody who's senior to me, and for you to tell me I can't do that denies me my agency." And I love that. I've already spent the past seven years being a fake journalist, a fake TV host, so, I might as well continue the tradition.

Judd: It's interesting, because people talk about this gray area a lot these days, especially when it comes to what they're allowed to do and say in public. What was once seen as normal is now seen as potentially problematic.

Hasan: People don't know this about me, but philosophically, I am a deep believer in speech absolutism. Like, to me, Noam Chomsky is a Dick Gregory–type figure, in terms of being an academic free speech thought leader. But what I try to tell people is, "Hey, the bears that I was poking through *Patriot Act*—[Indian prime minister] Narendra Modi, Trump, [Philippine president Rodrigo] Duterte, [President Jair] Bolsonaro in Brazil—these are guys that you're not supposed to make fun of. If you've come from our communities, you know that you should not do that publicly. And, quite frankly, dissidents and journalists in other countries get imprisoned, they get murdered or killed or chopped up in embassies, for saying these things. It is an incredible privilege that I am an American citizen and I can say those things. But I know that if I were to cross the border into another country, that those same things could get me in prison. In Saudi Arabia, I'm a cybercriminal for what I said on [*Patriot Act*]. So, if I have the right to say those things that are deemed dangerous, I also have to give space for other people to say things that they deem dangerous, even if I think they are uncouth and not particularly gracious, as much as I personally dislike them.

Judd: Everyone should be allowed to say anything they want to say, but you're also allowed to be criticized. It's good to have those debates, even with awful people.

Hasan: I remember doing this piece on *The Daily Show*, following the U.S. women's soccer team and their fight for equal pay. I interviewed Gavin McInnes, who is the head of the Proud Boys. I could tell from the moment we sat down—from the way he was wearing his suit, his talking points—[that] he knew what he was doing. He wanted to be a provocateur, and it was bad in the sense that he was able to rile up his base through that, and I should have known better than to sit down with someone who is a bad-faith actor. There's a difference between intellectual debate and provocation. That is an important thing to decipher. It took years to understand the way in which bad-faith actors can manipulate media and digital media to perpetuate a really bad message. What did people think of Andrew Dice Clay back in the day, who I see now as one of the early examples of this kind of provocateur?

Judd: I used to see him as a kid, when I was a dishwasher and a busboy at a comedy club. He was just a funny impressionist, and he wasn't yet doing that character. I think the audience almost collaborated with him to move in that direction, that the farther he went, the more they enjoyed it. There is a similarity between the Donald Trump audience and the Andrew Dice Clay audience. I think people debated whether or not it was just a character—you know, an idiot, sexist, New York moron. And I think what Andrew Dice Clay would tell you is that he was just doing a bit. Then it got so big, it became ridiculous, because people got some visceral thrill out of enjoying that kind of moron. Then the question always becomes: But does the crowd agree with the moron?

Hasan: When you first start stand-up, you learn that any joke that gets a laugh works. But when I got hired at *The Daily Show*, I would pitch jokes, and I remember [producer/writer] Steve Bodow would say to me, "That joke is funny, but it's not a sophisticated joke." He was like, "Some jokes are like top-shelf liquor, and then there are those that are just like college beer that you would have at a kegger, that almost tastes like urine." There are certain jokes that are done with a level of sophistication and panache, that are so good that you marvel at them. It taught me that all jokes aren't created equal and [that] we should all aim to that high level, the top shelf.

Judd: I know someone's good when I'm a little angry when I listen to them. Like, I would watch [John] Mulaney at the Cellar, when I started doing stand-up again, and he makes you want to stop doing stand-up. That's how you know someone's great.

Hasan: Do you feel that with film? Why do you feel that with stand-up, but you don't feel that with film?

Judd: I think because the type of movie that I like isn't made very often. I love *Diner* and *Fast Times at Ridgemont High* and *Terms of Endearment.* I feel like the world is not flooded with that, so there's room for me to try. It's one of the reasons why I work on certain projects like with Kumail and Emily—I just go, *We need this. No one's doing this.* Or [with] Pete talking about his pain and suicide and grief. No one wants to make that movie. But you're right, it doesn't really make sense. Maybe because it's so much more of a visceral failure when you fail at stand-up than when you fail at a movie.

Hasan: I can see that, because it's just you onstage. But I will say this, you put out the Shandling documentary, and what I loved about that documentary was that it showed us that comedy is not about whether you can top Adam Sandler or Chris Rock or Martin Lawrence or whoever the people are that have influenced you the most. You showed us that this art form is just about exploring who you are, and to bring it back to what Roy told me about Dick Gregory, what he said he loved most about Dick Gregory is that even before he died, he still had dates on the books. Dick Gregory had a weekend at Rooster T. Feathers. There's something really beautiful about that.

Judd: There's a feeling that you get when you get older, where you realize, like, kids don't remember *M*A*S*H*. They don't remember *Cheers* or *Family Ties*. And pretty soon, they won't remember *Friends*. You feel everything going off the cliff in a very Buddhist way. Whether you like it or not, you start feeling the texture of the nature of everything disappearing and that you really are only alive in this moment. That's what's so great about stand-up, which is a series of very direct, present moments. You must be present when you're doing stand-up, and then it makes you go, *Well, what do I want to talk about? What do I want to do if it's all disappearing?* And then you're trying to be present for your next thought.

Hasan: When did you get the financial security to be able to feel that you could finally just be present?

Judd: That is a big moment. Like, *If I stopped now, and moved to a certain state, I think I could live the rest of my life on this.*

Hasan: My *Daily Show* money will last me twenty years, and I don't have to do any dates. But I do have that fear of like, *Am I going to have to go back to OfficeMax?*

Judd: That's a good feeling, though, because it drives you. For me, what drives me is that no matter what you do, you can't be confident that the next one will work. I'm happy that there is that terror, because I am as terrified now, in prep on a movie I'm going to do in a few months, as I was on the first movie. And that's what makes me care enough. It's not a fear of going broke. It's a fear of humiliation, a fear of finding out I'm not good.

Hasan: You had movies that were massive hits and those that weren't. Does the same amount of work and love and attention to detail exist in both? And can you never really know? Or did you know?

Judd: You don't know sometimes. Sometimes you can sense when something is going to explode, but what you feel more often is *I don't know if they can convince people to see it, but I know that this is great.* And at some point, a certain amount of people will recognize that. I want any movie I make to be good enough that the people who like it think that it's amazing, even if it's fewer people overall.

Hasan: We always want to aspire to make somebody's favorite thing.

JEFF TWEEDY

January 2019

Judd: How's it been in this period, with both the record [*Warm*] and the book [*Let's Go (So We Can Get Back)*]? Are you scared of talking about yourself?

Jeff: I'm pretty lucky that, most of the time, I can be pretty selective about talking to people who aren't going to be just asking me to recount stories from the book. The thing that I can't tolerate is having to do interviews with the guy that was assigned from the daily newspaper to talk to Jeff Tweedy, and he had to figure out who he is. He's usually covering City Hall, and almost every question that they ask is something they could have found on Wikipedia.

Judd: And you know it's from Wikipedia because you know your Wikipedia.

Jeff: Or, they didn't even look at the Wikipedia. But in general, I look at it like—well, my dad worked on the railroad for forty-six years, I like talking about music in general, and if I don't necessarily look at it as being about me, if I can get into a conversation with somebody who spends their time listening to music, we can generally go in a cool direction.

Judd: That's why I like doing this, too.

Jeff: I think tons and tons of the recollections and the insights that were in my book would have only happened because of the book. Honestly, I'm not a very nostalgic person. I haven't spent a whole lot of time introspecting my past, and that forced me to do that.

Judd: Are you a therapy guy at all?

Jeff: I am. I'm really convinced that everybody has massive blind spots, and therapy is all about becoming more conscious of what choices are in front of you so that you could actually make a choice—as opposed to an addict, who is always compelled to do things without really realizing why. You know, *Oh, this is because of my mother. Well, too late, I'm high now.*

Judd: Do you think the *Warm* record was changed by the fact that you were actively working on the book? Did it change the writing?

Jeff: For sure. I feel like writing prose and writing lyrics are kind of photo negatives of each other. The way I feel like I've tried to get lyrics to work for myself is really similar to how haiku works, where you're trying to paint around the edges of something enough for somebody to see what's not there. What you *didn't* write. And then writing prose, writing this book, was the opposite. You have to be pretty concrete and just tell the story and not get distracted by all of those tantalizing details that are poetic, but [that] don't necessarily advance the story or make the picture clear enough for somebody to understand it. In other words, I depend upon the listener to really color in a lot, but if they're reading my story, it should be my fucking story.

Judd: Is it more difficult in the format of an autobiography than a song?

Jeff: I think that I had a lot of lyrics finished, and then, as I was getting more and more confident about writing the book, I kept going back to the record and going, *This isn't clear enough.* I couldn't really go back and forth anymore. I did way more revisions to get the lyrics to feel more direct, like the book, because that was the mode of communication I was really trying to stay connected to. But the interesting thing is that the inspiration isn't different at all. The emotions that I was trying to convey were the same. I just did more revisions so that they were a little bit more vulnerably open and [so that they say], *Well, this is what I'm singing about.*

Judd: As someone who has listened to a lot of your records, I just kept listening to it over and over again. And I don't listen to music that way, where it just rotates for a few hours. I thought, *I'm really getting pulled into this record*, but I wasn't sure exactly why, and then I started listening to the lyrics more.

Jeff: That's certainly nice to hear, to be honest with you. That's hard to do these days. People don't listen to anything repeatedly. There's so much to listen to.

Judd: There's also just the sound of it. It feels like when I listen to it, I wonder how many instruments he's playing.

Jeff: It's just my son Spencer on drums, and I'm playing everything else.

Judd: Is your other son, Sam, writing music?

Jeff: He's recording music now in the coach house. He claimed his own little fiefdom. He plays guitar, and he's really good at programming synthesizers and stuff like that. He came to it a lot later than Spencer. Spencer basically came out of the womb a drummer.

Judd: How do you talk about it with them? Because I had my kids in the movies, and I'm always encouraging them, "This is a good way to spend your life and a good industry." It's a healthy way to think about life in the arts. A lot of people just look at me like I'm crazy.

Jeff: I never understood people telling somebody not to do something that's given them so much joy. You have to have a really fucking shitty experience to think that your children should be protected from it. I tell them if they want to be famous and they want to be rich, they're going to struggle at almost anything they do, if that's what their goal is. But if you want to play music, that's an amazing thing to have in your life. And nobody can take it from you. You can find people to play music with or you can make music for yourself, and it's a great way to kill time without hurting anybody. I benefited so much from having this outlet for my creativity and something to do with myself. I could never imagine discouraging them from it.

Judd: It must create a much more intimate relationship with your kids, to share something like that.

Jeff: It's like the way we've played catch is to sit and play music together. I toured with Spencer, and they've both been on the road from time to time as kids, as early as they've been around. We didn't do the thing where we took them out of school and they traveled with us. Susie and I were really dead set on them having friends and a somewhat predictable lifestyle.

Judd: To tour in a band with your son—it's an experience people don't have with their parents. Personally, I can't imagine doing that with my parents. "What is your worst nightmare?" "Oh, I'd be touring with my mom."

Jeff: I think people were sold on this idea of there being a generation gap at one point in time. It was kind of a marketing tool for rock music, too. You can kind of blame it on youth culture as being conceived of as being more legitimate if it was distanced from the previous generation. I find that to be really culturally destructive. We have a lot to learn from each other always. So, I think we're much more like what you see in country music families, where it's just, "This is just a part of a continuum thing that we do, and you can be part of the family business if you want to do it."

Judd: Be like the Cashes . . .

Jeff: We were watching the Glen Campbell movie—all his kids play with him, and it's much more common in jazz and country. I think it's becoming more common in rock music, too, like [Ringo Starr's son] Zak Starkey and all these second- and third-generation musicians.

Judd: What are the main questions they have for you about music or writing?

Jeff: They're so much smarter than me; they don't ask many questions. His brother's pretty virtuosic, and Sammy's much more like me, where it's more like, *I'm learning what I need to learn to the minimum of what I have to learn to communicate.* So, he's more interested in those types of things, like the process of how do you come up with the melody? And we'll sit down: "Can you think of something? Can you hear a melody when you hear these chords?" And most people do. It's a matter of getting yourself still enough to hear it. "Oh yeah, I can totally hum along with this." If you can hold a tune, you can probably think of a melody. It's actually a very strange thing, to combine a bunch of virtuosos, especially in the rock context. Rock music has inspired amateurs, and at some point, the most powerful version of rock music to me is a bunch of people not knowing what they're doing at all but having a complete conviction of purpose. And bands are the rarest of all, if they can all point themselves in the same direction. The Ramones are a fucking miracle. They are. I mean how do you get that to happen? You couldn't conceive of that. They just—they just did it.

Judd: I got to meet Roger Daltrey. They were just really kids the first few years. They went to high school together, and Roger Daltrey made a guitar himself. He had no money, so he carved one. They just, you know, went for it in post–World War Two England. *I've got to get the fuck out of here, and this is my ticket.*

Jeff: They're all malnourished. Like the Rolling Stones. Have you ever met them? They're all the same size. They have, like, I don't know, a post–World War Two inability to gain fat molecules or something.

Judd: With writing, or writing jokes, you're often just sitting alone in a room and trying to believe that something will come. Does music require that kind of faith?

Jeff: I feel like it gets easier as you get older, because you have so much evidence that it does happen. Something does generally happen. And it's not the end of the world if it doesn't. But there's always something. I feel that there's always something to work on. If I go in the studio and I don't feel particularly inspired, that's kind of a relief, because that means that I can redo the bass part that I knew needed to be fixed on some other song. If you work on enough stuff at once—and I know you do that, too—that's a real luxury. It creates a lot of good work, to not have to focus on everything all at once, or one thing all the time.

Judd: They serve each other. When I was working with Lena Dunham and just talking to her about stories and the way she approached things, it made all my writing that I did without her better. Just listening to her.

Jeff: We would go and mix and help some other, younger band and record in the same week that I'll be finishing a lyric or something. It takes a lot of pressure off of each thing, to not be as precious. Also, when you stare at something too long, it starts to look weird. It's like saying any simple word over and over again. It's not meant to work like that. I'm a big believer in deadlines. I think you just have to abandon things. We get distracted by so many things. One of the things I talk about in the book is we deem certain things in the studio as "will not affect sales." You know, the hi-hats are not going to affect sales. You don't need to spend a day to get a kick drum sound.

Judd: It takes a lot of discipline just to clear your head enough to go into a space that has nothing to do with all the things happening in the world. To tune in to your own stuff.

Jeff: I'm just pretty conditioned to do that, because that's how I dealt with my own constitutional crisis. It's been a conflict-free zone for me.

Judd: Was that how it was when you first started writing songs?

Jeff: I don't think consciously, but definitely. I've identified after the fact that it must have been a real appeal to have something that centered me in the moment and helped me disappear. That's the way I describe it, and that's kind of the ideal scenario, when you get so involved in it that you feel like you've lost the burden of self. You're not really there.

Judd: I guess it's like something in flow.

Jeff: I'm pretty resistant to a lot of "Oh, I'm just a conduit for the universe. The universe writes songs through me." I'm pretty sure it's your subconscious.

Judd: It took me a very long time to realize that, a lot of times, whether I'm giving someone notes or writing myself, I'll have a problem, something I'm working out in my head, and the story would help me solve it. It might be a message to myself to work on something. Is there an equivalent to that in songwriting?

Jeff: The thing that comes to mind is *A Ghost Is Born*. That record was toward the end of my drug use and before I was properly treated for mood disorders, so it was really interesting to revisit that material right after I got out of the hospital and go tour on it. That seemed like it was way ahead of me. So, on some level, some stuff is getting worked out without there being a conscious direction to do that. But I definitely write songs as a reminder to myself when I come across some insight that I know could help me but I know I'll forget it.

Judd: So, you'll write it into a song?

Jeff: Even something like "Heavy Metal Drummer." I was just such a dick to the kids in the heavy metal bands, and they were having so much fucking fun. I was a dick.

Judd: So, you wrote an apology?

Jeff: An apology, but also, like, "Lighten up, Francis." Get over yourself.

Judd: One thing that I appreciate about comedy is when bad things happen, I always think, *I can put this to good use.* And sometimes the worse the things that happen, I go, *Wow, that will really make a funny movie or a good joke.* So, as a result, the worst things in life at least have some value. They're not just terrible.

Jeff: Oh no, you can't let your pain go to waste. That's actually a lyric I put in two or three different songs now. What a shame to have to go through shit and suffer and then not learn anything or accumulate any kind of wisdom from it.

Judd: With certain people, you hear a record, and it's great, and then you realize that it's only great because they just went through something tough.

Jeff: Sometimes I think a lot of art would be enhanced if there was a really easy narrative arc to it from the outside. People going into it know, *This is what she's going through.* If you did a walk through a museum with a really informed curator, that's the kind of shit they can illuminate: "This is done because he was born without a sixth toe." Then, suddenly, you have a story you can relate to.

Judd: What is a happy album you like? What's your happiest album?

Jeff: I don't know. I mean, I think of Fela [Kuti] records as being joyous and my ideal protest type of music, because it's like, *I'm going to dance and you can't take this away from me.* I'm not a dancer or anything. I just feel like if I could dance, that's what I would do. My son was telling me I shouldn't refer to my songs as being sad, because that could color people's opinion. A lot of times, maybe if they are sad, they're hopeful.

Judd: That's not a word that would ever come to me.

Jeff: I did a lot of touring this year, and I played a lot of outdoor festivals on sunshiney days, with people bouncing beach balls back and forth, and I don't feel like it's in my skill set to entertain those people with an acoustic guitar. They're just not up for my feelings.

Judd: I always, on some level, have an embarrassment or insecurity that anyone would care about anything that I feel, but then you do thousands of performances, and you go, *Well, people are interested.* Was that ever hard for you?

Jeff: I was the baby of my family, and I grew up almost like an only child, because my brothers and my sister are so much older than I am. And my mother really, really did not set boundaries for our relationship to where she wanted me to be her best friend and confidant, so I grew up pretty much believing that everybody was interested in every feeling that I had, everything I had to say, and then, at some point, I think I had that beaten out of me. So, this massive sense of guilt and some shame came with realizing that other people saw this as weakness or vulnerability.

Judd: What year did that happen?

Jeff: Probably high school, where you would typically go through some sort of reassessment of yourself. And then I feel like I worked my way back.

Judd: Who was the voice that you listened to? Was there anybody that you felt mentored you, or that you were paying attention to that you learned from?

Jeff: I do think some of it is innate. At some point, it was just too hard to keep repressing this desire to share how I feel. But then there are definitely affirmations from people like [the Modern Lovers'] Jonathan Richman. He's the one I always think of, because he was in the middle of the seventies, in the drug culture, singing, "I like my mom and dad." He was just so self-liberated to be Jonathan Richman. I've kind of come to the conclusion that most music that I respond to has some element of self-liberation. Like soul music and punk rock. Just some empowerment that someone afforded themselves, took for themselves. Rock and roll. *We're not going to do what our parents did. The world doesn't have to be this way.* What's the difference between an artist and nonartist? The artist has liberated and freed themselves to be an artist, and a nonartist hasn't had that chance or opportunity or conviction.

Judd: Who introduces those ideas to a young person?

Jeff: I think that making art is important and [that] the highest aspiration of any work of art is to get somebody else to make something. I just think it's harder to destroy things if you've been actively engaged in the process of creation, and this is about as religious as I get about anything. If you're on this side of creation, then you understand how sacred that is, and it's a lot harder to tear someone else's creation down or to be involved in destruction. Can you destroy things as an act of creation? Sure, of course. Some things need to be destroyed.

But I think that people are born creators. People are walking around creating all the time, and they don't understand that's what they're doing, but you need to be consciously connected to that and just allow yourself to make things like you did when you were a little kid. You didn't care if it was good or bad; it was just a fucking miracle that you did something and Mom and Dad hung it on the refrigerator.

Judd: If your kid draws something and you hang it up or you put it in a frame, it completely changes how they perceive the idea of being creative.

Jeff: One thing that was amazing was making the discovery that even though my father had worked on the railroad his whole life, he would go in the basement and, if he had something on his mind or in his craw, he would write poetry.

Judd: Did he share it with people?

Jeff: Occasionally, he would come upstairs and read it. And it was humorous sometimes.

Judd: That, on some level, must have completely formed your idea of what you do with feeling. I could see how that could just set up the whole machine of your mind.

Jeff: For sure. As far as, like, having a career arc that looks like what Wilco's looks like? I don't know if you set out to do that. Does it make any sense to set out to do that? I can reverse-engineer it and try to figure out the key elements.

Judd: What was your attitude at the very beginning?

Jeff: My attitude at the very beginning is the same as it is now: I can't believe that I ever got to make a record and a tour and a band. Because that was the highest aspiration. Honest to God. *You can put a record out and go across the country in a fucking van and play music and get to do this?* Once that was achieved, I feel like every step along the way has been a challenge to go, *Well, can I do this in a way that feels as good? Can I play on this bigger festival stage and have it feel true to who I am?*

Judd: I feel like I always had a thought in my head, when I was first starting out, that my biggest fear was not being good in the eyes of the people I respected, and that kept me from making choices to just get good money. I didn't want the people I respected to think that I suck. *I can't take that gig on that show because Garry Shandling will think I'm an idiot.* The idea of being true to myself—I don't think I even understood it at the beginning.

Jeff: I got over the selling-out thing pretty quick. Because we had some offer to allow some of our songs to be in commercials for Volkswagen, and it was a substantial amount of money, and I thought, *If I said no to this, how would I explain that to my dad?* I mean, selling out is a completely privileged person's luxury to even contemplate.

Judd: Even the Who made an album called *The Who Sell Out,* and had the theme [music] to every *CSI*.

Jeff: People that go to work every day at McDonald's don't worry that they're selling out.

Judd: But there's a moment early in your career where it can affect the actual birth of your work.

Jeff: It doesn't have anything to do with your work, but it could inhibit the perception that you're coming from a pure place, which is another kind of superimposed, exalted position to be in. To deem something pure or not pure, when most people really do have to work for money.

Judd: There is an embarrassment in getting to do what you want to do, that you enjoy, when other people work very, very hard doing what you don't want to do.

Jeff: Do you know Lydia Lunch? She was a provocateur, a performer, in New York around the same time as Sonic Youth. We were making this decision about these commercials at the same time we were in Spain, where she was living at the time. She's a paragon of iconic classic artistic virtue, you know, so I was hesitant to even bring it up around her at the time. And she's like, "Take their fucking money." It was pretty succinct, like, "Why would you not take their fucking money? If you take their fucking money, they don't have it."

Judd: When you hear Springsteen talk about his relationship with his fans over many decades, he's very Springsteenian, like, "We're taking this ride together." But what is the equivalent with you and your fans who followed you for a long time? What do you think people take from it, or do you have any sense of that?

Jeff: Wilco's a band that has a community that has grown up around it, but I don't see it as being as pinpointed as Springsteen's. I feel like [Wilco's fans are] pretty smart, and they don't want to be pandered to. And I think that they demand a lot of respect. The worst thing I could do is take it for granted that I know what they are or speak for them. I joked the other night that I look out in the audience and, some nights, I realize that there's only four of you that I really want to be friends with. And they can handle that. They would laugh.

Judd: They feel the same way?

Jeff: In a way, they identify. I have a lot of thoughts about the Springsteen cult, and I know from every account I've ever heard [that] he's a great guy and obviously a massive cultural thing that's part of our lives. But I've always felt a little confused at how easily people accept his version of what working class is. He really did a lot to perpetuate the images of working classes [as] being white, too. When people say "working class," you think white people, but working class isn't white; it's everybody. So, I don't know, maybe just write one less album about it. But at the same time, I get that there's a voice that he gave to a lot of people, that they feel super seen by him, and that's all good stuff, too.

Judd: It's fascinating that he wanted his dad to feel seen. His dad's depressed and unreachable; he makes all these songs about how he thinks his dad is feeling about his blue-collar life, to get some connection with him. It's fascinating. Your dad—what was his disposition, as a dad? Did he understand you?

Jeff: No. My dad's defining characteristic isn't working class. It's alcoholic. So, I never really thought of him as being working class. I mean, by the time I was around, he was a kind of company man anyway. He had graduated to being superintendent, but he was probably closer to being an entertainer than I was. I think if I really wanted to connect with my dad, I would have been a lot goofier. I probably would have gone into comedy. He would have been the guy with the lampshade on his head doing something less serious than music. Because that's what he was at every wedding reception we ever went to.

Judd: He was the life-of-the-party alcoholic.

Jeff: Until he wasn't.

Judd: Was that a scary thing as a kid?

Jeff: Totally, yeah. Adult children of alcoholics—that's something you identify later in life. We have a lot of anxiety, because you can't reliably predict the moods in your household and/or what's going to happen next.

Judd: Was it just wall-to-wall through your entire childhood? Was there a sober period?

Jeff: No. A minimum of twelve beers a day after he'd get home from work. He never missed work or anything. Over time, as I learn more about my own addiction, I've had to really question whether my dad was really an alcoholic. Because the trajectory of an alcoholic and addicts is generally worsening consequences, and my dad's life was completely stable. If anything, it got better because he rose in his profession. Then, much later in life, he had some surgery or something, and he had to stop drinking. I'm like, "Dad, you've got to tell the doctors that you are used to having a certain amount of alcohol in your system. Otherwise, you're going to have seizures," and he's like, "No, no. I'll be all right." He did end up telling them, but he didn't have any trouble not drinking.

Judd: When that happened, did it matter that he never stopped before? How did that all hit you?

Jeff: Was I mad? There were a lot of things that made me mad and sad for him. Knowing what my relationship with my children is like and how much he missed in not being present and not being engaged—because I think he would have really enjoyed it.

Judd: Was he [an] at-the-bar alcoholic or in the house?

Jeff: He was in the house. In the basement.

Judd: By himself?

Jeff: Yeah, but once he quit, he quit. And then he started having panic attacks. He said it was the first time he had a panic attack since he was a teenager, and that's when he started drinking. So, he self-medicated for sixty years or something like that. I'm like, "Dad, I can help you with this. I know what this is, and I think that we probably have the same diagnosis." And he started taking the same medications that I take, and then it pretty much worked. The other thing that was really striking about my dad later in life was that he hated Trump, and he couldn't even talk to his neighbors anymore. He was surrounded by all these people that love Trump, and he would call me: "You're the only one I could talk to about this motherfucker." A couple of nights after the election, I called him from Europe, and I was like, "How are you doing? I'm doing terrible. I feel sick." And he said, "I don't know what's going to happen, but I can tell you this: Of all the things that I've worried about in my life, only a tiny fraction of them have come true." It was actually pretty soothing. But I was just like, "Dad, that's really, really amazing. That really would have fucking helped me when I was in high school. What the fuck is wrong with you? Why did you wait until now?"

Judd: "You had wisdom to give me!"

Jeff: I had no idea.

Judd: My Jewish reaction is: Only a tiny fraction will come true, so that's proof that it's going to happen.

Jeff: I converted, so I have some of that. They accepted me pretty readily, so I have to assume that I have some of the cultural proclivities to catastrophize.

Judd: Your dad passed away recently?

Jeff: The summer before last.

Judd: You had some closure, and you were able to connect with him in a different way?

Jeff: He had a second chance at life after my mom died. He had a girlfriend for ten years. Looked almost like my mom, but was there with a beer, and anytime he crinkled a can, she'd have another one [there for him]. My mother would have never done any of that. "Get your own fucking beer." So, he had this sort of nice trajectory to the end of his life, and then he had the best death you can have: everybody around him, and we got him home. It was pretty heavy stuff for my kids, to see somebody die, but I feel really good about that, because I think we treat death really poorly in our culture. We really don't want to see it. We don't want to believe in it, and I think it's pretty bad for you to not come to terms with it, at least from time to time.

Judd: You talk a lot onstage in your solo performances and are really funny. How does that fit into what you do?

Jeff: I've always tried not to let getting laughs onstage go to my head, because I think having a guitar around your neck really sets people up to have their expectations subverted, which makes it easier to get laughs, because they're expecting me to be serious, and they're expecting to hear a song.

Judd: You seem to enjoy storytelling onstage.

Jeff: I do, when I'm by myself especially, but when it's with the band, I feel like there's five other people looking at their watches, going, *Oh my God, not this one again.* I've just gotten more and more confident from doing it over and over and over. Then, somehow, every night, my wife will go, "You're really funny." Am I? I think I have the added benefit of not having tried. Nothing worse than somebody trying to be funny.

Judd: So, you don't give it any thought?

Jeff: I do more so recently than I ever have, because I played more solo acoustic shows recently than I ever have, back to back, and it is starting to become a thing. Like, *I got some laughs with this bit the other night, maybe I'll say it again.* Because so many people come to see you repeatedly, and I'm really self-conscious about saying it the exact same way every night.

Judd: That's how I feel every time I go to the Largo. I assume it's the same exact crowd. And it isn't, but . . .

Jeff: Some nights, if I do back to back to back, I know everybody in the front row. I know them by their fucking names. And I'm looking at them, playing "Jesus, Etc." for the five-hundredth time for fucking Paul, and you can tell Paul's waiting for the new song or the song he hasn't collected yet. Paul's really sweet.

Judd: You have comedians opening for you. What is your connection to that world? There aren't many musical artists who also get a kick out of the role of stand-up.

Jeff: I love hanging out with comedians, because they make me look happy.

JIMMY KIMMEL

September 2020

Judd: You're really into cooking. Is that a recent thing, or were you always doing that?

Jimmy: I started when I was a teenager, when I would try to make my hot dogs exactly like Nathan's. I'd roll them on the frying pan, so that they got a little bit burnt, and then I would throw the sauerkraut onto the pan and put the buns on top of it, so it steamed the bun a little bit. That's where it began.

Judd: I feel like the food stuff is the flip side of the comedy nerd.

Jimmy: Maybe it's just about obsession, but I do think there's a real kinship between comedians and chefs. At its core, it's this: They're both really trying to make people happy and get compliments from them.

Judd: My obsession growing up was going home after school to watch *Dinah Shore* and *Merv Griffin,* and then I would stay up to watch Carson and Letterman. Sometimes it'd be *The Stanley Siegel Show,* or whatever. In fact, the biggest fight I got into with my parents was when we were eating in a restaurant. I wanted to go home to watch Steve Martin on *The Carol Burnett Show,* and they would not speed up their eating, and I missed the episode.

Jimmy: I had the opposite experience with my parents, because I grew up in Las Vegas. They rarely went out, but one night, they went to see Steve Martin live, when he was in, and my dad came home with a prop arrow through his head. This was the late seventies, and my dad had bought one of Steve Martin's albums, and he said, "Oh, you've got to hear this." I would just listen to it over and over and over again. But that's how I found out about Steve Martin. Dad came home with a prop in his head.

Judd: That was a big record for us, too. We used to drive fourteen hours to Hilton Head once or twice a year to go on vacation, and once, we listened to that record on a loop for the whole drive. I feel like you came to comedy the same way I did: starting as a hardcore, maniac fan.

Jimmy: Oh, absolutely. I'm always amazed when I hear these stories about you interviewing these big comedians when you're a kid, because that would never have occurred to me. Even the idea that I could ever be a writer for, say, Letterman never really occurred. It never occurred to me that you could get a job like that. I didn't know anyone in showbiz. The closest thing I knew was a lounge singer named Perfecto, who used to come to my aunt Chippy's house for dinner. If one person in my life had said to me, "Well, why don't you try that?" it would have blown my mind. I know if I had called Steve O'Donnell, who's the head writer of *Letterman*—he's nice enough that he would have responded in some way. And that would have been all the encouragement I needed. I probably wouldn't be a host. I probably would be a writer.

Judd: When Letterman started, were you aware of the morning show?

Jimmy: I was aware of it. I'd seen Letterman for the first time on an HBO special called *Looking for Fun*. My mom's friends owned a seafood store that I worked at when I was fourteen. They had HBO, which we did not have, and they showed it to me when we were over at their house. And then I started watching Letterman's *Late Night* show, but I never discussed it with anyone until my grandfather asked me one day, "You ever watch this guy Letterman?" and I almost exploded. I was like, "Yes, I love him." That was when I knew that I was obsessed, and I was obsessed to the point where every one of my school textbooks was covered with these *Late Night with David Letterman* book covers. I was known for two things in school: drawing and watching David Letterman's show. It became a bit of a burden, because it got to the point where there were some other kids who watched this show, too, and they would expect to get an update on what happened from me at school the next day. So, I had to stay up till one-thirty every night, and school started at seven-thirty. So, I was always very sleepy.

Judd: In school, were you more of a nerd or a popular kid?

Jimmy: I was definitely a nerd in that I never had any dates or anything like that. But I was popular among other guys, just because I was funny. And girls, too, but no one ever wanted to, say, go to a dance with me. But I was pretty smart in school, and I was pretty funny in a way that even the teachers thought was funny.

Judd: Did you have an emotional reason why you thought you were connecting with comedy so much?

Jimmy: I probably did. I'm not smart enough to explore that. I will say, for me, my house was very loud, and there was a lot of yelling, so comedy was an escape from that. It was an intimate relationship. I would just sit with my twelve-inch black-and-white TV in my bedroom. I had it on my desk, and I would sit there and draw, and I would watch or listen to the TV late into the night, every night. To this day, I can be in the middle of a very hectic and noisy situation and remain very focused on whatever the task at hand is. And I attribute that to drawing in the midst of all this madness that went on in my house.

Judd: Can you imagine if we had YouTube and could find anything we want?

Jimmy: I was a disc jockey in college, and I would always have to carry crates of records around and, sometimes, up many flights of stairs. The first time I saw a DJ in the iPod era, I was so angry and jealous that they had every song on this little device. They didn't have to carry anything. They didn't have to go to Tower Records and Warehouse Records, trying to find this song that this idiot bride and groom decided would be their first dance. We could go into how good the kids have it these days, but it probably all meant more to us *because* it was so hard to find, and *because* we would watch it so many times in a row.

Judd: What was the moment where you thought there was a way to be in show business?

Jimmy: I was sixteen and working at a clothing store called Miller's Outpost. One of the other kids that worked there was in college at [the University of Las Vegas], and he worked at the radio station KUNV, and he thought I was funny, so he went and told his program director about me. It turned out, years later, this program director became part of a pretty successful pop dance band called the Crystal Method. So, this guy said, "Yeah, bring him in." I went to his office, and he said, "Do you want to do a talk show for half an hour on Sunday nights?" And I said, "I would love to do that." He said, "We want you to bring people in and make fun of them." There was no other instruction. So, I just would go through the Yellow Pages and try to find things that seemed funny, and the first interview I did was [with] a guy who billed himself as the "Hairstylist to the Stars." I thought, *Oh, this will be fun. I'll find out what stars he's been styling hair for.* I called him up. It turns out, the only star whose hair he styled was [game show host] John Davidson. So, an hour of the interview was about that white spot on John Davidson's hair. The whole thing was about that. Then I started calling people who did local commercials, because there are a lot of great local commercials in Las Vegas, and I'd have them on the show. When I came home after my first show, my parents had been in the house listening to it, and they were so excited. Maybe there's something to being from a loud family, where you don't really get the floor much. So, to have everyone's complete attention was exciting for me. I almost instantly knew that what I wanted to do was radio. I'd been planning to be an artist since I was five years old, and just like that, I switched.

Judd: It hit you that all the hours watching Letterman were preparation for this.

Jimmy: It did. And not just Letterman, but my uncle Vinny used to send me cassette tapes of Howard Stern, because he loved them. I would get, like, one ninety-minute cassette tape every six months, and I'd feast on it. I'd listen to it over and over and over again, and whenever a new one would arrive, it was like Christmas and my birthday all wrapped up in one.

Judd: I remember, as a kid, when Howard Stern came to New York on WNBC, what a big deal that was.

Jimmy: Somehow, he makes things that should only be interesting to him interesting to everyone listening.

Judd: I interviewed him for my high school radio station. It was so fast—he gave me like four minutes. You and I, I think, are the exact same age. We grew up with the transition of Sammy Davis, Jr.–style showbiz into Letterman and Howard Stern.

Jimmy: In my case, quite literally, as Sammy Davis, Jr., was the first concert I ever went to. My best friend, who is now my bandleader—his dad was Sammy Davis, Jr.'s room service butler. He was with Sammy when he was at Caesar's Palace—he'd be with him the whole run—and they became very friendly. I was fourteen, and he took us to go see Sammy, and afterward we went to Sammy's dressing room and hung out with Sammy, which was pretty crazy. The two things I remember is, I was wearing my cousin's suit that had patches on the sleeves, and it did not fit me. And that there was a big bowl of potato chips, and I was starving, but I didn't know if it was okay to eat Sammy's potato chips. So, I sat there quietly on my hands.

Judd: Shandling had a great story about going to visit Sammy Davis, Jr., when he was playing Vegas early in his career, and someone offered to introduce him to Sammy, and he went backstage and said [Sammy] was really mean to him. It threw Garry off, and he didn't understand why he was so cold.

Jimmy: I didn't know Garry as well as you did, but I could also see Garry misreading that situation entirely.

Judd: Did you ever have Garry on the show?

Jimmy: Garry was never on the show. And it was interesting, because he would frequently email me to apologize for not being on the show. Even when we weren't asking him to be on the show, I always felt like, *You know what, I'm not gonna hawk him.* I don't like to bother people. I don't want to put them in an uncomfortable situation, and the last thing I want is for somebody to come on the show when they don't want to. So, I always just let him know that I was a big fan and that I hope I gave him the idea that he was always welcome, and I think I did, because every once in a while, he'd send me a nice email about the show and what he'd been watching and apologize and blame himself in an exceptionally detailed way for not coming on.

Judd: As someone who grew up idolizing Letterman, what is your relationship with him like now?

Jimmy: I don't feel like I know Letterman at all. He's very nice to me, and I think he understands how fragile I am when it comes to my relationship with him. So, he's always exceptionally kind, but it's not like we've ever socialized or anything.

Judd: You've never had a meal with Dave?

Jimmy: No, I wouldn't want to. I don't think he'd want to. And I wouldn't want to make him do something that he wouldn't want to do—I don't think that's the way you pay people back for entertaining you for many years.

Judd: As you've been doing your own late-night show, have you gotten a new perspective on how good Letterman and Carson were, and Dick Cavett and Merv Griffin—all those people?

Jimmy: I always felt that way. I feel like all of those people have more natural ability than I have. I have to work very hard to be off-the-cuff. I know that sounds like a paradox, but that is kind of how I do it. When I'm working on a monologue, I do it. Obviously, it's a different style than the way Johnny did it, or the way Dave did it, which was a little more traditional. I don't want my jokes to really *sound* like jokes. I want to feel like it's something that's coming out of me in that moment. So, if something is too clever or feels prewritten, I will move past it. I will reject it or alter it in some way. Sometimes I make it less funny and less clever. But what's most important to me is that it doesn't feel like a bunch of writers handed me a bunch of index cards that afternoon.

Judd: [Do you] feel that the world has gotten way more intense and serious, as a comedian and interviewer? As a viewer, sometimes you feel for hosts, having to address the darkness of the world. I can't remember Carson ever having a night where he had to deal with some tragedy. It seems like it's a new skill: to be grounded and sincere and [to] emotionally connect with the audience. Was that a hard thing to learn?

Jimmy: I don't think it was hard, but it's painful. I feel completely spent after a show like that. I dread having to talk about a school shooting or the death of a friend or anything that exposes my vulnerability. That is when I'm least comfortable. But it also now seems to be necessary. I'm not sure why, but there's an expectation that you can't just tap-dance past some of this stuff. For me, if I feel like I have something to say that is different from what everyone else is saying, then I'll want to say it. I don't feel like I need to say anything about everything, especially if another person basically said what I would have said—but yes, it is very different now than it was. And the old way was easier, for sure.

Judd: Is there a part of you that prays for a calmer political environment so you can just get back to being silly for a few years?

Jimmy: I long for the days when the big issue that I would rant about night after night was how long the receipts are at CVS. That sort of thing is pure fun, without any of the baggage. I know that people appreciate it when we talk about serious things, but a lot of times, I feel like it's not what I signed up for.

Judd: I remember, I was asked to go on *The Tonight Show* once, and I was the second guest. I get a call before the show, and they say, "Can you be the lead guest tonight? Bette Midler canceled because of the tragedy." I was so dumb that I didn't ask what the tragedy was. I was just like, *That's cool, I get to be the first guest.* I assumed it was something that happened in Bette Midler's family. But it was the day of one of those horrible shootings somewhere, a really bad one, and I find out literally while I'm at *The Tonight Show*. *Oh, that's why she left—because it's almost inappropriate to be here talking about your movie.*

Jimmy: I don't think it's incumbent upon the guests to also weigh in, but I don't know—maybe you would have gotten a ton of shit if that happened today.

Judd: The only time I've ever hosted TV was on *The Late Late Show*, when they just let a bunch of people host the slot before James Corden started. I did a few nights, which was a really fun excuse to get Sandler and Shandling out there, and [stand-up] Maria Bamford, but I feel like I only got a taste of the daily stress of a talk show host. You're basically shot out of a cannon every day.

Jimmy: Everything seems hard until you do it every day for a year. I think about how getting the newspaper delivered to my house in the morning is itself a miracle. It involved all these people. Not only did they write all these stories—some are long-lead stories, some were written last night—and then they send it to a printer, who hands it to a guy in a car, who then brings it to everyone's house. That, to me, is more impressive than doing a television show every night, but I know, to those people who do it, it's not so impressive.

Judd: At this point, you've built your machine, and the machine works great. What is the part that keeps it fun and engaging for you?

Jimmy: It varies from day to day, but the reward is always the laughs. Not just on the show, but just the laughs throughout the day, and being so lucky to be around people who are funny at such a high level. I love it when I can sit in with the writers and just fuck around. That's the part of the show that I love. The deadlines are the things that kill me, and all the other stuff you're asked to do to promote the show that makes it hard. You never want to get in a situation where the show is your second job, but sometimes, it feels like it is. And because it's so familiar at this point, it's easy to give it less attention than it deserves. For me, ultimately, I fear going onstage and not being as good as I could be. Some nights, the audiences are bad, and they don't give you what you deserve. And some nights, they're great: They give you *more* than you deserve. You have to remember that and enjoy the fun nights and move on after the ones that aren't as fun, and as you do the show more times, it does get easier.

Judd: Where you differ from a lot of the other talk show guys is that there was a deep dysfunction or darkness in them that also made how they ran their ship dark. You'd hear from the *Tonight Show* writers in the Carson era that he would pick up their contracts every thirteen weeks, and he made them sweat every thirteen weeks that they were not going to get picked up. But it sounds like, for you, the joy of doing the show is building a machine that you like, that makes you happy, surrounded by people you really enjoying being around all day. That is, oddly, a unique experience.

Jimmy: An advantage that I have that I don't think many of the older talk show hosts had is: I was once the writer. I was the morning disc jockey sidekick and producer, and I was fired a lot. One thing that I really disliked when I was an employee, on a TV show or a radio show, was when the host was moody, and I had to dance around that person's mood. So, I try my best not to be moody and to be consistent, so that I don't have a bunch of people having to guess. I don't always succeed—I can be moody from time to time—but I think it's a selfish way to go into the office every day, and I try not to do it.

Judd: And your wife is working with you? You're collaborators?

Jimmy: She gets the worst of it, because there's no hiding your moods from your wife. We talk about work at home; it's not limited to the workplace. I'll vent frustrations to her, and she will do the same to me. People often ask me what it's like to work with your wife, and I think they're expecting to hear something other than "It's great," but it is pretty great, because I know that there's at least one person who truly represents me. And even sometimes, when we disagree, I have to consider the distinct possibility that she might be right.

Judd: What is the dynamic of your [wife's and your] creative process and comedy writing together?

Jimmy: She definitely knows my sensibilities as well or better than anyone, but she also reminds me of what's important. Sometimes, I don't want to talk about something that's uncomfortable. Sometimes,

I would rather dodge it and give myself the night off from that kind of stress. But when she says to me, "You need to talk about this," or, "This can't just be a footnote on the show tonight; this has to be significant," I always know that she's right. I don't necessarily like hearing it, but I know she's right.

Judd: And when you're working together and raising kids together, do you think that ultimately makes the balance and the sanity of life easier to accomplish, because you're in the ship together on everything?

Jimmy: Having the same schedule is a great luxury. I have two older kids, who are twenty-nine and twenty-seven. I also have a six-year-old and a three-year-old. The first time around seems like a million years ago, but this time, I've learned a way of communicating that was totally alien to me, in which you listen to your children. And instead of immediately yelling at them, you explain why they shouldn't be doing something. These are all revelations to me, because it's not how it usually goes in my family.

Judd: And what are your kids into; what are their interests?

Jimmy: My oldest daughter, Katie, is an artist. She makes ceramics, and she's very successful—she has art shows all over the country and around the world. My son Kevin works at the show, and he also makes funny videos with his friends. I think he wants to do what I do, but it must be hard for a kid to say that out loud. But we finally reached the point where he's admitted it—not just to us, but to himself. So, that's fun to watch, and I try to stay out of the way and let him do his own thing. Then, my younger daughter loves to draw, and she's funny, and my younger son loves Spider-Man.

Judd: My kids always talk about what it means being in the shadow of someone who's accomplished something in the world they want to be in. It does, ultimately, bother them. I remember when I met [Ben]

Stiller, he had a chip on his shoulder about his dad, Jerry, and felt like he had to succeed and he had to do better than Jerry, so people wouldn't think he was just Jerry Stiller's son. It was the gas that made him work so hard in his career. But I'm always trying to tell my kids that people are glad that Michael Douglas is famous. They don't go, "He shouldn't be famous because we had Kirk." Nobody cares.

Jimmy: I'm sure that they will eventually know that you're right. But I can imagine that being in that situation is not always so easy. Because you feel like the last thing, especially in comedy, you want to be is predictable, and there's nothing more predictable than a celebrity's kid wanting to be in show business.

Judd: I would say we're like cobblers, where it's natural for the cobbler's kids to make shoes. This is the family business.

Jimmy: I do understand that hesitancy, though, and I think it's nice. I also find it helpful that there are people who are in a similar situation with their own children and would pull my kid aside and talk to them about it. Because I think it's a lot easier for the kids to talk about that stuff with someone other than their parents, but they also need to talk to somebody who knows what's going on.

Judd: That's the worst part, though. They'll talk to Lena Dunham all day about it, and they won't talk to me at all.

Jimmy: That's the best part.

Judd: When you're on your break with the show, what do you do with your time?

Jimmy: I always have to be doing something. Where my attention turned to this past summer was toward organizing my life. I've spent the last three months trying to organize my office, which was a terrible mess, and I have this fear that I will lose something important, whether it's videos or some audio. I used to tape my family with a cassette [recorder], and I found this audiotape of my aunt Chippy and uncle Frank arguing. It is just hysterical: They're arguing over a bottle of ketchup. He can't figure out how to pour the ketchup out of the bottle, and she starts yelling at him, then she realizes he has the cap on and just starts screaming. And she has a great line. She goes, "Frank, you've gotta open it before it goddamn pours out." And then she goes into this thing of, like, "He's so stupid, he'll never invent the lightbulb, he'll never invent the airplane, and he's lucky they even let him ride on one." That, to me, is just gold, and the idea that I had that in a box somewhere and I hadn't digitized it fills me with anxiety. So, I've been digitizing everything. I have all these magazines I was on the cover of, and I realized, *No one wants any of this stuff.* Maybe, if I'm lucky, I'll have a grandchild that gets a kick out of looking through it one evening—maybe I'll have a grandkid who's a comedy nerd. But my kids don't care about this stuff. I don't know why it's so important to me, that I maintain this museum dedicated to honoring myself, but I do.

Judd: I know my kids are not going to care about my three Paul Lynde autographs.

Jimmy: You know what's the saddest thing? When you think about those auctions that happen when some celebrity dies, and you get, like, Jerry Lewis's pinky ring, and it goes for eight hundred and twelve dollars or something. It's just like, *Oh, no one in his family wanted any of this stuff.* Isn't that sad?

Judd: Steve Martin had a very funny article about having all this stuff and how he didn't want to put people through that after he died. So, he decided to get ahead of that by auctioning a lot of that stuff off, and I bought the puppet that he would do ventriloquism with from his fly.

Jimmy: You mean the Great Flydini? For how much?

Judd: I could have paid like six thousand dollars.

Jimmy: What?!

Judd: But I think it was for charity, for the Motion Picture and Television Fund.

Jimmy: You're lucky I didn't know about it. That would have cost you eight thousand.

Judd: I always say to my kids, "The second I die, just burn it all." But then, when we were working on *Funny People*, I remembered how I used to videotape Sandler making phony phone calls, and I had, like, an hour and a half of him calling Jerry's [Famous] Deli complaining about the roast beef in the voice of an old woman. And I was like, *Yes! Hoarding pays off.*

Jimmy: Isn't that the best? I feel the same way, and I know that we're both wrong, but I still say, if there's a one-in-a-million chance that I'm going to need something, I want to make sure I have it. And you know what, both of us really need a young Judd Apatow or young Jimmy Kimmel to collect and treasure all our garbage.

JOHN CANDY

(Interviewed in 1984, backstage at the Lorne Michaels produced sketch show *The New Show*)

Judd: Have you done any formal acting training?

John: Only from a magazine ad that I once took out. That was only a twelve-week course, and it was only nine dollars, but I think it was a real course. But you know, it helped me out in my early days.

Judd: This is your third show with *The New Show.* What keeps you coming back to it?

John: Well, it wasn't the money. Don't get me wrong on this, it isn't the money. I had agreed that when we first got the show, that I would do three episodes over the thirteen that they were guaranteed for.

Judd: What attracted you to the show in the first place?

John: The people involved. It seemed like a good show with Lorne Michaels, and we'll have Dave Thomas again. I thought I was going to be on the show with Catherine O'Hara, but she did three other ones that I'm not in. But it's been varied. It's been a lot of fun, and it has a good cast.

Judd: You've also been busy doing films, and it looks like *Splash* has been a hit. What do you think is the appeal?

John: I think it's a nice family film in that there's plenty for everybody to enjoy. You care about the people, and it's not real schmaltzy. I'll attribute all that success to Ron Howard, because of his keen eye as a director and in the editing. It's just a good production all around. This picture is a pleasant surprise to everybody.

Judd: People seem to be especially drawn to your character in the film. Why do you think they like him so much?

John: In the film, I play Freddie, the brother of the guy who falls in love with the mermaid, and I'm kind of like the ne'er-do-well, the playboy, the guy with the devil-may-care attitude about life. And Freddie's a silly guy, he's got a good attitude. It's a pretty harmless character, really. He's just a good-time guy. People have met guys like him before.

Judd: When you're playing racquetball in the movie, how many takes did you need to do to get the shot where you hit the ball and it bounces back and hits you in the head?

John: Three takes. I was lucky. It was three takes.

Judd: They must have had the whole day set up so that they could just keep trying till you got it.

John: You got that right. They thought it was gonna be a long time. Not Johnny, though. It was three takes.

Judd: Did you practice that?

John: No, I was just real lucky. By rights, I should still be there hitting it.

Judd: So, you signed a three-picture deal with Touchstone Films after this, is that right?

John: It isn't signed yet, but yes, that's pretty much what I'm going to do. I'm going to develop three movies for them, as well as write and perform in the movies.

Judd: Did they approach you for this because of the success with *Splash*?

John: Most likely, and I'm glad they did. They seem like a very decent group of people who are bringing change to Disney, and with the Touchstone division specifically, they're going to go for more PG- and R-rated movies. More mainstream American films, like *Never Cry Wolf*, which was basically a Touchstone film, although it had a Disney label on it. If the film is not like a Disney-type movie, they'll all be under Touchstone, and it's nice. You're there from the beginning, which is also nice. This is brand-new, so you're right there when it's just starting to grow, which is exciting, as opposed to working with a major studio. Which, by the way, didn't bother to option any pictures. Touchstone were the only ones who did, so I guess that's why I accepted them.

Judd: What type of freedom did everybody on the set have? Did Disney have any control over anything?

John: They didn't bother us at all. The only suggestions they made were after the picture was shot, and they were positive notes. I spoke to the producer Brian Grazer before I even started negotiating my deal with them and asked him what they were like to work with. And he said they were just great, they didn't bother you at all, they let you make your picture. Which is rare these days, for an executive to keep his hands out of it.

Judd: What were some of the other movies that you did, other than *Stripes* and *Vacation* and *Going Berserk*?

John: I did a lot of pictures in Canada. [*The*] *Silent Partner, Fine Lady*—I was in a movie called [*The*] *Clown Murders.* I did another one called *Tunnel Vision.* And *It Came from Hollywood,* that short-lived film with Gilda [Radner], Dan [Aykroyd], and Cheech and Chong. It really didn't last—though, actually, it's doing very well in cassette sales, I hear. But no one really came out to the theaters to see it.

Judd: Well, it was a good film. It had all the conglomeration montages.

John: Yeah, I thought it was funny. It was also funny that it didn't last long. We shot it all in two days, all our segments.

Judd: What do you think about the fact that, when people walk into the theater and the movie starts playing and they see John Candy, everyone starts laughing? People hear your name, and they just start laughing. What do you think people like about you?

John: It probably goes back to SCTV, because people associate me with that show, and I thought that was a pretty funny show. If we instill that kind of spirit into somebody, and they're anticipating something good, that's very nice. And we definitely were trying to do that.

Judd: Will you be doing any more SCTV, like guest spots?

John: Not with the TV show as it is now, no. This is the last year for them. I think they're in the last six shows now. More than likely, I'll be working with the group again, in pictures or television specials, I don't know. But I know we're all good friends and we'll all work together again.

Judd: When you see the movies that you're in, and other Second City people are in, it always winds up with you guys popping up all over. Why is that?

John: Well, I guess you could call it nepotism. There's a core of us—Harold Ramis, Bill Murray, Dan Aykroyd, John Belushi—who hire each other because we know what we're going to get, and you know you're going to get something real good. There's also a shorthand in working with each other, whereas, with some actors, you bring them in, and you don't know what you're gonna get.

Judd: What do you think of the way that Second City got canceled by NBC right after receiving a lot of critical acclaim?

John: It's unfortunate. I guess NBC didn't feel like we were bringing in the numbers.

Judd: What were your most memorable characters and skits?

John: There are so many of them, and I just felt good about being a part of it, really. Each of the characters I did—meaning, the continuing characters and even some of the ones that you just do once or twice—we were allowed to have so much control over these characters that we created lives for these people. We did it so many times that each is special to me. Yosh and Stan Shmenge, they're brothers, and they have another life outside of that. Which is great. Which came into play with the show. Same with Doctor Tongue; Woody Tobias, Jr.; and Count Floyd. Their interactions with each other off-camera was just as interesting as what they're doing on-camera—even more so, actually. These two guys just bicker at each other all the time, but they still work with each other, they need each other. [Johnny] LaRue, Gil Fisher, all these characters—it was just nice to be able to do all of those, and we could do whatever we wanted.

Judd: What do you think of the way the Bob and Doug McKenzie characters from *Second City TV* took off into movies and records?

John: Man, that was great for them. Those two characters really caught on, and the album was such a big hit.

Judd: How did the movie do?

John: The movie didn't do too good. I don't know if a lot of people understood it. It's coming out on cassette, I think soon.

Judd: Are you interested in writing and starring in a movie?

John: I think the only way I'm going to get a lot of pictures is to do what I did in *SCTV*, which is write and perform. We know each other better than anyone else, and there haven't been that many offers coming from anywhere else. At least if we fail, we know that we did it on our own.

Judd: You should have made a movie with you and Joe Flaherty, blowing people up.

John: We talked about it. I don't know how it would last for ninety minutes, though. It kind of wears a little thin.

Judd: You could blow people up and have the police chase you.

John: I think with [Big] Jim McBob and Billy [Sol Hurok], it would be a little too much for two hours.

Judd: Martin Short said that he thought that Second City would have done really well in America in a ten o'clock time slot on a Friday night. Do you think that's true?

John: Absolutely, that's what we always wanted. But we were told that that's a sacred turf we'd never get, that they'd never put a comedy show in there.

Judd: But they did.

John: They did. You know, they also said that they'd give us Sunday at seven o'clock, opposite *60 Minutes*. And if that were the case, we would have had to change the format of the show. We would have had to have a child psychologist working with us at all times, because it's prime access. Most of our characters would have had to change drastically: LaRue's drinking and smoking would be out; Bobby Bittman would be out. And they were actually asking us, "Well, maybe Bobby Bittman could have a cousin . . . ," and Gene's reply was "Well, what if Bobby Bittman *doesn't* have a cousin?" It was all very foolish. I mean, that was their excuse for saying, "Well, we gave them a shot. They didn't want it," because there was a lot of heat on them. And when they dropped us, there were a lot of people going after them. There was no real reason to drop us from their format at all.

Judd: They're out to make money.

John: We just weren't in there with the ratings, but it's business. We didn't cut the numbers that they wanted, and that's what it's all about these days.

Judd: What about *Big City Comedy*? What type of experience was that where you had your own show?

John: It was a learning experience: I learned what not to do in the business, and who not to work with a lot of the time. It was frightening. I was naïve in that I thought I was going to have some control and some say on who the cast members were going to be, who was going to be writing the show, who was going to direct, and this and that. But the cast was good; we were fortunate that way. It was a good group of people. It just was—again, they put us in the wrong time slot, seven o'clock.

Judd: When you're doing the introduction to the show, you seem a lot more comfortable doing Mr. Mambo than talking up there as yourself. Why was that?

John: Well, I'm not a stand-up comic. And there's a real frenzied energy when you're on a show like that, that I had never experienced before. So, it's frustrating. I've stood in front of audiences many times before, but when you've got that kind of pressure on—you feel that pressure from these comics who are really trying, who want to make it. And this is their shot.

Judd: How is that different from the Second City stage show, when you have all these people helping you out?

John: It's just a feeling, just a different energy, that's all. We didn't have that killer instinct, where you're out there by yourself as a stand-up comic. There's a lot of pressure on them—they didn't want to blow their moment. I mean, this is a big time for them, and a lot of publicity. So, it's a lot on their shoulders. And they've got to make it count.

JOHN CLEESE

September 2020

Judd: Why did you decide that you wanted to write a book about creativity?

John: I'd been thinking about it for about thirty years. I got interested in creativity because I went to Cambridge and got into show business through the [Cambridge University] Footlights, but before that, I had always done science and law. I had no idea that I had any creative ability, and then, suddenly, I discovered I could write things that made people laugh. And I began to notice things happening. For instance, I'd work very hard at night trying to write a sketch, and then, in the morning, I'd sit down with a cup of coffee before I really got going, and the answer would be there within ninety seconds, and I couldn't even quite see what the difficulty was the previous evening, when I'd been stuck. And I came to the conclusion that my mind was working on the problem when I was asleep. Then I began to realize it was working on the problem in my unconscious while I was awake, so I began to take notes of what the unconscious was capable of. The problem with the unconscious is that it's extraordinary what it can do, but you can't order it about. You can't hit it with a stick. You have to discover how to coax it. What's your process when you sit down? Do you do lots of sharpening of pencils, making of coffee, and all that sort of stuff?

Judd: I like what you wrote about how boredom is essential. You have to allow yourself to be bored and, for me, I like to listen to music and try to let things bubble up. I'm a big believer of what they call the vomit draft, where you're writing fast—not wondering why you're writing it, just babbling, just, *Go.* Then I'll go, *Is there anything of value in this thing I just babbled out?* And a surprising number of times, there is.

John: I read about experiments that have been done by a psychologist called [Donald] MacKinnon at Berkeley in the seventies. And I knew a psychology professor who said that the problem about writing about creativity is that it's so much to do with the unconscious. So, what you can say about it is pretty limited. But this guy MacKinnon was very interested in professionals, and particularly in architects, because they had to be very efficient as well as very creative, because bridges need to stay up. What he discovered when he compared the creative architects with the noncreative architects was that the important difference was that the creative architects could play, and I began to see that so much of creativity was just playing, which is what you've been describing, when you just sit down and start any old nonsense and see if it leads somewhere.

Judd: I always think about the critical voice, how we all have that voice in our head telling us that we're terrible. And so much of being in play is to tell that voice to shut the hell up and have fun.

John: As my psychologist friend pointed out, if you're sad, you have sad thoughts. If you're feeling angry, you have angry thoughts. So, how do you get in a creative mood? That involves, I think, a little bit of meditation. It's the first time that you sit down and start to think, *What am I going to think about?* You think, *I should have called Tom, I should have bought a birthday present for the cat. I haven't mended* *the roof.* You have to wait for that to settle. Just like the Buddhists say: It's like a glass of cloudy water; leave it there, and it will settle. After about twenty minutes, then those thoughts—*I can't do this, I'm no good,* all that stuff you're talking about—that doesn't get in the way anymore. But it always does at the beginning.

Judd: When you're young, it's different than when you've had success, because when you're young, I think you're a little delusional. For a lot of people, there's a feeling when you're in your twenties that you can take over the world.

John: I think Americans are more optimistic and positive than the British. I always had the feeling I wasn't going to be any good. What I discovered, particularly working with Graham Chapman, is that we could average fifteen to twenty minutes of good material a week. We might have a terrible day Monday and not a great Tuesday morning. Then, suddenly, after lunch on Tuesday, it would all start flowing until about Thursday afternoon. And then we dry up again. Once you know there's an average amount that you can write just by sitting there, then when you normally get negative and think, *I'm no good at this,* you just see it as part of the whole process.

Judd: Mike Nichols once said that in order to have a good idea, you have to have a lot of ideas. I remember, when I was first starting out, there was this book by Anne Lamott, and she said she had a down/up theory, which is to get it down and then, later on, fix it up.

John: That's exactly right. And sometimes, when you go into the critical phase, one of the best things you can do is get away from it for a bit, put it in a drawer for a week and then come back to it. When Connie Booth and I were writing *Fawlty Towers,* if we got stuck, we'd just put the episode to one side and work on another one. Then, when you come back to it, two things happen. One, it becomes much clearer what's good and what isn't good, because you've been away from it, and that gives you a certain objectivity. The other thing is, your unconscious has been working on it while you've been away, so you actually come up with ideas quite easily.

Judd: Isn't it weird that your brain does that?

John: I'm fascinated by the idea of the two hemispheres. There is a book called the *Master and His Emissary*, by Iain McGilchrist. It's the most interesting book I've ever read. He says that the interaction between those two hemispheres is extremely complicated, and they're very interlinked, but you could say that they have distinct personalities. The left brain is the critical one that wants to know how to possess things and process them. It wants big things. Then the right brain is where the values come from. And I think we are going from one to the other.

Judd: I also look at it from the simplest point of view, which is, I wake up from a dream and it'll be so imaginative and so bizarre and emotional. I always find it so strange that, at night, my mind feels the need to create this little movie for me. What is that? And why in evolution would that happen?

John: We need ideas, and the hard thing is getting out of the left brain. These days, we have phones calling all the time, and interruptions, which is exactly what keeps us stuck in the left brain. It stops us from being creative. That's why I believe you have to sit down somewhere where you're not going to be interrupted. Go sit in the park. One of my friends was reduced to locking himself in the loo because he was in a family of six. If you're a CEO, you just say to the secretary, "Shut the door. Don't interrupt me unless the building is burning." You create a quiet place where you're not going to be interrupted, where the phone isn't ringing, and that's what enables you to sit there while the mind settles.

Judd: I read somewhere that when you check your messages, that you cannot return to a fully creative state for about twenty minutes.

John: I read twelve minutes. Interruption is the deadliest thing when you're trying to be creative.

Judd: I wanted to ask you about spirituality, because there are some people who believe in the creative intelligence of the universe. Tommy from Cheech and Chong was on the radio, and he said it's almost like some people have got a hose, and they can hook it into the big pipe and get all the ideas. Like Jimi Hendrix—he knew how to do it. Or Bob Dylan. Do you ever think of it in those terms?

John: I don't, because I don't have experiences like that. But I think those people and Mozart and other geniuses do. I once saw Ian Holm do *King Lear* twice in the same week because it was so good. I went back, and I said to him afterward, "How do you find the energy?" It's just such a long play and so dramatic in an acting sense. And he said, "I don't know where the energy is coming from." He said, "It's as though it's passing through me without touching the sides." But I've never had an experience like that. I noticed on *Python* sometimes, when we got together after we'd been writing on our own for a week, there'd be certain themes in everyone's piece of writing, as though in some strange way we'd been connected. I don't understand that. But then you discover that [Gottfried Wilhelm] Leibniz and Isaac Newton discovered calculus at almost exactly the same time. I think sometimes there are weird things going on. Do you have those experiences?

Judd: I do, and it's always connected to a stupid dirty joke somehow. I'll think of a dirty joke, and I literally feel like God gave it to me, because it'll come from nowhere. I always think about you and Monty Python as having had a similar experience to the Beatles, in the sense of a group of people holed up together, all with very different talents that served each other, and even though everyone was paying attention and loved you so much, you found a way to continue to grow and change and push the limits. Did you guys feel that?

John: I didn't realize the best team to build would be made of completely different abilities. Terry Jones's ideas for sketches were quite different from anything that Graham and I came up with; and Michael Palin, the same. At one stage, I tried to improve on that by actually saying, *Instead of my writing with Graham, why don't I write once occasionally with Michael Palin, with Eric, because then we'll come up with something that's slightly different.* But the force of habit overcame this. There were a small number of sketches that I wrote with Palin and Idle, and they were all, I thought, rather good. But we could have gone on longer and created more stuff together if we'd broken up the writing parts.

Judd: I was in college in 1985, and Graham Chapman was doing a college tour of America. He was showing clips of *Monty Python* and clips of the Dangerous Sports Club. It was really like an earlier version of *Jackass,* where these people would ride a bed down a ski slope or something. I was eighteen or nineteen years old, and I was one of the people in charge of the speakers at the University of Southern California. Graham gave his speech, and it was hilarious and wonderful, and then, afterward, a few of us went to go hang out with him and spent three or four hours chatting with him. It was a life-changing kind of night. He did something that really affected me, which is he was as interested in our stupid college lives as we were in his stories about getting hookers with [the Rolling Stones'] Keith Moon. He really was interested and was asking questions. We were all just idiots, and he was enjoying our company, but also telling us some of the funniest anecdotes we'd ever heard. He was just a very special, kind man.

John: He was extraordinary, and he was quite weird sometimes. I was talking to a theatrical producer who'd done a tour of his, and he said when Graham arrived in one city, he suddenly said he wanted six large salmon—fresh salmon, untouched. And the guy thought he must be on some strange diet. All he did was he came out at the end of the show with these fish and threw them into the audience. And the promoters said it was the biggest dry-cleaning bill he's ever seen. It's just a random thing that Graham would do. You have to be prepared to be random, because you don't know what your unconscious is going to throw up. The stuff that just makes people laugh and laugh and laugh is very often the pure, silliest stuff. Take the fish-slapping dance for Michael [Palin]—people can watch that again and again and again. It's absolutely stupid, and it means nothing. But sometimes, these ideas just have a pureness. You don't know where they came from.

Judd: When you were writing *Monty Python,* what kind of energy was it coming from? Was it coming from intelligence and confidence? Was it from anger?

John: Graham and I soon discovered that when we wrote from anger, it wasn't funny. If we got angry about something, usually something about the Conservative Party, and we would try and write about it, it just wasn't funny. We had to let go of the anger, and then, maybe later, a few days later, we could be funny about it. It was as simple as: We would sit there, I'd open up a thesaurus, and just read words to him. I'd say, "Cucumber." And then I'd say, "Plummet." And I said "plummet" once, and Graham said, "Well, a sheep would plummet." I said, "What are you talking about?" He said, "If she tried to fly, she would plummet." And that gave us a sketch, how there were sheep that were trying to learn to fly.

Judd: That's how you get a dead-parrot sketch, I guess.

John: That was more logical, because that was based on an experience Michael Palin had with a secondhand-car salesman. And we sat there for some time on it. We said, "Well, what could it be?" One of us said it could be an animal. That way, when you take it back to the pet shop, it's not working properly. Then we played around with what the animal would be. We go, "It can't be a mouse, because it's too small and sweet, and people like cats and dogs too much." So, then somebody said, "Why not a parrot?" I said, "That's great, because nobody likes parrots, so nobody's going to feel sympathetic." Then we wrote it about the parrot. I got the thesaurus back out and found all the synonyms for *dead*.

Judd: It sounds like you guys were playing.

John: Doesn't it? Einstein once said about science, if you're doing research and you knew what you were going to find out, it wouldn't be research. And that's a nice thought. The main thing in creativity is you don't know where it's going. My experience in the film business—and I really want to know what you think about it—is that when they commission a film, they want to see something immediate to know what they're getting. Whereas they would get something much better if they just said, "Go away and come back in four months."

Judd: You definitely need people who understand your process. I've been lucky enough to work with the same film studio for fifteen years, and they just know the flow of how it happens. Creative ideas, even really good ones, are often a difficult sell. Do you have advice for presenting creative ideas to others?

John: I think you've got to tell the story. You have to rehearse, and I think it's better to have a performer pitch the story to the executives. I'm so pleased you've had a good experience with studios, Judd. But my experience has been largely that the executives simply don't know what they're doing. It seems like, for you, the key is they trust you?

Judd: Yes. It's tough in the beginning, when they don't. When you're young and they don't trust you, then they want to be involved in your process. What was it like for you to have had the chance to do the reunion concerts with Python?

John: It was a very strange experience, because we got into financial trouble. We've always had hopeless managers, completely fucking hopeless managers. And we discovered we owed eight hundred thousand pounds in legal fees, because something had not been settled. We called in an old friend of ours from Cambridge who used to manage Queen, or still does manage Queen, and he said, "Why don't you just do a show at The O2 [arena]?" So, we did it for money. Eric had a few days off, and he put a very good script together of all the sketches that we knew were going to work. When we read it, it was a wonderful experience, because we started to laugh, really laugh. And this is material that's been around for forty years. But because we found it funny, we found that we were looking forward to doing the shows. Of course, the shows were very strange, because normally the people in the audience don't know the dialogue better than the actors. Very strange event, but very lovely.

Judd: And how was it, as friends, to work together? People don't always remember that you guys toured America doing these shows at places like the Hollywood Bowl. You traveled like rock stars in that period, which must have been a strange thing for all of you.

John: It's very strange because comedians on the whole don't do that in the way that bands do. Why doesn't it happen with comedians? I don't really know. All I can say is it was the usual thing: Sometimes we got cross with each other, but we always thought the material was funny. And the sound of laughter is one of the loveliest sounds in the world. It's hard to be very cross if you've just been in front of an audience who'd been laughing.

Judd: What are your thoughts when you look back at the amount of stuff you all continued to do together? I think all of us wind up in groups of one kind or another. I noticed that in my world, many of the people that I thought would work together their whole lives have split up, or they get into a fight. And some people come back together; some people don't.

John: I think we got together at exactly the right time. We went into the pitch meeting at the BBC, and the guy in charge of comedy, Michael Mills, said, "Well, what do you propose doing?" And we hadn't discussed it. So, we kind of ad-libbed a rather limp thing, and he asked us a couple of questions. "You don't have music and guest artists?" We said, "We never really thought about that." And then he looked at us and shrugged and said, "Go away and make sense in program." The most extraordinary thing. Nobody's ever commissioned a show before without knowing what they were getting. But the very fact that we'd not given a concept meant that when we got down to it, we weren't trying to fit anything into an idea that we'd had. And I think that was why it was so creative: because there was no sense that we had a mandate of *This is what the show's got to be like.*

Judd: Isn't it strange when something that was funny a long time ago is equally funny now? Doesn't its timelessness surprise you? I do equate it to the Beatles.

John: I was always envious of the rock musicians, because they made fifty times as much money as we did. I used to say to myself, *They're lucky: If they write a good song, people can hear it again two minutes later.* Whereas, if I tell you a joke and then tell it to you two minutes later, you're not going to laugh. Then something started to change: We suddenly realized that people were learning the sketches in the same way that people can quote Bob Dylan lyrics. Once, when I was onstage with Michael Palin, he broke me up and made me laugh, and I couldn't think what the next line was. I just said to the audience, "What's the next line?" and about sixty people shouted it out.

Judd: How does that feel? How do you view that connection between them and your work?

John: I always thought that Python was funny and that it was good for people to laugh. But I began to realize in the last ten years that we were doing a bit more than that, because people would come up to me after the show and shake me by the hand and say, "Thanks for making me laugh all these years," and there's a tear in their eye. It's meant something more than just laughter, and I think it's because Python is just saying, "Life is insane. This planet that we're on, it's ridiculous, nothing works, and nobody knows what they're doing." After about six shows, a friend of mine said, "What I love about *Python* is, after I've watched an episode, I simply cannot watch the news. I cannot take it seriously." And I think that's a really important thing that we do for people: say that we can't take this seriously. I think the turning point for me was when I went to Sarajevo for a film festival, and someone told me about how they had been under siege by the Serbians for four years. The Serbians were sitting up in the hills lobbing shells down, and people with telescopic sights were picking off people who were walking across the road. But in the evening, he found an underground garage, and they set up as a small cinema, and they used to go in there and laugh and watch lots of *Monty Python.* Other stuff, too, but they used to laugh especially at *Monty Python,* and what they said to me is, "We came out feeling better." Nothing had changed. Nothing about the shells had changed, but they came out feeling more optimistic about life, more able to go on. When I saw that the company has that effect, I started to realize it's more important than I used to think.

Judd: I would assume that's why people keep singing "Always Look on the Bright Side of Life." They need to hear that life is total madness. I had a similar experience. I was at a Mexican restaurant, and my waitress says to me, "I never say anything to people I recognize, but I want you to know that I was an interrogator in Iraq. We used to watch *Superbad* and *Knocked Up* at the end of hard days, to just relieve our pressure. And it really helped get us through. Thank you." And I was so moved, and clearly that was important to her. But then I thought, *Well, what did I do, give her more energy to interrogate and waterboard people?*

John: I think that the purpose of laughter, from an evolutionary point of view is to relax us after stress. Because once we're in the thrall of the left brain, we're worrying and planning and being resentful. And then, if we laugh, it simply moves us to the right brain, where there's relaxation and a sense of meaning and all these kinds of things that you simply don't get from the left brain.

Judd: It's meant to help us relax after a hunt. It also relates to what people need to relax, because there are so many different types of comedy. Some people like gentle and harmless comedy, and other people want really dark comedy. They can't get off unless you say the worst thing ever, which has led us to all these debates about political correctness. I know you had that experience where they took down one of the episodes of *Fawlty Towers*. What was the detail in the episode that they had an issue with?

John: We had the old Major [Gowen], who had been out there in the Indian Army or something like that, and he was explaining to his girlfriend the difference between these various insulting terms. Like, "We call the Spanish *dagos*, and we call the Italians *wops*, and we call the Egyptians *wogs*," and all these. He was explaining this in a very serious way, and of course the whole purpose of it was to make fun of the fact that he had these categories so clearly laid out in his mind. But people don't understand. You can make fun of things in two ways. You can either attack them or you can put the words that you don't like in the mouths of people that you then make to look very stupid.

Judd: We need the ability to have characters who are allowed to make terrible mistakes and say terrible things. You can't take away that the world is filled with mean people or idiots, and we should be able to mock them in whatever way we need to.

John: There is nothing funny about a perfect person. If you wrote a character who is really fine, intelligent, and thoughtful, and wise—no laughs there. An American once said to me, "You show me a sitcom about Saint Francis of Assisi, and I'll show you a bummer." Comedy is about things going wrong and people going wrong.

Judd: Tell me about your live performing now. I know you go out with Eric Idle and do some shows together sometimes. And you also go out by yourself. How's that for you? And what do you try to accomplish in those shows?

John: I just try to make people laugh. I used to like smaller theaters, and I've gotten used to places of two thousand, or sometimes two thousand five hundred. It's a very simple way of making money. Because after the show, the tour manager goes backstage and talks to the guy in the box office. It's all clear, you know what I mean? There's no studio coming out with huge expenses. It's very straightforward. There's something very satisfactory in the pure transaction of standing in front of people and making them laugh. I played a show at the Acropolis in Athens last year and stood there on the stage, thinking, *About two thousand years ago, people were standing exactly here and making the audience laugh.* There was lovely sense of continuity or history about it.

Judd: It's amazing to be performing as a stand-up comedian at this point in your career.

John: The *Python* show was a result of legal bills. My stand-up shows are really the result of my last divorce.

Judd: If there was a common complaint about you that all of your wives had, what would it be?

John: I used to be much more tense and uptight. Now I've gotten much more relaxed. I've also got a wife who I really like and love. I have a lovely group of friends. I don't feel I have anything much to prove now, and I'm much less anxious. Somebody once said, "Very few things matter much, and most things don't matter at all." And somehow that opinion covers my life. I don't expect things to go right.

Judd: You've been interested in psychology and your own behavior your whole life. What is the main wisdom that you have now that you may not have had forty years ago?

John: The realization that you can't get things right most of the time. When you make mistakes—sometimes a big mistake, sometimes small mistakes—you can usually correct them before very real damage is done. So, don't spend your whole time trying to not make mistakes. The English are like that. There was a speech in *A Fish Called Wanda,* when I said, "Do you think you know what it's like being English, going through life just trying to get everything right and not upset people?" Whereas, if you can just let go and say, *Well, there's always going to be some people who hate me anyway,* that frees you up. And when you're trying to present an image to somebody that you're really a super person all the time and very kind and intelligent and that you earn more than you do—all that ego stuff puts us under pressure and makes it much harder for us to actually be ourselves.

Judd: How does that affect these friendships that you've had for fifty, sixty years, when you guys are all together and laughing and talking about your journey of creativity and humor?

John: It totally depends on whether I'm talking to my English friends or I'm talking to my American friends, because I find my American friends are much more interested in the strange stuff. With my English friends, the conversations are very warm, but we're old-fashioned, and we probably talk about less controversial subjects.

Judd: And what have you learned over the course of your life about how to be a good parent?

John: I think it's the hardest thing in the world, because you never get any immediate feedback about whether you're getting it right. You've got to try something and then, in fifteen years' time, you think, *that worked* or *that didn't work.* There have been difficult times with both of my daughters, and I'm very, very happy now that the relationship with both of them is really warm and accepting. That, and a nice wife, and four good cats—well, what else would you want except a bit of money?

JOHN MULANEY

January 2018

Judd: You were on *Fallon* recently, and you talked about going to a Steely Dan concert with your wife and Pete Davidson.

John: I'm a huge fan. I've always felt that people always say they don't like Steely Dan, but they don't even know what their music is like. I'm like, "I think you're talking about the Doobie Brothers. You're lumping it together with bands that it's not." I talked to my wife before I went on *Fallon*, and said, "I'm going to talk about when we all went to that Steely Dan concert with Pete Davidson, but I've never publicly talked about how much you hate them. What do you want me to say?" She said, "Say I hate them. I hate the music, I hate the lyrics, and I hate everything about them."

Judd: My wife really hates Steely Dan, too. That's one of the reasons why, in *Knocked Up*, Seth Rogen's character goes off about how much he hates Steely Dan. There's a scene where we're sitting around at the table, and Seth says, "If I have to listen to any more Steely Dan, I want you to cut my throat with an Al Jarreau LP." I always felt bad that I insulted Steely Dan, who's actually in my top-three bands. My wife doesn't like me talking about this, but she hates guitar solos. All guitar solos. If a guy is shredding, she's like "I can't do it."

John: I remember, in junior high or high school—and this is such a blanket statement, it's not fair—girls didn't like Kurt Vonnegut. And I was like, "You don't like *Slaughterhouse Five*?" It was Phish, Kurt Vonnegut, Steely Dan . . . it was just these proud nerds of summer.

Judd: Were you a nerd in high school?

John: I'm interested in how you define *nerd*.

Judd: I always think of nerds in an admiring way. They were different. They usually weren't athletes. They liked weird stuff and took some shit for being different.

John: I would say no, then. I was bad at sports, but basketball was so popular in Chicago that from ages nine to thirteen, I had to play basketball. And I was terrible.

Judd: It was popular there because of Michael Jordan?

John: Yes, and no one played football, because there wasn't room for football fields in the city. So, I had to deal with aggressive basketball schedules starting in fourth grade. By high school, I think I had enough defense mechanisms about the things I wasn't good at.

Judd: In high school, did you have a sense of "things are working out for me"?

John: Things *were* working out for me, but I couldn't wait to get out of Chicago. It was not a small town, but I still had the attitude of *I've got to get out of here and go to New York*. And like, *This school is bullshit and small.*

Judd: What did your parents do?

John: My dad's a lawyer, my mom's a lawyer. They were sophisticated—we saw a lot of theater. They went to the symphony.

Judd: Did you know you were going to do something creative?

John: Yes. And I was quite surprised with some of my friends who liked comedy when we were little, because I'd be, like, "So, when we grow up, we're all going to be in a comedy group like this, right?" and they'd be like, "What, why?" I would think, *Why wouldn't we? Don't you want to do this professionally?* I thought we were all going to be a sketch group. I even thought that with my college improv group at Georgetown. When we were graduating, I was like, "Do you want to be a duo?" And this guy I collaborated with a lot, and who I did a lot of scenes with, was like, "I'm going to theological school," and I was like, "Then why did we do all this?"

Judd: Nick Kroll was at Georgetown, too, right? You eventually got him to do it.

John: Kroll, I knew, was serious, but he was also four years older. To get face time with Nick was a big deal to me. He was already established in my mind as a wildly cooler older brother.

Judd: Did you stay in touch after he left?

John: Oh yeah. I bothered him a lot. I think we made a short film over the summer when I was between my junior and senior year. He and Mike Birbiglia were actually doing it, making it in the comedy world. I followed Birbiglia to a club, and I was like, *Okay, he got eight hundred dollars, and I know his rent is, like, six hundred dollars* . . . And the documentary, *Comedian*, about Seinfeld, came out around the same time, so that life became a thing that was no longer impenetrable.

Judd: What have you learned from Seinfeld? Was he the number-one guy for you?

John: I realize I don't say it enough, because I think of it as a given, like saying you like the Beatles. But his voice was in my consciousness so early. Him and Stern. Conan O'Brien, too, especially, was a beacon for me.

Judd: He's an example of a smart, normal person who's talented and funny. He proves that you don't have to come from a hellish situation to do something creative and great.

John: It wasn't like, "Oh, my dad died when I was two, and my mom had a heart condition, and the doctor was like, 'You better make her laugh.'" Which is some people's real story, but there was none of that for me. I definitely had a lot of embarrassment about being from a family that was well-off, and nothing other than personal problems that I had to deal with. My drug problems were basically fun until they weren't, and I took care of them rather quickly.

Judd: So, were you guys doing stand-up and sketch comedy at the same time in college?

John: We were in an improv group that we took very seriously, like long-form improv. We thought the Harold [improv structure] and all that was awesome. We'd come up to New York and go to the old Upright Citizens Brigade Theatre, on Twenty-Second Street, and we would do student shows where we'd do forty minutes of improv games that audiences loved. Then we'd do a Harold, and we'd basically lose the audience.

Judd: That's ballsy.

John: Most people can't follow how a Harold actually works. If you don't know how it works, it's very confusing. And we were also sticking to the most regimented form of it.

Judd: Were you doing theater in college?

John: No, because once I could do comedy, I was like, *I don't want to be in* The Importance of Being Earnest.

Judd: What was the dream in college? Was it to go write for *Conan*, or was it to start doing stand-up?

John: I think the surprise to me was I didn't realize how much I'd like stand-up. I'd gotten so into *Conan, The Simpsons, The Ben Stiller Show, SNL*—all that stuff, so I was like, *Okay, there's TV writing.* I was like, *Wow, Buck Henry had a cool career.*

Judd: That's such a nerd connection we have, as a guy who watched Buck Henry when *SNL* was airing in the seventies. Even as a little kid, at nine, I was attracted to Buck Henry more than Burt Reynolds hosting.

John: I'd seen a lot of those best of '75, best of '76 videos. Then I remember seeing him in *The Graduate*, and I remember seeing that he wrote *The Graduate*. So, he was a writer, but he also did things. Conan is a writer who then they brought on camera.

Judd: That's such a specific track. When I was a kid, I wasn't aware that this was a career you could choose. Like: *Can you do all these things? Can you write variety, can you write a movie? Can you do stand-up, can you act in something?*

John: Would you be as happy writing and seeing your joke on the Golden Globes as you would performing it? And kind of, yes. Because I'm like, *That's mine.*

Judd: My first job was writing the Grammys. And having Shandling do a joke or two. When somebody walked onstage and performed what I wrote backstage, I was so happy. I had no friends who wanted to do that. I was the only one who was willing to write jokes for other people.

John: That reminds me of when I was at camp in Minnesota; it was called Camp Lincoln. It was on a lake, and the girls' camp was through the woods. My brother was also at the camp, and he was older. He finished reading [Bob Woodward's Belushi biography,] *Wired*, and he says to me, "Read this. You'd like this. It's about John Belushi. Read it." I remember reading—at some point in the book, he says something like, "I was a sarcastic guy on the back wall who'd lob some good lines into the scene and then Belushi came in and he was like a tornado." I remember thinking, at eleven, *I'll never be a tornado. I'll definitely be the guy on the back wall lobbing in sarcastic comments.*

Judd: What does it feel like now when there's an argument that you have evolved into the Belushi guy?

John: I feel like it's so nice that everyone's watching me do this. But I worry that in the back of their minds, they know I'm just a writer and that someone could be saying this better.

Judd: That's not how people think of you. The last few years of your career is a rare thing in comedy, where you're recognized purely on the quality of the work alone.

John: That's very nice to hear. It is really nice when people are like, "I like this joke of yours," or, "I like this story of yours," the way they'd say, "I like this song." I like that you heard the material first, then later connected that that was me.

Judd: How did it feel to have already done so many different things in comedy, and then have your stand-up explode, and the Broadway play explode?

John: Even on Broadway, I was like, *Nick [Kroll]'s an actor and a writer, and I'm a writer, but I'm the only one who can do this character.* With *Oh, Hello*, I'm like, *I should do it because I don't want anyone to mess up the other characters.*

Judd: Would you say you saw any of this coming?

John: The only time I felt it was when I saw the *Comedian* documentary, and at the end, Seinfeld's doing a two-thousand-something-person theater or something. I remember thinking, *I want that*. Like, *I have a hunger, an ambition for* that. And when I was onstage in St. Louis last fall, and it was like a three-thousand-seater, it was mid-show when I thought to myself, *Well, this is bigger than anything I ever anticipated. We're in St. Louis, and this is sold out.* And I thought to myself, *I have no need for this to get any bigger.* This is it. Not in a "I'm done" way, but, like, *Wow, this is the thing I fantasized about and it is actually happening. Wow, I get to do a theater.* It doesn't go beyond that, I don't think. Or Bill Hader telling a reporter, "The guy that writes those sketches is John Mulaney." That meant as much to me as anything.

Judd: Bill was always really good about that.

John: He was extremely good. So, I had a rare case actually, now that I say it out loud. With *Saturday Night Live*, there was already some adulation, because people knew some of the things I was writing, mainly because Bill was extremely kind about sharing credit.

Judd: In this moment, when you have more options, where does your brain go in terms of what you want to do next? What is that conversation like in your head?

John: There's a natural self-protective feeling of, *Go away for a while, so that people aren't sick of you.* You know when the goods are gone. I'm not going to be asked to host the Oscars, but let's say they did. I'd be like, "I don't know if I have that this month." It might actually be modesty, but it's probably not. It's some instinct of, *You've been around too much. Back off.*

Judd: In stand-up, backing off still means writing.

John: One issue I do have is I always need a specific role model, and as a pure stand-up, I look at someone like George Carlin, and I'm like, *That's the life of a king.* However, I also want to be able to write a movie for Fred Armisen and Bill Hader, or I want to be a writer on *Documentary Now!* I guess you have to tell me, how do you also keep up with writing and learning about how to do stuff behind the camera?

Judd: Did you see the Quincy Jones documentary? I feel like that's a version of it. I'm a trumpet player. Maybe I should also lead the band? Okay. Maybe I should be an arranger? Maybe I'll produce other people? Maybe I should write stories for movies? Maybe I should produce the movies? Maybe I should produce a miniseries? There's that need to keep looking for spaces, creatively.

John: I'm not Quincy Jones, but I really identified with that. I feel like my generation was told that anyone would have wanted to be Johnny Carson, to be a talk show host, where that's your job forever. But I think everyone my age is kind of like, correctly or incorrectly, *Well, if you take that job, it's that for life.* And there's this weird hesitancy about a fucking golden job.

Judd: My trajectory is slightly different because I started doing stand-up too young. I was seventeen when I started, but I left college by nineteen to do it full time. I lacked a vision or a style, I didn't really have that much charisma, and I was not about to reinvent the form like some of my friends were. When it came to stand-up, I thought, *I don't think I'm going to be doing what they're doing.* And that made me open to doing everything else. I could write Roseanne's act with her because I was giving up what my primary dream was, because I felt like the universe was telling me, "You can do all this other stuff. Maybe you'll write a movie."

John: Did you look at any of the very successful comics—like Robert Klein, George Carlin, Tom Dreesen—and think, *Maybe I could do that?*

Judd: It was Bill Maher for me, before *Politically Incorrect.* I thought, *I'm like a half-assed Bill Maher.* I thought that would be the bar for me. But then I realized that when I sat with Jim Carrey kicking around jokes, and he did them, he would murder, and my confidence as a writer built. Was it like that for you, when you wrote sketches for Hader?

John: Yeah, writing for Bill and Fred was like writing for Jimi Hendrix.

Judd: I always enjoy people's later years at *Saturday Night Live*. Because I feel like in the early years—and I've tracked this with a bunch of people, but most recently with Bill and with Pete—they're trying to make a name for themselves, but then they start getting on too much, and they get a little burnt out. And there are a few years where they lose all anxiety about the show, and they hit a higher plane of fun.

John: Where it dawns on you. It's been either intimated to you or you have been explicitly told that you can perform on this live network show every week for as long as you want, and it suddenly dawns on everyone, like, "Oh, we have this amazing platform."

Judd: It's the same with stand-up when it all comes together, where you think *I'm not nervous on the stand-up stage anymore. I get what this is. I'm enjoying it.* When you were on *SNL*, what did you think about writing for the show, rather than performing on it?

John: It sounds disingenuous, how much I try to convince people that I did not want to be in the cast because of how rewarding it was to be a writer. One of my biggest takeaways is that this is not something people will ever believe. If you're lucky enough to be there and feel the comfort and feel that you have a little bit of agency, that amount of freedom and fun was so great, and how much you learn about television is so insane that I find myself overexplaining when people ask, "Were you bummed you weren't in the cast?"—to the point that it sounds like I'm lying and I've just convinced myself it was a better existence. But I genuinely think, if not better, it was unparalleled.

Judd: I believe everybody has a different experience. For some people, they're fitting into the show machinery well, and so, their whole experience is very gratifying. For other people, it's the most painful time.

John: I know. And I went in thinking it would be the most painful time ever. Because when I was hired, it was not in my plan. I was doing *Best Week Ever* a lot. I was doing stand-up, and it's kind of fun to be on TV every week. I remember this girl didn't want to go out with me, and I was taking the L train home to Brooklyn, and I thought to myself, *At least I'm on TV tonight.* I was not covetous of Letterman or *SNL*, because I thought they were unhappy, cold environments.

Judd: How did you get on *SNL*; was it a sketch packet?

John: No. I auditioned.

Judd: You auditioned to be in the cast and got hired as a writer?

John: Yeah. Kroll and I were in L.A., pitching a movie with Tracy Morgan, who had left *SNL* already. This is the summer of 2008. I got a call to audition for the show, and since I was in L.A., they thought I lived in L.A., so they gave me a hotel. I lived in Brooklyn, but I took the hotel. And T. J. Miller, Nick Kroll, Bobby Moynihan, Donald Glover, Ellie Kemper—we were all auditioning.

Judd: That's a strong run of people.

John: And I liked my audition. It was stand-up I was already doing that had some characters in it. I was like, *I'm not going to get this, but I think what I'm putting up is funny, and I'll get to tell the story of the one time I auditioned for Lorne Michaels.* And I auditioned, and it went really well. Everyone beforehand was like, "They don't laugh, just so you know," and then they laughed a lot. Then Seth [Meyers] called me and hired me as a writer, and I remember thinking, *I don't want this to end.* It was so exciting to audition, I want this high to continue. I'd already written for *Important Things with Demetri Martin* and a show for Comedy Central, but I did go into *SNL* being like, *This is going to be hard. This is going to be a cold year.*

Judd: What is a highlight of *Oh, Hello* being on Broadway?

John: Nights that it'd be going great, I'd just take it in, and this is, well, like I'm on the moon. It's working so well, and we're not supposed to be there. Quite literally. That's not modesty—it's very hard to get a Broadway theater.

Judd: Did you ever think that's where it might ultimately land?

John: The joke was always, "What are you going to do next?" and we said, "*Oh, Hello* on Broadway." Then we were like, *We should do that.* We were happy doing Off-Broadway while talking about how we should be on Broadway. Then, when we were given a Broadway theater, we knew it was fortunate, we knew the timing was great. But I don't think we fully appreciated how many shows with much bigger names than ours are in Connecticut or working out in DC and won't get one of the super-theaters. I remember thinking, *I genuinely don't know how we got here, and I also don't know, when we leave, if we can get back.*

Judd: I've felt that way, too. I had *Freaks and Geeks,* I had *The Stiller Show,* and you think it's crazy that it all has happened. The weird, nerdy kid who dreamed of hanging out with Rick Moranis. But then again, a lot of my career has been motivated by revenge, just to show people that they were wrong about something. You hated *Freaks and Geeks*? Then I'm going to make Seth Rogen a star. But the main thing that I wanted to ask you about your style of joke writing, because it seems like you're doing two different things: You're doing modern observational comedy, but then you're also doing very personal stories. You go deep.

John: I always have. It is very funny for me to drop extremely personal bombs on people in what is otherwise an upbeat, "Don't you love entertainment?" tone.

Judd: How did you land on, like, your general vibe and style?

John: I think opening for Birbiglia for a couple of years, but especially over this one thirty-day stretch on a college tour. He did this campus tour, and it was thirty days on a bus. It was like a boot camp.

Judd: Watching Mike and doing the show?

John: I had a phase in the beginning where I so wanted to be a comedian, but I was not aggressively booking myself every night. I wanted to have already done it. I was like, *Why aren't I already a comedian? I don't like this middle stuff.* So, that stretch, with thirty straight days, and then followed by a dozen other days—you have a show every night, sometimes two shows a night, and you're the emcee, and you have to be good. Which Mike actually said to me, and I still credit him for it. He was like, "If I take you on this tour, by the way, you have to be good."

Judd: Now you're in a place where there are people who can do impressions of you. You have a distinct cadence in the way you express yourself, but how long did it take you to figure out who you are and what was funny about you?

John: It is a presentation when you're a comedian. I wore a suit for the first time at [the] Helium [Comedy Club], in Philadelphia, in 2012. I'd just been at the Laughing Skull [Lounge], in Atlanta, and I was wearing a plaid button-down shirt and jeans, and there were, like, four openers. We all were twenty-six, and we all dressed the same way. The audience was also wearing plaid button-down shirts and jeans, and I remember thinking onstage, *This isn't right.* So, I was like, *I think I'll wear a suit for this special.* I'd never worn one onstage, and I wore one to Helium. It sounds dumb, but that was it. I'm now showing you what I've always wanted to be, which is Desi Arnaz.

Judd: What does Desi Arnaz mean to you?

John: On the surface level, that meant to me that you get to be home all day when you do the show at night. But I was like, "Boy, to do comedy in a suit and tie in New York City. If only." And then I thought, *Well, why don't you do that?*

Judd: That's a very Seinfeld thing, too. You suit up for the job, you take this seriously. Did anyone intimidate you as a comic when you first were dipping your toe in the scene? Who made you feel like, *Wow, I don't know if I can ever be as good as that person?*

John: A lot of people. There's a guy at the Strip who had a long bit where he impersonated Willy Wonka yelling at the kids that got [into the] fizzy, lifting drinks. And I just remember it destroying at the Strip after I'd eaten shit there. So, anyone who was doing well, it was just something like, *Goddamn, how did they do that?* How did they walk up and look like they were in charge?

Judd: How many years did it take for you to feel confident up there?

John: I would say I'm still not fully confident yet. Lately, I've been like, *Does this persona have to change? Do I want it to change? Will people get bored of it?* Or is it like, "I'll be here if you need me." I've been reading *Born to Run,* Bruce Springsteen's book, because I've been thinking about this a lot lately. I'm getting past "Tunnel of Love," when he's very wealthy and he's at a loss, and he said, "I didn't want to be this rich man in a poor man's shirt."

Judd: The guy who could say, *I think I'm the person that needs to make that album about 9/11.* Imagine if you really believe that in your soul. *I think I'm the person who can turn this into art and help people somehow*, and he completely pulls it off.

John: Or [Springsteen's album] *Wrecking Ball*. That is a multimillionaire singing about the recession, and he means it.

Judd: I have a pure technical question for you.

John: Of course.

Judd: I've seen you do shows where you come with your notebooks, because a lot of your bits are longer, and they're intricately woven. I'm always interested in how much time people spend at a typewriter or thinking through the whole thing. How much time in your act, when you're crafting a story, will you sit and try to take a run, on paper, at the whole story?

John: I've almost never done that. When you do *Live at Gotham* or other TV things, they would ask for a full transcript and were writing out the jokes word by word in paragraph form. I remember, I was like, *This is so not funny, seeing it written out.*

Judd: But do you go onstage and babble? If you're doing the Trump horse bit, how much do you have when you first get onstage?

John: I at least have to have A and Z.

Judd: What are the bits that you're most proud of?

John: What was meaningful to me was the end of that *New in Town* special, which was a story about when I tried to get Xanax from a walk-in clinic across the street from the office that Pete Holmes and I shared. It was forty-five minutes of my life that was just humiliating, and then I collapsed because they had drawn blood and I hadn't eaten all day. Also, what I didn't say in that story is when I walked out of that clinic ashen from having fainted, I bumped into someone, and it was Elijah Wood. I went right onstage and told that story, and it did okay, but I was still literally sweaty from fainting.

Judd: I've noticed that when I'm writing other things, like a movie, I have to shut down the part of my brain that's paying attention to things to see if they could be stand-up material. Is that a part of you that's always on?

John: I feel very uncomedic when I'm dragging my bulldog down the street in thirty-degree weather, and she wants to walk, but I just need her to pee. Genuinely, I'm sometimes amazed at how little a sense of humor I have about life.

KEVIN HART

May 2021

Judd: People don't know our vast history. I met you when you were nineteen or twenty years old. Your manager, Dave Becky, said, "You know who you need to know? Kevin Hart." And you're just a young man. You're a child. You're not drinking age at this point. I was doing a television pilot called *North Hollywood*, about a bunch of people who live outside of Hollywood trying to make it in show business. It was Amy Poehler, you, Jason Segel, January Jones, Judge Reinhold, and in a small part, Adam McKay. And this was your first foray to Hollywood to do a TV pilot.

Kevin: I remember when Dave first brought it up, and he was telling me, "Look, there's a guy. He's the hot guy in town right now. One of the best creators/producers. I feel like he's just the guy, and he's going to be the guy for a long time." And I was at that point in my career where any information was the most amazing information that you can receive. If somebody chose an opportunity, everything was the opportunity. *This is gonna be the one, this is gonna launch me.* So, when he told me that he had a conversation with you, and it was about putting myself on tape for you to see, that became my moment to come to L.A. It ended up being the best thing ever. It was the best opportunity with the best group of comedic actors and actresses. And it came so long ago, but so early in my career, that I just wish it [had] worked out. But then, at the same time, I'm glad it didn't. And not because of where I am now. I'm glad because I stayed in your Rolodex, right? Our relationship continued. And you were very persistent in the opportunities that you were bringing to me. What I realized later on is that what's going to be, will be, but if you surround yourself with the people who truly are about the work, then the work is going to find you, and you're going to find it. I became a fan of yours because you really did the work. You showed me the benefit of sitting down, creating, writing, and then seeing that material come to life. I got to watch you do that from the front seat.

Judd: I saw it as my own personal failure that I knew every great person in comedy that deserved to be a star, put them in the same pilot, and I couldn't get it picked up. It was all single-camera, and there was this moment where Jason Segel's character had an audition, and he was nervous about it, and he's dry-heaving into the toilet. And while we're shooting it, because he's fake dry-heaving, he starts bleeding out of his nose. And it's gushing blood. I find it so funny, so we don't cut, and we're like, "Let's shoot this scene with real blood gushing out of his nose." And then I hand it into ABC, thinking they would find this hilarious, and they did not find it funny.

Kevin: Horrible. It was a horror film in there.

Judd: And your persona on the show was a young actor who had money because he was on a beer commercial.

Kevin: I'll never forget it. A beer commercial. That was the best big beer commercial.

Judd: And you kept saying, "I'm going to be the next Chris Tucker because you can't understand him, but you can understand me." And then you talked about how you wanted to be in the next *Beverly*

Hills Cop, and it'd be you and Eddie Murphy. And he'd be like Scooby-Doo, and you'd be like Scrappy-Doo.

Kevin: It was so amazing, because it's so aligned with my trajectory, if you look at my success and where it's come from. Me saying, *I'm gonna be the next Chris Tucker, I want to be as big as Chris, and I'm going to, and here's why,* it was really what I thought and believed would happen. And in that show, you gave me an opportunity to echo my real feelings.

Judd: What was interesting for me is that, back then, you were fresh from New York and Philly, and you had this belief in yourself, which was comically gigantic. It made us laugh how sure you were that you were going to make it.

Kevin: I truly believed I could accomplish that and get to these places, because I knew that once the opportunity came, there was no world where I was going to drop the ball. There was no place where I felt like, now that I've gotten an opportunity, I'm not going to make the most or make the best of it. It was always, *I'm gonna knock this out of the park because I'm ready and I'm prepared. I know what's going to happen once I get that opportunity. And once I'm in position to go full steam ahead, I'm not going to look back.* Because I believed that I put the work in, and I believed that I was really good at my craft. That was a real feeling. And that's what ended up happening.

Judd: I remember that you would have outfits and call them sets, like, "You like my set? Isn't this a good set?" And we found it funny that your pants and your shirt have been thought through in advance. As schlubby guys, we didn't understand that concept. But you lived with Jason Segel. I asked you to live with him, just so that you guys could figure out what your comedic rapport would be.

Kevin: What I love about Jason and myself staying together is that, when it was presented, it was, "Hey I want you guys to get to know each other, spend some time together before we start shooting." Looking back at it now, I couldn't believe I had all of these people around me in the same space. I had no idea who I was around: I had Seth Rogen, I had Jason, I had James Franco, January Jones. We hung out in this genius comedy bubble without even realizing it. Jason was always creating, and he had bought a new camera. He was shooting sketches before sketches were a thing to shoot, before social media, before YouTube. Jason was just shooting and directing his own sketches. And we were doing them from the house, because he was excited about the new camera that he bought. That was not only the space that I was in, but where I learned what would ultimately help further my career. I thought, *This is what the people who want to get here do, Kevin. You've got to learn to do this as well.* And that's why Jason and I hit it off. We had a great relationship, man. I still owe him money, Judd.

Judd: I'm sure you do. Weren't you saying that since you had nothing to offer him in the relationship, you would make him breakfast?

Kevin: Yeah, I made him breakfast. Pancakes, eggs. Jason would always say, "Kevin, you are so nice." And I was thinking, *Well, that's all I can be, Jason. I have nothing else to do. I got no money to give you. So, I need to be a nice guy and show you that I appreciate this.* And when I finally got some money, I remember writing a check, and I had, like, a great presentation. I was giving him the check to say, "Thank you for letting me stay there and covering these things." And he wouldn't take my money.

Judd: When you're young, and you get your first show, you really feel like, *This is it, I'm about to make some money. My life is about to change.* They tell you how much you're going to make every week when you get a TV show, when you sign the contract—say, twenty grand an episode. But then it doesn't happen; the pilot doesn't get picked up. Then you're back in the clubs. What was that like?

Kevin: It's tough, because you get thrown a vision of what the life is, or what it can be. And then you go, *Wow, it's over. It didn't get picked up. Now I have to go backward and go back to the road. Back to the life of the struggling comedian.* And that's a hard transfer. It's not until you get a firm understanding of the business that you're able to process the back-and-forth.

Judd: Was that a depressing period?

Kevin: Yeah. But I got up, and I was like, *This is it. This is where I need to be.* And when the show wasn't picked up, I went back home to the East Coast, but I was like, *I can't come back here after seeing what I saw there.* So, I made the decision to move to Los Angeles, even though there wasn't a plan in place. There wasn't a blueprint laid out of how I was going to pay these bills or where the money was going to come from. I had a little bit of money from that pilot and a little bit of money from a deal that I got at Montreal, and I was like, *I'm bored and I'm moving to Los Angeles. I'll figure it out.* I put all my eggs in that basket. And thank God, I figured it out. But I just said, *I can't see what I saw and not chase that.*

Judd: There are people who are really funny, and then there are certain people who will just sit alone in a room and write a pilot or write a movie, and they have a vision to take it to the next level.

Kevin: I think you need to get a nice balance of the two, and I definitely developed that at a younger age. As a result, I was able to constantly stay in a good headspace. I never got rocked too far this way or too far that way. I stayed in a space of positivity, and it's because I saw high levels of negativity early on in my career.

Judd: I feel bad when things don't happen. I'm very empathetic, to a fault, for the life experience of actors and actresses and how the success or failures of projects affect their lives. I don't just move on, I have a kind of Jewish guilt about it, where I always think, *Damn, it* *didn't work for them.* So, I always was looking for ways to work with you at that time, and to not have destroyed your life. I felt that way with all the *Freaks and Geeks* kids, because a lot of them relocated for that show. Seth moved here from Canada. It changed their lives, and then, suddenly, the show is gone. But then we worked together again on *The 40-Year-Old Virgin.* And you came in and did a scene for that movie, too.

Kevin: That was a defining moment for our relationship. There's this expectation that you'll get an opportunity because you just know someone, and with *The 40-Year-Old Virgin,* I auditioned for the part that Romany Malco got. I was like, *Wow, this is the one. Judd is going to give me this part. I'm going to knock this audition out.* I remember when Romany got it, I was like, *Dang. I lost out. Shit, I really wanted it.* But I instantly understood that Romany was probably better for that part than me. I couldn't wait to see Romany's performance, because there's something I'm either going to learn or see, but ultimately, I'm going to know that he had something that I didn't have. Later on, you guys are about to go to production and film, and you just call me randomly to do a scene. That made everything okay, and this is why the positive mindset has always worked for me, because things always worked themselves out. That scene ended up doing so much for me that it was ridiculous. Romany Malco destroyed that part in *40-Year-Old Virgin.* He was a more polished actor, and he had things that I didn't have yet at that young point of my career. I said, *I need to take some acting classes. I need to make sure that I'm ready for these opportunities when they come.* But this all came from the school of Judd. It all came from being underneath that umbrella that you knew you held for all of us.

Judd: That scene was also such a natural space for you to be yourself and show the world, "This is how Kevin Hart works in a movie." We did a DVD of the extended version of the movie, and I added like seventeen minutes, which you really shouldn't do. But there were so many funny things that were too short. So, I extended your fight with Romany by, like, another minute, and most people remember that version of it.

Kevin: That's the way it floats around in social media.

Judd: I was reading your book, and you talked about when you would go into auditions, and you used to think, *It doesn't matter if I get this or not. I'm going to be so appealing that even if I don't get it, these people are going to like me, and it's going to pay off at some point.* I think for most young actors and actresses, those auditions are so terrifying. They want it so badly that they melt down in the room a fair amount of the time.

Kevin: You're going to get an opportunity to be brought up in conversation again, and it's your choice as to how that conversation goes. Some people approach every audition as a possible job, and that's great; you should. But my approach was, *I want to be the best that I can be. I'm going to show them who I am. I want to be likable, and I want to give a good read. And regardless of whether or not I got that part, when I leave, they're going to go, "That guy was cool, I like that guy."* That's it for me, because eventually, when you see me again, you're going to remember that moment, and that moment is going to act as a motivating factor to make the next moment happen. Sometimes, you got to lay that groundwork, and it can be a lot. You might have to do a shitload of undercoats before you actually apply the paint job, but those undercoats are going to make that paint job pop. That's how I approached my auditions, and that's how I approach my career to this day: I'm still the people person, I'm still the guy who will shake all the hands. And that's worked for me; it's been very beneficial thus far.

Judd: I remember when we first met, you talked about knowing Jay-Z a little bit. What was that relationship like? You've said before that he inspired you to not just think of yourself as an actor trying to get a gig, but as more an actor trying to build a business. You were the first person I met that had that type of a mentor.

Kevin: Hova, he's my guy. He's who I go to when I have real questions, or when I've got an idea and I'm having trouble figuring out how to make it a reality. I remember our conversations back then were about where he was versus where he was going to go, and there was never a moment where he looked at himself and said, *This is all good right here, I'm great.* It was always the mindset of the greatest, always the mindset of taking over, of changing the way this genre of music is identified. It was always the mindset of CEO instead of coworker. I somehow managed to duplicate his mindset and his persistence. When you've got a good mentor or adviser, you're able to dissect and process their wisdom, and use it how you feel it best fits or suits you. And that's what he does for me until this day.

Judd: You made a choice to be that mentor to anybody who wants to read your books or listen to you talk. You encourage them to think that they can be the greatest, they can be the next Jay-Z or Walt Disney.

Kevin: I don't think we give enough information to each other, and I truly believe in sharing information. For us, as older people, we've got to equip these younger people to be better than us, to be able to surpass what we've done. The best way for the world to get better is to give the people who are coming up behind us an opportunity to make it better. I don't take that lightly.

Judd: You have one of those rare minds that allows you to switch gears to funny Kevin, or creative Kevin, and you can also switch to inspirational or business mode. I find the reason why a lot of comedians don't get very far is because they might be hilarious, but they do not have that business acumen. It's rare that someone can switch from comedy to work on a clothing line, or self-help books. Most people can't do both. I find when I have business calls, my comedy mind shuts down. How do you look at that for yourself in terms of how you organize your day, or your mind?

Kevin: For me, the best thing is the merging of those distinct worlds. I try my best to create a complete circle—all of those things have to connect somehow. My business has to complement the things underneath it, which ultimately should be driven by my personality. Regardless of the venture, regardless of the project, regardless of the task at hand, my personality should never disappear, because whatever it is that I'm offering, I should be offering it as myself. Merging those things so that I'm not always tugging and warring with myself has seemed to work.

Judd: As someone who's so busy and takes so much on, what has the experience of COVID, of this "chill-out" moment we've all been forced into—what has that been like for you?

Kevin: It's amazingly positive. I'm happy that I get to spend more time with my kids, and it makes you understand and appreciate the value of quality time. You think you know your kids, your wife, and your household, but when you're able to be there every single day, all day, you discover more. And you love more; you love harder. Yes, I still love my job, and I'm looking forward to getting back to doing what I love, but I'm never going to overlook the high level of love that was developed through this time, when we were forced to sit down and all be together. It came right on time for myself, my wife, and my kids. So, I'm extremely thankful.

LIN-MANUEL MIRANDA

August 2020

Judd: My daughter Iris wanted you to know that she sang "A Very Good Day," from *Working: The Musical*, in high school last year.

Lin-Manuel: It's a very heartbreaking song. The songs that I wrote for that were kind of my *In the Heights* methadone, because I spent my twenties writing *In the Heights*. I started writing it when I was nineteen years old, for a college project, and then we opened on Broadway when I was twenty-eight. I'll never make a leap that big again. I went from substitute teacher to Broadway composer. I don't have another leap that big in me.

Judd: Is that how you were making money, as a substitute teacher?

Lin-Manuel: I started teaching seventh-grade English at my old high school. They offered me a full-time position, and I got scared of the *Mr. Holland's Opus* version of my life, because I really liked it. I enjoy teaching. But I said, *No, I can make rent by subbing, and then I have more time to write.*

Judd: Were you going out on acting auditions and trying to have that life as well?

Lin-Manuel: I went on lots of voiceover auditions and acting auditions, and the only thing I booked was *The Sopranos*, as a bellboy; I say "I don't know" twice. I'm so green you can see me look down at my mark. Watch it if you get a chance, because now people are like "Lin-Manuel's cameo on *The Sopranos*!" It wasn't a cameo. I wasn't even in the union yet.

Judd: Who were you in the scene with?

Lin-Manuel: Gandolfini and Paulie. My one story about Gandolfini was that he stayed and did his sides even though it was the end of the night. He had no need to do that. He stayed and did the scene for the scared-shitless Puerto Rican kid in the bellhop outfit. The other thing I remember was that he sat on the steps of his trailer the whole time. He was never locked up in this trailer; he was just out, and people would talk to him.

Judd: It's a powerful lesson as a young person. "Oh, you respect everybody, you care about the work, you're not playing star." It's weirdly meaningful to observe one of the greats on a set. You're also the leader of a giant crew when you do these shows. When I worked as a producer on *The Ben Stiller Show*, I didn't know how to do it at all. I thought, *I'm so young. His whole crew is older than me. They must hate my guts.* I was just a terrified boss, and I would read, like, business books in my office, like *[The] Seven Habits of Highly Effective People*. I didn't really know how to be a leader of a hundred people. How was that, for you to realize that's your role?

Lin-Manuel: I think the biggest gift I had is [theater director] Tommy Kail, because I've gone through it twice with him. With *Heights*, we did so many readings and workshops with the same actors over and over, for no money, in the basement of the bookshop, that it was very easy for the actors to see me as just a cast member, and I disappear for rewrites. I was also such a kid that we were all kind of in it together, and because I'm the writer but I don't run a department, I don't really hire or fire people. I weigh in on casting, but it's Tommy's show. So, I had the best position, that I got to play with everybody. I do have to say it was different on *Hamilton*. I think I was expecting it to be more "Hey, it's just me, I'm one of you guys," but because *Hamilton* became this *thing*, I felt a little more isolated. I was isolated by the praise. The cast was fantastic and lovely, but it wasn't the same. We were all strapped to this rocket ship together, hanging on for dear life.

Judd: I always remember the first time we met—this was maybe five days before the official opening of *Hamilton* on Broadway. That energy right before had that feeling of *It's working*. In a few days people will see it, but we're still scared shitless. What is it like for you right before? Are you in a meltdown state? Are you just riding it?

Lin-Manuel: You're just trying to stay on top of it. The weird thing about the show was that it solved its own problems. The two and a half hours where you're performing is so intense that it actually forces you to shut out the world. The thing that is causing you the most anxiety is your moment of Zen, because if you space out onstage, the turntable will throw you into the pit, or you will get hit with a chair, or a dancer will kick you in the face. These are all things that happened. The nerves are around the whole two and a half hours you're doing it, because it's a meal. It's a fourteen-course meal. You live the whole life. It's a joy, and it takes everything out of you to do it, and that, I think, is also what kept us sane and kept our energy, because you also have to pace yourself for another two and a half hours living life.

Judd: As a comedian, you can change all the words in any moment, so there's this tension of, *Am I going to run the act or completely bail and go into free-flow mode, or do both?* Whereas, you do improv—and you do rap—and you cannot miss a beat.

Lin-Manuel: I find that the tracks in my brain—the one that knows all the words to *Hamilton* and the one that is open and receptive and listening to suggestions—are really different. So, the few times I've had to improvise within *Hamilton,* I feel like I lose a year off my life. We did a performance in Puerto Rico, and there was a young lady in the fourth row, and she was filming, and this is a performance that was just for the university students. So, I'm coming down the steps in that opening number, and I just see this, and I'm like, *All right, I'm not gonna say shit. It'll probably go away after the opening number.* Then, I come around with Aaron Burr, into the bar, and it's still there, and I'm getting distracted because I also know if it were any other show, there'd be a moment where I could go offstage and tell the stage manager, "Hey, someone's filming in the fourth row." That's how I handle it ninety-nine percent of the time, but Hamilton doesn't leave the stage.

Judd: So, you go full Patti LuPone.

Lin-Manuel: But I don't want to stop the show, so I think up, "I got a scholarship to King's College / I probably shouldn't brag but, dang I amaze and astonish / Hey, lady filming in the fourth row, please stop it / I got a holler just to be heard / Every word I drop knowledge . . ." and I just kept going. I was so covered in sweat just having to think of the line while the show was going on, whereas in the freestyle show, the whole thing is just being open and saying whatever comes into your head. On *Hamilton,* it was really hard switching gears.

Judd: Jay Leno always talks about when he's onstage and he's running his set, sometimes his brain can split so much that he can count how many people are in the comedy club while having a good set. It almost becomes a meditation.

Lin-Manuel: That happens over the course of the run. Camera spotting as an example, especially with the [Richard] Rodgers Theatre. It's a very steeply raked house; I can see nineteen rows back. I'll be doing the show, and I'll tell the stage manager, "Tenth row, five seats in."

Judd: Or Bryan Cranston is there that night.

Lin-Manuel: That's the shit that bugs you out. I like to know beforehand, and I'm not limited to the odd Tom Hanks—it's like, "You're Robert Goulet," or, "You're Tony Randall." So, I'd like to know in advance. The hardest one was early at the Public: Busta Rhymes, front row. Honestly, no one's opinion means more to me than Busta Rhymes's. Everyone else can go fuck themselves. I was like, *Don't look at Busta Rhymes. Don't look at Busta Rhymes.* And he's a big guy, and he's in the front row. So, I looked up to not look at him, and Mandy Patinkin was sitting above, who you could argue is the Busta Rhymes of musical theater.

Judd: In my house, he is. Do you feel that your improv skills, your freestyle skills, affect your ability to get into flow as a playwright and as a songwriter?

Lin-Manuel: For me, freestyle is the ultimate version of being present. And what you want in your characters, when they're talking to each other, is to be present, speaking in a way that feels spontaneous and feels real. So, absolutely, I think it's made my writing better because I'm always chasing the most honest impulse. It's also the ultimate excuse against writer's block—you can't lie to yourself and say, *I have writer's block,* when you've just done a ninety-minute show based on the verb *gesticulate,* or whatever the fuck the main audience said that night. You made a show out of nothing last night, so get to the page and don't lie to yourself. It cuts out my internal bullshit and excuses not to write, because I know that if I'm in the right setting, I can just generate it.

Judd: But you also make the choice to mainly be a songwriter who writes alone.

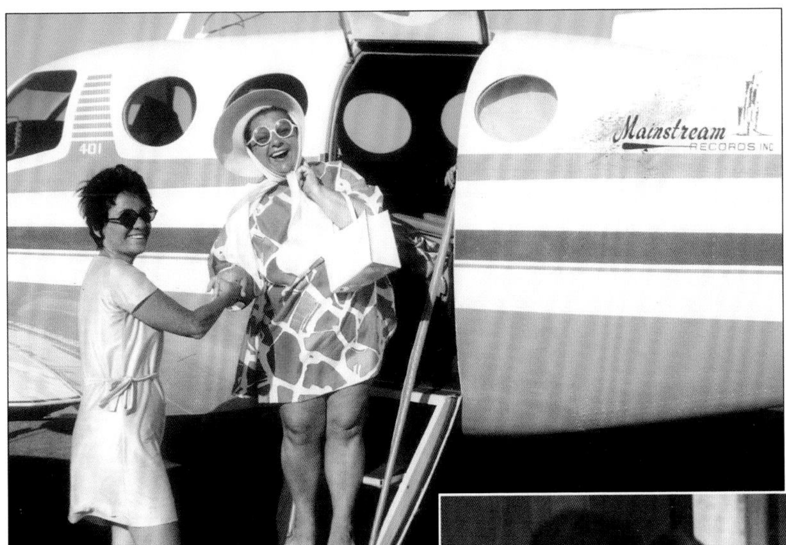

My grandmother, Molly Shad, and her friend, the great comedienne Totie Fields.

My sister, Mia, and brother, Robert, backstage with Totie Fields.

Bar Mitzvah Life. Long Island, New York, 1981.

Gary Frank with me in a Fila sweat jacket.

Interviewing Paul Reiser.

Showing the infamous book to Steve Martin.

Sorry Judd—
I didn't realize
you were _The_ Judd
Apatow!
Your friend
Steve Martin
3/80

Steve Martin's apology after refusing to sign an autograph for me after I showed up at his doorstep uninvited.

Kevin Hart at a party for the lost pilot *North Hollywood,* in 2002. *(Gabe Sachs)*

Me and Kevin Hart onstage at the Comedy Cellar in 2019.

On a break from writing the 1994 Grammys, I forced Bruce Springsteen and Garry Shandling to take this photograph.

I clearly snuck into this photograph with Larry David, Martin Short, Bill Maher, David Steinberg, and Eugene Levy.
(Mark Seliger)

Open mic night at Governor's Comedy Club, 1985.

Performing in my 2017 Netflix special, *The Return.*
(Mark Seliger)

Comic Relief benefit at UCLA with Dweezil Zappa, Michael Winslow, Paul Rodriguez, Bob Goldthwait, and Colin Quinn.

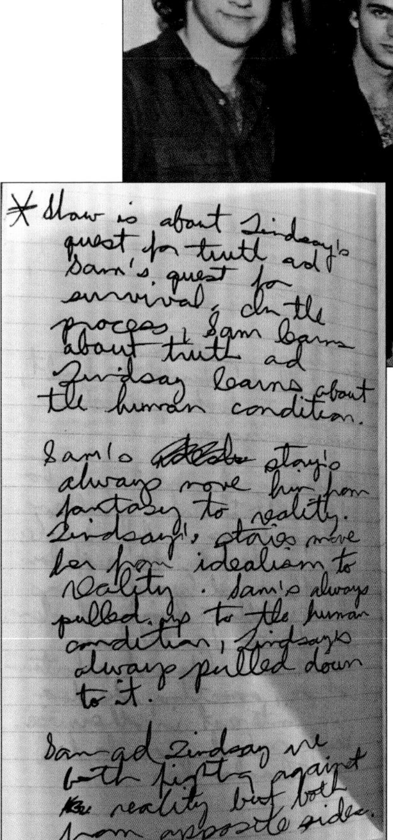

* Show is about Lindsay's quest for truth and Sam's quest for survival. In the process, Sam learns about truth and Lindsay learns about the human condition.

Sam's ~~[illegible]~~ story's always move him from fantasy to reality. Lindsay's stories move her from idealism to reality. Sam's always pulled up to the human condition, Lindsay's always pulled down to it.

Sam and Lindsay are both fighting against ~~the~~ reality but both from opposite sides.

Paul Feig's original notes conceiving the concept for *Freaks and Geeks.*

Visiting Scott Davidson's old firehouse, Ladder 118. From left to right: Eddie Greene, Robert Forte, Andrew McCord, Pete Davidson, me, Barry Mendel, John Sorrentino, Bill Burr, Dave Sirus.

you have to
Be and Bring Joy.

may be your comedy
is natural gift to
be given to others
with joy to help
them through this
impossible life, and
you sharing it,
with no desire of getting
anything

Pete Davidson and Maude Apatow on the set of *The King of Staten Island*.

A note from Garry Shandling's journal.

The world of Apatow Productions as drawn by Tom Richmond of *Mad Magazine*. *(© and ™ E.C. Publications. All Rights Reserved.)*

Mugging my brains out with Jimmy Kimmel.

Backstage during the previews of *Hamilton* with Josh Gad, Lin-Manuel Miranda, and Jonathan Groff.

Trainwreck set with LeBron James, Chris Rock, and Bill Hader.

The cast of *The Bubble*. Back row: Pedro Pascal, Galen Hopper, Danielle Vitalis, Harry Trevaldwyn, Maria Bakalova, Keegan-Michael Key, David Duchovny. Front row: Nick Kocher, Iris Apatow, Guz Khan, Karen Gillan, Vir Das, Fred Armisen.

This photo doesn't apply to this book. It's Maude Apatow, dressed as Bob Ross, meeting Drake on the set of *Euphoria*.
(Eddy Chen/HBO)

Headshot day with Adam Sandler.

Thirty years later, performing at Carnegie Hall. *(Lloyd Bishop)*

Failing at a first pitch while Jacob deGrom looks on horrified. *(Hoo-Me/SMG/Alamy)*

Our family and the *Oh, Hello* family (Nick Kroll and John Mulaney).

Nathan Fielder and I share an awkward moment.

My mentor, the great David Milch.

The *Trainwreck* Live concert tour hits L.A. with Colin Quinn, Norman Lloyd, and Amy Schumer.

Leslie Mann, Melissa McCarthy, Paul Rudd, and Megan Fox pose for their *Vanity Fair* cover. *(Mark Seliger)*

The first time I met Kumail Nanjiani, Chris Gethard, and Pete Holmes, at a taping of the *You Made it Weird* podcast at the SXSW Festival. *(Bradley Dugdale)*

Eddie Vedder and I singing a song we wrote about Garry Shandling at Bonnaroo Music & Arts Festival. *(FilmMagic/Getty)*

Paul McCartney hesitating to give me his email address, as he should.

Talking mental health with Maria Bamford, Patton Oswalt, and Gary Gulman at Largo. *(Jim Bennett/Photo Bakery)*

Press conference prior to the USO's 75th anniversary show with John Mulaney, Hasan Minhaj, David Letterman, and Jon Stewart.

Sacha Baron Cohen's Bruno models with Ben Stiller, Clint Eastwood, me, and Leslie Mann.

A normal day on the set of *Anchorman 2*.

Attempting to show Roger Daltrey how to swing a microphone at the Teen Cancer America benefit.
(William Snyder)

President Barack Obama tells a pretty good joke.
(Alex J. Berliner/ABImages)

Leslie and Judd on a very early date with Garry Shandling at the MTV Movie Awards.
(Jeff Kravitz/FilmMagic/Getty)

From Garry Shandling's journals.

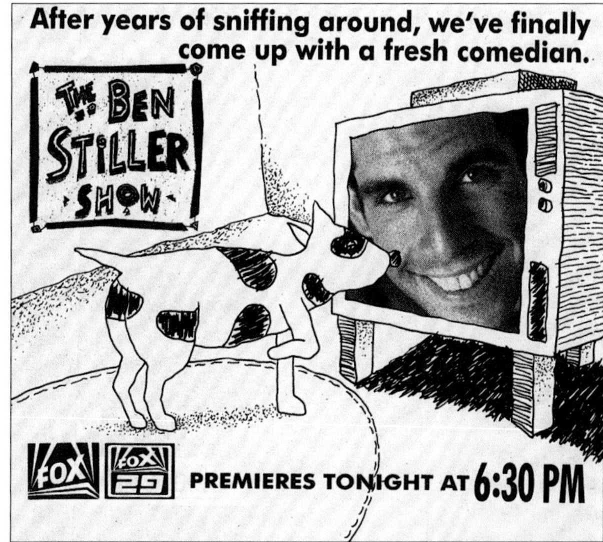

Solid marketing for *The Ben Stiller Show*.

On a writing road trip with Owen Wilson. Making a pit stop at Disney World.

Love table read. Back row: Me, Dave King, Tracie Thoms. Front row: Chris Witaske, Mike Mitchell, Paul Rust, Gillian Jacobs, Claudia O'Doherty.

Opening for Adam Sandler in Los Angeles with David Spade, Nick Swardson, Rob Schneider, Tim Meadows, and Norm Macdonald.

Crafting comedy with John Cena on the set of *Trainwreck*.

Lin-Manuel: I always see the freestyling as exactly the opposite muscle group, because it is collaborative. It's also your first best impulse. There's no time to be like, *Wait, I have a better punch line.* It's gone. Train's left. It allows you to honor that first impulse in a real way. Then I think they feed each other. It was really ideal during *Hamilton,* because I knew the moment I had that idea that it was going to take fucking forever to finish it. I was like, *Oh, I have to now go do homework and learn the social studies I never learned and do research,* which I didn't have to do on *In the Heights,* or any project to that extent.

Judd: Did you like that world before, or did you just happen to stumble upon something that caught your interest?

Lin-Manuel: I like biographies. I like dipping into someone else's life. I think the only other really big historical biography I'd read prior to Hamilton's was *Team of Rivals.* But even that—it was more the conceit than the historical biography, like, *Oh, this guy hired the people who opposed him.*

Judd: So, it wasn't like, "Lin loves Founding Fathers books."

Lin-Manuel: On the contrary, none of those stories were interesting to me. They were just iconography. What got the book off the shelf and into my hands was that I remembered that I'd written a paper in eleventh grade, and I knew [Hamilton's] son died in a duel, and then *he* died in a duel in the same place three years later. I knew that more as a piece of trivia than anything else, and I was just like, *How do you not see that coming?* It felt like the most avoidable mistake of all time.

Judd: I tried to read the Ron Chernow book—I didn't read all of it—but what kept coming up was how religious Hamilton was. A lot of it was this faith that God wouldn't do these things to him.

Lin-Manuel: It's interesting, because it's in his early writings as a teenager and then in his later writings, after he's experienced loss and death. I think it's something that was really drummed into him as a kid, and then he went and lived his life and came back to it. Which I think is how a lot of people experience religion—all right, here's the things you're supposed to learn, then you live your life and shit happens, and as you're on the back nine, you start, like, going, *Oh, I'm finding myself praying. I guess all that scaffolding my parents put in, it's still there.*

Judd: How many years was *Hamilton* from the first thought to Broadway?

Lin-Manuel: I picked up the book in summer 2008. And then we opened summer 2015.

Judd: When you're in an eight-year run of work, what makes you not lose your touch with what it is? Because this is your second show, right?

Lin-Manuel: I also co-wrote *Bring It On: The Musical.* That was the miracle baby, because it was two composing teams, so it came together really quickly, and it was really fun and good.

Judd: It's a strange trajectory, for your first show to win the Tony, and then for *Hamilton* to be the same, but way bigger in terms of success. What do you think prepared you to not lose it both then and after? Because nothing has changed in terms of your work. It hasn't gone off the rails. What about your life or how you were raised allowed you to be able to handle this?

Lin-Manuel: A couple of things. I think if the *Hamilton*-level success had happened on *Heights,* I'd be a lot more fucked up, because I didn't really have my shit figured out yet. Vanessa, who is now my wife, and I were dating, but I don't know if the tsunami of attention would have hit me in the same way. By the time *Hamilton* happened, I was married and had my first kid. He was born two weeks before rehearsal started.

Judd: Trying to get sleep is your main concern.

Lin-Manuel: I'm trying to get sleep. I'm going home. I'm going to the show, and I'm eating by five-thirty P.M., so I don't burp during any of my reps. All of the stuff I learned on *Heights*. I used to try to do a matinee of *Heights* on a muffin and a cup of coffee, and then I'm like, *Why am I lightheaded?* Because I didn't know anything about nutrition or maintaining my body—I learned all that stuff on the first show, like, *Okay, I become a monk for the time I'm doing this run. This is the food that gets me through the show, and this is what I need to sleep.* So, all of the other noise and the things that derail folks, like getting invited to the party and the famous people saying, "We want to do this," I had to say no to ninety percent of it, because I had a show the next day, or I had to sleep eight hours and I knew I was gonna wake up twice and change diapers. My family really saved my ass, because I think that's how you lose it.

Judd: I think I've seen the show five times, and it was fun to watch how it morphed. The first time I saw it, it hadn't opened officially. The next time I saw it, it was giant. It was more of a rock concert. Now they're applauding when the song starts.

Lin-Manuel: And then the audience starts knowing the words, which puts a different kind of pressure. Because you know you're gonna see that tweet about the line you fucked up that night.

Judd: I think we saw one show where we thought, *Lin looks fried.* It's still great—most people don't notice—but it was maybe eight months into the run. I went again the last week before you all left, and it seemed like the cast was luxuriating and enjoying the moment and present. Like, *We're probably not going to do this again.* I felt the energy explode again. Is that what it felt like to you?

Lin-Manuel: I'm grateful that the streaming version that most of the world is seeing was like a week and a half before we left, because we know what we're doing. We know it's finite. So, it's the energy of savoring it, but it's also really dialed in. There's lots of puppy energy in previews, like, *Let me try everything!* I always laugh when I see dancers in the workshop space trying really crazy shit. I wander behind them, like, "Eight shows a week, eight shows a week, eight shows a week." I know you're showing Andy how many spins you can do, but you're going to have to do this a lot of times.

Judd: I remember going to see *The Book of Mormon* very early and watching Josh Gad going crazy. Then, after six months, he could barely walk. His back might have been completely out. I remember him telling me right at the beginning of the run, "This is a nightmare for me. Because, in my mind, I get really bored. It's almost unbearable to do it so many times."

Lin-Manuel: It's a hell of a thing. I can really stay lasered in, and Tommy makes fun of me because I'll tell him the same story fifty times, including one memorable time where he was like, "That happened to *me*. I told you that." But he also said, "That's why you're cut out for theater, because you'll tell it like it's the first time."

Judd: Did you find that there was a giant adjustment, when the show ended, in terms of getting your work done? When people win an Oscar, they tend to make fewer movies after, because on some level they overthink it. One of the most important pieces of advice I ever got was from Ron Howard. He just said, "I don't look at any of my movies as more important than any other movie I've made. I just think there's an art gallery with posters of all the movies I made, and I hope some of them are good." That's how he framed it. You're working with him now, right?

Lin-Manuel: He's so level-headed. The theater version of that advice is how [Harold] Prince would always say, "Start working on your next thing the day after opening night." A couple of things happened after *Hamilton*, or during the end. I don't make any decisions without my wife. I can't be like, "I'm going to do this, honey." There's no world in which that happens. But the thing you need to know is my wife's mom is Austrian, and her dad is Dominican, and she was born in Sweden. If it were up to her, we would live in every country in the world for a year until we die. I wrote a whole show about how I don't want to leave the block where my apartment is and where I can see the George Washington Bridge. So, that's a big difference, and when that call came to do *Mary Poppins Returns,* it was exciting because it was, *Oh, I can work for Rob Marshall and see how musical films work.* It was not so much *Mary Poppins* as seeing the director of *Chicago* do what he does, and we get to live in London for seven months, with a kid who's young enough that it's fine. So, that was the next big move. It was the balance—what's right for my family and *What do I want to learn next?* Because to go right to work on a new musical made no sense. Rodgers and Hammerstein, after *Oklahoma* opened, were like, "We can't write another musical with ourselves; this thing's a fucking hit!" So, they went into producing.

Judd: How did that affect the *In the Heights* movie? And you're doing *tick, tick . . . Boom!* [the Jonathan Larson biopic].

Lin-Manuel: Those are the film schools I didn't pursue. I went to Wesleyan to study film, and then I fell into theater because it was a much more affordable option. I was not gonna be able to afford a senior film that gets into a festival. Whereas, with theater, you put up three hundred dollars for the lights and the costumes, and you can make as much theater as you want. I remember, from your first book, you talked about how your parents' divorce was the thing that made you be like, *No one's minding the store. I gotta get my shit together.* My version of that in college was I keenly felt my parents' financial burden. Their thing was, "Our present to you is we're gonna work our ass off." My dad quit his nonprofit job and, like, went into for-profit stuff, and my mom took on more patients—she's a psychologist—so that I'd have as little debt as possible getting out of school. My sister had to do an extra semester of college, and when she came home and was like, "I'm not going to graduate in four years," I remember my mother bursting into tears at the table. I wrote a ton in college, because I was like, *I can't just leave with a degree that says "Theater" on it. That doesn't mean anything.* I was just like, *I'm gonna leave with three scripts.* My version of your epiphany was, *My parents are killing themselves so I can be here.* I felt that really keenly.

Judd: I had the opposite of that. I needed six grand for tuition for the third semester of my sophomore year, and both my mom and my dad, who were divorced at the time, did not have six grand. So, I quit college.

Lin-Manuel: So much of the plot of *In the Heights* is about that financial pressure and how no one preps you to be an adult on your own, and the culture shock if you go from being the star in your neighborhood to being one of many. All the stuff Nina goes through—it's all from that anxiety.

Judd: The strange thing, as parents, is we realize that the thing that motivated us was this neurotic terror, so we have this insane, workaholic energy. Now we have kids, and we want them to have that fire, so how do you fuck them up in the right way?

Lin-Manuel: The thing that I worry most about as a parent is empathy. To understand that the things you have are hard to come by for so many people, to have empathy for that and to understand and recognize the enormous privilege. Putting yourself in other people's shoes—to me, that's the magic bullet of existence. It's what we do as writers: put ourselves in someone else's life and then try to speak honestly from that place. That's the trickiest and hardest gift to give your kid. Have you ever read a book called *My Name Is Asher Lev*, by Chaim Potok? It was a book I was assigned in eighth grade, and it's actually the first musical I wrote. It's the reason I started writing musicals, because we had to teach three chapters on it, and I decided to write a song for each chapter. Like, bad *Les Mis* a cappella. The whole point of the book is: This kid, who's incredibly smart, so his father goes, "I don't know how he will understand the suffering of other people, so I'm going to raise him in absolute silence." It's the most fucked-up thing, and it works. The kid is keenly aware of suffering and keenly aware of pain in himself and in others because his dad froze them out, and my terrible eighth-grade version was: "Now I can hear the silence . . ." And my eighth-grade teacher, who's kind of the guy who changed my life, was like, "You should be writing plays and not bullshitting in the back of my class."

Judd: Isn't that amazing? All it takes sometimes is just one person.

Lin-Manuel: One person who is not a family member. We had a student-run theater group called Brick Prison, and he was like, "I don't know if Brick Prison's ever done a musical. You should write one." And that was it.

Judd: An English teacher in eleventh grade for me. This teacher, who was not cool but a nice lady—and you would never think that would be the person that puts some seed into my head.

Lin-Manuel: It's about being seen, right? You hope that you are a little clever, or you hope that someone else sees it.

Judd: I know, when I speak to a film class, I'm not going to reach everyone. But in ten years, two of those kids are going to walk up to me randomly on the street having done something pretty cool, and they'll remember something I said. What's the main thing you think about as you're trying to communicate to a class of kids?

Lin-Manuel: That's the reason I've only ever done two graduation speeches, because they take it out of me so hardcore. I remember being as hungover and terrified as I've ever been on *my* graduation day and knowing I really haven't packed enough, and I've got twenty-four hours to get my shit and fill an already marijuana-filled U-Haul truck with actual things and move to New York. I really try to put myself back there: What's real and what's actionable? What can I say that will break through the fog of these kids' self-regard? They've got their families behind them. I remember having my grandparents when they were still alive. My mom's parents didn't show. They're from Jersey. My mom's parents lived in New Jersey, and my dad's friends lived in Puerto Rico, but the Puerto Rico ones were the ones that showed up for everything. The other ones couldn't come from East Brunswick.

Judd: Traffic that day.

Lin-Manuel: Both the Wesleyan and the UPenn speech, I remember them really well. I was in the library the night before, until four in the morning, at Wesleyan, being like, *I can't believe I'm writing another fucking paper for Wesleyan, and at the last minute.* That's how it felt to me. I'm really pulling from a deep place. For UPenn, I felt, *You have to dig personal if it's going to break through to this audience. Because they're going through their own shit.*

Judd: You had a great story in that speech about dating someone and having to break up with them, and feeling guilty because you realized, through her lens, you're just the idiot she had to get out of the way to find the right guy and be happy.

Lin-Manuel: She was studying abroad in the Dominican Republic. I wrote *In the Heights* while she was away, and when she came home, I couldn't stop cracking my shoulder. Like to the point where I was getting pain in my shoulder and my neck. It was a nervous tic. My mom looked up back doctors in *New York* magazine and took me to some guy who was one of those seers. I remember he had thick glasses and he looked at my shoulder for a second, and he went, "Well, there's nothing wrong with your shoulder or your back, but there will be because you keep clicking it. You have a nervous tic. Is there anything stressful in your life?" And I burst into tears in his office that I broke up with my girlfriend that night and I went into therapy the following week. In my head, I was a good guy, and good guys don't break up with their significant others while one of them goes off to study abroad. The story I was telling myself was being physically rejected by my body. The punch line is she started dating a guy who was friends of ours who lived on her hall, like sophomore year, and I was not the Jim and we were not the Jim and Pam. I was Roy.

Judd: Yeah, you were the bullet dodged.

Lin-Manuel: I was totally the bullet she dodged.

Judd: I realized that I was that way where I never broke up with a girl ever. I would ride it out till she ran away screaming for the hills. And I would never ever think I could break up with someone. I didn't have the self-esteem to go, *I'm unhappy. This isn't right.* I just couldn't believe anyone was there. And then I realized that that's what I was doing. And this beautiful woman liked me, but I didn't think I liked her enough. But I was terrified to just tell her. I'd never done that. And then one day, she bought me a pair of pants. And I was like, *I gotta end this because now she's so sweet and she's buying me pants.* And so, I told her I couldn't do it anymore. I think I may have said, "I don't think you're the future Mrs. Apatow." I think I said that, which is awful. And then she said, "I can't believe *you're* dumping me."

Lin-Manuel: It reminds me of your Steve Martin story, one of my favorite stories. "I'm sorry. I didn't realize I was talking to *the* Judd Apatow."

Judd: I was in a meeting with Steve Martin and someone asked me to tell that story. And I told it. And at the end, they asked Steve if that was how he remembered it. And he said, "In my memory, I knocked on Judd's door."

Lin-Manuel: That's a nice coda.

Judd: Who are your mentors? I saw that you translated *West Side Story* with Stephen Sondheim. Who were the people for you that gave you some time and had a real effect on you?

Lin-Manuel: It was a couple of folks. My interaction with Sondheim is interesting, because it was the second brush with him. The first one: I was a kid, and I was directing *West Side Story* at my high school. We got him to come speak to our cast, and the only reason that happened was because [lyricist] John Weidman's daughter, Laura, was a good friend. Weidman wrote *Assassins* with [Sondheim], and *Pacific Overtures.*

Judd: You had an in.

Lin-Manuel: We had an in. [Sondheim] came and spoke to us on a lunch break. I had changed some of the things to the movie version, because I liked them better, which you're not allowed to do. But I did a girl version of "America," and I remember one of our cast members asked [Sondheim], "Which do you prefer, the stage or the movie version?" He was like, "Oh, girl version is better in every way." Then, the other thing I remember, was he talked us through the creation of the Prologue from *West Side Story,* and he discussed all these lyrics he'd written with Leonard Bernstein. Like, originally, Riff was named "Riff" because he came in holding a trumpet and started singing these snatches of lyrics to us. As you and I know, there are no lyrics in the Prologue, so weeks of [Sondheim's] work went into the wastepaper basket. That was my first glimpse that these are not stone tablets from on high, these musicals. You revere these people, and here's Steve telling us, "Yeah, I really wanted them to say, 'Fuck you,' but they wouldn't let me, so it's 'crap.'" Giving us process.

Judd: That's a real guy. A guy in a room with the pencil.

Lin-Manuel: It's real the same way you became a kid reporter to talk to these folks. We got him on a lunch break.

Judd: Like, there's a person who does this, and I'm a person, and I guess that I seem a little like them. Right?

Lin-Manuel: Right. Then my second brush with someone in this world—one of my best friends in college, his dad was the cocreator of *Ain't Misbehavin'*. Those were Fats Waller songs, but he wrote some additional lyrics, and he was also a lyricist. He gave me two pieces of advice—well, he actually gave me money for my senior thesis and recording it, but he also said, "Join the Drama Guild as soon as you graduate college, because they help writers, and it doesn't cost that much, but if someone says, 'I want to produce your show,' you can go to the Guild and go, 'What do I do?' And two, get the Clement Wood rhyming dictionary." He said, "You're good, you have rhyming; you don't really need it unless you're stuck. But he's got a great essay at the beginning about what rhyming is and what it isn't." Then, the other piece of advice he gave me, when he saw my senior thesis, was like, "These are a bunch of songs, but it can sing and not have to be a song." Look at *Hamilton*—that advice bore fruit in a huge way. You don't just throw a song at every moment. Sometimes people sing, but it doesn't have to be an ABAB chorus. So, those were nuggets that my friend's dad gave me, and then, when I met Sondheim later—this is later, with *In the Heights*—I told him about that *West Side Story* lunch meeting, and he said, "Oh, that's the one where I sang the Prologue lyrics."

Judd: Incredible that he remembers that. He's a steel trap.

Lin-Manuel: Insane mind. He was one of the first people I told about *Hamilton*, because he asked what I was working on next. At that point, I just had the one song, and he threw his head back and laughed and said, "That is perfect. No one will expect that from you." And that laugh was enough to power three years of writing.

Judd: I had that once, when I was starting out. I introduced Jerry Seinfeld at the Improv. I was the emcee, and you try to slip in a couple of jokes before you bring him on, and he came onstage. He just looked over at me and went, "That was funny." And I knew he doesn't give that up for people. Two years on "That's funny."

Lin-Manuel: It's the way writers talk about living high off a personal note on a rejection letter.

Judd: What about having the movie out there now? In the last month, more people have seen *Hamilton* than have seen it in all the time since it came out. Suddenly, millions and millions of people seeing it.

Lin-Manuel: It's great. I mean, it's a weird déjà vu. Everything is louder—the people who love it love it; the people who hate it hate it. What I'm most grateful for is that one of the biggest digs against *Hamilton* was that it was so hard to get to see it—even though we grew five companies as fast as we could out of a desire for people to see it—but now that's gone. The person who bragged, "I saw the original cast!" well, so did this guy for six ninety-nine.

Judd: I thought they did an amazing job with it, as someone who's seen it a lot. And I really enjoyed watching the performances up close, to see your acting and Leslie [Odom, Jr.]'s acting—tight.

Lin-Manuel: There's a reason all of them have gone on to become movie stars. They are comfortable with the stage, and they're comfortable with the cameras an inch away. It's the same performance. That's just a testament to how incredible that original company was. They really were. But also Tommy [Kail, the director of the filmed version of *Hamilton*] had four years. He would edit it, and then put it in a drawer for a year, and then look at it again. We had the foresight to make it ourselves and finance it ourselves at the last minute, before the principals started to leave.

Judd: People never understand how hard it is to decide when to be tight and when to be wider, when editing something like that.

Lin-Manuel: There are some sections of that where we are so fucking sweaty, where we'd joke about the gift of going wide. I was like, "Thank you for going wide in that moment, Tommy, because I'm covered in sweat and I have the weirdest look on my face."

Judd: "Where's the CGI sweat-removal guy?" The show came out during such a political moment. Suddenly, the world had changed, and everyone is looking for new ways to interpret work and decide if it fits what they think is appropriate. But I saw one interview you did where you said they didn't talk about slavery that much in the musical because they didn't talk about slavery enough back then. Like, "I'd be lying if I put it in there."

Lin-Manuel: I wrote that third cabinet battle and put it on the mixtape. It was incredibly cathartic to write Hamilton being like, "Washington, you motherfucker." I had to write it, because I was struggling with it. But then you get to the end of the song, and it's like, *None of these guys are doing enough.* Can we afford four minutes that might make the audience feel better but [that] doesn't move the story and doesn't really accurately reflect any debate that these guys were having about this, because they literally put a provision in the Constitution saying we're not discussing slavery till 1808? So, it was something, like so many things in the show—what do you put into two and half hours of a musical?

Judd: Because you're saying, *Do I change the vibe of this to be really disappointed in these people?*

Lin-Manuel: It's the live ammo of playing with real lives, right? I don't think Hamilton comes off as a saint in our show. Pretty relentless and flawed motherfucker, but when it comes to that question, specifically of slavery, none of them did enough. So, how much time can we meaningfully spend on it when there's no other boot that drops? The weird thing about the show is that because it deals with the origins of our country, people who are rah-rah about our country are rah-rah about the show, and people who go, "We've never been represented," go, "I'm represented." The big thesis, if there is any, is that when it comes to talking about America itself, it's the same contradictions. We're having the same fucking fights, and that can be a source of comfort, or that can be a source of dismay, depending on your mood that day.

Judd: There was an Obama-era sense of change: *This is getting better.* Then, suddenly, someone ripped it all away and revealed, *It's fucked.*

Lin-Manuel: I think a lot of people who wrote about the show said, "This is the Obama-era show." There's a Black president here, and there's a Black president onstage, very one-to-one. I was as stunned and depressed by Trump's election in 2016 as anybody else. I saw this show go from the show that the president likes to the show that the president attacks. Then people came out to support the show because Trump hates the show, but also the death threats. Weirdly, the show contains that. Hamilton comes to power; he falls from power. He's outlived by all his enemies—they all become president."*

Judd: There's a line that I felt appropriately summed up this entire debate: that the country is a "work-in-progress."

Lin-Manuel: That's the big thesis. I think it's in the end of act one, where they say the Constitution is a mess, and it's full of contradictions, and it needs amendments. The ideals have never been enacted. Life, liberty, and the pursuit of happiness has never been true for all Americans, ever. When the thesis is ancient, unchanged from the 1700s until now, it's gonna resonate. Different things are gonna pop. The Trump/King George thing—"I will kill your friends and family to remind you of my love"—is a terrifyingly resonant line from the guy saying, "Maybe herd immunity is not so bad."

* Except Burr

Judd: What is your daily writing routine? How do you carve out your time, and where do you do it, and how do you get focused?

Lin-Manuel: I'm pretty deadline-based. I wrote those graduation speeches the night before. That's one of the benefits of working with Tommy [Kail]: He just sets a meeting every week. So, if the meetings are on Friday, I'm writing Thursday night. The tricky thing is carving out time. The work-life balance is a universal thing. My parents were both workaholics, so I want to be as present as possible. Yet, the thing you learned when you grew up—you're like, *Oh, my dad loved his job.* He wasn't like, "I wish I could be home with my kids all the time." He really *likes* his job.

Judd: There's a certain guilt for enjoying your work. Because if you come home and go, "This was the best day of my life!" your family's like, "We're here."

Lin-Manuel: You cracked it nicely: You made movies with your family.

Judd: We've enjoyed doing that. And that was part of it. I needed the collaborator with Leslie [Mann], so we could both go deep and talk about each other from a different point of view. But also, we had something to think about together for years.

Lin-Manuel: Most people just get a house.

LULU WANG

August 2020

Judd: What do you do to let go and try to access your creativity during the pandemic?

Lulu: Gardening has been helping, because it allows me to be present in a moment and try not to think about all the things we can't do. I try reading books. I don't know if you are dealing with this, but I signed up for a bunch of projects before the pandemic hit, and now I have to execute them. But when I go to execute them, I'm like, *Does anyone care about this?* All the drama that was interesting before feels completely out of context. I've had to find ways to reassess or reposition those narratives so that they're relevant without making them about COVID.

Judd: I have always had trouble believing that anybody cared about anything I had to say, but right now, with everything that's been going on, it's especially easy to go, *Does anybody want to see this? Is this what we should be talking about right now?* But then, at night, we turn on the TV, and we spend forty minutes trying to find the right show or movie. I realize that people must still need that stuff, because I'm watching *90-Day Fiancé* for the third time today.

Lulu: I just finished watching *Indian Matchmaking,* which I binged in about two and a half days. And I thought it was great. Some people will criticize it and say that it might be playing into stereotypes about Indian culture, but I have friends who live that reality, and it is interesting coming from a more traditional culture. Chinese culture is very different, but still, I see why you might have to think practically and honestly rather than just sentimentally about your life choices. It's like, yes, we have to talk about money, we have to talk about class, we have to talk about colorism. What does the world value? How does that position you in the world? We can pretend that romance is just romance. But the show plays with that. And also it's just really fun.

Judd: I feel like people have a much bigger hunger to see those stories like *The Farewell* than the studios want to acknowledge. There's always been a bias in how studios pick projects, what they think will make money. Was it hard to get financing?

Lulu: Very hard. It's funny to answer this question now, because I think that our culture has definitely shifted since the pandemic. This is a global pandemic; we're looking at the world as a global culture and how we're dealing with it *as* the world. Even before the pandemic, I think that Hollywood has shifted directions. But when I was trying to get financing for *The Farewell,* between 2015 to 2018, all of the studios kept comparing it to either *My Big Fat Greek Wedding* or *The Joy Luck Club.* Of course, those are the only films those studios could compare it to because that's all most people knew of ethnic comedy. So, I got a lot of notes along the lines of, "Maybe somebody would give you more if you did X, Y, and Z," trying to push it in a different direction. It wasn't until I did an episode of *This American Life* and really grounded that story in reality that producers responded to it.

Judd: You had a script for *The Farewell* before *This American Life*?

Lulu: I have so many versions of the script. Before going on *This American Life,* I had some version of the movie that we saw, but it had been through so many iterations because of the influence that I got from the outside, where people kept saying, "Can you make it broader? Can Billi have a white American boyfriend that she brings home? Can she be the bride?" I would try these things because, as a filmmaker, you think, *Maybe they're right.* And it's like you said: We already struggle with that doubt of *Who cares about what I have to say?* But when I wanted to make *The Farewell,* people saw this script for a movie about an eighty-year-old grandma, who's Chinese, and were like, "What are the stakes? She's eighty. So, she has cancer. She's gonna die at some point." As if we don't all have grandmas or somebody older who we love, right? And the script was bilingual, which was another issue. I tried to write that studio-friendly version of the script, but it just didn't click. It was a compromise between my vision and theirs, so it was neither here nor there. I had to just scrap all of those versions and start from the beginning.

Judd: How did the *This American Life* piece happen?

Lulu: Neil Drumming is a producer at *This American Life,* and he was just about to start that job when we met. He's a filmmaker as well, and we met at this film festival in New York, where I was screening my short film *Touch.* He said to me that he saw his role at *This American Life,* as one of the few people of color, to bring underrepresented voices and stories that we haven't heard before. He said, "Do you have any stories that Hollywood is not letting you tell? Can you bring that to me?" And obviously, I had been pitching this film about my grandma for years, and nobody would let me make it. I immediately thought it would be perfect for *This American Life,* because I had even toyed with the idea of writing it as a short story and sending it to *The New Yorker,* so I had a very rough draft of that and sent it over, and that's how it got set up.

Judd: Did the process of crafting the radio version of the story help you find its tone?

Lulu: Absolutely, because it's a fact-based show, so you can't make stuff up. Normally, you walk into a room to pitch a movie, and immediately you're trying to make it more dramatic and more interesting. But with *This American Life*, it's like, "Okay, what happened? And how did that make you feel? And then what did your mom say? And then what did she do?" There were certain questions that they asked, and I said, "I actually don't know why she said that. Let's go talk to her." So, we interviewed her. Neil and I flew to Atlanta, where my parents live, and we spent a weekend with them and interviewed them. And those pieces of that interview ended up in the show. We interviewed my great aunt, who was the instigator of the lie about my grandma's diagnosis, and allowed her to have a voice. You saw all these different perspectives. And we could argue about how I felt, and: "How did you feel back then? Did you think that I was a threat to telling her?" The process was all about finding the drama in what exists, finding the shape, finding the main character. Finding the narrative drive without making something up is a really great exercise, because you're shaping it rather than resorting to easy answers. We don't want the easy solution. We're trying to get to some exploration of some truth.

Judd: There are so many different people and voices that you have to contend with during the process of making a movie, and sometimes that can make you lose sight of that sense of exploration.

Lulu: I got really lucky having the experience at *This American Life*, where it was all about protecting the story, protecting what I wanted. And then meeting producer Chris Weitz, who in the first meeting that we had said, "I see my role as the person who's going to protect your voice from whoever finances the movie." I think a lot of filmmakers wonder, *How do I know that this is going to be a company that* *is going to protect my voice if I don't get final cut?* So, Chris actually said to me, "I will fight so that we all share creative control." And we all shared final cut.

Judd: That's a very hard thing to get, and it really is everything. It reduces your level of terror, because you think, *No one is allowed to make me screw this up.*

Lulu: Totally. And in the end, no one had to use that clause. How to protect one's vision is the question I get the most from young filmmakers. I remember hearing Ava DuVernay give a keynote speech many years ago, where she talked about something she called "the cloak of desperation," and how she realized that she was wearing a cloak of desperation whenever she would walk into pitch meetings, and it stinks from a mile away. Nobody's going to want to work with you. But how do you remove that cloak when you actually *are* desperate to get a movie made? For me, yes, it's important to remove that cloak of desperation when you're pitching, but then, once you get the yes, once you have people who are interested in working with you, you have to ask yourself, *Is every yes a good yes?* When you're desperate, both to make money to pay the rent and also to move your career forward, how can you say no to an opportunity? I think people will often rush into these partnerships without really vetting them beforehand. They feel like *they're* the one being vetted. *Oh my God, somebody said yes and was willing to give me money. I'll do anything.* But that can be tricky, because if you get into a situation where it ends up not being your voice, and your name is on it, then what? Where do you go from there, if it's not representative of what you want to make?

Judd: I remember when we set up *Freaks and Geeks* at NBC, at the time there was no head of NBC. That person had just stepped down. The higher-up person, who wasn't as creatively involved, green-lit the show. In the middle of us working on it, NBC hired a new head, who didn't really get what we were doing. So, when notes would come down, we were always like, *Do you take notes from someone who isn't even excited about it?* Years later, we did a documentary about the show, and they interviewed that person, and even after all the acclaim for the show, he *still* said he thinks he was right. I thought that was funny. How do you avoid people who ultimately are going to intrude and say, "I don't like this casting," or, "Add this person to it"?

Lulu: Intrusion is possible at every step. I was just talking to a friend about this, who had been trying to get her film made for so many years, and the financers didn't let her do the casting or have a say in who was controlling the casting. I have another friend who went through this with his first feature film, where they wouldn't let him hire the department heads. He couldn't bring his own DP [director of photography], and it's his first feature film. I can't imagine making *The Farewell* without my team, because that's who you turn to when everyone is doubting your creative vision.

Judd: It took me decades to find the people who understand what I do. In the beginning, you don't always have that luxury. *The Big Sick* was a five-million-dollar movie, and a lot of that had to do with the fact that we really wanted a partner that would let us make the movie that Kumail and [screenwriter] Emily [V. Gordon] and [director] Michael Showalter wanted to make. And Film Nation were great partners, because they believed in the team and let us make the film. Most of our other movies cost anywhere from twenty to forty million, so that was the concession that had to be made.

Lulu: *The Farewell* was supposed to be a one-point-five-million-dollar movie, because I think there's sort of this unfounded belief that it's cheaper to shoot in China. But we ended up making it for three million, which is a pretty substantial budget for an indie film. I'm curious: Do you see your role more and more as one that shepherds newer voices and protects them—sort of in the way that Chris did for me in *The Farewell*?

Judd: On some level, I felt like my early years were difficult for reasons similar to what you've described. I didn't have that productive collaboration most of the time. So, I think it's great to work with someone who's just getting started, and save them from the pain I had. I want to save you from everything that broke my heart. I don't want you to even know how brutal this business can be. I want you to be clear-headed, so that all your energy is going into your creativity. When I met Lena Dunham, when we were starting *Girls*, the first thing I said is, "I want you to know you have final say on everything with the show." I wanted her to feel fully empowered. I think that everything comes out better when you do that, because when people get watered down, it gets weird.

Lulu: I think one of the best questions that I've ever been asked was just, "Why is this important to you?" My editor and I work this way, where he'll make me defend scenes and frames. He'll ask me, "Why do you want this to be forty frames instead of three? Why can't we just get out of this moment?" And if I'm like, "Because it's pretty," then that's not enough of a defense. When I worked with Chris [Weitz], it was never like, "This sucks, why don't you just take it out?" You have to assume that the creative put it there for a reason. That reason may not be coming across, or maybe the execution isn't working, but it's worthwhile to dig and find out why it's there. And you might land somewhere really unexpected, and come up with a better solution of how to communicate this idea. Chris was often asking me that, and just being able to talk out loud about it made what I was trying to do clearer to me, even if it wasn't working on the page. I don't think most people experience that kind of creative collaboration during development. It's often just like, "We don't like this, can you remove it?"

Judd: Can you talk a little about why this particular story was so important to you?

Lulu: After I made my first feature, *Posthumous,* I was really focused on making my next movie something that I could stand behind and say, "Yes, this represents my voice." I love to tell stories in my daily life—when I talk to friends and people I feel comfortable with, I have a particular sensibility, where it's darkness and humor, all combined. I wanted to learn this skill of putting *that* into a film, which is really a lot of different elements. It's about putting it on the script so people can read it and get *that.* It's putting it on the screen through camerawork and lighting, and then it's casting, and then it's working with your actors to find that right balance of not being too big, but not being too little. When this story happened in my real life, and I told my friends about it, it was like, "Oh, this is so classic Lulu. This is such a classic thing that would happen to your crazy family." In telling the story over cocktails, people would be laughing, people would be crying—so, I knew I had a good story. The challenge for me as a filmmaker is, *How do I get that into a film?* And if I can do that successfully, then it's going to work, because I know that it's working. The story itself isn't the problem.

Judd: Did you feel like it was important that your way of looking at the world would get across to the viewer?

Lulu: It kept me up at night. Since I had already made my first feature, and I knew that I wasn't going to get that many more opportunities to really establish my voice and show what I could do, I felt like even if I had to make this movie for very little money, it had to be a film that I could completely control creatively, so I could really balance the tone that I wanted. I would describe my vision to people where they're like, "Is this funny or is it sad?" I'm like, "It's both, just like life." And they're like, "Well, do you want the audience to cry or laugh?" I'm like, "Both. I want them to be laughing as they're sobbing, because that's how I felt through this entire wedding, funeral, reunion, goodbye, whatever."

Judd: I had the most joyful experience watching the movie. I just thought, *This is everything I love about movies.* This is a way of presenting humanity that I so related to. And we had a history, which I didn't really remember, which is that that you worked on *Pineapple Express* briefly?

Lulu: And you fired me.

Judd: Well, not me; another person fired you. We won't call them out. What happened?

Lulu: *Pineapple Express* was my second job in the industry ever, and I was a terrible assistant. I didn't know how to make coffee, and ultimately, I didn't understand studio hierarchy. David Gordon Green was the director, and he comes from the indie world. So, he and I were just always like, "Let me see your film. Let me do this. Let me do that. And let me help you." That's probably not what you're supposed to do on a studio set. Lots of lines were crossed as far as the hierarchy. But David was incredibly supportive, and that was one of the great things that came out of that experience, where he said, "If you want to be a filmmaker, don't work on a film set. Get the experience, and then go and figure out your story. Because if you do this for ten years, you're not going to have any stories to tell." He worked as a janitor and worked like three different day jobs and then lived under somebody's stairwell and wrote *George Washington.* That was actually his advice to me. He said that it was okay if I was a bad assistant and didn't want to work on a set. So, I left and started writing scripts. And then, right before I went off to shoot *Posthumous,* I saw you at an award ceremony, and I said, "Hey, Judd, you guys fired me. But guess what? I'm about to go make my first film."

Judd: And I think I said that to get fired was the best thing that ever happened to you.

Lulu: You said, "Congratulations, that's a great badge of honor."

Judd: That's a funny thing about the business. These moments that feel so terrible can spin you off into a completely different journey. I remember, when I was at USC, John Milius came and spoke, and he just said to the cinema class, "Quit. Quit college right now. Go live your life. Otherwise, you're going to have nothing to write about." And that's hard advice.

Lulu: When I came to L.A., my parents were so terrified. They were like, "You don't know a single person in the industry. We have no money. We can't help you. How are you going to do this?" And I didn't go to film school, so it felt like the question was: How do you break in? It's a legitimate question; you have to find a way to break in. I thought I broke in by being on that set, but I wasn't there in the capacity that I wanted to be. So, now I think, anytime that you're learning or gathering stories, great. There's a lot of different ways to sustain a living while you're able to write. And set life is really hard. I had done another movie before I worked on the set of *Rush Hour* 3, so I went from one movie to another, and it was, like, sixteen-hour days. I was just exhausted and wondered, *When am I ever going to have time to be creative or be a writer and have stories to tell?*

Judd: I think when you have those experiences—like when you were talking to David Gordon Green and he's excited for you—it makes you go, *Oh I can get in this club. I can figure this out.*

Lulu: I think most people know a novelist or a journalist, but not many people know directors. There's something about directing that feels like it's put on a pedestal and it's this inaccessible thing. Particularly for me and my parents, it was like, *There's nobody that looks like me doing that.* So, that's like a whole other step. When I met David Gordon Green, it meant so much to me that he's like, "My assistant said you made a short film and it's pretty good. Can I watch it?" And I'm like, "Oh, my God, this is the coolest thing." So, I just went up to Video Village. It was like, "Here's a DVD."

Judd: And then . . . ?

Lulu: I got fired.

MARGARET CHO

August 2020

Judd: Did you ever do that stand-up show *The Half Hour Comedy Hour*?

Margaret: Yeah, I remember Janeane Garofalo couldn't take the microphone out of the stand, because she didn't remember how to. So, she was just holding it and walking around with it, sort of like it's a compass or something. It was just so hard to take the mic out of the stand.

Judd: That show was a big deal. I was living with Adam Sandler at the time, in the Valley. I lay out in the sun and got a tan for it. I've never been tan in anything, ever. And my set was so stupid and pointless.

Margaret: I noticed that our voices are very different now. The way that we speak is very different.

Judd: Yes, I had a Long Island accent back then. It's a little shocking. I remember starting out at a bunch of comedy clubs in Long Island—Chuckles in Mineola, Governor's in Levittown, and the East Side Comedy Club in Huntington, which was one of the first clubs on Long Island. I washed dishes there in high school because I wanted to see comedy. But then I realized, *I'm in the kitchen, I can't see anything*. Then I became a busboy, so I could be in the room. And that's where Rosie O'Donnell was starting out, and Eddie Murphy still came in a few times. He was twenty-one years old and exploding the comedy scene with his brilliance. What club did you get your start in?

Margaret: Probably the Holy City Zoo in San Francisco. I lived across the street from it so I could emcee there. I would go there every night after I would do shows everywhere else, and just watch everyone. And I could do a set there anytime anybody dropped out. It was really fun, too, because that was the one club that when we were all young, everybody lived close by. So, one block away was the apartment where Patton Oswalt and Blaine Capatch and Brian Posehn lived. And then, on the corner, was the Toy Boat café, where Jeff Garlin and Robin Williams would always stop by. I think Ron Lynch lived about ten blocks away, in a house where Alex Reid lived at first, and then it was Dana Gould, and then Jim Earl also lived there—all of these comics lived there at some point. Did you ever live in one of those houses?

Judd: I used to visit one of those houses deep in the Valley when I was an eighteen-year-old at USC. The house was a total crash pad, and you'd go there, and Joel Hodgson would be there, or Rich Hall. There was an amazing crew of hilarious people there, and I couldn't believe they would let me hang out. I was just a nerd wanting to be a comic. I used to host at the Improv, but it was like Ellen [DeGeneres] and Paula Poundstone and Leno and Seinfeld and [Paul] Reiser. It was star-studded and terrifying. And then you would hear about San Francisco, and it always sounded way more creative and fun. But I never spent much time up there. I just remember opening up for Jim Carrey at Cobb's, when he was on *In Living Color.*

Margaret: I was there for that. He was so great.

Judd: That was before he got really big, and even *In Living Color* had only been on a few months, and he just started doing the road a little bit. But that scene in San Francisco—I was very jealous of that scene. It seemed mysterious at the time, and now I'm friends with so many people who started there. It must have been amazing to have landed there at that moment.

Margaret: We were just doing drugs. We were just stupid and were doing stupid open mics. What I loved about it was, in the beginning, the Other I was still open, which was the really good club. You'd get to go see Paula Poundstone there, and she would do these shows where she wouldn't really do any jokes. She would just fuck around with the audience the whole time, which is so funny and so crazy. She still does that. And that, I think, was amazing. Or you could be at the Zoo and watch Jeremy Kramer and Robin Williams on one side of the stage making fun of Perry Kurtz trying to do a set on the other side of the stage. The best part of comedy was before any comics were tied to any kind of family obligations, before everybody was married or had kids. We could spend all of our time watching each other and making fun of each other. That was a good era for comedy, because nobody was really successful or anything. After a certain amount of time, people start to get successful, and then there's a real sense of bitterness that creeps in. And success is actually pretty meaningless in the end. When you look at how much it affects things, and how it affects you inside, it's weird. Also, the people who are really talented often never get what's due. Some of the people I thought were the funniest never quite achieved the success I thought that they would. Or they didn't want to. And that's fine.

Judd: Because there's talent and there's ambition, and not everybody has every part of it. Some just get the business side of things, while other people are geniuses, but they have no idea how to interact with the business side of comedy.

Margaret: I mean, everybody has a particular genius, and there's very few that have everything. But there are some people that are always my perennial favorites, that I love to watch. I always love Andy Dick. I love him. He always makes me laugh, even really mundane, stupid things like hanging up a payphone.

Judd: Someone like Andy is a good example, because he's also been in his share of trouble. You feel for them, because you know their story, but as we get older, there seems to be more and more of those situations, especially in this era when the MeToo movement has revealed so much about people, people you've known forever, and you're like, *How do I file this? What does my relationship with them become in the aftermath of their transgressions?*

Margaret: There are a lot more opportunities for bad behavior to be witnessed now. Before, we didn't have smartphones, so we didn't have as much accountability. The only time anybody would get in trouble for anything is if it was reported, or you got arrested or something like that. Now it's constant accountability for everything, which is better—it's safer for people. At the same time, if you are going through a hard time and you want to talk about it, going public with that kind of personal difficulty is now seen as a new kind of strength. Our society values a whole different set of strengths, where bravery is now about opening up. Vulnerability becomes very powerful in this era of accountability. It's a different landscape from the hypermasculine world of the nineties. The comedy scene that you and I came up in is very different from what we're looking at today.

Judd: So much of what is happening now is stuff that you've been talking about for decades: diversity, MeToo, childhood sexual abuse. This is stuff that you started hitting head-on, way before other people were talking about it.

Margaret: People are starting to be more aware of these issues, but you also want people to find their way through it and find a purposeful way to talk about it, because I don't have all the answers. People think that I'm the expert because I've been vocal about these issues in the past. I was interviewing this author about a traumatic experience, for example, and it was really hard, and I felt like I didn't do the right thing. When I talk about sexual trauma with people, I feel like I should be equipped to do it in the right way. But I'm not sometimes, just like everyone else.

Judd: Part of the problem is generational. When we grew up, no one talked about anything. But I look at my kids, and I see all their friends, and they're very open about all their pain, all their trauma. I think about all the people I went to high school with in the eighties and how *no one* talked about their issues. We might have talked about our parents getting divorced, but there wasn't one person who came out or talked about their depression or their eating disorders. It was a very different era.

Margaret: Everything was really shut down. There was that movie *Ordinary People*, with Timothy Hutton and Mary Tyler Moore, and it's all about how they can't talk about anything. There's one point [when] Timothy Hutton goes and hugs Mary Tyler Moore, and she's just so brittle, it's like she's going to break. That's our generation: Nobody can talk about anything.

Judd: Why do you think you were able to make the leap to being an open, expressive, creative person? When did you realize that comedy was a place where you could find your voice?

Margaret: I've always just really loved the art form. And I got lucky because my dad is a comedy and a movie fan, so he would let me watch movies that I probably shouldn't have seen, like *Jaws*. We also saw *A Clockwork Orange* together, which is very adult. We also loved movies like *Blazing Saddles* and *Young Frankenstein*—all the Mel Brooks movies, which were just hugely important to me.

Judd: It sounds like your family exposed you to all sorts of good stuff.

Margaret: They were big laughers. They didn't approve of the Three Stooges, though; they were too violent. But my parents were, overall, very permissive about television, because they weren't home a lot, so they were glad that I could be entertained by something. We got a VCR pretty early on, and we would watch Richard Pryor, which was also very adult for a kid to watch. I got to watch *SNL*, and Joan Rivers hosted one week, and that changed everything, because I wanted to be a comedian after I saw her. Watching Andy Kaufman and Steve Martin host *SNL* was also so influential to me, and they were the comics who made me want to be a comedian. I was obsessed with *SCTV* and *SNL*. Really, really obsessed with *SCTV* more than anything, and mostly Eugene Levy.

Judd: I'm still obsessed with Eugene Levy.

Margaret: Me, too. So, when I started doing comedy, it was a very natural thing, and I just never thought to stop.

Judd: You also starred in your own sitcom, *All-American Girl.*

Margaret: That was an interesting experience. I'm glad that I went through it, and it would be interesting to try it again, even though I don't know exactly what that would look like now. I like the format of, like, multi-cams. I like the tradition of it—I love an old-school Norman Lear–style show. I like the audience, the live energy. It's really special. There's a real science to making it work, like trying to figure out the right combination of people and finding the right network. But it also depends on the context, the moment in history, that would allow you to successfully execute your vision. Even though the sitcom has reemerged in recent years, there's still something traditional about it that I think is ready for true reinvention, where it can be fresh, but at the same time, very traditional. I like *Taxi* because *Taxi* had a film look to it, but it still was a multi-cam, so there was a melding of formats, and there was also a melancholy as well. I'm not sure what it is, but I think it has something to do with the immigrant story of love.

Judd: It's Judd Hirsch's existentialism. It has to do with the things that the characters are not getting from their lives. They drive other people around, but they don't go anywhere themselves. We could update that to Uber drivers, but Uber drivers are not centered anywhere.

Margaret: It's like, what do we do when we don't do anything? Where do we go when we don't go anywhere?

Judd: Where do you feel like you stand now, in terms of what you're doing and what you want to be doing?

Margaret: I've always liked the way that Greg Proops would frame it. He said that I was going to be a lot like Ella Fitzgerald: Somebody who gets better with age. Somebody you'd go and see at the Venetian on a night out because they're a class act to go see.

Judd: When you look back at all your sets over the years, how do you see your comedy evolving?

Margaret: I think I hit a high point around 2000. I was really great in 2003, and then it's gone up and down since then. Sometimes, you're like, *Oh, my God, I was amazing.* Or, sometimes, I'll go back and look at my past work, and although it was great, I'll still think, *Oh, that was terrible.* I haven't done a show since the beginning of March, so that's weird. I don't know about you, but if I don't do a show every week or so, I get really freaked out.

Judd: I didn't do stand-up for twenty-two years, and then I started doing it again in 2014. I realized I really missed it, because this is the fun part of comedy, not sitting in the editing room all day long with my editor for years. All the fun is that interaction with people.

Margaret: That energy that you get from performance is very vital, and I didn't realize how much I got from it, because it was such a part of my daily life. It's like working out. I didn't realize how much I missed going to the gym—which is unfortunate, because I complain about it all the time.

Judd: When people talk about how much your work means to them, what do they say to you?

Margaret: It's different for different people. But it's mostly that it was the first time that they've seen somebody who looks like them talk about things they understood, that they've personally seen the experiences I talked about. That's really meaningful. Other Asian American comedians say that I inspired them to do comedy, which is really awesome.

Judd: Because you didn't have that person as you were coming up?

Margaret: I did, in a sense, because I had people like Joan Rivers, who, even though she's not Asian, is still somebody I looked up to and was like, *I want to be like that.* So, I did have somebody that I could really admire. But the fact that there are other Asian comedians who really look to me for that, I would say that's my greatest achievement.

Judd: I just thought whoever is funny is funny. I didn't really have any thought about representation. Only when I started working with people like Lena Dunham did I realize how meaningful it was for people to see her on television. You don't often see a woman who is so comfortable with every aspect of herself, comfortable with herself sexually, and who's a writer, and a director, and a producer. There are other people who've been able to break down that wall, as I saw when I worked with Kumail Nanjiani on *The Big Sick.* I don't think I put much thought into it, other than, like, *Kumail's hilarious.* It was almost after the fact that you realize the significance of a movie or a show that breaks boundaries in terms of what's represented in Hollywood.

Margaret: It's that lack of visibility which is the hardest thing to even quantify. When the problem is invisibility, it doesn't even come to mind as discrimination, because it's not even there, so it's hard to feel it.

Judd: I remember, when we were trying to sell *The Big Sick*—we worked on it for years, the script was great, but it was hard to get someone to finance it. Most studios didn't believe it would sell to the masses, but it did. They were stuck in an old way of thinking.

Margaret: There's a deep-seated racism that is not perceived as racism. It's this idea that if it's only about a certain race of people, then it's only applicable to that particular race or that niche audience. But that's not true, because we all want to see stories of all kinds.

Judd: Or the idea that men won't go to a movie about women. But it's not true. I know from working on *Bridesmaids,* where maybe fifty-five percent of the viewers were women—it wasn't that skewed.

Margaret: All we want to see are good movies, and nobody really cares about what it is or who it is. Race, gender, sexuality—all of those things matter less than the quality of the stories being told and how well they're being told.

Judd: Do you consider yourself political when it comes to these things?

Margaret: I think it's about inclusion. I think it's about seeing ourselves in the way that we are in the world. It's fairness, it's equality in a very plain way. It's not so much political for me, although it's seen as a political thing by others. It's more important than ever because of the way that COVID-19 has caused this surge of racism toward Asian Americans, but in general, I just want to make it where we can tell our stories or see ourselves in the same way that everybody else does.

Judd: Was there a comedian who inspired you?

Margaret: Greg Proops—nobody is better. He is so funny, and he's always been that funny and smart. His mind works in a way that I still can't really figure out. I love Patton Oswalt. I loved Mitch Hedberg, and loved working with him. He was really special. Paula Poundstone, of course. She's probably my favorite.

Judd: What's the history of your love affair with tattoos?

Margaret: Growing up, my parents owned a gay bookstore, and all of the people that worked at my parents' bookstore had full-body tattoos from Ed Hardy, who made the famous T-shirts that are worn by the *Jersey Shore* people. They all were getting full-body tattoos in the eighties. So, when I was a kid, I knew that was going to be my destiny. When I was in my thirties, I went to get my first Ed Hardy: very large stomach and back tattoos. That was the beginning, but I knew that I was going to get my full body tattooed eventually. That was the plan from when I was a kid. I hadn't gotten around to it till my thirties because I thought I was going to be an actor. But now I'm almost completely tattooed.

Judd: How does it feel now that you're almost done?

Margaret: I don't think I'm going to get any more, because there are enough now that I could still probably cover them if I'm in a suit or something. That's probably good enough. If you have them all the way up to your neck and your wrist, people just know you have tattoos. You can't really hide them. I want to try to maybe hide them sometimes.

Judd: How did your family come to own a gay bookstore?

Margaret: They wanted to have a bookstore like City Lights, because my father is an author. In the seventies, one became available that he could buy, and it happened to be a gay bookstore. So, we had a gay bookstore in the seventies, and that's where I grew up. It was a great place to grow up and a great place to emerge from. There was a gay comedy club upstairs from the gay bookstore, called the Rose and Pistol. I did some of my first sets there.

Judd: From those sets above your parents' store until now, how have you seen the comedy scene change over the course of your career?

Margaret: I think comedy now is so much more sophisticated and grounded in a truth that is more profound, and I feel like we as a generation have really elevated the entire game. It's all of us, we've had to push it all forward. There are different philosophies around it now. Even the whole idea of alternative comedy: that we could just take away microphones and do comedy without a microphone. Or without shoes on. There was this whole movement of doing sketch comedy, doing these shows, where we could be out of the construct of a comedy club. Comedy audiences are just a better judge of what's funny now, and I think it's up to us to keep that bar high.

MINDY KALING

May 2020

Mindy: I mentioned to you that I subscribed to MasterClass because I wanted to see your class. After I watched yours, since I had that subscription, I watched David Sedaris's, and I was excited to see that he talks a lot about how he works. I'm obsessed with process. I would read a book that was just about people's workday. In his master class, David Sedaris talks about how he works from, I think, ten A.M. to one P.M., every single day, seven days a week, and I thought that schedule sounded really good.

Judd: I used to be someone who wrote at night, and I loved writing from, like, ten P.M. till two in the morning, and I haven't been able to do that for twenty-two years now.

Mindy: Are you working on something right now?

Judd: I produce a lot of things that I like, to be a part of other people's writing process. But I don't very often have an idea for a screenplay I want to write. Someone once said that at some point, you mine yourself completely, and then it all turns to mining other people or your imagination.

Mindy: I loved your master class. Your anecdotes are great, but your advice is so practical, so attainable. I'm so mad that I'm forty and I'm only learning this now, which is that any great comedy story is actually a drama that you can make funny—as in, it has to have real emotional stakes for all the characters, not just the leads. Otherwise, they become bad secondary characters. Everyone has to have a story, and it has to work as a dramatic story. I would have saved myself countless, countless hours if I had known that earlier, even going back to when I was at *The Office*, approaching an episode of TV that way. I thought that was so wise.

Judd: When I worked for Shandling I just got the sense that every scene that he was either writing or approving was a gem. That was the word that kept coming into my head, like, *Oh, he's trying to create these little gems.* So, anytime we switch spaces to another character, another problem, even exposition, he's finding some way to have a great beginning, middle, and end to every moment. Making every moment special in some way.

Mindy: That has a lot to do with laziness, which no one really talks about. You'll hear a joke in a movie or a show, and it sort of seems funny, but it also seems like no one on set or while they were writing the screenplay took the time to ask if it was funny, or if it was just three quarters of the way there? In comedy, it's not about like getting things three quarters of the way there. You have to get everything one hundred percent all the time. It's backbreaking perfectionism, which is maybe why you only write movies every five years.

Judd: When I was on set, it helped me to imagine that I was in the editing room, so that I was always thinking, *If I hate this, why will I hate it?* Will I wish he had given me more joke options? Would I wish he got me a dramatic version instead of just a goofy version? And because I'm so neurotic, I usually try to give myself all of it, so in the editing room, I have options and can modulate it to my liking.

Mindy: When I watch your movies, the experience feels like you're seeing the greatest hits of the scene, like you've done the work of culling it. And in addition to being funny, your movies often feel very personal and dramatic, because I know that working with Amy Schumer and Seth Rogen and Pete Davidson on their movies, they were tapping into something that was really true for them.

Judd: Now, Mindy, we have a shared history which we never talk about. You're in *The 40-Year-Old Virgin*, and that was your first movie. How do you look back on that moment and where you were in your life at that time, way back in the early aughts?

Mindy: It feels like I had this great opportunity and I blew it, because I didn't know what it was like to be on camera. I only shot for two days, but I have two really vivid memories of that movie. One was that I was sitting across from Paul Rudd, who, for the record, is ten years older than me but now looks fifteen years *younger* than me, so *that* I don't love. But I was sitting across from Paul Rudd, and I was supposed to be talking to him, but I started looking into the camera. And I remember, at one point, you had to come over and really nicely tell me, "Hey, you can't look into the camera." And I didn't even know I had been doing it. I was just so nervous—I couldn't believe that I'd been picked to do this with all these funny people. The second memory was in Video Village, and it was you and Seth and Paul and Elizabeth Banks, and you all had such a great rapport. I didn't want to seem like I was hovering and trying to laugh along, so I sat a couple of rows back and watched you guys. I love the movie, but whenever that scene comes up, I fast-forward through it.

Judd: You scored every single time in the movie, and my memory is only of you being hilarious and great. But I guess the only thing you had done on camera before was the first season of *The Office*, which was like a half season?

Mindy: And I probably had just four or five lines on camera, so *The 40-Year-Old Virgin* was a huge experience for me. I also remember that I didn't know you're supposed to hire a stylist for the movie premiere. I had a frenemy at *The Office*, and I asked this person, "Hey, what do you wear to a premiere?" And they said to me, "Oh, just wear jeans and a T-shirt. It's L.A. so nobody really gets dressed up for these things." I was like, *Okay, cool,* because I didn't want to seem thirsty wearing a gown while everyone was dressed down. So, I showed up in a tank top and jeans with some earrings, and everyone there looked so good—they had been styled to perfection—and I was like, *I've been fucking duped by this frenemy of mine.* That also felt like a missed opportunity, and then after that, I became really into fashion.

Judd: I also did not know that you paid people to help you dress for Hollywood events, because usually the studio pays, so you don't dress like an idiot to things. But in all these early pictures, I'm wearing a collar that is sticking out over the suit, and everything is wrong about how I'm dressed. What was your path into comedy?

Mindy: I'm so inhibited compared to someone like Andy Kaufman or Robin Williams. And I think that when you're inhibited and shy, and you really care what people think about you, those people just seem incredible to you. I loved, loved watching them. I don't know if this is the way you were as a kid, but I couldn't tell the difference between watching an Albert Brooks movie and a Gilbert Gottfried stand-up special. I wasn't a snob; if you were trying to do something in comedy, it was worthy of me watching it. And I grew up in that time where Comedy Central would do random stand-up shows with little clips. I didn't have a favorite; I just loved how everyone was trying something with it. Then, as I got older, I got really into *Kids in the Hall,* to the point that I'd seen this one episode five times and written out the specific sketch, because I wanted to know why it's funny. Then that evolved into my really loving *Saturday Night Live.* Stand-up was less exciting to me, although I was still in awe of it.

Judd: I did that, too, for *Saturday Night Live,* where I would write the sketches out and try to understand why it was funny. It's a specific kind of comedy nerd that goes *that* far. I know Bill Hader also talked about recording *Saturday Night Live* on audio, to hear it and try to understand it. When did it become a job for you? When did you think, *I could have a career in this*?

Mindy: When I was a teenager, Conan's first show was really big. I remember I would tape it, and I would freeze-frame on the list of writers. I was like, *So, this is something you can do*. At that point, I think he pretty much had all guys who were writing for him, but I thought, *That must be heaven*. I didn't know what that was actually like—there weren't books that existed as they do now, telling you what that would be like as a job. I just remember the credits on *Conan*, and the credits on *SNL*. It wasn't like two people, it was like twelve, fifteen, twenty people wrote it. I thought, *Maybe I have a shot*. But this was pre-Twitter, pre-Instagram, so you couldn't just tweet at Colin Jost and be like, "How do you do what you do?"

Judd: Do you feel relieved that social media wasn't around when you were younger?

Mindy: The thing I'm relieved about is I thought I was funny, and I did have a good sense of humor, but it wasn't until I was on *The Office*, when I was around all these other funny people in a writers' room, where I realized, *Those kinds of jokes are kind of hacky, and these observations have already been made*. I was already twenty-four when I felt like I was starting to become more sophisticated. I just think that, as a confident sixteen-year-old kid who was a comedy nerd, I probably would have been tweeting Lorne Michaels really lame things, and it would have ruined my career.

Judd: And people would still be able to find them today.

Mindy: I'm so happy there's no physical evidence of me on the internet from before I'm twenty-four.

Judd: I always say to my kids, "If you want to find something mean on the internet, you're going to find it." You really need to have some discipline to not go online and look for that.

Mindy: I have a show that came out on Netflix about three weeks ago, and I think it was well reviewed, and it felt like a lot of people were watching it. It has an all-Indian cast, and I'd never done that before. I was riding this wave of all this positive feedback, and the tweets I was getting were so nice, so I just kept looking. I should have stopped looking, because I found a website that was written by a group of anonymous Indian and South Asian writers in L.A. and Hollywood, and every fifth tweet was about how much I sucked and how I don't do anything for Indian people. I was like, *I just put this show out; what are you talking about?* I spent so much emotional energy on that. I spent a night writing a rebuttal, but I realized I shouldn't tweet it because they'll never be happy. I'm forty, so I still haven't learned this lesson. I couldn't just stop at the people saying nice things. I had to look and find the criticism.

Judd: As comedians, we're always looking for the two people in the room who aren't laughing. I tell everyone I work with, twenty percent of the world hates everything. If you look at the movies that have won Best Picture for the last twenty years, I probably hate twenty percent of them. And if you search [for] "the Dalai Lama" on Twitter, twenty percent of the tweets will be hateful. No one's exempt from that hate, but it doesn't stop it from being really painful. How has working on *Never Have I Ever* been otherwise?

Mindy: It's really fun. I found that with some other comedy shows with diverse characters, a lot of times you feel like you're getting a civics lesson. Like they're putting in these diverse characters just to show that they're a woke show, and it's not actually funny and it doesn't help the story. What was cool about this show is we spent so much time casting it that we were able to find truly hilarious people. You've done this with a lot of young comedy people—maybe they didn't quite have the chops yet, but you still saw something in them. We were able to find this immensely funny cast of actors of color and then got them acting lessons and got them experience, well before we started doing the show. There wasn't the phenomenon where white characters are funny, and the characters of color have the setup lines because they couldn't find a funny young Latin actor or something like that. It took a lot of hard work, but I think that's why people are responding to it.

Judd: When we did *Freaks and Geeks,* one of the things we decided to do was to assume that all the great people didn't have agents because they didn't think they could be in show business, so we did open-call auditions. We said, "Anyone can come." We went to Vancouver and Chicago and New York and Toronto. We just let any kid show up. If we find an interesting kid, we will teach them how to act.

Mindy: *Freaks and Geeks* came up constantly when we were doing this. It's the gold standard for teen shows. They're all stars. They're all so funny and completely different. I didn't know you went to these open casting calls in Vancouver and everything. That must have taken a really long time.

Judd: I was just like, *Where are all the weird kids like me?* Well, they wouldn't have an agent. They wouldn't think they could be in show business. They wouldn't think they could act. They wouldn't think they looked like an actor or an actress. So, let's just open it up to them. But the key thing is, even though I felt like a weirdo and an outsider, I still felt represented on television; I saw people like me. So, the idea that I could get on TV seemed possible. How was it for you, not being able to see people who looked like you on television?

Mindy: This might just be a defect in my personality, but I just thought, *Even though I don't look like these white actors and actresses,*

I'll still be accepted in Hollywood. I don't know why I felt that way, but that confidence followed me through my career—the belief that sensibility and a sense of humor are much more important than the way we look. I don't know why I thought that, but I just did. I feel really lucky that I have that personality defect, because I think a lot of people don't. There are a lot of people who looked at TV and comedy at that time, who are Asian or Black, and just thought, *I really like it, I'm a big fan, but how would I explain this to my parents?* For whatever reason, with my family, they just saw my determination. They got used to the idea that that was my passion, so they got on board. But not that many people are lucky enough to have that with their parents. The one thing you've talked about, too, is how if you're not obsessed, it's not going to happen. And I was obsessed as a kid. If you're someone who just thinks that show business is kind of cool, but there are a couple other things you want to do, and you don't want to stay late, you don't want to work hard, then it's just not going to happen. There are far more people who are less talented but who are obsessed who will make it than people who are super talented but don't have the patience to put in the time.

Judd: The hardest worker has the best chance of winning. One of the things I always tell people is that most writing in Hollywood is terrible. It's a funny thing about the industry, which is that there might be a hundred thousand people trying to get the writing jobs, but there's still probably only about eighty people who are actually great. And if you worked really hard to be one of those eighty, you don't have to worry about getting work. It's so obvious, and there's not too many of them. Even on the greatest shows, you might have twelve writers, and maybe three of them aren't doing much.

Mindy: I can't believe you say three. I've worked on shows that people love and would look around the room and think that four people were doing all the work, and the rest are just there.

Judd: You show that in your movie *Late Night.* I was laughing at how it was cast—that all-white writers' room is so real—but also I thought, *Oh man, I'm one of those guys.* I've been in those rooms. Most talk shows didn't have a single female writer until five years ago.

Mindy: I learned so much about the late-night writers' room world. The first Black woman wasn't hired on a late-night talk show until 2016. It was on Seth's show. These are shows that are set in New York City, and they couldn't find a Black woman to write on a late-night TV show in New York City until 2016? I was lucky because, when I was in New York prepping the movie with Emma Thompson, I asked all the women on all the New York shows if they could come to the table read and tell me about their experiences. I think that the late-night rooms have an edge and a competitiveness, whereas there's a clear hierarchy in sitcom writers' rooms—there's a staff writer, a story editor, a supervising producer, and so on—so people aren't really trying to one-up each other. It's counterintuitive, but I think people do really well when you know where you are in the ladder. You know when you should be in line to get food. If you're a staff writer, you're not going to be first in line for dinner. You have to wait. And it's good. I think I do well when I know what the hierarchies are. But I think in a room where everyone's a writer, like for those late-night shows, whether you're a fifty-two-year-old guy or a twenty-two-year-old just out of college, that would feel like it'd be more of a struggle.

Judd: I also think that with a talk show staff, they're not writing anything that's emotional. As a result, it's a different kind of vibe. Because a sitcom staff is talking about emotions and feelings and love and caring, and there's none of that in a talk show.

Mindy: That is such a good point. It's all about one character, which is the host of the show, which is more likely than not a man making funny jokes. Whereas, in sitcoms, if it's a good sitcom, you learn a lesson. It's impossible on a sitcom to not have that emotional stuff come up.

In writing late-night shows, there's an emphasis on a kind of boy humor, which is really cerebral, well-worded and -crafted jokes. A lot of my friends who come from the *Lampoon*—that sort of humor is put on a high pedestal. Whereas being really in touch with your emotions, or having a character say, *Hey, what scares me? Where's my place in the world?* That stuff is considered not funny and sort of lame.

Judd: Isn't that part of the arc of what we learn over a long career? That we all get into it, and we're just trying to be funny, but we don't really know ourselves yet. We don't realize how much of comedy is about deep personal exploration.

Mindy: What I love about your movies is that they're so often about someone who is stuck at a crossroads, where they have to decide whether they're going to keep going down the path that they're already on or switch directions. A central question for your characters is *Am I going to be brave enough to try and change?* And if you talk about it like that, that doesn't sound like a comedy premise; it's a really intense drama premise.

Judd: It's funny because they say that most filmmakers or writers write the same story every time, even if they think they're doing something different. I noticed that with my work, and I'm trying to not be ashamed of it. It must be just what I want to work through, because even when I think I'm doing something so different, it ends up still being about that stuckness that you described. What has writing and telling stories revealed to you about yourself?

Mindy: It feels like I'm writing something that I cannot see, and I felt this way especially with *Late Night* and *Never Have I Ever.* I write something because I feel like I can't see it unless I do it. With *Late*

Night, I wanted to see Emma Thompson—who is one of the greatest comedy actors of all time, and gorgeous—not in a period movie, where she's playing a grieving grandmother. I wanted to see her be funny and sexy in New York City with a high-powered job. And with *Never Have I Ever,* I wanted to see a corny, dorky Indian American girl who isn't a quiet side character. So, lately, I'm writing what I want to see. But I think what you said about telling a story that will somehow heal me—that's a deeper and more honest answer, I just hadn't thought of it. So, now that's going to be my answer for *my* master class.

MORT SAHL

August 2017

Judd: How are you, Mort?

Mort: Good, man.

Judd: I watched your Periscope last night. And it was fucking hysterical.

Mort: Thank you for looking.

Judd: Oh, my gosh. You were tearing it up.

Mort: Well, we turned the corner there. You know, we've been doing it for a year. And you can feel it now.

Judd: I really enjoyed watching it. But I want to go back to the beginning with you and track your career a bit. You wanted to be a comedy writer first, and then, when that wasn't working out, you became a performer. But when you were in high school, were you interested in comedy?

Mort: No, no. You know, when I was in high school, the war was on and I was interested in—Roosevelt was the president and I wanted to be a paratrooper and I wanted to get the girl. I was in the movies. All that stuff. When I came out of the military, I didn't fit in anywhere. I liked jazz a lot and hung around the Kelly Band and eventually, when the singers would take a break, I would get up onstage. I wasn't an instant hit. Everybody wondered what I was trying to prove and it took a long time. And then I followed a girl up here to Berkeley and—romance was always in the way. She said to me, "If you can do this, we'll have a better life. If you can't, we'll have a terrible life and you'll blame me because you can't do it."

Judd: Yeah.

Mort: So she sent me over to Hungry I. It was a folk club. I got up to do it and it was a disaster for a long time. *Long* silences. Finally, I threw the suit away and got the sweater and began to talk personally, and that's when I realized there was a constituency out there that isn't heard from. I don't think it would have happened in another town.

Judd: The owner of the Hungry I believed in you even when you hadn't figured it out yet?

Mort: That was Enrique. He used to run the sound system. At first, he tried to fire me, but then he was the one who said: Take your tie off, take your coat off. And I began to go against authority. You know, McCarthy was around then. Nixon was around then.

Judd: Good targets.

Mort: Yeah. And I began to talk about the blacklist of the writers. That was the first real breakthrough.

Judd: What were the jokes?

Mort: They had just sent the ten writers to prison, Trumbo among them. And the joke was, every time the Russians put an American in jail, we put an American in jail. That was the breakthrough.

Judd: That's funny. Were there other political comedians at the time?

Mort: Not that I remember. Nobody. And that was one of my first disappointments with the Jewish people. I thought they were the guys who were gonna speak up! They didn't. They were doing what they considered commercial.

Judd: Who was the hot comedian in the clubs when you were first starting to do political comedy?

Mort: They were all guys in suits. Paul Gray. And of course, Gleason. Danny Thomas. And most of them worked what they call blue, which is the bedroom. Now it's the bathroom. So again, it was a fight. You know: "It's too intellectual. Nobody will understand it." Finally I went to New York and did the Blue Angel with Jonathan Winters, and Pat Weaver came in. He was a great man. He said, "No, everybody will understand it." I did *The Steve Allen Show* while I was there and Steve was a saint.

Judd: He supported all the great smart comedians.

Mort: The best. The best guy of all time. And then of course everybody wanted to come to the Hungary I, so I brought them all out. I brought Woody out here. I brought Cosby out here. Cosby, that great American. Who's carrying the quaaludes, you know?

Judd: I hear it was a lifetime hobby.

Mort: Oh yeah. Forever.

Judd: What do you make of, like, a guy who is almost like a pedophile priest and presented himself as this pure person?

Mort: Have you ever known any entertainers who couldn't get a date after the job?

Judd: Exactly.

Mort: *I'm in love.* The rock guys didn't have any problems finding a girl.

Judd: Well, I guess it wasn't about that.

Mort: He's about him.

Judd: Yeah.

Mort: When I went to work for Jim Garrison in New Orleans, Cosby was eating dinner in my house with servants. Eating dinner. I had gotten him the television show. I had gotten him the Playboy jazz festival. I had gotten him into the Hungry I. And he stood up and he said, "Well, where you're going, I can't go. I've got a wife and kids." And he left the food.

Judd: Because he didn't want to support your investigation into the Kennedy assassination?

Mort: Actually, nobody did. There was a tremendous break there. Everybody said I was crazy, which is easier than recognizing a national malady.

Judd: After all these years, where are your thoughts about the assassination?

Mort: Exactly where we were. You know, I was a credentialed investigator in the office and I've got a plaque here from the four DAs. It says, "To the best friend Jack Kennedy ever had." And Garrison said to me, "Too bad he'll never know it." But as I told the audience last night, the CIA killed the president. We took a few bumps along the way, and Garrison said to me, "If you go public with that, they're gonna say you're paranoid." But we had a lot of problems. They dropped LSD on me. The wheels came off my car. Garrison was chased by Cubans in the men's room of the United terminal at LAX. That's a long way from the stage of the Hungry I.

Judd: What do you think is the main piece of information that the public ignores about the Kennedy assassination?

Mort: That the president did not want to proceed in Vietnam. He fought with [Curtis] LeMay and the generals. In other words, he double-crossed them. They thought they elected a fascist.

Judd: Let me ask you a question, Mort. Do you think, when they assassinate the president, is it because on some level they think they're fighting the communists? Or is it for financial gain?

Mort: No, it's strictly buying guns. Just like Cheney did. Just like Obama. They don't care whether they win. They just want it to be perpetual. Even though it sounds absurd for a comedian to be opposing the military industrial complex, I didn't know why everybody else didn't want to.

Judd: If you were a religious leader, what would you preach? What have you learned about people and what would you say to people about how they should live their lives?

Mort: Well, you should be in love if you can possibly work it out. You shouldn't be by yourself. You should stand up for what this country is. Jefferson's America. The place that my grandfather came from Russia.

Judd: So it all comes down to—I mean even through all of the attacking of politics . . .

Mort: People using each other.

Judd: Who do you think has explored that territory well?

Mort: Jonathan Winters. He's a total individual. He was a goy, a Republican, didn't curse, but had no mercy about exposing the manipulators. A total original.

Judd: Who made you laugh the most?

Mort: Herb Shriner. Remember him?

Judd: Absolutely.

Mort: I liked Herb Shriner. I thought *The Fred Allen Show* was good. But nobody really busted me up because they all thought the audience was dumb and you had to be kind of commercial. I'm not sure the audience is dumb. I think it's a rationale for not giving them anything.

Judd: What are your favorite movies?

Mort: Hardly any now. There's nothing. First of all these guys—they're filmmakers. They're not guys like Richard Brooks, or Robert Aldridge. Look at why we won. We were the good guys. And what did we win? We won the girl. Who's the girl now? I mean it's all very pessimistic.

Judd: Did you ever hear about Bill Hicks?

Mort: Yeah, I did.

Judd: Did you enjoy any of his work?

Mort: No. I thought it was on the nose. In other words, we're noble and they're the bad guys. It was on the nose. You know, I was a great friend of Lenny's.

Judd: Lenny Bruce?

Mort: Yeah. And he's totally misinterpreted. He liked girls and jazz and dope. He said to me, "I don't know how a bright guy like you would think there's a difference between the two parties. They're all hustlers."

Judd: What did you think of Lenny Bruce's politics?

Mort: He didn't have any. I knew him very well and he had none. I thought he was far from profound. But they talk about him like he's Jesus.

Judd: What do you think that's about?

Mort: He took a chance and got crucified. But nothing he did was profound. I want to emphasize that. Nothing. He was all right. By the way, the audiences used to walk out on him. It was kind of rank. Now it's rank and it isn't funny.

Judd: Does it blow your mind a little bit that you seem to have interacted with everybody?

Mort: Well, that's the miracle. That's the miracle of America—that you can get up with an idea and you can do that.

Judd: You were friends with both Kennedy and Reagan. What were the similarities and differences between them?

Mort: Kennedy was highly intellectualized and a little bit skeptical. And he had his trouble with me 'cause he said, "You really love Adlai Stevenson. You're working here but you really love Stevenson." He was hoping eventually I'd come to love him. He was very very subtle, you know. Reagan was straight up. And he knew audiences. Before I did my show at the White House he said to me, "They're not gonna laugh. Don't get discouraged. They're gonna look at me as an authority figure and when I laugh, they will laugh. It's gonna be fine." And he had one other thing on his side: His wife really loved him. Nancy Reagan once told me that Gable said to her, "No matter how well he does at Warner Bros. or as governor, be at that door when he comes home for dinner because that's what we all dream about."

Judd: What did you think of him as a politician?

Mort: Well, the fascists had their fun. Look at Grenada. Look at the Contras.

Judd: Yeah.

Mort: The other side was doing it all: Jim Baker and the Bush side. I knew him pretty well, too. As a matter of fact, when George Bush ran, Jerry Weintraub threw a party for him in Malibu and I was the entertainment. And at the end of that show, we were waiting for the car parkers to bring the cars around. Carson and I made up, because Carson had thrown me off over the Garrison stuff and didn't talk to me all those years.

Judd: Did Carson apologize to you?

Mort: No, no, he was very withdrawn, as you remember.

Judd: But he really hurt you, though.

Mort: It was like ten years of not being able to make the rent.

Judd: Carson was another one of those guys that presented himself in a certain way but was a really dark guy.

Mort: Oh yeah. I mean, antisocial out there in Malibu. He came from game shows. Remember, he never worked live like we did.

Judd: A big drinker, right?

Mort: And everything else.

Judd: Do you think that all of those guys—like the Rat Pack, and Carson, and Jerry Lewis—were they just on a rampage of bad behavior? What would they do if there was a YouTube back then?

Mort: Lewis was crazy.

Judd: Were they a bunch of good guys or a bunch of just narcissistic lunatics?

Mort: Sinatra kept romance alive in this country for fifty years. He was talented. But when I got on the wrong side he disappeared on me, too.

Judd: And he had his problems with the Kennedys as well.

Mort: Uh, yeah. We went bananas when Jack wouldn't stay at the house. Because the old man wouldn't let him. So he went to Bing Crosby's house. And by the way, Crosby and Bob Hope split up over Kennedy.

Judd: Really? How so?

Mort: Because they were both Republicans. Crosby was a Catholic on top of it. But he's gonna vote for the Irish Catholic. So they split. So did Poitier and Belafonte. And afterward, there wasn't anybody around except me, the enemy.

Judd: Do you generally have a good feeling about people? You're pointing out all of these problems and hypocrisies, but overall: What's your feeling about human nature?

Mort: I think it's gonna be like *It's a Wonderful Life*. I think we're all gonna rally to Jimmy Stewart by the third act.

NATHAN FIELDER

January 2020

Judd: What makes you laugh?

Nathan: I laugh a lot when I'm uncomfortable. And I put a high value on comedy that gets me to laugh out loud when I'm sitting alone.

Judd: What's an example of that?

Nathan: *Curb Your Enthusiasm* was a show that consistently made me do that. Also, a lot of dumb stuff on YouTube, like, people falling and farting.

Judd: That's always the funniest.

Nathan: I know. And that's the thing: No matter what you do, you can't compete with comedy like that. Even though we had stuff we planned or wanted to do [on *Nathan for You*], we were always chasing the unquantifiable moments that would emotionally make you laugh and you don't know why. Those moments are so hard to find. I don't get that feeling with scripted things as much. You have to do a bunch of stuff and just hope they happen. I'm not really trying to make any political statement, or trying to provoke in that way.

Judd: Are the people who end up on your show generally happy with how they're presented?

Nathan: We've actually never had anyone who, after the show aired, has come back and been like, "You guys tricked me," or, "I'm upset with how this went." Their main worry is how they're going to be portrayed, but we've actually edited out the hateful stuff people have said, because we don't *want* the audience to hate them.

Judd: When I watch the show, what I tuned in to the most is the loneliness. There's a lot of material that feels like it's about your character's loneliness, or people trying to reach out and connect. So, underneath the laughs is something that's really powerful. You are captivated by it because, deep down, you hope they don't go bankrupt or fail in some way.

Nathan: The recession of 2008 was the first economic collapse I'd experienced in my lifetime. My parents had been through something like it before, but I really thought the world was going to end. I read so much about the housing crisis, and I came to the conclusion that running a successful business is about finding that legal loophole that no one has patched up yet and exploiting that for profit. When that loophole gets patched up, they'll find the new one. It made you feel like anyone who's not at these big companies that are doing this really have no chance.

Judd: Because they don't know how to do it.

Nathan: Or they're put in a place where they have no ability to win, no matter what. There are so many confusing messages, and people are telling you, "Here, you can do this. Here's a loan." Everything was based around tricking people. So, when I met these business owners, I felt that as long as what they were doing was legal and it makes money, then there's no reason not to do it. You can tell that a lot of these people don't necessarily think it's right for them, but at the same time, they realize that this is just the world that they exist in, and if they don't embrace these practices, they might be left behind. You come to see how unnatural or how disconnected from real emotions the business world is, and I think it makes it hard for people to connect, in general.

Judd: Did you find that most of the people who came to you had to be particularly gullible or ignorant? Or did you find that a range of people fell for it?

Nathan: A lot of people watch my show and think, *Oh, if I was in that situation, I would just laugh or I would say, "That's absurd."* But I don't really think that's the case. First, there's a lot of pressure when there are cameras around. And at the same time, given the right sales pitch, most people would agree to do stuff to save or make money. Then it just keeps escalating and escalating to the point that there's no way to bail.

Judd: Do they know it's candid comedy, or do they really believe that it's sincere?

Nathan: We try to avoid people who ask a lot of questions, and we try to find people who seem to be open to an experience outside of their day-to-day existence. We definitely don't say it's a comedy show when we book people or anything like that. As time goes on, people do get a sense that there's like something a little *off* about this, but also businesses become so absurd with their marketing that I was always able to justify it as something that would get attention. We walked the line between comedy and marketing.

Judd: What was the pitch for the show?

Nathan: I initially pitched this show as me being a consumer advocate. Then we turned in a draft of that version, and I don't think it worked quite as well. It's hard when you're attacking businesses, because unless you're doing all big businesses, you don't want to say anything bad about someone's small business. I just have a hard time criticizing, or punching down, that way.

Judd: When did you discover what it was?

Nathan: At some point, Comedy Central said it just didn't feel *big* enough. At first we were like, *That's so annoying. They obviously don't get it.* And then we thought, *What if we just sold people, like, poo?* We had the idea of poo frozen yogurt as almost a joke. The more we thought about that concept, though, we started to realize that that could work, and that Comedy Central was right. We had already figured out we wanted to help businesses, but then they pushed us to come up with bigger ideas that would anchor the show, and then I could still do all the more subtle, human moments that I liked. And it was great. Comedy Central saved me from poverty.

Judd: How did you develop your persona on the show?

Nathan: I first started doing this stuff with real people in Canada. I got hired to do work on a show called *This Hour Has 22 Minutes,* which is kind of like *The Daily Show,* where I was a correspondent who did these consumer advocate pieces. I noticed they would screen the show in front of a live audience. I had stuff in there that I thought was funny, but people would also laugh at stuff that I didn't intend to be jokes. There was something about how I was acting that people were finding funny. I generally have a fairly flat demeanor, and I just kind of leaned into that.

Judd: You realized that you were part of the joke.

Nathan: I was going over the top with trying to be funny, but then people were just like, "Well, you as a human are so sad and pathetic that we find *that* funny." With time, I leaned more and more into that with the show. I didn't say anything not truthful about myself. I use my real name, my real background. A lot of interactions are structured in a way where it's not awkward. When you're talking about something business-related, you can interact comfortably. But the second you start to have a personal conversation, it gets really weird, because that's not the reason those people are there. The subtext was always that this whole show is born from my desire to just be around people. I'm trying in little ways to create friendships, to see if people actually like me as a person, or if they're just there for this other stuff. People come up with extremely roundabout ways to accomplish very simple things, because no one teaches you how to be social. I got a business degree and learned all sorts of things, but no one is teaching you how to be close to other people. It's one of the saddest things to say.

Judd: I'm so interested in why this kind of comedy works. *Why am I enjoying this?* I think that's why that format interested people so much.

Nathan: The series finale of the show was this feature-length episode, almost like a movie. And there was this Bill Gates impersonator we met in the second season—a seventy-eight-year-old man who's also named Bill—and in between the times that we shot with him, he would come around the office and talk about this woman he dated when he was twenty, who he really regrets not marrying and had recently been trying to track down. That was just in the background for so long, and we were like, "Well, maybe we can incorporate this into the show in some way." Of course, we didn't know how she would react to him and what we would end up with for the episode. As things go on, you're like, *Okay, what can we do with this material? How can we adapt?* Sometimes it's not till the edit where I really realize what something's about. I would like to think I had amazing foresight, but a lot of the time we just plan broad strokes.

Judd: And that could have taken a much darker turn, or just had no ending.

Nathan: We try to think through various ways that it could play out, like, "Okay, if this happens, what's our plan? If that happens, what's our plan?" I can think through all those scenarios, but oftentimes what happens is something very different than what we expect. And my weird instinct is to feel like I planned poorly, rather than just realize that life can't be controlled.

Judd: And in the end, when he found her, she was kind to him.

Nathan: She was. I mean, she's married, and she has grandchildren. I think, in his head, Bill thought that she still wanted to be with him, and he was very much living as his twenty-year-old self, even though he's in this old-man body. I really got caught up in that whole thing while we were filming, and it also made me think about my own life, because Bill had been all about his career and prioritized his career over his personal life. He moved from Arkansas to L.A. to be an actor. That's why that relationship with the woman [had] ended. A lot of it's unclear, since I can't get a clear story of everything from him. I've tried to think a lot about what about him makes me laugh so much. He just has this rhythm and cadence that really gets me; he's almost the embodiment of something that I don't understand why it's funny, or why it's interesting.

Judd: What did he make of it afterward?

Nathan: For his whole life, he wanted to become an actor. And he never quite had a career of it. But when the episode screened, we did a big premiere with, like, fifteen hundred people, and at the end, everyone gave Bill this big standing ovation. I think he was really touched by it, and I don't know if he sees it the same way I do, but I think it brings him back to those moments—of her and him, and his regret. And I think he was happy with it.

Judd: What made you want to end the show?

Nathan: I felt like I had cornered myself into something that I couldn't really keep doing. Basically, every season of that show, I thought, *This is the last.* We just got so lucky every year. Outsiders are like, "Oh, this is great. Can you do more?" But it's very hard for an episode to work out. There needs to be a lot of things that happen, and that took a lot out of me, because I'm performing this version that's twenty percent my real self, and I had to get my personality back after each season. We started to feel the constraints of it being a show about business, where the ideas that we were most excited about as time went on were the nonbusiness ones. And if it was going to become a show that wasn't related to business at all, I was like, *Well, why keep doing it as this show?* I also wanted to end it because I had this fear I was going to screw it up.

Judd: This is the type of thing where, if you ever had an idea, you can always bring the character back.

Nathan: If I'm doing more stuff like this, I think it'll be me and some other type of environment. But I was watching your Garry Shandling documentary around the time we did the last episode, and what really resonated with me was when Garry talked about how he was always just trying to find projects that would allow him to be closer to himself. That really stuck with me. I think, over time, you start getting more comfortable as yourself when you're doing comedy, and then you home in on who you are. That was my experience with the show, where I felt that, as time went on, it was harder for me to be further from that self.

Judd: Shandling always said that it's just so hard for people to connect, to open up, and be real and love each other. He said that all stories are obstacles to love. That's why it's fascinating to hear how you didn't necessarily know that your show was pulling you toward a certain direction, and then it ends with this episode that's beautiful and compassionate toward this strange man. It becomes as universal as it ever could be, because on some level, we're all Bill.

Nathan: A lot of people have said that they've made changes in their lives after watching that episode, because they realize they don't want to work their whole lives to accomplish this one goal and [then], in their old age, find that they had left all this stuff behind that they actually cared about.

Judd: But you're feeling your way through that, as you do it. You're not philosophizing as it's happening.

Nathan: I really just started with like, *Oh, poo is funny, how can we do a poo joke?* And then, from there, a world evolves around that joke.

Judd: I remember that episode, where this one guy is on a date at a fast-food restaurant. And you were feeding him lines to say on the date, through an earpiece.

Nathan: That was Solomon. Basically, Comedy Central came to me and was like, "Quiznos wants to do product placement in your show." I had already been talking to Solomon about his love life, so we were already planning on doing something with him. And when we told Comedy Central that, they were like, "Can you do his date at a Quiznos?" I was like, "Can the Quiznos rep be in the show?" They agreed; so we did it. [Solomon] was trying to make the date work, but he also had to say these Quiznos taglines, like "Mmm, toasty."

Judd: But what was weirdly powerful was that his date seemed very warm and positive with him. You're enjoying the comedy of the moment, but it's not cruel. It's kind of the opposite. It's about acceptance.

Nathan: People do think that I'm trying to take people down a notch or make fun of them, but really, it's not about the other person or me.

The joke is in the space between people, where we're struggling to be on the same page. I really believe it's impossible for two people to be on the same page. When I was younger, social anxiety was the number one stress for me. As a high school student, I was into magic, which obviously is something you do to try to break the ice with people. There are always these excuses to talk to people—you can never just go to someone and say, "Do you mind if we have a conversation right now? I'd like to talk to you," because that's weird. So, you need a trick to talk to someone, you need an excuse.

Judd: That's why people become the funny person in school.

Nathan: That's probably part of it. Most of high school was just awful for me, but then, in college, I went in the opposite direction, where rather than trying to hide all my insecurities, I leaned into them more. I would try to exude confidence I didn't have, and it was really awkward—people could see through me. But I was just like, *All right, however people see me is how I am.* And that was a turning point. Because then, no one has anything on you.

Judd: I find that part of it fascinating, where we find ourselves and drop our fears. And then the world says, "This is great. I love that." That's the lesson. We're all trying to learn in some way that we're okay.

Nathan: That was also a large part of the show, where no one is saying what they're thinking. That's the heart of the problem. Without ever saying what you're thinking, you're always just playing a game, and you're never able to really form connections.

Judd: Shandling would always say that, in Los Angeles, everyone's wearing a mask. No one says what they're thinking, no one speaks the truth. When they do, it's a huge deal.

Nathan: That's true. Even now, there's this underlying stress in my chest about talking about myself. I'm terrified of being on camera, that I'm going to humiliate myself all the time. That's a real motivator for making sure something's good.

Judd: I feel that way about work. The thing I like about making things is that anything you made in the past has no bearing on whether your new thing will work. That fear of humiliation is always terrifying, but it wakes you up and makes you want to work hard. But then I started having anxiety when I was watching TV, because I was burnt out, and I felt like I was bored of stories and that I'd seen them all before.

Nathan: That's another interesting thing about how the show developed. I was very aware that comedians had done shows with real people before. I was aware of the Sacha Baron Cohen stuff, *The Daily Show*, et cetera. So, it was almost a process of elimination, where it's like, "Well, we can't do that, can't do that, can't do that . . ." We couldn't do any joke that felt like it could be on those other shows.

Judd: What were the ones you thought came together perfectly? What are your moments of pride now?

Nathan: My favorite moments are the ones that went so differently than what we planned. Where we scrambled to figure it out. That's what I love about it: inexplicable moments between people that are somehow funny but don't follow any of the normal rules of why something's funny. There was that one episode that was about a gas station rebate, but to claim the rebate, customers had to drop it off in person at the top of a mountain. But then, when they got there, the rebate box was hidden, and people stayed overnight. That was the first one we did that was really elaborate. But then, I think, once we did that Dumb Starbucks one, we realized [that] just skirting around the law actually gives you a lot of story to work with. Like, *How do we make this legal?*

Judd: What's next for you? I know you're directing and producing, but how do you approach your creative career?

Nathan: I've always tried not to have goals. Instead, I make sure I like what I'm doing, and then once I stop liking it, I stop. But I have a couple of shows for HBO, one I'm producing and then one I'm going to direct and act in. It has elements of *Nathan for You*. It has a real-people element to it, but it's a different thing. I'm also doing something with the Safdie brothers [Joshua and Benjamin]. I'm trying to make more things, and just have more things going on, and I'm doing better at it.

Judd: It's funny. When you're open, things just present themselves.

Nathan: When I first moved to Toronto and started doing comedy, I had this video camera, and whenever I would have an idea, I'd just go out and do it. I would shoot it in a day, with no planning. There was something so great about being able to execute an idea just like that. When things go on for a long period of time, it sucks out some of that energy a little bit, but I try to hold on to that. I guess that's the appeal of the reality-based stuff. It keeps that sense of *Well, anything could happen any day.*

PETE DAVIDSON

February 2020

Judd: People might not expect it of you, but you have a great love of film and a great education in film. I know, because the whole time we made *The King of Staten Island*, you would always say to me, "After work today, let's go to where I live," which is in the basement of your mother's house, where you had built a man cave. And you would always say, "Tonight, we're going to watch movies." And then I always would not go.

Pete: You never went.

Judd: I didn't really need to see [*The*] *King of Comedy* at two A.M. on a shooting night.

Pete: On mushrooms with me and my homes. Steve Buscemi came to the cave. The cinematographer Bob Elswit came twice. He had a really great time. He signed the wall.

Judd: Your grandfather was the guy that got you interested in movies?

Pete: His father owned a movie theater back when that's all that existed, so he grew up watching every single movie ever. And he had to babysit me all the time, so he made me watch a bunch of movies, his favorites. So, I know, like, Ernest Borgnine and all those old guys from the forties. When my grandfather got a camera, we started making our own movies. And my mom got really mad, because we would make a version of *Mission: Impossible* where I would jump off of shit, or come down from the ceiling in my cowboy boots. I was, like, six years old. I was in constant danger, and [my grandfather] would go, "What? We're making movies here!" I did that till I was about nine or ten, and then I got my own camera. Then me and my cousin and my friends started making movies like *Jackass*. I think every kid does that in high school. We would also try to make some sketches.

Judd: What was the most dangerous *Jackass* stunt that you did?

Pete: It was all done in Staten Island, so there's not a lot you could work with. But we jumped through a thorn bush in our underwear. We went right through it, and we were like, "This is some shit. If only the *Jackass* boys could see us."

Judd: Now, with [*The*] *King of Staten Island*, how was it for you to make a movie without your grandfather?

Pete: It was cool to do, because now I have something to show him. He was always showing me what we made, and now I got to show him what I made. He's in it, and he arguably gets the biggest laugh in the entire movie.

Judd: How was it having him on the set?

Pete: You really got the best of Steve Davidson, for sure. It was great. It's fun watching him on set because he didn't know that one scene takes eight to twelve hours sometimes. He'd be like, "Peter, if you move any slower, this picture will be done in 2030." It was just adorable for him to be on set and see how things are actually done.

Judd: He felt I was abusing him, I think.

Pete: Halfway through, he went, "This director that you got over here, Mr. Apatow. I don't know what he wants from me. I'm very sweaty, and my Parkinson's is about to kick in." And you'd be like, "And action!"

Judd: What's it like for you now that the movie's over? What was your hope for it versus what it became?

Pete: I wanted all the people in it to crush more than anything. We just have such a good group of people. I'm lucky all my friends are hilarious. I was so glad that we got to put them in a place where they could hit home runs, and they all did.

Judd: Do you remember when we first met? I was working on *Trainwreck*, and Amy Schumer was talking to me about you. I'd asked her, "Who's funny? Who should we consider putting in the movie?" She said, "You need to see this Pete Davidson kid. It's crazy how funny he is at nineteen." So, I said, "Let's put him in this little scene in the hospital, just so we can say we were the first people to put him in something."

Pete: I was so happy that it wasn't cut. That day was so crazy. I'd never shot anything before, so I didn't know that you get there and then you just sit in your trailer. I didn't bring much stuff with me, or deodorant. I was just sitting in there and started smelling like shit, because it's the middle of summer in Manhattan. Then they're like, "You're wearing a tank top in this scene." And I was like, *Fuck.* I was super in my head about stinking up the Apatow set that entire time.

Judd: My monitor was far away, so I didn't notice.

Pete: I was very lucky. But it was so much fun. I got to improv with Bill Hader, the year he left *SNL*. It was just super crazy.

Judd: Then Bill recommended you to Lorne, and I bumped into Lorne and talked about you. Then, suddenly, you're on *SNL*. Afterward, we talked about making a movie together.

Pete: I remember we tried to write one script, but our writing wasn't there yet. Then there was another idea that we had that was floating between us for a little bit. Then we wanted to do something where we could get my mom involved, but there wasn't any heart to it. In the end, we combined these two ideas.

Judd: In the beginning, you wanted to write something about a guy whose mom hasn't dated in a long time and about how you wanted your mom to be happy and to be in a relationship. I remember, in our conversations, I kept saying, "But wouldn't you *not* want her to be in a relationship?" How did you feel when we started kicking the script around, and it became more and more personal?

Pete: I've always been pretty open, but I think it's much easier to talk about your past than it is to make a movie about it, because you're doing a version of yourself, so you don't want to be disappointed in yourself while you're watching yourself. That part was weird.

Judd: Did it feel strange to write a fictional version of your life and your family?

Pete: It was pretty accurate. We just switched jobs and the thing that I was aspiring toward. The hard part was being in the firehouse, because I don't *go* to the firehouse. I had to hang out with those boys again. The only time I would ever stop at a firehouse was if I ever had to go to the bathroom. I would be like, "Hey, my dad died in 9/11. Can I take a shit in your bathroom?" And they're like, "Yeah, he's a hero. Right this way."

Judd: How was that for you, having your dad's friends as extras and as actors in the movie?

Pete: It meant as much to them as it meant to me, because I just wanted to show my appreciation, and we also wanted the movie to be as authentic and real as possible. We all had the same mission, and it was great. *We all just want to make this as real as possible.*

Judd: You've told me how you've spent a lot of your life avoiding all these people. I remember, there was a day where we have a scene in a bar, and we decided to have a lot of your dad's friends in the bar. And before the scene, you were worried about it. But on the day of, you seemed to like having them all around.

Pete: It was really nerve-wracking at first, because we get to deal with emotions all the time through watching movies and making stuff, and we heal through that. But these guys haven't seen anything in twenty years, and they haven't seen me in all that time, so all of this is just a fucking straight shot to them. I was really worried about them. But then, having them there made me more emotional and made me want to do a better job and put me more in the zone. So, I think it helped a lot.

Judd: All those guys really loved your dad.

Pete: They meet for drinks on his birthday every year. They listen to Creedence, his favorite band, and they do this every year. Every time they cough or anything, everybody just stops for a second, because they were all down there doing Ground Zero duty. It's a real brotherhood. And I wanted people to see that these guys aren't just fucking around. There's this common misconception that they are just sitting around and that there aren't that many fires. Do you have any idea what a fucking fire is? I think we really showed that, when the bell rings, it's time to go. And there's a chance that not everyone will come back.

Judd: There's a scene in the movie that was a hard scene to shoot, where, for the first time, your character goes with them on a ride-along and watches them put out an apartment building that's on fire. That was one of the harder days for you.

Pete: Even though it was fake and all set up, it was still just, like, "Wow." This is what they're doing five days out of the week. It's them, leaving everything behind just to go in and save people. It was really seeing that for the first time in person and on camera. That was a lot.

Judd: In one of the first conversations that we had, as we were trying to figure out the emotional life of the character, you talked about how you felt like firemen shouldn't have kids. You told me that that's something that you felt as a young person.

Pete: I did feel that way, and this movie made me feel differently toward it, because you get to hear the other perspective. Previously, I just shut out that other side. I remember being at a Christmas party at the firehouse when I was five or six, and everybody's having a good time, and then, all of a sudden, that bell rings. And then all the kids are just sitting there, and you're like, *Wow, I hope they come back.*

Judd: So, your reaction to losing your dad was *Why does he have this job? Why would he have taken a job this risky?*

Pete: There was a little bit of anger. When he died, I wondered if he [had been] doing this or that, would he still have died? My parents [had] just got divorced, and he moved out, so his work schedule changed. So, I would ask, *Would he even have been working that day? Is it my fault? Should* he *have called in sick that day?* There's a million scenarios that you play in your head. You drive yourself nuts. I was just seven years old. You're not supposed to learn what death is until you're in high school. I was literally trying to be, like, a detective. Then I'd watch TV, and certain people give their answers of what happened that day. I should have been watching cartoons. I didn't understand anything that was going on.

Judd: Seven is a hard age for that to happen. If you were five, you're almost too young to even realize what's going on. Seven is just old enough to be really confused.

Pete: You're just starting to be a person at that age. It was so weird. But it would have been worse if it happened now or when I was a teenager, because of the accessibility to drugs and stuff. It would have been so bad. I already wanted to kill myself when I was seven. If I wanted to do that when I was seventeen and had the access, it would have been a wrap for sure.

Judd: What were you like when you were five or six, before your dad died?

Pete: I was bouncing off the walls. I was a big Jim Carrey and Adam Sandler fan, so I was always walking around being weird. For the most part, we were just a normal Staten Island family, where there was a lot of love, but couldn't stay together. Parents got divorced, split time with the kids. It was pretty chill. I had a very chill childhood up until that day. My parents got divorced six months to a year before 9/11, and that's when I was starting to understand, *Oh, so he's not going to be in this house anymore.* I was still just getting used to not seeing him at home every day, and then I didn't see him at all.

Judd: When my parents got divorced when I was a kid, that screwed me up enough to do the things that I've done. It made me want to be creative and to live with a chip on my shoulder.

Pete: It fuels you. You almost think, *If I kick ass, maybe they'll get back together.* There's just so many things you think as a kid.

Judd: You were telling me that the week before 9/11, you switched schools?

Pete: It was a Catholic school. I was there for a week and was not making many friends, and then 9/11 happened. Nobody's nice to the new kid, but after that happened, everyone would *try* to be nice, but kids don't know how they are coming across. So, they would say to me, "Hey, I heard your dad died. You want to be friends?" And I'd be like, "No."

Judd: You also sent me a video of you, where you were playing football. It's two weeks after 9/11. And the coach gives this really bizarre speech, about how we need to respect Pete, but also he's berating the parents for getting too emotional about the games, and using 9/11 as a way to convince them that they're getting too crazy when they root for their kids.

Pete: He made it about him, which is my favorite thing. Nobody knew how to deal with it. And because it was New York, there are cameras everywhere. So, if I'm playing football, there's going to be people there. Everybody wants the 9/11 family's opinion for that little blip on the news. I met the president when I was seven. He gave me a medal. I just went, "Thanks, Mr. President." And he said, "Stay in college." That was it.

Judd: Where was this?

Pete: This was at the White House, on the front lawn. They gave everybody the Medal of Valor. We all got to receive the medal on behalf of our lost loved one. And I got to shake hands with George Bush. It was just weird. I watch clips of it now, and I'm like, *Oh fuck, that's horrible.* I can't believe this is what they thought would be helpful. And then my sister, who was five years old, fainted, because it was like three hundred degrees outside, and Laura Bush carried her into the White House.

Judd: At the time, did you think this was all weird?

Pete: I didn't get it at all. I was like, *Wow, my dad must have been some guy.* That's all I thought. *This guy must have been the coolest if I'm shaking hands with the president.* But I couldn't really grieve on my own. People were always inserting themselves. That's the New York way of dealing with things. It's like, your dad's dead. Got a PS3 with the new *Madden,* though. Ultimately, it's just distraction, and then you never deal with it.

Judd: You've said that it was just such a bizarre aftermath. My mom died eleven years ago, and no one ever mentions it after that first week.

Pete: 9/11 is mentioned on a weekly basis, in comparison.

Judd: Does it feel like you can never get over it because it just never goes away?

Pete: I've still never fully dealt with it. I still don't remember all that went on. When I was little, I blocked a lot of it out. I think it made it impossible for me to grieve, because there was such a fucking spectacle. But comedy saved me. It gives me a purpose and stuff to do. The first time I was ever happy was going to an open mic and just trying out a joke, and it got a little bit of a giggle. That feeling was the best.

Judd: You were sixteen when you started doing stand-up, which is crazy. In some way, you developed a dark sense of humor from just having to deal with all of this.

Pete: That, and I had no friends. I ripped my hair out all the time from anxiety, so I was a bald sixteen-year-old with braces, acne, pores everywhere—so, I just thought, *What do I have to lose?* Then I started doing stand-up, hanging with older dudes and meeting people who were troubled like I was, but they had normal lives and girlfriends. I found this whole other outlet and this group of people that kind of saved my life. It wasn't in Staten Island, so I had to take the ferry. It felt like, *I'm leaving the island to go hang out with people who get it.*

Judd: Your mom had to make a deal with you that she would allow you to go to Manhattan by yourself as a child if you agreed to stay in school.

Pete: My senior year at public school in Staten Island, you would get out of school at eleven A.M., and my mom was like, "That's not happening, you're coming over to the school where I work, and you get out at three P.M." So, I was like, "I just won't show up to school," and she was like, "You can do stand-up as long you get up in the morning and go to school."

Judd: So, she let you roam the city alone.

Pete: I was in weird bars at four in the morning when I was sixteen years old.

Judd: You found this group of comedians who are accepting of a super weird, partially bald, depressed child. Did you feel like you found a world of acceptance or parental figures?

Pete: I could tell these people how I feel. Because all the open mics were just people trying stuff out, so it felt like an AA meeting for me, but with jokes. Then, if you get a little giggle out of telling a joke about your dad's death, it became a nice, healing moment. And no one knows who the fuck you are, which is great. No one from Staten Island was there; it was all random people.

Judd: Do you feel like [*The King of Staten Island*] is an extension of that in some way?

Pete: The movie is my love letter to my mom. It's my trying to end that part of my life, because she and I maybe got to a place where we can finally let go a little bit. And there's art to it.

Judd: What does your mom think about what the movie was saying to her?

Pete: I think she got it. My mom's been going out since then. I don't know if she's going out on dates, but she's like, "I'm going to hang out with friends. I'll be back at like two, three in the morning." The last month or so, she's been really social, so I think she got the point. The movie was me saying, "I don't want you to blow your life for me." That's pretty much where it is. And it's also saying, you know, "I made a movie, so you should go date now."

Judd: And you and your grandfather—I would assume after making all those movies with you, it must blow his mind a little bit to see this.

Pete: As soon as he gets paid for it, he's going to be thrilled. That's a real text from him. I wish I was joking.

Judd: What do you think your dad would make of this movie?

Pete: He'd be thrilled; he would get a kick out of it. He gets a kick out of shit like this. The last movie we saw together was *Rush Hour* 2. He loved comedy, and I think he would be thrilled, because some of his buddies are in the movie. It's really real and full circle. He liked real stuff.

Judd: Your dad's friends all talked about how funny he was. They would say, "He was kind of like Pete." He was the funny guy at the fire station.

Pete: He was always hilarious. He was the guy that would show up late, and people would be like, "You fuckin' asshole." Like, nobody would be mad or anything like that. He was just the life of the party.

Judd: You said you were really happy when you learned that your dad drank and partied and did coke back then. Because it freed you from the idea that he was perfect.

Pete: It gave me a little insight into the divorce. It made me realize that he had his own issues; he had problems just like everybody else. But it also made me realize that even with all that, his morals were still intact, and none of that prevented him from being a hero. It made me feel good on two different levels.

Judd: We put in that dedication to your dad at the end of the film, and I think when you see that photo of you and your dad, you realize that even though that's a fictional character, it's a real thing that happened and that [that] little kid in that picture grew up and made that movie. He ended up okay. Now, Bill Burr's someone you've known since you were first trying to be a comedian. You met him when you were really little.

Pete: I met him when I was sixteen at Carolines and I just was like, "Hey, I'm trying to start stand-up. Do you have any advice for me?" And he just said, "Don't sign anything." I thought that was hysterical. He's like, "If they want to work with you, they'll work with you." And then my mom took me to [Atlantic City] for my seventeenth birthday to see Bill Burr tour with Jim Norton and Jim Breuer, Artie Lange, and I ran into him there, and I just kept saying hello. Eventually, I started doing stand-up, and we started meshing a little bit, and then I got him to bang my mom in a movie.

Judd: It came full circle. Would you say that Bill was a mentor for you growing up?

Pete: Yes. Anything he says, I don't take lightly. He has a deep knowledge about the game. He's been doing stand-up for thirty years, so he's the shit. Having him play my father in the movie was amazing, and he really cares about the acting.

Judd: How do you prepare to act in a movie like this when you're playing a fictional version of yourself?

Pete: You just try to believe the other guy's story, which is a little different. He's a tattoo artist; his friends are complete scumbags. He's selling weed and pills and stuff. He doesn't really have a lot of options. He doesn't have a safety net. He's still with his mom. You just put yourself in that position. I had to put myself back as an eighteen-year-old. This was the version of me if I didn't get into stand-up or escape to the city. I'd probably be robbing pharmacies with my boys and getting more tattoos.

Judd: The opening of the movie is you driving in your car and closing your eyes. That was something you told me happened years ago in your life.

Pete: There was a time in my life where I wasn't trying to kill myself, but I was testing it. You close your eyes for fifteen seconds, and if you die, it's supposed to happen. Or, just, like, putting yourself in a place where you can't be in control. I did that a bunch. I thought, *I can't hurt myself because that's not fair to my family*—that was my rule. But I could accidentally get hurt, and then I thought my mom and my sister could live with that, if it was just a bad accident. That's how fucking psycho I was.

Judd: Does it feel different now that you're twenty-six?

Pete: It's starting to get a little easier. Your twenties suck. Growing up is really hard. It's really awful. Especially in front of the world.

Judd: Let's talk about your friends in the movie.

Pete: In Staten Island, I hung out with guys who were like three, four years older than me. They introduced me to weed, and we used to smoke weed all the time. And then they started moving on to harder drugs, selling them and pushing around. Luckily, I realized I had to get out of there. So, my mom helped me find an apartment in Brooklyn, and I decided that I was going to go full into comedy. And I never spoke to those people again.

Judd: That probably saved your life. How is your relationship with Staten Island now?

Pete: Much like my public relationships. They're really good for three months, and then, all of a sudden, right down the clogger. I love Staten Island to death. I still live there. I just have a lot of issues with the way it's starting to change. They're starting to get a little blue over there, and are more aware of the socioeconomic crises, but in many ways, they're still stuck in the eighties or nineties. It's like an old suburb. Staten Island is the sister to Long Island, where it's just for families, and if you want to be more fast-paced, you go to Brooklyn or Manhattan.

Judd: Do people like you on Staten Island?

Pete: I think it's fifty-fifty. I think some people like me, and they get that anything I say about Staten Island comes from a loving place and [that] I genuinely just want it to be better there. The other fifty percent are just like, "Fuck you, dude. I hate you."

Judd: How is the movie different from the experience of making *SNL* every week?

Pete: With the movie, I had a little bit of control for the first time, and I really liked that. I appreciated that people would listen to my ideas. At *SNL*, it's a little more competitive.

Judd: Is it intense to be on a TV show that's part of the national conversation every week?

Pete: Yeah, especially when you don't want to be a part of the national conversation. When you're trying so hard to be quiet.

Judd: Yet, on the show, you'll talk about going into rehab. Why do you share that on the show?

Pete: I don't like people to be surprised about me; I like people knowing things. So, if they see me being sad or having issues, they're like, *Oh, I know.* Rather than being in the dark about what's wrong with me. Also, I'm not the greatest sketch guy there. There are fifteen others on the show who are the greatest sketch guys. The best that I could bring to the show is to talk about my personal life, or to do stand-up at the ["Weekend] Update" desk.

Judd: You've talked about how, when you have a father who's a hero, in a lot of ways it makes you afraid to take risks, because you think, *I'll never be able to do what he did.*

Pete: I also just don't want to insult the Davidson name. There's not much higher you could go after giving your life to save others. It always instilled this fear in me. *Don't ruin the family name, because it's all we've got.* That's just a very Staten Island–type of motto to live by. Don't ruin your fucking name.

Judd: I know when we put the dedication to your dad at the end of the movie, it made you uncomfortable.

Pete: I get why it's there. It's just a dedication, like before certain *Law and Order* episodes. But it makes me feel weird.

Judd: You don't want people to think you want sympathy?

Pete: Yeah, I'm not looking for sympathy at all. I'm just hoping you enjoy the movie and that you could maybe relate to it in a certain way.

Judd: I think, when you see the dedication, you realize that even though that's a fictional character, it's a real thing that happened. And that little kid in that picture grew up and made that movie. He was able to make that movie and—

Pete: That's our way of saying he's okay.

RAMY YOUSSEF

September 2019

Judd: Your show *Ramy* has been getting a lot of attention, and it seems like everything has happened very quickly for you. Does it feel that way, or does it feel like it's happened at the right time?

Ramy: It's interesting, because I moved to L.A. with a job, but it was just so under the radar that no one knew that I was on a show. I did this Nick at Nite sitcom, [*See Dad Run,*] for three seasons. Otherwise, I wasn't really getting cast as an actor, because I was kind of a difficult type: I wasn't quite the lead; I wasn't quite the best friend; I wasn't quite ethnic enough; I had an Arab name, but not the vibe that they're looking for. But all that did was just keep driving me into stand-up, which I had only done a handful of times before I moved to L.A. And then I came out here, and all my sketch comedy partners were in New York, and I realized, *Okay, I really want to hit stand-up hard.* By the time I got into development on my show, I'd been doing stand-up for about six years, which is still not that long. But it certainly feels like it's been coalescing as it should. Although, I still can't believe all this is happening.

Judd: Do you feel like Hollywood has changed in those eight years since you got the Nick at Nite sitcom? Was there suddenly a demand for more diversity?

Ramy: A couple of years before I even sold my show, I remember thinking, *Oh man, who's done this before? A show about anyone who is practicing Islam? There must be someone, but I don't even know them, and there's no real connection that I have to them.* I knew I wanted to make something in that vein. I didn't know what it would be, but I remember going into my management company at the time and telling them, "I want to do this story about a Muslim family," and they asked me, "Well, what if they lived next door to a white family?" or "What if it's one kid, and he's kind of, like, displaced?" It was all really like, "How do we make this something that a non-Muslim would be interested in?" Now they need to be as Muslim as possible, like, "Let's show the whole thing in Arabic, and if you're Egyptian, let's have the whole thing with hieroglyphics subtitles." People are so down to go down that path now, and everyone is really sensitive about representation.

Judd: It's a funny moment in comedy and television, because there's finally a demand to have more diversity in the writing rooms and in TV shows. It's always hard to know how much of that is sincere and how much of it is business. How do you perceive it these days, as someone who's in the clubs and hiring people for your show?

Ramy: It's interesting. It's almost like being like a white writer in Hollywood now is like if you were a writer of any minority before, which is, you have to be the best. I've seen it even in ways that I've constructed my shows. There's nothing wrong with this on a certain level, but a lot of the time, you just make stuff with the friends that you're with. And a lot of the time, your friends are like you. So, you kind of have this club that gets developed where a lot of the people who've been in it, who are friends, who are making things, are white guys. And that's fine. I don't really think there's a problem with that. I think that now it's this thing where there is this desire to have more diverse voices, I think that can really make you stronger. With the amount of streaming services we have, and the amount of outlets to make things, it's just more interesting to have these new stories. A big part of it is there's this pressure to tell other stories, and maybe some people are afraid of being called out on Twitter or something like that, and that motivates why they would do something. But for me, none of that is really a motivator as much as "What is the story?" We're now decades and decades into audiovisual storytelling. How can we start talking about things that we haven't yet?

Judd: You also need people to understand what you're writing about. It's like when we did *Freaks and Geeks*, I hired Jon Kasdan to be on the writing staff, because he was eighteen, and I thought, *He'll remember high school*. We hired Seth to be a writer at *Undeclared* because he was the age of someone in college, and we just thought that would somehow add something to the soup. Do you think writers and comics can grow from this moment?

Ramy: Overall, the demand for more diversity changes what people are looking for, and I think it can be really positive. But there are probably going to be some growing pains as to why people are doing what they're doing. That needs to be examined, and I don't think someone can just be in a situation because they check a box. I don't think that's fair to that person, either. The thing that I'm afraid of is that we hire people just *because* they're minorities, because if someone doesn't get the opportunity to get rejected for a job, they don't get the opportunity to grow. You grow most as an artist from being rejected, so I think there needs to be this healthy balance of just making sure that we're really doing due diligence in meeting the right people and making sure that they're getting a chance to be read and getting a chance to audition. The main responsibility, to me, is to make sure you're casting the net in a genuine way. And then you really do have to make the hiring choice that you feel will inform your storytelling most accurately and to the highest ability.

Judd: When I started out, I didn't see goofy, nerdy, not-classically attractive people on television. And on some level, I thought, *I'm not represented here.* I'm curious to hear how it felt for you, as a kid, to be completely unrepresented in the culture for so long?

Ramy: On one level, the only cultural reference point to being Arab was *Aladdin*, and that was it. Or else, it was in the news. So, you were either a cartoon or a villain. There's nothing really human there. And then I feel like I have a grounded spiritual practice—that's another thing that's either very villainized or cartoony. It's hard to find an honest expression of religion that isn't caricatured. I think with both of those things, it was very much feeling like, *Yeah, there's not really anything that looks like me,* and I think that's when you have actual violence happening to certain communities, because of the misunderstanding that proliferates. You look at the spike of hate crimes against anyone who's perceived to be Muslim or brown in this country—it spikes at various points in the political cycle, when it's weaponized. When people know so little about you that you can be weaponized every time there is an election, that's a problem. That's a problem that I felt personally. When you're making things, or if you're a network that wants to green-light something, I think you look at that political reality and you're like, *Television is about having a conversation.* Here's a group of people we're talking about, but we're not talking *with*. And so, why not make a show so we can talk *with* the people who are very much being talked *about*.

Judd: Who are your influences?

Ramy: I don't know if I've told you this, but *Knocked Up, Superbad, 40-Year-Old Virgin*—that's the shit I watched in high school. I graduated in 2009, so when I really got into making things, my thing was always like, man, *I love Apatow movies, and I love Tarantino movies. I love how slanted Tarantino and the Coen brothers are, how weird those worlds are, and I love how relatable Apatow leads are.* So, when I got into writing, I was like, *I want to put in the likeable Apatow lead that I feel like I am, even though I'm a Muslim kid.* I watch Michael Cera, I watch Seth [Rogen], and I'm like, *Fuck, I relate to this dude.* And I want to throw that into the weird Tarantino-y world. That was always my approach to what excited me about writing and what I was into. All of that stuff came out when I was really getting the love for comedy in high school.

Judd: I'm someone who has been in similar situations, in the sense of having to run a show, to be the boss, without much experience. How did you know how to do this?

Ramy: A lot of running the show has been on the fly, and I've learned a lot from season one versus season two. I wasn't the showrunner on season one. I've learned what I want a room to look like based on trying to adapt what I like about stand-up. Because so much of stand-up is you go to a show and you try some jokes, you see how the crowd reacts, and then you walk around feeling sad for a while. Then you go back, and you try it out again. I kind of wanted to set up a writers' room like that. Instead of being in the room from nine A.M. to seven P.M. and eating lunch together and doing all this stuff, I want to get together for short bursts of time. So, we were meeting for just three or four hours at a time, not much longer than that. And that was me experimenting, trying to make it feel like other processes that I knew. I've just been trying to embrace a lack of convention and trying to find a recipe that can fully utilize how *I* think, which feels important for a show that's semiautobiographical.

Judd: That episode where you take your friend, played by Steve Way, to hook up with a girl, and she turns out to be sixteen years old and drunk. He has muscular dystrophy, and he says, "I don't have a lot of options." I thought it was a really daring episode. How did you guys conceive that story line, and what were you trying to do?

Ramy: That was actually something that I had talked about with Steve for years, about how he could get away with anything because, as a society, we kind of put people who are disabled onto a pedestal, and we assume that they must be good. I think that the characters on my show, and in anything that I would want to make, are spiritually inspirational. That might look like faith, but, really, what it means is just that they're trying to do the right thing, and they're trying to be themselves. That's really at the core of where they're at. They want to be good, and they're trying to grapple with their ego and their desires and what's "right." That is such a small goal, but it can really expand into so much comedy if that's all your character wants. As a writer, you can then just dress it up with like, *This person is trying to do the right thing but also grapple with their desires. Let's enter the most fucked-up situation that we can.* We just got excited by the prospect of testing audiences' morality and what their threshold is in terms of acceptance. For us, as creators, how do we draw the line in a really firm way where it couldn't go either way—we want to be on the right side of it, but we also really want to show the wrong side of it and show how tempting that might be. Anything that seems fucked up? Our job is to make whoever's watching it, if they were that person, think, *I might have done the same thing. I might have fucked up the same way.* How can we put the audience in that place? And so, that was the scenario that episode was born out [of]. It emerged from the question "What are the lines we can push?"

Judd: How do you relate that to the current climate in stand-up, where everyone is debating what is appropriate?

Ramy: I think there are two parts to this. I wish that, as a society, we could demarcate between the honest thought processes we all have and something being presented as a challenge or as a fuck-you. Because, for me, the best comedy is someone walking you through the honest thoughts that hit them, even if those thoughts are messy. We should be able to share those messy thoughts, because if we act like they're not there, then we'll never actually accept the group that needs to be accepted, that might feel like they're being attacked. So, I think we need to draw this line between "When are we thinking something out together as a society?" and "When are we attacking as a society?" There's a version of any show that can come from a thoughtful place, and you can really pull off anything. I don't think anything's untouchable. I do think that certain subjects are much more of a tightrope walk than others, and the reason they are is because at the other end of them are communities who feel like, *There is violence involved in me being misunderstood.* So, if you are a trans person who is hearing about trans people being murdered all the time because that's your community and that's what is being talked about, it's not that you can't hear a trans joke; you actually *want* to hear one. You *want* to hear one that is actually in line with helping and with understanding what's going on, even if that joke encompasses the lack of understanding people have. I think some people will still find that funny. I've done trans jokes, and they don't fall in this place where everyone's upset. I mean, some people are sometimes, but I find that if it's rooted in something thoughtful, that will get you really far. That's one part of it. The other part of it that's important to me is this idea of what we should be expecting from comedy. I think that from growing up watching *The Daily Show*, my generation is very much at this place of "Comedy should be facts." Because when people watched Jon Stewart on *The Daily Show*, there was this thing that I heard people say all the time, which was, "I don't get my news from the news. I get it from *The Daily Show*." Which is kind of fucked up, because now you're putting comedy in this position to tell you what's going on. And it puts this unfair weight on comedians to feel like, *Am I supposed to be telling the truth? Is that what this is? Is this supposed to be educational?* I think that's wrong. Comedy doesn't have to be right. It doesn't have to be a fact. Comedy is about someone just being honest about what they think, and that should look messy and can look messy. By no means should you get your news and facts from comedy, because none of us went to college.

Judd: I think there are a lot of comedians now who see their performances as being about kicking the tires on what's happening in the world and having fun with the audience, discussing issues and how the culture is changing. They are just trying to toss it around. But sometimes it's in a dark way, sometimes in a hurtful way. Sometimes there's a sloppiness to it.

Ramy: I think it's our job to find a personal connection to whatever we're talking about. Otherwise, it feels like you're adding fuel to a random fire, because it's already lit. I think that's what's infuriating to people. There are a lot of people who feel like they're edgy and boundary-pushing, but they're really just being opportunistic, because they don't have a unique point of view on the subject that's being debated. They don't actually have a connection to this issue that actually needs to be talked about. They're just doing it to do it.

Judd: Do you think there's still room for roast humor out there?

Ramy: I think what captivates people about roast humor is that everyone's on the same stage, and they get to say something back. We get to say these nasty things, making fun of someone for anything, but then that person gets to respond. There's an even playing field with a roast, even though it's not something I've ever done. Nor do I think I'd be very good at roast humor. But the thing I like about it, when it's good, is that people are really going there, but then the other person who's being made fun of gets to go there, too.

Judd: Sometimes, I wonder if comedy is in a precarious place right now, or if you just have all these comedians who are saying it is, but then they're selling out arenas. I don't know anyone whose career has really ended who was doing normal comedy.

Ramy: No one's really been silent. Even Chappelle was talking about critics and the media, and he was talking about it in, like, his fourth special in two years. So, he's getting to say whatever he wants to say, and I think he's very funny. There seem to be very few instances where a comedian is actually being wronged by the crowd. Ultimately, I think a comedian's job is to be super aware of the climate we're in. Maybe the level of difficulty has gotten a little harder, but if you're a comic, that should be fun. That should be what you're aiming for.

Judd: So many people are working from a place of neurosis and anxiety and depression, but you seem so grounded and thoughtful and centered—why is that?

Ramy: I appreciate that. I have my anxieties, I have my bouts of feeling depressed, all those things, like we all do. But, obviously, I've made this show about a Muslim family. I don't make it because it's a cool filter to sell a show. It's just who I am, and it's a big part of my life. When I think about my goals, the highest thing for me is spiritual actualization of who I want to be and who I know I'm not yet. That's what I'm really struggling for. And, genuinely, anything under it is cool, but I think it's important that your goal is to do something that will challenge you until the day that you die. I don't think I'm ever going to reach the goal that I have for who I am as a human. There's almost, like, teeth in that for me. I never want to feel like my show or a stand-up set or a special rules my life and my sense of self. I give everything to what I do, but it's not the thing that's going to tell me who I am. And I think that's the only thing that keeps me from going crazy. Because, like you said, a lot of this stuff has happened very fast for me. I think that the only thing that's helped me with that speed is that I know there's something bigger than this, and so, I'm just going to go along for the ride and try to maintain my humanity.

Judd: Can you explain how your sense of purpose as a creative person is connected to your religion and how you look at the purpose of your life?

Ramy: There's this Islamic saying: The purpose of life is to know God, and the only way to know God is to know each other. I really feel there's something at the core of comedy that can help us know each other in a unique way. That, to me, is tied in with any spiritual path, and certainly with mine.

Judd: Is it heartbreaking when a lot of people in our country have an impression of your religion that is so the opposite of how you see it?

Ramy: It's heartbreaking mostly because it has real-life consequences that hurt people. It's tough growing up, because when you're an adult, you have your rationalizations, and you're like, "There's this idea against Muslims because it's part of a larger tactic of dehumanizing people in order to justify certain political or military actions . . ." You can rationalize the shit out of it when you're an adult. But when you're a kid, you're just scared. I had such a fearful childhood, where I was actually afraid of myself and afraid of my family because I believed things I heard, and then, in turn, [I] had doubts about who I was. That is something that I don't want to happen for kids growing up. I want kids, regardless of what they are, to be proud of what they are.

Judd: What do you think this show has done to help change that misrepresentation of your culture, and what would you say is the mission statement of your show?

Ramy: The mission statement is super simple: Expand the conversation. Even if not a ton of people are watching the show, for me the goal is: How do we extend the conversation, even if it's just on an industry level? A real reaction to my show, from industry people, is that it is really specific. It was about a Muslim Egyptian guy in New

Jersey, and we were so zeroed in on what we were doing, that I think we could do a show about a Black Muslim woman in Michigan and it would feel completely different. The thing that excited me is I think it expanded the palate; it expanded the appetite for comedy and the different types of stories we can get into. I keep hearing from people all over the world who are watching the show in areas where it's not even distributed or officially available. I was kind of blown away when I saw that our show was being pirated and that people were putting subtitles in their languages. We didn't even do that. It was just out there with other languages subbed on it. It's so amazing that someone would care enough to make sure that people understood the show in their language and feel connected to those scenes.

Judd: With *The Big Sick*, I always thought the reason people didn't think the movie would do well is probably the reason why it will do well. Most studios who turned it down just thought, *No one wants to see this community*.

Ramy: They look at it like toothpaste or something, right? Like, there's not enough Chinese people, or there's not enough Muslim people, to form a real audience for this. They're coming at it from this marketing standpoint of product-per-seller, like that's the only group of people who would buy this thing. But what's really cool to me is when you ground a film or a show in a character that everyone can relate to. So, when you put a particular cultural filter on it, it's just a filter. The core of it is what everyone's feeling.

Judd: What does your family make of your show?

Ramy: It's been amazing for my family, because so much of what happens in the show are conversations that I feel our community has a hard time having. A lot of them around sex. I wanted to make something that would help us open up conversations that I don't think we have in a clear way. The conversations this family is having on the show—some of them, I never have with my own family. People reached out to me and were like, "Your show helps me have this conversation that I never have with my dad," and I'm like, "Yeah, me, too." I use my show to talk to my dad, and that's kind of blowing my mind. That's so much cooler than anything else that has come of it. My family feels closer to me because they're seeing this story that's not fully autobiographical or anything, but they're seeing my point of view. My show and my special came out within a month of each other, and my parents had never seen any stand-up that I did outside of a five-minute set that I did on Colbert.

Judd: Why is that? Because that was the case with Aziz [Ansari], and Hasan Minhaj also told me that his parents had never seen him perform in person. Is it something specific about stand-up that is uncomfortable for your parents, and maybe for the Muslim community more broadly?

Ramy: I don't know if it's stand-up specifically. In my case, I really care about what my parents think, because I love them and I care about their opinions, and I didn't want to have their opinion influence what I wanted to talk about onstage. I didn't want them to see my stand-up because I didn't want them to say no to it. It's better to just do it and apologize later, rather than ask for permission and have them say no. I wanted to protect this incubator, and I didn't want them to see it, because their silence, or even their laughter, was just going to influence me too much. That was the reason for me.

Judd: And what becomes the purpose of your stand-up when you're putting so much of your creativity into the show?

Ramy: They kind of feed off each other. The first season of my show was based on all the stand-up I'd ever done. Pretty much every episode had a scene that was based on my stand-up, or at least the subject matter. Now I've been in the process of making a TV show, so I'm doing less stand-up. The interesting thing for the show is the characters are alive now. They're like these people we made, and they can grow into their own story lines. They don't need my stand-up as much.

Judd: As you approach the next season, what are your ambitions for the future of the show?

Ramy: To continue to remain nervous about what we're putting out there. The more you do something, the more you get a little desensitized, and I want to just make sure that I'm continuing to dig into the things that are making me uncomfortable. It's not about being insatiable. It's about stripping away at things that bother me and making sure that's in the forefront of what we're making. We put out the first season and realized that there was certain backlash, but for the most part, everything was more than okay. That's exciting, because that encourages me to dig even deeper and know that everything is going to be fine. Like, just go for it.

ROGER DALTREY

October 2018

Judd: How exciting is this? I've waited since I was ten years old to do this.

Roger: What? Sit on this stage?

Judd: To grill you in this way.

Roger: Hold on. I just got to adjust the hearing aids. You're too loud; it's like being back with Entwistle. That's better.

Judd: You know, I've got ringing in my ears as well. I went to a Lou Reed concert, and my ears rang, and they haven't stopped for the last twenty-five years. And I saw him somewhere, and I said to him, "I saw you, and my ears have rung for twenty-five years," thinking he'd laugh, and he just looked at me.

Roger: Yeah, that was Lou.

Judd: He was not amused. The book [*Thanks a Lot, Mr. Kibblewhite*] is fantastic. It was really fun to hear your point of view. Did you enjoy looking back and writing it?

Roger: I didn't know if I had a good book in me, and all I wanted was a good book. If it hadn't been a good book, I wouldn't have gone to a publisher with it. So, I worked with a friend who's a journalist. He had followed me around for the day, and he wrote this article in *The Sunday Times*, and I'm having Sunday breakfast, and Heather, my wife, falls on the floor laughing. I'm like, "What's the matter?" She says, "I'm just reading this article on you by this guy called Matt Rudd, and he totally gets you." It was indeed a very funny article.

Judd: What was his take on you?

Roger: I'm completely mad. I won't have an iPhone, so I still have my old steam phone, and it was taking me ten minutes to do a three-line text. But that's me. I just refuse to have an iPhone. I find them sucking up your life like a vacuum cleaner, and it disappears into this thing. People are spending their lives looking down instead of up.

Judd: And they found a way to suck all of your royalties away.

Roger: Well, yeah, the internet. I've never been very pro. It's useful in its ways, but it seems to be bringing out a lot of bad in people.

Judd: Me at two in the morning.

Roger: But Matt got it. I just said to Matt, "Would you like to work with me to see if I have a book in me?" He did interview after interview after interview for about four years. He even did an interview with me when I was in the hospital with meningitis, when I didn't think I was coming back. He thought, *You better get one last one in.* He wrote the interviews down exactly how I said them, and then, of course, speech isn't grammar, so I had to write it over and rejig it. You have to give it a thread. And because I did it the way I did it, I could insist on the title [*Thanks a Lot Mr. Kibblewhite*,] which the publishers fought against. I don't know why, but they seem to think every biography just needs to be called the name of the person with the face of the person on the cover.

Judd: What I found so fascinating in the beginning of the book is how you grew up in post–World War Two England, what that experience was like and how it shaped you.

Roger: One of the hard things to do through our whole career is to get Americans to have any idea of what we grew up in. My mother started to go into labor on the twenty-ninth of February, 1944. In the area we lived, which was West London, there were lots of arms factories, and by now, Hitler had designed the V-One bomb, which used to just come over, *boom, boom, boom, boom,* making this thudding noise, which would then stop, and then, before you knew it, there'd be two tons of high explosives falling on your head. So, my mother went into labor during one of those raids. And she was determined I wouldn't be born on the twenty-ninth of February—so, well done, Mom! She had waited till after the air raid was over.

Judd: Because she didn't want you born on a leap day. I like that during World War Two, *that's* what your mom was thinking about.

Roger: She's strong, and that's what they were like. Just imagine what our parents went through. My dad was in the army. He got off the landing craft on D-day, [was] immediately blown up by a motor bomb, and fortunately survived. He had the shrapnel in him until the day he died. But they were terribly traumatized by the war. You've got to remember, your 9/11 event, how it traumatized you, how you sat there in that hopelessness. That feeling in the gut? Our parents—Pete [Townshend]'s parents and my parents and John [Entwistle]'s parents—they were going through that kind of event every night for four, five years, because we were being bombed for that long. You'd go on down into the shelter, and you'd come up, and maybe your house wasn't there. My mother came out of the shelter, and both ends of the street had disappeared. Just gone, flattened. So, you can only just imagine what that must have done to the way they were in their lives. And it was only later on in my life [that] I realized that they were probably shell-shocked for their whole life. Every time there was a thunderstorm, my mom would scream like a banshee. Run under the kitchen table like she was back in the bombing.

Judd: How did that change how they parented you or how they felt about you running around?

Roger: It created a kind of silent, incredible loving, but there was a distance I found with my parents, and a lot of people I talked to found it with theirs. We've all come to the conclusion they'd all been through the same trauma. When we grew up, we had very little food. During the war, it was rationed, as you know. A pound and a quarter of meat was the rations for a family of four for a week.

Judd: I just had that at the Palm earlier today.

Roger: Exactly. That was a family of four's meat for a week during the war. And when we got to 1945, we then had to share that ration that we had with the German people, who were in even worse straits than we were. In 1945, half of our loaf of white bread was made of chalk, to pad it out. That's why a lot of my generation are very short. I've always blamed Hitler for my legs, because these fucking legs wouldn't stop a pig in a passage.

Judd: But it seems like one running idea throughout the entire book is how much you appreciated your success and how responsible you were to keep it going even during difficult times. You just had this work ethic that came from growing up like that.

Roger: People say we were poor. We were not poor; we were incredibly wealthy, because the war brought families very, very close together, and they were big family units in those days. The workforce was far less mobile than it is today. And one thing that got people through was singing, which Hitler could never work out. The more he bombed us, the more we sung. The louder we sung. There was singing everywhere. Every factory you'd go past, the workers would be singing. The builders on the street would be singing. It gave us this ambition and this willingness to strive for what you wanted. I couldn't afford to buy my first guitar, so I made it. Keith Richards made his first guitar. Quite a few other people from our generation made their first instruments, because to buy one was impossible. It was a terrible guitar but it worked. As long as you've got six strings and you learn to tune it, the intonation of it is not really important until you get up high. And all we needed in those days to play the music that inspired, the music of Leadbelly and all those other early American blues singers—you could learn the three chords that you could use to play most of those songs. So, immediately, you could start a band. You get a tea chest, which was a two-foot-six box of plywood with an open button, you put a string through the middle and a broomstick. But a good player could make that sound like a double bass. I'm serious. Every street had a band, with people singing. It taught us to do things for ourselves and not have it given to us.

Judd: Doesn't that seem like a miracle [that] it all worked out?

Roger: It's extraordinary when you look at the bands that came out of that period. Elvis and Little Richard and Jerry Lee Lewis and all those great guys would come in to us through our ten minutes that the BBC allowed us, because this music was dangerous. It'd be hidden away on a Saturday night or Sunday night somewhere. But we'd managed to find it, and of course, when everybody saw Elvis, even my age—and I was about ten or eleven—immediately, it was going out to get the soap to slick the hair back. We couldn't afford Brylcreem or any of those hair products, but the soap worked wonders. You could slick your hair back, and it would stay there, and we all thought we all looked like Elvis with that soapy hair. Until it rained. But then we saw this guy called Lonnie Donegan, and he was singing all this Leadbelly and early America folk songs in a way that was primal. And he was really square, because he used to sing in a dinner jacket and a bow tie. But it was the way he sang it.

Judd: How did he sing it? Give us a little Lonnie Donegan.

Roger: He'd start a song: *Ham and eggs, pork and beans / Could had more pork, but that cook was so mean.* Kind of chain gang songs, but then he'd get halfway through it, and he'd start wailing. Often he'd sling his head back and he'd wail, and it touched me in a way that Elvis didn't. Elvis looked great, but Lonnie had a primal thing in him. I thought, *I'm going to do this. This is good.*

Judd: When you first thought, *I'm going to do this,* did you have any real vision it was possible to get outside of your small town doing it?

Roger: No, no. You do what you do, and I got up onstage at the local youth club, did my version of "Hound Dog" and "Midnight Special," and suddenly, there was a row of girls down in front! I was eleven years old. I didn't quite understand what that was, but you understand that there's something about singing that attracts friends. I always felt more comfortable on the stage than in the audience, so that was the start of it. Then I started a skiffle band, like every street had. And later on, when I started working in a factory, I made my first electric guitar, and going home from work one night, I bumped into a guy who'd made his first bass guitar, and that was John Entwistle. I managed to talk him into joining my band by telling him that we were getting paid. We had been paid once, and not a lot, but we had been paid. It wasn't quite a lie, but it wasn't quite the truth. He started to play with me, and I thought, *This guy is great.* At that time, we had a rhythm guitarist who was not very good. I was the lead guitarist, and the rhythm guitarist had the amp—the one amp that John and me and the rhythm guitarist had to go through.

Judd: So, he had to stay.

Roger: So, we couldn't afford to get rid of the rhythm guitarist. But after six weeks of putting up with this, John said to me, "I don't know whether I can go along with Reg playing this rhythm guitar. I've got a friend that would suit us much better. Do you mind if I bring him along and give him a try?" So, I had a serious talk with Reg. And to his credit, Reg loaned us the amp and gave up the rhythm guitar. Which was a relief.

Judd: Because he was sure you were going nowhere.

Roger: Then John brought this guy along who I'd seen at school, because you could hardly hide him in a crowd of a thousand, or even a hundred thousand. Because, in those days, we were all incredibly skinny—and I don't mean it as an insult, but in those days, Pete really was a nose on a stick. I love Pete. I love Pete. I think he's got a fabulous head. He's grown into his nose. I'm just trying to give you a picture of why you could not miss him. Anyway, John brings this guy along with another handmade guitar, but it had a machine-made neck. Where the body had gone, I'd never bothered to ask. And it was Pete Townshend. And immediately, it was quite obvious that this was a budding genius. He was playing chord shapes that we'd never seen before, not even the professional guys on the TV. He was playing all these diminished things; I don't know what they're called now, even. These shapes that you could only go, *What is he doing?* And his rhythm action was so different than anything else, and I think that came because, in the trad [Irish folk] band, he was playing banjo. Pete joined the band, so there we are the three of us. I'm playing lead guitar, Pete's on rhythm guitar, John's on bass guitar, and my oldest friend from the first day at school, Harry Wilson, is on the drums.

Judd: How old are you at this time?

Roger: I think just turned sixteen, and they were just turning fifteen.

Judd: Was Pete popular in high school?

Roger: Because I'm small, I was bullied at the grammar school, quite badly bullied. I'm sure Pete, because of the way he looked, didn't have an easy time, either. At that age, all boys' schools can be quite cruel. I broke my jaw when I was about eight years old. I was playing on a building site. We used to play on bomb sites. I remember finding the tail end of a bomb once. You've never seen ten kids run faster in your whole life. There were no safety things. A bricklayer had left one of his lines out for the night, and over I went and smashed my jaw. I didn't realize it was even broken until about a week later. I was kind of a funny-looking bloke—still am—but then, a *really* funny-looking bloke. And they gave me some very cruel names. So, that was our years, and we would just progress as this band playing pop music of the day, playing clubs and pubs. But then we got lucky. Betty Townshend, Pete's mother, was instrumental to the success of the band in the early days. She managed to get us gigs, and an agent who got us better places to play.

Judd: They were in the music industry, his parents?

Roger: She was a singer in a band, and Pete's father was the saxophonist in a RAF band called the Squadronaires during the war, so a very accomplished musician. Betty Townshend managed to get us an agent, who then booked us into an officers' club for the American army in London, called Douglas House. We used to play there every Sunday afternoon, and of course we came into contact with all these GIs. They would start requesting music that we'd never heard before, stuff like the blues, like Johnny Cash and Chuck Berry, all this material, and you'd be expected the next week to play at least one of them. So, that started our musical journey into other music than what was in the Hit Parade at the time. We had another singer with us at that time, who used to think he was Cliff Richard, and he used to do all the Cliff Richard songs, and I used to sing all the other songs. I would do the Roy Orbison. I would do the Johnny Cash. When I look back, it was probably only about a year. And then we started to get into the blues, which Pete heard from his friend at art school. A guy called Tom Rat, dear friend of ours, had an amazing collection of John Lee Hooker and Howlin' Wolf, Jimmy Reed—all those people that we were introduced to. Pete wanted to immediately become a blues band. And I thought, *Well, if we do that, overnight we'll lose our audience.*

Judd: They didn't want to be depressed.

Roger: But, slowly but surely, we became a blues band, just like the Rolling Stones. Then we found a manager, and he thought we had something special. By this time, we found this strange drummer. I can't tell you how strange he was. They don't come any more strange then Keith Moon. It's impossible to describe to anyone who didn't know him and didn't spend lot of time with him, through the good times and the bad, what Keith Moon was like. He was an extraordinary character. And when he joined the band and started playing with us that first night, that first audition, I knew that something big would happen. There was something that locked together. Pete, John, and myself had it. But we could never find that missing drummer, that missing piece. But when Keith joined, he was the key that started the engine. And just—*poof*—it was perfect.

Judd: So, he comes in and he auditions at the end of a gig?

Roger: No, he came halfway through.

Judd: So, in the middle of the show you're like, "You want to do one with us?"

Roger: In the middle of the show, he came up and said, "I can play much better than that drummer you got." He was a cocky little son of a . . . We didn't hire him that night, but we thought we better try him out in rehearsal. It was quite obvious that he was going to be the one. He said he was never asked to join the band. Perhaps he was, perhaps he wasn't. We didn't need to ask him. We invited him to the rehearsal and said, "Would you like to do the next gig?" So, I reckon that's pretty much being invited to join the band. I'm trying to make a film of him at the moment, but I'm determined not to make a biopic.

Keith Moon deserved a proper film. Because Keith's personality was so enormous. Every facet of his personality was enormous. He could be the most generous, the most mean, the most caring, the most uncaring, the most loving, the most hateful, the most spiteful.

Judd: How did you learn that?

Roger: He was wonderful guy, and he was the funniest man that I've ever met in my life. He was one of the few people in the world that could make Peter Sellers laugh. Keith could have you belly-laughing until you had to leave the room because you were aching so much from laughing. I don't know if you have ever had that in your life, but I'm not kidding you, it really hurts when you can't laugh anymore and you start to cramp up. When Keith would get on a soliloquy, he'd go off, and he had a vocabulary way beyond his education, and he could pull it out of the air with subjects that went off of tangents, absolutely extraordinary stuff.

Judd: Where did his personality come from? What do you think was the root of what made him that type of guy?

Roger: Depends on what drug he was on. Apparently, his mom said he was a normal child. Dear Kit Moon—what a sweetheart she is. I doubt if Keith was ever normal. What a one-off. If I ever do allow my picture to ever be made of him, I guarantee you it'll be something you'll not expect him of, and worth your while.

Judd: What was that scene like in London in '62, '63, right when you had your first singles, and the Beatles were around, and the Rolling Stones and the Kinks? Was it a community? Did you guys do shows together? Was there a camaraderie?

Roger: I mean the Beatles' "Love Me Do" was the record that really was the ignition of the swinging sixties. And then, of course, the Stones came with "Come On," Chuck Berry's song, and they looked very different than the Beatles. But then this movement started up which this new manager we got talked us into becoming the figureheads for, which was the Mod movement in London, and they all rode scooters and dressed in trendy, trendy clothes. Of course, I was really a teddy boy, which was not even a rocker. Teddy boys wore Edwardian dress: long, draped, finger-tipped jackets, velvet collars, kind of smart. I liked the Mod thing when it started, because that was smart, too. It very quickly turned into a kind of mess, but in the early days, it was smart. Anyway, Pete and me took this long-haired Rolling Stones–alike band into the barbershop, having walked in as the Who, we walked out of the barbershop as the Mod band called the High Numbers, with these very short haircuts, looking very different indeed, but of course, inside exactly the same.

Judd: So, he created an image for you guys in the beginning. And then you were doing your first singles?

Roger: Pete wrote "I Can't Explain," which was a kind of tribute to the Kinks. You got to remember, in the process leading up to this period, we'd supported every one of those bands. We'd supported the Beatles in Blackpool, we'd supported the Rolling Stones a few times, we'd supported the Kinks a few times, and every band that was out there, Gerry and the Pacemakers, you name it. Dusty Springfield. We'd been on the same stage, but as the support act. So, we were cutting our teeth in a pretty good way, but then, once Pete wrote "I Can't Explain," it was quite obvious that he was writing songs from a different perspective. They were writing music for girls; Pete was writing music for blokes. Rock and roll was music to make love to, but rock, which the Who was doing and still does, was music to fight to. Pete understood that. So, he's writing these songs for *My Generation*, and it's got an arrogance about it that isn't there in rock and roll. And the beat is on the one.

Judd: It was very angsty at a time when music wasn't angsty. He was talking about being a teenager.

Roger: I recognized his talent very early on, and I was just happy to be the guy that was lucky enough to be in that position on the stage with these songs to present to an audience for the first time. How lucky was I?

Judd: What do you make of the songwriting when he's writing songs like "Pictures of Lily" and "I'm a Boy"? It was very different than what anyone was writing.

Roger: That's when I had to really get to grips with Pete. Prior to that, it'd been easy. It was blues, it was aggressive, and I could sing it in much more of my natural voice, from a point of view that I understood really easily. Then he presented "Happy Jack," and I don't get where this is coming from. So, I had to learn then to really gain an empathy for Pete's interior motive for writing these songs, and what he was going through inside, and feeling. So, I had to kind of climb into Pete in a way.

Judd: What was he going through? What do you think it was that he was struggling with that made him write that type of music at the time?

Roger: I just think he had this imagination that was so wild. If you read anything about Pete, you know he had quite a lot of abuse when he was young, and like I say, I think he was probably bullied at school. He is incredibly intelligent. He has a mind that goes off at tangents all the time, twenty-five thoughts at once. And he's incredibly vulnerable at times, but he likes to put that in right in front of himself, which is incredibly courageous. So, for things like "I'm a Boy," I had to climb inside that, and I really struggled to find the voice. But when I listen back to it now, it's kind of interesting, because there's a haunted quality about it. You really do feel that you're this boy going, "But Mom, I'm a boy, not a girl." And there's a quality to my voice that was obviously mentally trying to tune in to where Pete was when he wrote that. Then *Tommy* and "I Can See for Miles" and those things happened, and that gave me the vehicle to develop the voice that I ended up with.

Judd: What I thought was interesting was that you were the only person in the band who wasn't imbibing and partying and drinking and drugging. You were the person keeping the trains [running] on time. In the book, you talk about flushing their stash down the toilet. And they fired you. Then, when you join the band again, after they took you back, you say that they were mean to you for years as a result of this.

Roger: It was really a feud between myself and Keith and John. John had a side to him that could be quite spiteful. He had this side of him that was dark. The reason I flushed their stash was that we did that first tour of Europe, and they managed to get ahold of this bag of amphetamine tablets. I tried them early on in our career, when we were doing two shows a night. We worked from eight to eleven at night—this is after a day in the factory, by the way—and then from two in the morning to five in the morning the next day. So, it was quite a long day, and I tried doing it just to help me stay awake, and all it did was dry me up, and I couldn't sing. All I ever wanted to do was be a good singer and deliver a good show. I'll tell you the reason for that: I went to see Cliff Richard and the Shadows at the Chiswick Empire, and I remember how many Saturday mornings I had to work to pay for those tickets. And if Cliff Richards and the Shadows had been shit that night, God help them. I really realized then that, as the person on the stage, you owe it to an audience to turn up. You do not ever dial it in. And what these pills were doing, because the band could take them, they were starting to speed the music up, and they were starting to make the music louder. And in those days, we had no monitors, so it was very rarely I heard myself singing. By the end of about five or six shows in Europe, they were not only taking one pill before the show, they were taking I don't know how many. We ended up at a show where I could not get the words of the songs in. It was ridiculous, and it was so loud. I've spent four years managing the chemistry of this band, and I'm listening to this stuff falling apart at the seams, and I think, *This has to stop, because they're far too good for this.* So, while they're busy gleefully smashing up the equipment at the end of the show, I go off the stage and I find Keith's stash in his suitcase and flush it. He comes off the stage, immediately looking for the stash, which is now gone. And he says, "Where's my stash gone?" And I say, "Well, it's down the toilet." And he attacked me with a tambourine. Which sounds very gentle . . .

Judd: It's like razors, right?

Roger: He didn't attack me with the skin of the tambourine. He attacked me slashing with the bells. Needless to say, he didn't get very far. I was thrown out of the band for fighting, and I was out of the band for about four weeks. And they did a few shows without me.

Judd: Who sang in those weeks?

Roger: I don't know. I don't really care. I've never asked Pete about it. I've never talked to them about it. I really didn't give a shit.

Judd: You were talking about starting your own band during that time.

Roger: That was how it was then. I felt, *Well I've started this band. I'll start another one.* By now, I knew I could sing. We'd had a hit record, I'd a following, I knew my voice was doing something, and if it was to be in a band that had potential but we're throwing it all away because of this silly bag of amphetamine, I don't want to be in that band anyway. Anyway, after a month, the management comes knocking at the door, and they'd had a talk with the band and told the band, "You're not working without Roger. It's just not happening." Apparently they'd been booed off. That might not be true, but I've heard that. They said, "We've talked to the boys, and they've agreed to take you back if you promise not to fight." I said, "I'll tell you what. I'll go back, and I'll promise not to fight again, but they have to promise not to do any drugs before a show. I don't care what they do after the show, but they go onstage straight." And they lived up to their half of it, and I lived up to my part of it, but for those two or three years after that—because Keith and John knew that I had promised not to fight, but they knew my red mist and how it could come down—they would do everything they could to antagonize me. I used to just think of myself as a duck, and I would just let it roll off my back.

Judd: Did it make you feel isolated in the band, that they want to party like that?

Roger: I've been isolated all my life. It didn't bother me. I've always wanted to be the dog and never one of the sheep. So, it never bothered me.

Judd: Were they bonded in a way that you weren't with them?

Roger: Once the drugs kicked in, I felt isolated, because I didn't do any of it. I got to be very good friends with Owsley Stanley, the maker of LSD, Purple Haze, and all that. Great chemist. He said to me, "Roger, whatever you do, never take any chemical drugs. They will not agree with you." I got on great with Owsley, and for some reason or the other, because he was so respected by everybody—the Grateful Dead worshipped Owsley—I listened to him. He said, "Just smoke the pot. That will never hurt you. Here's a present." And he gave me this joint that was about this long, and it was wrapped in the Stars and Stripes. I said goodbye to him, and the next day, we traveled down to Monterey, where all the others after the show dropped acid and were tripping, while I spent the night smoking this mentholated Stars-and-Stripes thing that Owsley had given me. And it was wonderful. I woke up in the morning, and I was fresh as a daisy and straight. The others were somewhere in outer space, looking at everything, and I had to get them back to the UK all the way from Monterey, through the San Francisco Airport and New York, and then get them through immigration when they're all like this. Oh God. You got no idea what it's like to be on a plane with them. Pete spent his whole time looking at my caftan tan coat, but apparently, according to Pete, that's what led him to write "I Can See for Miles." He looked like he could.

Judd: It also seems like it would be hard to conceive of *Tommy* if you didn't do that.

Roger: What that whole journey did for him was it turned him off drugs, and he got into Meher Baba, into religion, really deeply into it. Pete never does anything by halves. His work ethic is extraordinary. He got into Meher Baba and went completely antidrug for a very long period of time. Right up until after Keith Moon's death. So, that was the most creative and the most joyous part of the Who as the originals, with Keith in the band. That part of our lives was the most fantastic time.

Judd: Can you talk about a press conference where you guys brought in all the music journalists to tell them about *Tommy* and then played part of *Tommy*? Can you tell me that story?

Roger: It sounded ridiculous. We'd written a rock opera, and it's about a deaf, dumb, and blind boy who plays a pinball machine, and of course, [the reporters are] just getting drunker and drunker in a tiny little club in the West End of London. They all seemed very disinterested in the spiel. So, we thought, *Let's just play the music.* And we played most of *Tommy*, and we flattened them, and they went out with their heads spinning, and the reviews they gave us were incredible. So, it just shows, you can do all the talking in the world, but if you can play a good piece of music well, you'll move mountains.

Judd: Do you remember the first time you heard what the premise of it was?

Roger: The premise was a very simple idea: What would life be like if all you experienced were vibrations? I thought that was very interesting, because music is vibration. And this thing's carried through Pete's life and quite a few of his things, like [the rock opera] *Lifehouse*—that's the theory that if you ever find the true spark that sparked up the universe and the cosmos, it will be a music note. That to me is magical, and it was the same thing with *Tommy*. So, we slowly but surely pieced these songs together, and Pete would go home, write demos, and bring them in two days later. Kit Lambert was instrumental to the narrative of *Tommy*. He wrote a film script. It was very much like the stage play. And it was just a magical period where we were free to rule our own lives creatively. Unlike the music business today, which is kind of ruled by the accountants and the lawyers.

Judd: You were taking gigantic creative swings. With the *Lifehouse* project, some people said he was almost envisioning some version of the internet.

Roger: He had this idea of the grid rather than the web. It was the search for this note, the meaning of life, and it was incredibly futuristic. It's almost like we're moving into *Lifehouse* at the moment, with virtual reality and all that stuff. Pete had written about experience suits and things like this.

Judd: Where did he get that from? Were other people talking about that, or did he conceive of it?

Roger: Other people weren't. But instead of him just writing the music and it being whatever story you wanted in your head, he'd written this film script about this vibration. And Pete is not a film script writer. That's a different skill. So, none of us could get our heads around it. And we'd have meeting after meeting after meeting, and it'd usually end up with us all very, very drunk trying to understand it, and Pete getting very frustrated. But in the end, he had the fabulous songs, the wonderful songs, which we experimented with. We did some live stuff at the Young Vic in London, where we'd play all afternoon with people just coming in off the street. No charge. We just thought, *Can we find this thing that Pete's looking for?* We did that for two or three weeks and then decided, "Let's go out and do a few shows with it," and we did a few live shows. We're experimenting with the tape machine, putting all the synthesizers on "Baba O'Riley," all that stuff. It went down incredibly well with audiences. That's the only album we've really ever recorded where we had the songs quite a long time before we got in the studio.

Judd: Was it considered a disappointment that you couldn't figure out how to put the whole thing together like *Tommy*? Because the album it became, *Who's Next,* is that the biggest of all the albums?

Roger: *Tommy*'s the biggest of all them. *Who's Next* is a strange album. It should have been a double album and never quite made it. Of course, individual songs on that album—"Baba O'Riley," "Won't Get Fooled Again," "Behind Blue Eyes"—they've become kind of legendary. But as a continual piece, it's not as strong as either *Tommy* or *Quadrophenia.* I don't think, anyway, but fans will argue with you anyway, just for the hell of it.

Judd: You've told this story before, in the early days, about Pete's guitar smashing into the ceiling, and he seemed embarrassed as the reason why he started smashing the guitar.

Roger: You'd have to ask him about that, but from my perspective, over my left shoulder, it was kind of a weird moment, but then it was an explosion of anger. It was a Rickenbacker as well. My heart was bleeding. I thought about all those hours it took me to make my first guitars, and there was this Rickenbacker he's destroying. I could have repaired it, it would've been all right! But the effect it had on the audience was extraordinary, and of course, Kit Lambert, who was then our manager, recognized it to being the key to us getting noticed. It was like how to write your name large on a wall and get people to see it.

Judd: Did they ever get bored of doing it?

Roger: We got very bored of doing it. I got more bored of the fact that no one ever wrote about the noise and only ever wrote about the visual. Because the noise, for me, and the sound that it created, this whole auto-destructive art thing, the noise was the important thing. Incredible. The guitar used to scream like an animal being sacrificed. It used to howl and scream. Moon's drums would thunder. Entwistle's bass [was] going double, and [the] feedback. And I used to do a thing with Keith's cymbals on the microphone. The sound was just too immense. Never once did they ever write about the sound. All they ever wrote about was "They smashed their instruments," and I found that very dull.

Judd: And it was expensive.

Roger: It was very expensive.

Judd: One recurring thing in the book that I was surprised by is, in every chapter you talk about going on tour, they would break the guitars, they would trash the hotel rooms, you would every once in a while be arrested for stuff *they* did, and then you would come home and find out you'd lost money on the entire tour.

Roger: It was really extraordinary. Because there's something about having a hit record. Immediately, all your friends overnight think you're a millionaire. Of course, we'd had hit records for six years; people thought we were millionaires. We didn't have any money. We did a tour in 1971. We came home from it, and our accountant said, "You've done great this year, you've done really great: You started the year with a debt of six hundred fifty-five thousand pounds," he said. "And now I'm happy to tell you it's down to six hundred *thirty-two* thousand." And you'd go, *Well, this is mad.* This is how stupid it all was. Because you've got to remember that kind of money now would probably be twenty million dollars. Of course, Keith Moon, hearing this news, immediately stripped bollock naked and laid his balls on the table.

Judd: What was that meant to signify? What was his message?

Roger: I'm thinking it was his fuck-you message to the accountant. I'll leave this to say that his balls were upside down, because he was standing on his head on the chair.

Judd: You've said when you're twirling it around onstage, the mic sometimes flies into the crowd.

Roger: The few times, the lead is broken. I tape them on really well, to make sure it can't come off from the plug. But there's two times the lead's broken, and where the mic was going, I wonder if it's come down yet. Because when it's spinning, it must be going probably a hundred miles an hour.

Judd: People are injured right now somewhere.

Roger: I've been waiting for lawsuits.

Judd: In this period you've been doing a bunch of tours, big triumph tours and the Super Bowl and the amazing performance at the [Concert for New York City]. What does it feel like in this era for you?

Roger: We're having the time of our lives, Pete and I. For the first time for a long time, since Keith died, the band feels like it's doing the music in the right way. We're progressing. It can never be the same. We can never have the energy of our youth, but the music is still there, and that was what was always important to me, and I know that's what was always important to Pete. Every time we play those songs, Keith and John are there with us. The noise they made in their life is still echoing, and every time we play the music, we ground it again. So, they've never left me when I'm onstage; they're still there in my head. They always will be.

Judd: I saw the *Quadrophenia* show a few times, and it really was remarkable to see you do the entire album.

Roger: I love doing *Quadrophenia*, and it's a tough one to sing. It is a tough one to sing for any singer. There's been a few tribute nights to the Who where guest singers come up, and they all come up to me afterward and say, "How do you do it?" And I realize there's something about my voice that doesn't sound very high, but the songs are incredibly high. They are up in the high Bs and the high Cs, some of the notes. But I just love it. I just love Townshend's music. I think he is one of the most important rock composers, or any popular music composers, of the twentieth century. In my opinion, he should be out there with the Lennons and McCartneys. If not as popular, but in the quality of his music. He writes in a classical manner. There's something else going on in Pete's songs that is nowhere else out there.

Judd: As a teenager, *Quadrophenia* was the kind of album that got you through that period of your life. Listening to songs like "I'm One," which we used in *Freaks and Geeks* for a sequence. And I talked to Eddie Vedder about it—that was the record where we felt like somebody understood what was happening.

Roger: Pete's genius is that. It still happens today. The audience, when we play *Quadrophenia*, goes from eight years old to eighty. And it speaks for every generation going through. Now, that is pure and utter genius.

Judd: How was it doing the Super Bowl?

Roger: I hated it.

Judd: Is it terrifying?

Roger: It's not terrifying. You're completely out of control of anything. And the dressing room smells of jock strap, as you probably know.

Then the stage has to be set up. And of course, you have to do a recording of it, in case they lose transmission to the stage, because everything's done so quickly. So, you have to do a recording of it first, and you also have to sing it and do it live, but you never quite know what one they're using. And you think, *Why?* It is a big honor, I understand that, but the Who aren't really up for medleys. I did my best putting that piece together. It was left to me to do it. I thought it gave an indication of the kind of stuff that we've done through our whole career. Although I don't like medleys generally, I think it flowed as a single piece.

Judd: How about the [Concert for New York City]? Because that really was a remarkable performance.

Roger: That was a tough cookie. Just emotionally for everybody, for the Western world, surely. It was traumatic. Wonderful but sad. All your emotions were amplified a thousand, maybe a million times.

Judd: You talk in the book also about when you had meningitis, and you looked back on your life and you were happy with it.

Roger: Well, you could hardly be sad with it, could you? From when I got kicked out of school to where I was laying in that hospital bed, really thinking I was going to die. They couldn't find out what was wrong with me. I was getting worse and worse and worse. I had tubes coming out of everywhere. The pain was horrendous. And I just thought about my life, and I was in wonder of where it's taken me and what I've done and how lucky I've been with my family. All the things that I've achieved. And I just thought, *Ya know, Rog. It doesn't matter if there's no more.* Because I was calling people up saying goodbye. The only thing I could work is a finger to push a Skype button. And I really didn't think I'd make it. So, I laid there and I thought about it. *It's all right, you won't leave anyone in trouble, let go.* And I don't know if they had given me a drug or what, but an incredible peace came over me, a calm like I can't describe. There were no lights at the end of tunnels, there was none of that, but my brain did have a thought: *Why fear?* And I thought about how everybody views life as an exit, and I thought, *If you're on the other side of that door, Roger, it's an entrance.* So, now, every time I meet anyone that feels they're on their way there, I say, "Head for the entrance."

SACHA BARON COHEN

January 2019

Judd: How has it been returning to television with *Who Is America?*

Sacha: Bizarre, because this is the first time I've shot something simultaneous to releasing it. I'd be filming, and then I decided to reedit while I was filming. I looked at the show at three o'clock in the morning the day before I left Morocco, which is where we'd been filming, and realized I got it all wrong. So I started reordering and reorganizing everything.

Judd: I bet Showtime loved that. They're like, "We already did closed-captioning!"

Sacha: Something I've noticed with all corporations is there's a point where something is just "good enough." They've done the budget, they've worked out roughly what it's going to do for them, and the difference from its being good and very good, or very good and excellent, isn't really worth the hassle. They just go, "Okay, this movie's going to make sixty million. If it's ten percent better, it's going to make sixty-two million."

Judd: They did it on *Superbad.* We knew the movie was good, but it needed more support from the studio, so we called Amy Pascal at Sony, and we said, "You have to throw a lot more money at this. We'll put out the first five minutes of the movie on the internet, just so people can get the sense of it." And she did that.

Sacha: Our experience was the opposite in that they wanted to launch a traditional long marketing campaign. And I said no. "I want no marketing campaign. I don't want you to announce the show." Every two months, Showtime would say, "So, we're going to announce it now, right?" And I said, "No, no, no. We're going to *drop* the show."

Judd: Like a Beyoncé album?

Sacha: Yeah, but what I didn't tell them was that I didn't mind whether the show was a success or not. My aim was that the show was as good as it could be. And I knew that if we did a normal publicity campaign, [the real] people [in the film] like Roy Moore and Joe Arpaio would sue or try and get an injunction. Or they would start getting calls from the White House.

Judd: They would have too much time to find ways to fuck with the show.

Sacha: They could get a court order or start suing and could basically shut it down. And part of the appeal for the show was we were getting powerful people. And once they start suing, the networks start thinking, *Wait a minute, is this worth it? Do we really need Bernie Sanders?* But the network was actually great, because they kept it secret, which is quite incredible, considering who we got. And secondly, they were tough when there were objections. We shopped this show around a bit, and one of the conditions for a channel buying it was that I could speak to the head of the channel and ask them, "If you get a phone call from Washington saying we want this thing pulled, are you going to say yes or no?" And David Nevins at Showtime got on the phone and said, "I'll stand by you."

Judd: And did that call from Washington eventually come?

Sacha: Yes. We're in DC, our first interview is with Bernie Sanders, and I'm doing this character, Billy Wayne, who's a conspiracy theorist. It's my first time as this character, so I'm not deep in character; the accent's not quite there. We sit down, and it's chaotic. We know we've only got an hour with Bernie Sanders. He's late. And he gets pissed off within five minutes, when he realized that he was with this idiot. He didn't think it was part of a prank; he just thought, *This is not the show that you told me that we're going to make.*

Judd: What did you say it was going to be about?

Sacha: I can't remember. We said it was for Showtime, about great political minds.

Judd: And then everyone says yes because they wanted to be on the show?

Sacha: Yes. So, with Bernie Sanders, he comes out of it, and his team are really good. They immediately call up CBS, who owns Showtime, and they go, "What the hell is this? We're going to the press with this. Who was this?" And the good thing was CBS didn't know what it was. So, they asked Showtime. They go, "Do you know anything about this show?" Showtime said, "Yeah, we're making it; it's legitimate." Sanders's people said, "We don't know. These could be terrorists, and if you don't pull the interview we're going to go to Congress and get a congressional hearing on this terrorist group that's going around DC." His team is tough. Sanders didn't know whether it was a right-wing show trying to destroy him or what.

Judd: And it's funny, because you're getting to see a side of politicians that most people don't see, which is not even necessarily what you're putting on the show, but their *protectors*.

Sacha: Bear in mind, this our first morning in DC, and I have to survive there for two weeks.

Judd: In that character?

Sacha: We did three characters there. During those two weeks, no one in DC can know that I'm there. But right away, Bernie Sanders already thinks something's up. If he goes to the press, everything's destroyed. We wouldn't be able to get all the rest of the guys that we wanted.

Judd: What was your philosophy on what you wanted to accomplish by goofing on the Ted Koppels of the world?

Sacha: We were thinking in the writers' room, "What's the modern Ali G?" Like, who's the modern stupid interviewer? And we thought, *Actually, those guys are the conspiracy theorists.* Because of the internet, they have as much status now as respected journalists. It's absurd that Ted Koppel, one of the most respected journalists in America, should sit with one of the worst journalists. This character is basically the worst possible journalist in America. But because of the internet, he can possibly be on Breitbart.

Judd: It's not shocking that [that] guy would have a show—and a show that people would want to be seen on, too.

Sacha: Well, Ted Koppel didn't. We had the simple philosophy that this character, the interviewer, is a guy who believes every lie that Trump has said. So, Trump says he had the biggest inauguration crowd ever? This guy's going to prove it. And he's got a bunch of fake evidence, and it's pretty bad faked evidence. And Ted Koppel had enough integrity to say, "You're an idiot; you're spreading lies. I'm not going to sit for this anymore. I'm leaving." There are different styles of comedy that we were looking at, and I think some of the reviewers missed that. They said, "Oh, this one failed with Ted Koppel because he didn't get his ass out and scream, 'America!' like another guy on the show."

Judd: And then you have the rich character who's like Trump.

Sacha: Gio Monaldo. Guys like Trump have their Roger Stones, the facilitators who let evil stuff happen. Weinstein had that as well. They go, *If Harvey Weinstein wants to rape somebody, how can I get the girl that he wants, because it's going to be good for my career.* The idea was to have a look at what evil things people will do out of greed. And it was all done by hidden camera. We had one interview, in Las Vegas, where we made Gio worse than Weinstein. We went, "Let's say this guy has sex with children, and we're going to get a concierge, one of those guys that help rich people in Vegas, and see how long it will take him to walk out of the room once he realizes that the rich guy in front of him has had sex with an eight-year-old boy. How many seconds is it going to take to get up and go, 'I'm out of here and I'm calling the police'?" The shocking thing we found out was that this concierge that we spoke to not only didn't leave the room; he helped the rich guy solve his problem. My character said, "There's this eight-year-old boy, he's victimizing me; he's threatening me. He sent me these Snapchat messages that he wants tickets to the Criss Angel concert, the bastard!" The concierge goes, "We can get the Criss Angel tickets, not a problem." Then I go, "Can't we get rid of the boy? Can we murder the kid?" And he goes, "Unfortunately, we can't do that in America." By the end, he's helping me fix the problem of the boy. And I go, "Thank you for helping fix the problem. I want to have fun tonight. Can you get me someone for me to play around with tonight?" And he goes, "All right. How old?" I go, "Under bar mitzvah, but above eight." And he's like, "Okay. I know somebody who can get you something for tonight."

Judd: Wow, and that didn't air.

Sacha: It didn't air. And it's incredible. It's journalism rather than comedy. We ended up turning over the footage to the FBI.

Judd: At some point, there's no humor in it at all. It's just pure art. It's horrific. Because you think, *Oh my God, these evil networks exist. In this world of the super-rich, they can have anything.*

Sacha: Exactly. But what was happening, at least for this concierge— I think the FBI looked into it and thought he probably didn't have a network. He probably was just trying to get some money out of me. These guys think they're going to be in with a billionaire. When we were researching *The Dictator,* I spent a bit of time in the United Arab Emirates, and there was a philosophy there of like, "We can get any actress we want to fly over, and we'll have sex with them, and we'll send a private jet and five million dollars and send them back." There's always been this network of people with incredible money.

Judd: I've heard you speak a little bit about your interest in history, and your studies about the Jews of the world and the civil rights movement, but at some point, these interests eventually turned into comedy. How did you decide that this is the kind of thing that you would do? How did this idea evolve from when you were a kid?

Sacha: I was ten years old when I met my friend Johnny Popper, and I thought, *He is the funniest guy I've ever met in my life.* Then, at eleven, I find out about Monty Python and realize that Johnny had stolen all their jokes. I still stayed friends with him. The first sketch that I wrote was with Johnny. I was nine years old. We performed it for a bunch of fifteen-year-olds at a Jewish Youth Club, and they all found it really funny because we were nine-year-olds trying to be funny. Then I became obsessed by sketch writing. I just loved getting people to laugh. Eventually, I applied to Cambridge for university, because Monty Python and Pete and Dudley, who I love, had all come from the Footlights group in Cambridge. I applied just to get into the Footlights, and obviously, I don't get into the Footlights. I audition again; I don't get in. I audition again; don't get in. In the end, when I left university, I went to the president of Footlights and asked, "Why did you never let me in?" And he mentions a year when I had come up with a character called Solo, who's an idiot and just the biggest fucking twit ever. It's the type of comedy that we hadn't been playing with there, which is a clown, a complete moron. So, I do a sketch as this character at this Footlight event, in front of five hundred people. And they are in hysterics. I'm going on for fourteen minutes, fifteen minutes, and it killed. But later, the president of Footlights said, "You never knew when to get off. You always milked it." That was why he never let me in. He was mad at me for staying onstage for too long.

Judd: On some level, there are some people who see others who are really good, and they're just not cool with it.

Sacha: I think it was a class thing as well. When I went to Footlights, they were doing imitations of Python—they were kind of upper class about their comedy. They were doing the the Dead Parrot sketch while I came in, and I'm this sort of ethnic kid who, for my first audition, took my top off and played with my nipples. I remember there was one woman who was in hysterics, but she came to my room afterward and she said, "You're never going to get in."

Judd: How do you eventually turn your rejection from Footlights into a first gig?

Sacha: I don't know how this happened, but I get offered the lead in a Chekhov play at university. That weekend, the director goes, "I'm sacking Sacha. He's terrible; he cannot act." Which is obvious. I'd never acted until then. But the rest of the crew really liked me, and they're like, "You sack Sacha, and we're out." So, I went ahead, and I did the play and actually turned it into a comedy, and it went well. Then I start getting lead roles in other productions. It actually taught me how to act, which was useful. And then, one of the actors I'd been working with tells me about an amazing course he had done, called a clown course. He did it outside of Cambridge, with a guy named Philippe Gaulier, who's the world's foremost expert on clown. At the end of Cambridge, I go and study with him, and I realize I was doing a clown character when I performed as Solo, at the Footlights event. This style of humor is clown humor. Philippe also specialized in something called the buffoon. And he's one of the few guys to teach it, and his explanation was that it's nasty satire. It's really hard-hitting, horrible satire from people who have been historically dispossessed.

Judd: Do you feel like the mistreatment of people really bothers you? Because it's in all of your work. Most people don't get bothered enough to make it a big part of their life's work to continually point out that something is wrong.

Sacha: I've become more and more preoccupied with it. And I say "preoccupied" because it's not something that's conscious. For example, the situation with Syria is very depressing. When I was a history student at university, one of the big questions that we could never understand was how could the Holocaust [have] happen[ed]? One big theory was, "Well, no one knew about it, and so that's how it happened." But then, with Syria, you say, "Actually, the whole world knows about it; they just don't give a shit." People are prepared to do things if it serves their own interests. So, there's a new conclusion to that older question, which is: "The Holocaust happened because of greed and because people didn't give a shit." So, I have two priorities when I make comedy. Number one, I'm trying to make people laugh; and number two, I'm trying to get this stuff out of what's in my head.

Judd: When you look back at *Borat* and how big it was, but also what it was about, what are your reflections on why it was so popular?

Sacha: I did *Borat* during the Bush era, and at that time, I had problems with a lot of stuff that was going on in America, and I wanted to expose it. I also just wanted to make a really funny film, so I gravitated toward this idea of being an ignorant foreigner who could get people to show the extremity of their views.

Judd: When did you first come up with characters like Ali G and Borat and this style of comedy?

Sacha: I had stumbled into this form of undercover character comedy when it didn't yet exist in England. I was the host for a live cable TV show, which was a program for teenagers. I was twenty-four, and I said to myself, *Okay, I'm going to do this live show but I'm going to perform as these characters who are going to comment about the show.* One of the characters that I did was an early form of Ali G, and as we're shooting him, I see some guys dressed like me. With a skateboard in my hands, I go and talk to them and start doing bad tricks on my skateboard and falling off. After about three minutes of them laughing, I said, "Guys, see, I'm joking, I'm kidding around." They were surprised that I was playing a character, and then, at that point, it was literally an epiphany for me. That was the moment that changed my life. I go, *Oh my God, they believe me.* And then a double-decker tourist bus pulls up, I look at my director, and he nods, so I jump on the bus. The camera follows. I get to the top deck, and I start freestyle rapping into the tour guide's microphone. Then the bus takes us over London Bridge, we get off, and there's a pub there, and I start breakdancing in the pub. They call the police and kick us out. Eventually, it gets to be two-thirty, and the show goes live at three, so I quickly change out of my costume. We go live on the air. I'm interviewing and doing some live discussion. Then we link to the first video clip of me from earlier that day. The kids loved seeing me interacting with real people. It's a new style of comedy for them. Then the show ends, and I get a message that the head of the channel wants to see me, and they say, "You try this again and you're sacked." Cheekily, I later take over another guy's news show for one day because he's sick, and two hours before I go on, there's going to be this fox hunt. I couldn't stand the upper class, and I hate the idea of chasing foxes just for amusement. So, I go down to where the fox chase is happening, and I go, *Okay, I'm going to play some foreign character.* As I'm driving down there, I look at what I've got in the car, and I've got a hat from Russia. I stick it on my head, and it's basically the beginning of Borat, and I start interviewing people as this foreign character. I came back from that, put it on air, and it kills. Eventually, we come up with an idea for a documentary series, and it's going to be me as Borat, undercover, living in a house with students, and there's going to be hidden cameras, and we're going to live there for three months. And this was before *Big Brother.* But the channel that I was working for ends up going bankrupt and has to close down. I pitched it to Channel Four, and they said no. That was it, and I ended up unemployed for a while.

Judd: And then someone else eventually let you do it?

Sacha: I end up traveling for a bit, and as I'm on a beach in Thailand, I'm thinking, *This is great. I could live here for one pound fifty a day. I'm never going back to England.* Then I get this phone call from my agent, for an interview, and she convinced me to go back. I ultimately didn't get that show, but while I was there, I showed the producers a bit of Borat. And they go, "We love that, we want that, have you got any other characters?" I came back the next day with Ali G, and they loved it. The next day, we shoot an interview with Ali G and the head of the London School of Economics, and we come back with it, and everyone in the office is crazy. They think he's hilarious. And that changed my life. Ali G went on the air, and the next morning, I was famous.

Judd: Why do you think Ali G became so wildly popular?

Sacha: The rise of Ali G was so fast because he wasn't a traditional white English character. People didn't know what his ethnicity was. Different people would claim him. The Greeks were claiming him; some people thought he was Black. The pirate radio stations go, "You got to check this guy out, this guy Ali G." People thought my name was Ali G and that Ali G was real. There was a bit of controversy when finally someone finds out my name is not Ali G, that I'm Sacha Baron Cohen, and I'm a Jew. So, they ask ten Black comedians, "Is Ali G racist?" Eight of them say, "No. We love it." One of them said, "I don't know," and one of them said, "Yeah. It's racist." The headline around the country becomes "Ali G Is Racist." This shocks me to my core and offends me, because I'd been interested in antiracist movements, I'd been involved in the antiapartheid movement, I studied this in university. I wanted to go out and speak, but we decided to be quiet. Luckily, the original journalist came out and said this is ludicrous. He's not racist, he's actually exposing racism, and this is great political satire. But by the end of that week, I was properly famous in England.

Judd: And you made a choice not to do any interviews as yourself for a really long time?

Sacha: Yes, so there were a few years where I did nothing. There was not a photo of me out. No photo of me as me, or interview as me.

Judd: I think, these days, it would be much harder to do zero promotion as yourself. In general, it's interesting to think what the reaction would be if you were to create these characters today.

Sacha: We experienced some of that with *Bruno*. GLAAD came out against *Bruno*, and that was very depressing, because we were doing the movie to expose homophobia. And I risked my life pretending to be a gay guy in the [American] South, and almost got killed a few times. We even shared the movie with GLAAD before it went public, and we asked them what they thought of it. The two heads of the group loved it. Then, a week before the movie came out, they asked us to make a couple of changes, and that was the first time in my career I made changes for an interest group. But then those two heads get sacked two weeks before the movie comes out, the new guys come in, and the first thing they do is they come out against *Bruno* as a movie. I was so upset.

Judd: Was it because they felt that you're having fun with gay stereotypes, or that a straight person shouldn't be able to goof on certain parts of gay culture?

Sacha: I don't know. I'm not going to speak for the gay community. I don't know if anyone *can* speak for the gay community, because it's so diverse. But *Bruno* exposed how difficult it is to be gay in that part of the country. While we were working on it, we realized early on that *Bruno* is essentially a gay rom-com. So, we knew there had to be a scene where he gets back together with the boy, and we're like, "Where is the funniest place where they make up and get back together? Where we can get the funniest reaction?" It's amongst the most homophobic people in the world, and they're going to kiss and make out and almost have sex. So, the funniest place to do that is in a steel cage match amongst about two thousand people who would happily kill the people who are making out.

Judd: Did you think, at the end of it, *I have pushed this too far*? That you had lost your mind a little bit with the risks you were taking?

Sacha: *Bruno* was too extreme for its time. I think if you released it now, it would be more acceptable, but at the time, it was this hardcore gay rights movie that had a lot of sex in there. We got reports from the middle of the country, where people went to the cinema with their families. There'd be a sex scene ten minutes in, and ninety percent of the cinema would get up and leave.

Judd: I sometimes look back on things I've made, where there was maybe a mess around it, but when you get ten years past it, you're so happy you did it.

Sacha: Oh, I'm really happy. Something like the cage match, I think, is my best reality set. We managed to pull off a scene that should have been impossible. We sent it to the lawyers to make sure we wouldn't be arrested or charged for inciting a riot, and we interviewed ten security guards, just to figure out how to get me out of this cage that's surrounded by two thousand people who want to beat me up.

Judd: How does this kind of thing compare to when you do scripted work as an actor? Because when you focus on a movie, whether it's scripted or unscripted, it seems like you go deep.

Sacha: I get too committed. When it comes to looking ahead to how to pace out the next project, I'm very bad at planning. And then I get terrified of committing to anything, because I know I'm going to go nuts deep.

Judd: Do you ever really fight for something, and you're sure it's the best thing ever, but then it just doesn't work at all?

Sacha: Of course. That is the insecurity of any artistic business where it's not a science. We've just got hunches. Sometimes you're wrong. I think there are two things, and they're not necessarily connected: There's the product, and then there's the ability to sell that product. There's a difference between whether the product is good and whether the marketing campaign is good. We could have made *Borat* in England, and it could have made three million dollars worldwide.

Judd: Sometimes you just catch a different wave. Or a wave is going against you, and you don't even really understand why.

Sacha: Unless you're Disney, and you're putting out existing brands, a lot of that stuff is luck. The sad part is that our work is tied in with money. We're not allowed to lose money. However, you look at any sort of creator, and you'll see that it's a really important part of the creative process to put out disasters. Look at Peter Sellers. I grew up idolizing Sellers and still do. If you look at his IMDB page, he does movie after movie that is dreadful, but the ones you remember him for are *Dr. Strangelove* and *Being There*. This guy's a genius. It's important to have the flop. It's important to have the disaster and go, *Yeah, I'm going to do something different.*

Judd: I remember we all loved and felt really good about *The Cable Guy*, but it didn't do well, and we took a big beating for that. But now these movies get these afterlives on Netflix or somewhere else, where suddenly the world goes, "Wait a second. That movie is hysterical." They put out a twentieth anniversary Blu-ray with all these extras, and we're like, "Wow, they still think it's worth putting out." Even *Heavyweights*, the first movie we did with Ben Stiller, is still coming out in all these different editions. But when it was first released, it made no money. For some reason, people still watch it.

Sacha: It'll be interesting to see what is remembered, if anything, when we are old. Or the people who liked our stuff when they first saw it, will they still like it years later? I remember my dad trying to get me to watch Jacques Tati. When I finally watched it with him, he goes, "Yeah, it's not so funny anymore." But I think that's okay. I can talk now about satire and the importance of the work and the desire to change people's minds, but a few hundred years ago, we were the court jesters. I would be running around with an inflated pig's bladder bonking people on the head. So, the idea that I could have any influence, or somebody would invest money in the court jesters, is ludicrous. The reason you and I are sitting here talking about our important work is because of technology, the advent of radio and TV and the internet.

SAMANTHA BEE

September 2020

Judd: How many episodes do you do a year now?

Samantha: We've been doing thirty-four or thirty-five. I think if we get picked up for a sixth season, I'll try to do less. It's okay to speak your mind just thirty times.

Judd: That's also a lot to be in charge of. It's a weird thing in comedy, where there are the comedians who are pure energy and joy, but they're also on the verge of disaster. And then there are the rare ones who know how to run things. Jon Stewart's like that. [Steve] Carell, [Stephen] Colbert, Amy Poehler—people who are so funny, but they are going to finish exactly on time.

Samantha: I think I fall into that category, too, of, like, workhorse. *We're gonna make this work. These are the ingredients. Let's do this.*

Judd: If somebody had asked you when you were a kid what you were going to do with your life, what would you have said?

Samantha: I never really had an answer. I liked theater and all that stuff, but I didn't really start performing until much later in life. I was the first person in my family to go to college, so I wanted something that was going to be financially stable. I kind of assumed I would go to law school, just because the only thing I really knew was that I wanted to have a good job.

Judd: When did you start performing?

Samantha: I took a theater class in college because I thought it would be so easy. One of the things you had to do for this class was work on a production, so I auditioned for a part, and I got it. I had to sing and be onstage, and I didn't know anything about acting. I didn't care about it then. So, I walked onto the stage with absolutely no problem—I wasn't particularly nervous—and I sang a solo and just did the part. As I was doing it, I realized, *Oh, I love this. I choose* this. Then I just resigned myself to a life of poverty.

Judd: In Canada, what's the path to a career in theater? What did you think you would need to do in order to break into that world?

Samantha: I didn't really know. I was totally disconnected from that world. I'm actually an intensely shy person. I switched to a more conservatory-style school in Toronto, where I thought I would be able to make connections, but by then I was in my late twenties. I thought, *If I don't try this, I'm never going to do it.* So, I got a job doing regional theater for teens, which involved a lot of traveling theater shows. Awful, dreadful shows. But I did one show that toured high schools, and the people that I met in that show did sketch comedy, and they asked me if I wanted to replace a girl in their troupe. At the time, my now-husband was doing tons of sketch comedy and was very successful at it in Toronto, so I reluctantly consented to join them.

Judd: You didn't see what he was doing and think, *I'm going to get into that*?

Samantha: No, it seemed like a miracle to me. I didn't really understand how he made shows happen. He's a great sketch performer. They were really, really funny. I would go to the shows and just didn't understand how they did them: Do you just call up the theater and say, "I want to do a show"? How do you even start writing a sketch? I was intrigued to try it myself, but not through [my husband] Jason [Jones]. We understood that there were certain boundaries that we shouldn't cross with each other. When I finally tried sketch comedy, the moment people started laughing at the sketch, I realized, *I should do this. I thought I wanted to do theater, but I actually want to do comedy.* After that, I started seriously doing sketch comedy with an all-female troupe and thought I would just do that forever. *We won't make any money at it, but I'll just always have this trunk of props in my car. And we'll just do this until we're eighty, I guess. We'll just keep performing in bars.* We were called the Atomic Fireballs.

Judd: What was that life like in Toronto, as a traveling sketch show? How do you make a living?

Samantha: I had other jobs. I worked in restaurants; I waitered a lot. Then, toward the end, right around the time that I auditioned for *The Daily Show*, I was working at an ad agency. I wasn't copywriting or anything like that. It was actually working on the technical side, the print shop side. I was so bad at it. I didn't know what I was doing. I left a trail of destruction, because I got hired for *The Daily Show* while I was working at the print shop, and I just walked away from the job. For sure, there was a cascading series of ad-related problems all over western Ontario because I didn't follow up on so many different projects.

Judd: So many comedy nerds spend a lifetime dissecting and obsessing over everything comedic and how it works. What was your relationship with comedy at that point?

Samantha: I didn't have an aspiration to work in the world of comedy, but I was a big consumer of comedy. So, I had a very steady diet of watching people do comedy. It was a very important part of my life, except that I didn't think that it was ever possible for me. So, when I started doing work with the Fireballs, they actually had a preexisting approach to putting on shows that I slid into. And I really liked it. We were really disciplined about writing. We would all write a certain number of sketches, and then we rented a space to rehearse in, and we put on shows all the time. So, we were actually very industrious and busy, and it taught me a tremendous amount about writing for myself. We were writing constantly, and we never rejected anything because we respected each other's ideas too much. We should have said no to each other a little bit more, probably. But we wrote a lot, and we made a lot of shows happen. I was doing my day job, whatever my day job was, but at night, we'd put on these big shows. And it was so "do it yourself." We would contact venues, put together a whole lineup, talk to our graphic artist friends to make us a poster, and then we would plaster the city with posters. I would make a playlist, and we would put a whole night of comedy together. And we did that for years.

Judd: Was there a lot of political comedy in the group? What do you remember of the type of sketches you would do?

Samantha: It was not at all political. It was just observational and fun stuff that we loved. Personally, I was very interested in political comedy, because I watched *The Daily Show* religiously. We had a special zone in our house where we watched *The Daily Show* every night. We were huge Jon Stewart fans. We really didn't watch a lot of television, but at eleven o'clock every night, we would retire to the room where the TV was and watch the show together. Are you getting the impression that I fell into my career? Because I think I did. Because as I lay it out, I kind of fell face-first into it.

Judd: There are definitely people whose careers reveal themselves to them. But there's also so many people that, in their late twenties, have friends go, "You should go up on open-mic night." And they find out that they're just hysterical. And it just hits them, *I can do this.*

Samantha: Even as *Full Frontal* came into being. When I was working at *The Daily Show,* I wasn't thinking that one day I'd have my own show. I truly didn't think that at all. I thought, *When this chapter of my life is over, we'll move into scripted comedy.* I thought that that was the next move. Not this.

Judd: When did you join *The Daily Show*?

Samantha: Two thousand three. I don't pretend to know why this was the case, but they were searching for a woman. They could only ever have one woman at a time, so they were looking very specifically for a woman. Of course, we had Second City in Toronto, and that had this huge reputation, so the casting people came to Toronto to see the women of Second City. I was not one of those women, but there was only a handful of women there, and the producer who put on that showcase audition didn't want to just put on a day with four women, so he asked his agent friends if they had any women who could fill out the gaps on this Saturday at a casting agency. So, I was a gap filler, but I had a forensic knowledge of the show. I was such a dedicated fan, and no one else there had ever seen it. *The Daily Show* was kind of a niche product in Canada at the time. It was barely available and was on a really small channel. I remember, there was one woman at the audition who I knew from the Toronto comedy scene, and she was like, "Which of these funny character hats should I wear?" And she'd brought a selection of hats. I was like, "I don't think they're looking for, like, hats. I think they just want you to do the material." And she was like, "I think I know what I'm talking about."

Judd: What did you do in that first audition?

Samantha: In the first audition, I just read two scripts that they gave us to read. One of them was a Stephen Colbert piece that I had seen on the show, and one was a Steve Carell piece that I had also seen on the show. So, I knew exactly how to do them. It was just fully organic for me, because I understood the tone of the show. I just did my best impression of Stephen Colbert, and they had me cold-read something else that I had also seen, like I had seen every episode. So, they had me come back.

Judd: How did they know that you can write or go in the field and interact with people?

Samantha: They didn't know. I don't know what their audition process is now, but it was terribly inadequate at the time, which I very much benefited from. It's fine to read a script there. But the reality is that you need to be able to interview people, because the majority of the work that I did was out in the field. So, I was terrified when they hired me. I was sure they'd made a terrible mistake. Jason stayed back in Toronto, because we both just assumed it wasn't going to work out, and we needed to be practical. We're just very pragmatic Canadian people.

Judd: You weren't going to buy the Manhattan townhouse yet. So, they throw you in the field, and you see what the job really is—what was that adjustment like?

Samantha: It was so scary. Again, I am very naturally shy. I'm really good at pretending over the years, but interviewing people is difficult. A conversation can take any turn. In the context of *The Daily Show*, you're trying to not only mark the beats of the story that you're trying to tell, [but] you need to add jokes on top of it that don't really make any sense in the context of what you're doing. The skill of both listening to the person you're interviewing *and* being able to pivot so that the conversation stays focused is something that took me a really long time to learn.

Judd: Did you eventually get to a point where you knew what people were going to do? Did it ever become predictable for you?

Samantha: You definitely try to predict what they're going to do. But you always have to build in the possibility that they're not going to go where you want them to go. I had to be told again and again to just listen to what the interview subject was saying. It's a skill set that maybe you learn in journalism school; I don't really know. It was not natural for me.

Judd: You were also developing a comedic character at that time. How did you eventually figure out your persona's point of view?

Samantha: For the first couple of years, I was probably doing an impression of Stephen Colbert. Just to have a basic level of competence. I was awful in my first few pieces. They're still so painful for me to watch. I *look* as terrified as I felt on the inside. It took a couple of years of constantly being in the field for me to feel remotely grounded, and I was always scared before every single interview. I'm *still* always scared that something's going to go wrong. So, working on a character, as you say, was so distant from my mind at the time. I remember the executive producers were telling me, "We should work on your character a little bit. So, what would your character do?" I told them, "I don't know what the fuck you're talking about. I'm just trying to survive. I have to go to South Dakota today and talk to somebody who's trying to take people's rights away. What character are you talking about?" I have to make comedy with this, spend the whole day with this person who's so odious. The thing that was very difficult during those times was that we didn't have a two-camera setup; we only had one camera. So, you would have the camera on the other person, and you would film them, like, for two hours of just sitting with them and trying to get all this material out of them. After that, you'd have to do a whole reset of the room, turn the camera around, and shoot me asking them all these questions. You would see this realization across their face of *Oh, I see what the game is.* In those moments, they started to see what you were doing. They could see the game. It was so awful, and it took hours.

Judd: Because, in the early days, a lot of the people that were being interviewed still didn't know what the show was.

Samantha: They did not know the show, which was so helpful. And they didn't know the show for most of the time I was there.

Judd: How was it adjusting to not only being on television, but also dealing with the newfound fame?

Samantha: I would say that the first two years were really, really hard. I had never really been on television before, in that way. I would google myself. It was so bad. Everyone hated me. I felt like I was failing at the job for so long.

Judd: Do you think that's just the internet, though? In the sense that you can always find something mean about yourself out there?

Samantha: You can, but you don't know how to handle that. It took me a long time to figure out that that was separate from me, and that I didn't have to take every criticism on board. It was mind-blowing that strangers would have an opinion about me. It still actually blows my mind a little bit to this day. One thing that was good about it was that, at the time that the show was at its peak, we were also having babies. So, that was very grounding. Upon reflection, I'm not sure that Jason and I fully went on the celebrity ride. I'm not sure we enjoyed as many highs as we could have enjoyed, partially because we're pragmatic people, but also because we were young parents and very, very focused on our kids. For us, it truly was a very good job, but we treated it as a job. We must sound like really boring people. But I do think that we were trying to always have a measured approach to all that stuff.

Judd: You and your husband seem like two peas in a pod.

Samantha: Oh, thank you. I do think we are very aligned. We can definitely finish each other's sentences, which does not mean that we do not argue about things. We for sure do. But we are career-aligned. I think we are always practical. He's such a hard worker. He's always writing. We got married in 2001, and we were already making stuff together. We made two movies that we shot in our house, on a small budget with some friends. And it was a labor of love. The only difference now is that the scale, the budget, is a little bigger. But it's the same basic process along the way. We've always kind of fluidly filled in where the other one was not working. Like, he worked a lot in Toronto, and I did not work nearly as much as he did. He got tons of work and filled in the gaps when I wasn't really working. Then I started working, and I filled in the gaps when *he* wasn't really working. So, it has cycled through a lot of different versions, where one of us was earning, the other one wasn't. When he would go away to shoot, that would be super challenging. It was very challenging for me to work on *Full Frontal* while he was in Vancouver shooting *The Detour* because we were taking care of the kids on our own. So, for me, it was full-on solo parenting, with getting everybody up, having breakfast, walking kids to school, then going to work on *Full Frontal*, shooting the whole show, coming home, making dinner. That was a lot of work, and I would go to bed every night at eight-fifteen—so, tired for months.

Judd: I want to talk about the kind of daily commitment it takes to make a show like *Full Frontal*, or *The Daily Show*, happen. What did you take from Jon as you had to create your own style of show and the structure for it?

Samantha: I obviously took away a lot from him. He was always the hardest worker in the building. He was usually the person who got there the earliest and the last person to leave—his work ethic is incredible. I definitely took that away and found that very inspiring. It took me a while to understand this, but I also took away a sense that everything that is on the show was his. Everything was marked with his presence. The show was filtered entirely through his editorial viewpoint, including pieces that I would shoot for him. He was totally involved in pulling them together, totally involved in editing them, watching the piece along the way to make sure that it represented his point of view perfectly. And I know that a lot of shows don't operate that way. I think that rarely exists. I love Oprah, but I filmed something for her show, and I asked the producers what Oprah thought of the material as we were going along. It was a piece about being a working parent, and it was pretty cute. And the producers were like, "I think she'll watch it when it airs." So, I learned that kind of deep involvement from him, I learned to care about every single second that's on the show, which is a very annoying way to be. It's disruptive for me to watch a piece and go, "I don't think this is working. Let's try to figure out a way to fix this." I'm extremely involved in the show on a very micro level, and that's hard to do, and probably lots of people don't like it, but I do. I like to be proud of what I'm doing.

Judd: You become the editor. You're the showrunner. I remember when I first ran my own show, I was just so embarrassed that I was allowed to tell anyone what to do. I had a hard time feeling comfortable with the crew, with all the departments, and the Teamsters. And it's hard to grab the mantle of that.

Samantha: It's hard because you see yourself as a worker, not the boss. Managing other people is really difficult. It's a whole discipline unto itself. People go to college for that, and they get really good at it. There are entire schools of thought around management. But when you fall into a comedy career, you are essentially this independent contractor. You're never managing anybody, and you never think about what it means to tell someone to do the thing you want them to do when they don't want to do it. They think they did a good job, and they probably did do a good job—but it isn't *you;* it has to represent you. It has been very uncomfortable at moments for me to tell people what to do. I've had to learn from watching Jon. I learned from watching him both enjoy my pieces and not enjoy them. Because fifty percent of the time, he'd be like, "Oh, what are we gonna do with this massive footage?" It's really painful to sit in the edit room with someone who doesn't like what you've made, while they reformat. *And* they do a much better job than what you did. It's painful. It's painful to watch the footage that you collected. It's painful to watch yourself on camera, and I learned how to do all of that.

Judd: And you learn how to be kind in that process of telling someone what to do.

Samantha: Totally. How to be assertive about your opinions when people don't listen to you. Sometimes I ask people to do something, and they literally don't listen to me. Then I have to say it again, and then they don't listen to me again. The third time, I'm like, "You're not listening to me." You have to be able to do that.

Judd: And to be funny while doing that, even as you have to hold that strength and be clear-eyed—that's what I find most difficult, because it feels like a different part of the brain.

Samantha: It's a totally different part of the brain, and it's unpleasant. No one goes into comedy to go, "Check it out. I'm gonna manage a whole bunch of people who come from different backgrounds, and we're all going to work together, and I'm going to try to keep them happy." It's so hard. I think everyone who works for me would agree that I fail as a manager sometimes. But I also succeed as well. It's just about taking those moments where you really failed to communicate something, but still having everybody logged onto a Zoom so you can tell them even more stuff. You have to find that inner capacity to go, *God, I hate this part of it. But I'm still going to try to also make everybody excited to do the show.*

Judd: Your show seems to be your vision of what you think a modern work environment should be. How did you design that?

Samantha: It's certainly a work in progress. You end up having all these huge ideas at the beginning, where you think, *Oh my God. This will be so great.* For instance, at *The Daily Show*, the intern program was so full of rich kids, because they're the only ones who could afford to take an unpaid internship while also living in Manhattan. When I went to create my own show, I wanted to design this wild intern program that takes people from economically diverse backgrounds. We would have a mentorship program, where we would bring people in who don't know the first thing about TV but have aspirations to work in it. And then you go, *Wait, but we also have to launch this new show out of nowhere, and we have to make thirty-four episodes a year.* And you also want to have someone who's still learning the ropes of comedy, where you promise to teach them everything you're doing while *you're* also just learning how to do it yourself. Very difficult. All these ideas are so great at first, and then you kind of lose the thread of them, and you have to pick those threads back up again when things are more stable. I feel like we're actually in a place where we can do that; it's more achievable now. It's very hard to put on a TV show thirty-four times a year.

Judd: What drives you to do it? What's the mission? Is there a chance of winning over the Fox News crowd, or is that not really the point?

Samantha: I don't think it can be; you would face failure every time. I don't think that we're out there changing people's minds; I really don't. I think occasionally we present information that people aren't familiar with, and that's a valuable service, but, mostly, for me, I think it's catharsis. That's certainly how I felt as a viewer of *The Daily Show* when I wasn't on it. I would watch the show and go, *Hey, I'm not crazy to think these things. He's saying it, and that's what I think.* You need that every once in a while, to just go, *Yes, the world is fucking crazy. This is nuts. This can't be real.* And then a commercial break happens.

TIG NOTARO

December 2020

Judd: Your story is that you left high school? Or middle school?

Tig: I failed eighth grade twice. Then they moved me up to ninth grade, so I wouldn't, like, toss myself out of a window. Because I would have been in eighth grade three times. So, they moved me to ninth grade, I failed that, and then I dropped out.

Judd: Looking back, do you go, *Oh, it was this learning thing*? What do you think it was?

Tig: I don't know if it was a learning thing. I still have it—there is a letter sent to my parents, an envelope that says, "To the parents of Tig Notaro." They said, "Give it to your parents; don't open it." And I got on the bus, and I opened it, and it had me checked off for all of these tests for special education, and I was like, *Oh, oh no.* So, I just hid the letter, and my parents never found out. I was eleven years old. I was so confused by that letter. And so, I hid it. So, yeah, I don't know what my learning disabilities might be. But I had a lot going on at home. I was very much the rebellious, mischievous one and the typical class clown.

Judd: I had a letter home like that, from sixth grade, that I was the cause of all sorts of trouble. My parents were fighting. I remember gluing all the chairs to the desks when no one was around, and there was a letter to my mom which said, "Judd refuses to accept punishments." They were really scared about it. Like I was a sociopath. But I do remember being young and thinking, *You can't break me*.

Tig: Right back at ya. My wife, Stephanie, is also a high school dropout, but she dropped out her senior year with a four-point-one [GPA], because she knew she wanted to act and write and has worked ever since she was eighteen.

Judd: I felt that way. I thought, *I function better in the world and not in these classes*. I'm the dumbass in the class, but when I get in the world, I kind of do well.

Tig: That's how I feel. When I lived at home, I used to always sketch out a one-bedroom apartment and where the different furniture would go. I was just excited to get out into the world.

Judd: You were in Houston mainly when you were a kid, or Mississippi?

Tig: Lived in Mississippi, and then we moved to Houston and Dallas. I lived in Austin as a young adult. We lived in New Jersey for a couple years. But I would say mainly Texas.

Judd: When you say that there were a lot of things happening at the house, was it divorce?

Tig: There was divorce. I was very close to my mother, but we had a very roller-coaster relationship, because she was the epitome of the mother that was cool, and she liked to stay up all night and have friends over, and she was an artist and a dancer, and she was really, really funny and just wild and shocking, and she didn't give a damn what anybody thought, and it was great. I think it molded me and who I was, but it also made me a little, like, "Um, could you take it down a notch?"

Judd: 'Cause she's big.

Tig: She's so big. I used to always tell people that if I said, "Have you met my mother?" nobody would say, "Huh, I think so. Maybe. I don't know." It's just not possible, because she was a force and a presence. She was a debutante, raised to be a New Orleans socialite, but she also rebelled against where she came from and the beliefs of who you're supposed to be as a person or a woman. She was also very beautiful and stylish and very dynamic. We clashed a lot, but we loved each other so deeply. When she would party, she would party. People partied at our house. My mother drank. There is this guy that used to come visit us, a friend of ours from England. He came to visit us maybe once a year and overdosed in our house.

Judd: How old were you when that happened?

Tig: He didn't die, but I remember being, like, "What's wrong with Chris?" I was probably maybe six or seven. If my stepfather was out of town on a trip, my mother might put us to bed and head out for the night. Stuff like that. It also gave me another version of *I don't give a shit.* I remember us calling our family in Mississippi when we were in Texas, like, "We're alone." It was just the party never stopped.

Judd: What were your mom and stepfather doing for a living?

Tig: My stepfather was an attorney, and my mother was a stay-at-home mother. So, we were her job, and she worked hard at it. She also took breaks. Like, she really took some breaks.

Judd: Did you talk to her about it later?

Tig: I think she copped to all of it. Just: "It was a different time and I loved you guys, and I didn't know what I was doing. I was doing my best." It was a lot of that kind of apology.

Judd: Was she a young mom? Did she have kids early?

Tig: She was maybe twenty-five? Pretty typical for the seventies, I would say.

Judd: People didn't helicopter parent back then. My mom never stepped in my high school once, other than me getting in trouble. I don't think they ever talked to a teacher or a guidance counselor. You'll see the amount of time you spend interacting with schools now. In a week, I talked to the school more than my parents did my entire childhood.

Tig: I'm curious of what my mother would think of my parenting, because we are so involved with our kids.

Judd: It's also the strange part, because on some level, you go, *I guess it worked. I'm here. I'm a nice person. I'm doing okay.*

Tig: My stepfather was military. He was the structure in our household. Because my real father—he and my mother were too similar for that to work out.

Judd: Was your father in the same city as you?

Tig: No, he was in Jackson, Mississippi, and then he moved to Maryland because he had other kids, and he decided that he wasn't gonna mess up again, and he was going to be in their lives. And we were kind of like, "Oh thanks. Good for them." He passed away like a year after my mother died. I went to say goodbye to him before he died and met a brother of mine for the first time, who was eighteen. I had seen my father here and there when I was on tour. I was taking a train once through the East Coast, and I stopped in DC, and we had a meal together in the train station. And he surprised me at a club in Virginia once, that kind of thing. But my stepfather was definitely who I was raised with. My real father didn't hold a steady job and had a lot of kids and got sober finally. To picture my mother and father together, I'd have no idea who I would be.

Judd: How old were you when they got divorced?

Tig: They split up when I was six months old. We lived on the Gulf Coast, and he would drive down to see us. Or, when we would go see our grandmother, his mother, in Jackson, we'd go visit him. It's so weird. He always lived in a not-very-nice apartment and didn't have a bed, slept on the floor. Had a card table for a table, with his loose change on it, and had guns everywhere, rifles. He carried a pistol and always had a gun or a knife in his cowboy boot. He was just like that. Anytime we were visiting our grandmother in Jackson, we would see our father. It would always be at her house, or we go see him in a motel room. And I wonder if it's because of his living situation, I don't know, but I feel like I was always in a motel room when visiting my father.

Judd: My parents got divorced, and my mom left my dad, and then she really struggled. She was very upper middle class, but suddenly she was broke and waitressing and miserable and in a rage about it.

Tig: For so long, I didn't really think about it. I just thought, *Oh, my father is broke.* Ultimately, I feel very thankful for all of them and love them all very much. But it wasn't really until I was probably eighteen that I really started to think about, like, *What is this all about?*

Judd: My parents hated each other so much. They didn't stop fighting in court until they both literally filed bankruptcy. So, it made me think, *Oh I gotta get a job. And I got to take care of myself. I don't think they can take care of me.* It made me very hypervigilant to pay my bills and have the right job while I pursued comedy. I got hyper-organized from their madness. I was really afraid of chaos. As a result of that, it made me a producer.

Tig: That's so interesting, because I've explored different avenues, from acting to writing to directing, and producing is one of the things that brings me the most joy. When I first got into stand-up, I would never have thought that's what gets me going more than anything.

Judd: Feels good to have things go right and not go fucking crazy, right?

Tig: And to connect the dots. I am definitely somebody that, when there is chaos or crazy or disruptive people or things in my life, I'm like, *I cannot have this around me.* And so I retreat, for sure.

Judd: When you were a teenager and you're out of school, what were you doing? How was your sense of humor developing even before you knew you want to do comedy?

Tig: You have to understand, my mother and stepfather watched *Saturday Night Live* every weekend. My mother was obsessed with *Laverne and Shirley* and *I Love Lucy* and *Sanford and Son* and *All in the Family*, all that stuff. We were watching those things together and very much connecting in that way. My mother was one of the funniest people. I remember, after she died, her best friend came to a show of mine, and she came up to me and she said, "You think you got this all yourself? That's from your mom." And I was like, "Yeah, I know." There was rebellion to comedy and all of that, but I can't ignore the influence my mother had on me. And my stepfather is very funny. He's very, very subtle and very dry. And my father was very funny. When Stephanie went to Mississippi and New Orleans and met my family, she was just, like, "I can't even comprehend that these people are real." That's what's so interesting, bringing somebody back to where you're from, because you think, *Oh, this is normal.* And then you're like, *Oh, right. I guess I haven't seen this outside of my house or my town.*

Judd: So, when you're high school age, what were you doing? Did you get your GED?

Tig: I got my GED, and then my cat ate it. I have that framed on my wall. I started working in childcare—which is hilarious—because my very close friend worked at a childcare center. She was going off to college, and of course I wasn't, and she was leaving her job, and I wanted a job. I was just seeing it as a job.

Judd: Were they school kids?

Tig: They were elementary school, like fourth grade, and the age where girls want to sit on your lap and braid your hair. And I was just not that kind of person, where I was going to welcome a bunch of children to sit on my lap and play with my hair. It was a daycare. I also worked at a pizza restaurant down the road from my house, and that was delivery. But I'm very thankful for that [childcare] job, because it really made me get in touch with my love for children that I had so naturally as a child. I loved teaching school to little kids in the neighborhood; I like to be nurturing in that way. But I became so rebellious when I got older; I think the Chrissie Hynde in me came out, and I just didn't give much attention to kids. They weren't really in my world. But that job made them be a part of my day-to-day. It reawakened this side of me that was like, *Oh yeah. I love children.*

Judd: I remember when my daughter was, like, one, and we would be playing on the floor. I just thought, *This is so weird. Being on the floor with a kid wanting to play blocks for three straight hours—you haven't really done that since you were one.* Then, at some point, your kids grow up and are like, "Yeah, no. I'm gonna be in my room." And they shut the door, and you're like, "What?" It's appropriate and devastating. I knew this was coming, but I can't believe it's true. Then you're like, *This is so brutal.*

Tig: I know. I hate hearing about it.

Judd: And then they drift back in a different way.

Tig: A different form.

Judd: It just keeps evolving into something different. You got into the record business a little bit? Music?

Tig: I started playing guitar when I was nine, and I was obsessed with the Beatles as a kid. Like, really obsessed. And even though I knew the Beatles had broken up, and I knew that year, when I turned nine, [that] John Lennon was assassinated, I still would listen to their records and think, *My goal in life is to become the fifth Beatle.* Because whenever the record was on the turntable, I was like, *I'm going to be in that band. I am going to be in the Beatles.* I'm crazy. So I got really into music and really into playing guitar, and I would sit in my room for hours at a time and play. Then, as I got older, I tried to pursue music. The two or three times I got onstage, my hands were shaking. I couldn't. I was so uncomfortable onstage.

Judd: Like an acoustic performance? What were you doing?

Tig: I played with some people in garages and basements, and some of it was acoustic-type stuff. Maybe somewhere along the line of the Breeders-type stuff. Just kind of all over the place, maybe a little country here or there. I tried to get onstage maybe three times, and I really did not like the attention on me. I was very nervous, and I had this vision of myself very different from what happened when I got onstage.

Judd: You're not going to be in the Beatles. I can't believe it.

Tig: Here I was, in the nineties, finally accepting that I wouldn't be in the Beatles. So, I thought the closest thing that would maybe make me happy would be to start working in the music business. I started booking bands, and I started working as a representative for different record labels, to promote new albums and companies in the record business. My friends owned a coffee shop in Denver, and they had this big basement in their building. They just let me set up shop down there. So, I had this office in a coffee shop basement in Denver, and I got to look legitimate and just scrape by with that job. I represented a lot of bands in the Denver music scene and booked them. It was definitely fun, but there was this little part where I was like, *Something's missing.*

Judd: When you're doing that, is the idea of comedy not there at all? Or are you aware of the stand-up scene? Is it a secret dream, but you just don't have the courage to do it?

Tig: Oh, I'm fully aware of comedy. In fact, I remember driving girlfriends of mine insane, one in particular, because I wanted to constantly repeat jokes and stories of comedians, ones that I'd already told her. I remember, she would say, "If you massage my back, I will let you tell me another Paula Poundstone joke." I was very, very aware of it. I was still following it, and it was my secret dream, but with bands, I could track the trajectory of a band or a songwriter because I'd done it. I could not track how, when I turn on HBO, I would see a completely unknown, to me, comedian walk onstage and get applause and fill a theater. I was like, *I've never heard of them. They're hilarious, but how did they fill that with thousands of people?*

Judd: You'd never met a comedian.

Tig: No.

Judd: When I was a kid, I started interviewing comedians because I wanted to know the answer to that question. I was obsessed with knowing, *What is this path? How do you do this?* Did you meet a comedian before you got onstage for the first time?

Tig: I was housesitting for those friends of mine that had the coffee shop, and they had cable. A girlfriend of mine at the time was housesitting with me, and we were watching TV, and I watched Roseanne Barr's *E! True Hollywood Story.* I turned to my girlfriend—because she knew I wanted secretly to be a comedian—and I said, "I feel like I could do this. I feel like I want to try this." Roseanne made it seem like I could touch it, you know? Then that girl and I broke up. And I lived in Denver with my childhood friends that I've moved everywhere around the world together with, and they were on their way to Los Angeles. I was not going. I had no interest in Los Angeles. I thought L.A. was just an episode of *Cops*, and I was like, "No, thank you." But then my girlfriend and I broke up, and I said, "You know what? Maybe I'll come with you just to get away from her for six months, and I'll move back to Denver." Then I got to L.A., and I saw the open mics in the *L.A. Weekly* and started going to see those every night for two weeks, and then I got onstage.

Judd: So, you watched people, which is kind of fun, too, because most people are terrible, which gives you confidence, right? There's not that many good ones. You're like, *I could do this.*

Tig: That's exactly what happened.

Judd: Where were those open mics?

Tig: I went to the Comedy Store. I went to the Laugh Factory. I went to coffee shops. I went out to Hermosa Beach. I went everywhere. I went every single night, and I made it a goal of mine. My childhood friend who I'd moved out there with went with me every night. And then I said, *I'm going to get onstage after two weeks.*

Judd: And then you did.

Tig: And I did. And I have been doing it ever since, until the pandemic.

Judd: What was the place where you did it the first time?

Tig: It was a lesbian coffee shop, Little Frida's, in West Hollywood, and they had an all-female night of comedy. It wasn't even an open mic. It was a book show, and somebody had fallen out on the lineup. I just said, "Can I get up onstage?" And they're like, "Sure." So, I got up onstage. I had been talking to myself for weeks at home in the mirror, and I didn't account for laughs because I had been alone, so when I got laughs, it scared me. I remember that. I was like, *Oh.* I had my monologue of stuff I had written, and then when I got a laugh, I was truly startled.

Judd: So, it went well, the first time?

Tig: Of course, I would never want to see that footage, but it went so well that I signed up for a competition my second time. My friend and I drove out to Hermosa Beach, and I signed up for a competition to win a hundred dollars, and I bombed so painfully that I walked offstage in the middle of my set. And that was the beginning of what is stand-up comedy.

Judd: A lot of people—their second show is a bomb. The first show opened a little better, and they're way more self-conscious for the second one. Did you have to work a day job while you were doing all these open mics?

Tig: Oh yeah, they were not paying the bills, for sure. I got a job at Sam Raimi's production company. My friend was working on the Universal lot—my friend who I grew up with. She moved out there with a job, whereas I didn't, and I was just sleeping on their couch, and I needed a job. I also got a job at that coffee shop, because I wanted to be able to get onstage every week. That was my first job. I thought, *This might be a good way for me to have a social scene, too, if I work in a lesbian coffee shop.*

Judd: Did that work out?

Tig: A million percent. It was my dating service.

Judd: This is a wise plan, well executed.

Tig: That coffee shop really launched me into Los Angeles. Then I felt like, *Oh, I don't want to leave.* Because my goal was to get back to Denver and do stand-up back out there.

Judd: When did it start going well? When did you connect with your generation of comedians?

Tig: I'm an odd person in this world, because I didn't move here for comedy. I moved here because I love my childhood friends, and I didn't know how to separate from them. So, when they all were moving out here, I moved out here. I kind of always thought I was doing well. I didn't have any goals—I wasn't trying to get a sitcom, I wasn't trying to become famous. I wasn't trying to do any of that stuff. I used to sit at open mics at the Comedy Store and watch big-name comics come in, do drop-in sets, and then leave, and I remember thinking, *That's so weird.* I can't imagine not wanting to see everybody's show. I can't imagine not wanting to sit through all this, because I just loved it. I loved hearing everybody's jokes. I loved getting up for my three minutes. Being a failure and a drop-out, I just didn't have high expectations for myself. I didn't ever see myself living in anything other than a studio apartment. I didn't imagine having success.

Judd: You're with your friends and having enough money to live, like, *Oh, this is just fun that we're all together.*

Tig: I did not have a single complaint, sir. I was so fulfilled. I wanted to get onstage every night, and I did. I would say six or seven nights a week, I was onstage. I did not have a car. I rode my bike everywhere. I was devoted. So, I felt successful when I was doing open mics, and I remember when people started saying, "Oh, do you want to do my bringer show?" or, "Oh, try out at the Improv." I'd be like, "Yeah, yeah, sure, sure." I thought I was successful when I was doing one-night gigs in Oregon and Washington State, and those Tribble runs.* Are you familiar with Tribble runs? When I started doing Tribble runs, I was like, *Oh my God, I'm on the road.* I just couldn't believe it. Then I was going through Idaho, and I knew there was a Funny

* Dave Tribble is a comedy booker.

Bone there, and I called, and I said, "Can I do a guest spot?" I did a guest spot, and the owner or the manager of the club said, "We have a fallout. Why don't you stick around and do two weeks as a feature?" And I was like, *Oh my God.* Then she called the guy Dave Carlo, who booked the Funny Bone chain, and said, "You should see Tig." So, he said, "Come out. Do a showcase in Indianapolis." So, I went and did a showcase in Indianapolis. And then he was booking me as a feature around the nation. Then I take that and sent that in and got a half-hour special on Comedy Central. You know what I mean? I had those little moments where I was like, *Awesome, awesome. This is great.* I didn't have any reps, though. I was just doing my thing, but I felt really happy the whole way through.

Judd: When you say "feature," do you mean middle or headline?

Tig: I was middling.

Judd: And you got a half-hour special in that era.

Tig: That half-hour special bumped me up to headlining. When I say it happened fast, I was obviously no Aziz Ansari, or one of those people that really exploded. But it happened where everything handed itself to the next moment very nicely and smoothly.

Judd: What were you learning about your style in those years? Because you have a unique style. How did you figure out how you wanted to do it?

Tig: I rode my bike everywhere, and I wore a backpack, and I would bring this little video camera and tripod every time I performed. I wouldn't just audiotape myself; I would *video*tape, because I wanted to see. I remember seeing a video of myself, and I didn't look like I performed the way that I thought I was doing in my head, and I was a little shocked. So, I filmed myself from there on out, and I would watch my five-minute sets every night when I got home.

Judd: Nothing harder in the world than doing that. Most people could not tolerate watching their set.

Tig: There is no part of me that enjoyed watching myself. I can't think of anything worse than seeing myself, and I also felt that way back then. But I do feel like it helped me move faster. I was enjoying myself, but I wasn't quite sure where this was going. When people are asking about my late-night set, or showcasing, or reps, or what would my sitcom be, and all these kind of conversations—I just was so amused by that. But I also started to think, *Yeah, what am I doing?* Because I feel like I'm good enough to do something, but I was also getting this feedback that I wasn't mainstream enough and that I took too long. I didn't have enough jokes per minute for late night; I was too slow and dry. I remember being told, when I was trying to get representation, that nobody was going to want to watch *The Tig Show* on Thursday night at eight or nine o'clock. He said, "I think of you as like a Margaret Smith, and you're going to eventually become a writer." And I was like, "Oh, okay." So, in my head, I thought, *I guess I'm funny, but I don't really have a future in stand-up. So I'll just do this as long as I can, until I have to become a writer.* As though this manager decides. I don't know why I listened to that.

Judd: There's power to that. I remember, when I first started, there was an agent who came and saw me. I was maybe twenty or twenty-one years old. And he's like, "I'd love to send you out on pilot season to audition to be in pilots." He goes, "Let me send you to an acting coach to see where you're at with that." I had never taken an acting class, and I couldn't hack the teacher. He gave me these scenes from the TV show *My Sister Sam* to read with him—I couldn't even understand where the jokes were. I was terrible. He told the agent, "Yeah, he can't act." And I never acted again, off of that.

Tig: And it's because of that.

Judd: Because of that. Probably my dream since I was ten years old. "One day, you'll be Bill Murray" or something, and all it took was one numbskull to say, "He can't do it." I knew how to be a comedian. But I never knew what the path was to learn how to act and was so quick to give it up in one millionth of a second. Done forever.

Tig: Why don't you audition for Judd Apatow?

Judd: Exactly. I gotta get in with that guy.

Tig: I took it very seriously. When I say I felt successful doing open mics, I'm being very honest with you. But I know that, obviously, when I did my Largo set in 2012, that was the point where people knew me more and paid more attention. Then it just became comical—my slow way or quirky way or different way was now my strength.

Judd: It's the part we'd never thought. I know, for me, I just thought, *Oh, I'm just trying to be funny.* And I never really thought showing my vulnerability or being really deeply truthful is actually the thing that the audience wants the most.

Tig: As I tell people all the time about that show, there was no part of me that went onstage that night thinking about all the other performers and the audience who would be tweeting about the show or blogging about the show. I had seen how quickly life goes away, in that I had [had] three deadly illnesses at one time, and my mother tripped and died out of nowhere. And I was just deteriorating physically. I just thought, *I love stand-up so much that if I am going to die*—and I thought it would be in a couple of months, mainly because of my intestinal disease—*I just want to go onstage one last time. And I want to take that risk even if I bomb and this is my last performance ever.* It also amused me that people would be saying, "Yeah, I was there for her last performance, and it was a bomb." But that risk was worth it to me. I would never have shared that information if I thought it would go worldwide. I would never have done that, because of who I was and where I was in my life at that time. It busted me open, and it took me a couple of months to agree to put out the album, because I felt like it was a you-had-to-be there moment. I felt so fragile for so long after being so sick and emotionally in pain that I didn't think I could suffer through bad reviews for that album.

Judd: Because there's always a backlash to anything. You had *C. diff*?

Tig: I had pneumonia. And then I had *C. diff*. And then, through that, I didn't know I had invasive cancer. So, the doctors were kind of confused because of how sick I was. I remember them saying, "It's so crazy, because typically, people that are elderly or young children or immune-compromised get *C. diff*. And you have a very severe case." Nobody knew I had cancer. I was just lying there with invasive cancer, and I was like, "Yeah. I don't know."

Judd: At the time, when you found out about your mom passing, you didn't know you had cancer?

Tig: Yeah. The ironic part is I got out of the hospital. I was discharged, and even when you're discharged, you still struggle a long time with pain and [not] being able to eat. My mother tripped and hit her head and was on life support literally a couple of days after I was discharged from the hospital. I had to fly home to take her off life support. And when I was home after I took her off life support, after her funeral, my health just really started to deteriorate. I was stuck in Texas at my mother's house, and my girlfriend at the time was back in L.A. The ironic part being *C. diff* isn't a well-known disease and especially wasn't in 2012, and I used to say to people, "I wish I had cancer, so that I could explain to people, so they would just understand how sick I was."

Judd: When you found out you had cancer and then you went onstage, it was like a day or two later, right? It was pretty fast from the diagnosis?

Tig: Yeah.

Judd: When you went on to do that set, how much had you written? What was the process of preparation like?

Tig: I had these appointments, and I kept being told, after my exam and after biopsies, from doctors and nurses, and from friends who have had biopsies and scares—they're like, "I'm sure it's nothing." And I was like, "Oh, I have no doubt." I didn't think I had cancer. I thought there was something in the universe where *Of course, the universe knows I just got out of the hospital. My mother just died. I just broke up with my girlfriend. There is no part of me that thinks I have cancer. So, I'm fine. Don't you worry.* So, when the doctor told me, I of course laughed right away. I was mortified. I was terrified. I was every part of scared I could be, and like I said, I had seen how quickly life slips away. But I felt immediately inspired, and I started writing. I am not somebody that writes comedy. I write a word down, and I go onstage and I work it out in front of everyone. And then [Largo owner Mark] Flanagan said, "Are you going to do this show?" Because I told him there's no way I'm going to. He said, "You know you can cancel five minutes before, but let's just leave it open, in the event you do want to perform." I thought he was crazy. I thought Ira Glass was crazy. He was saying, "Go onstage and talk about this." And I was like, "You're both abusive, terrible people."

Judd: Because you thought it might be a piece for *This American Life*, and then Ira said, "Maybe you should try it live"?

Tig: No, I didn't find any humor in anything at this point. Ira said, "Why don't you go onstage and work this out?" And I was like, "Did you not hear what I'm going through? I weigh like fifty pounds. I'm so sad, I don't know what to do with myself. And I have an invasive cancer. I am so rock bottom." I was kind of offended. But he had the best of intentions. I know he loves and cares about me. I think he thought that it might be a therapeutic thing, just as Flanagan did.

Judd: Also, comedy makes us happy. We all know it's a joke, but endorphins and laughter and being with people is good for your immune system. It's the Norman Cousins of it all, right?

Tig: Yeah, but I couldn't see that. People think of 2012, when all this happened to me, as being, "Oh, that was a crazy year for you." I'm like, "No, it was four months that all of that happened in." It was back-to-back-to-back-to-back. So, I called Flanagan, because he'd texted me, and he said, "Are we going to do the show?" And I said, "Yeah." So, I did it. And I asked them to record it, because I told Ira that I was going to do it, and I said, "If there's something there, I'll send it to you." Because he wanted me to do another segment on *This American Life*. I'd just done this story about Taylor Dayne that had been kind of instantly popular on his show, and he was like, "Send me some more stuff."

Judd: Was it your show, or were you doing a spot on someone else's show?

Tig: It was my show. And my childhood friends that I had moved out there with? We all went out to a diner and stayed up all night on this crazy wave of what just happened. Because that show . . . I was floating. I didn't know what had just happened. It was that kind of performance, that kind of evening. And I'm not saying it like *that* kind of performance, like, "Oh my God, wasn't I so great?" It was really intense and tearful and funny and uncomfortable. So, we were out at the diner until two or three in the morning, just, *whoa*. And then I went to bed. I always tell people I felt like a great-great-grandmother when I woke up, because I had turned my phone off. I cannot have anyone think I'm exaggerating when I say that my mailbox was full. I had hundreds of emails. I had book offers. I woke up to that at noon the next day.

Judd: How did people even know about it? Because it wasn't broadcast.

Tig: Everybody was tweeting. All of the comedians on the show were tweeting. All of the audience members were tweeting. People were blogging about it. I wasn't on Twitter; I didn't understand it had gone viral, because it wasn't out there. That was the first time I really understood how social media works. Everything changed. I remember, before I went to bed, I emailed Ira and I said, "Hey, Ira. I did a show tonight and I did record it, and maybe there will be a couple of minutes you could use." And it ended up becoming, I think, the number-one-selling comedy album of the year around the world. There's no part of me that set out to do that. It obviously became the more famous part of my success.

Judd: I can't imagine listening back to it for the first time to decide if you wanted to send it, or what you made of it when you heard it.

Tig: Honestly, I didn't like it. I understand now, with distance, that it's helpful to people going through similar things, having a sense of humor. But as a comedian, I listened to it, and I thought, *Well, that's not my best work. If I had been given time to work that through, it would have been so much better.* I understood in time that it's also the feeling, for people, of eavesdropping on a moment that somebody's going through. But even to this day, when I hear it, I cringe. Not because it was a hard time I was going through, not that. "Oh, poor Tig." It's also hard when I say, "Hello, good evening. I have cancer." It's a subtlety in my voice—I can tell I'm about to cry, and I think that's hard for me, because it's so subtle. I don't know if people would know, but I know that thing in my voice. I was about to cry out of the gate. I was so scared.

Judd: I know when I worked on *Funny People*, I was writing about the fact that my mom had just died of ovarian cancer. She died right when we started shooting and, years later, I thought that was kind of crazy. I didn't even know that's what I was doing. At some level, I was aware, but I didn't realize how deep the grief was that I would spend years writing a movie while it was happening, after it happened, to just deal with what was rushing up that I didn't understand how to process.

Tig: Wow.

Judd: But sometimes, the only way to deal with it is to go to the one thing, the one language we understand. At the time you're doing this, you're about to go in for more treatments? You're not doing the set because it's over . . .

Tig: Yeah, I don't know what's to come at that point. I remember, people would say, "Oh man, you must be so mad that you finally get your big break, and it took you getting cancer." I would hear people say that to me, and I would think, *What does that mean?* Then I thought, *Actually, no. I was doing stand-up. I was doing what I do.* Of course, the topic was cancer, but I was doing stand-up. That's what everybody responded to. Obviously, the subject matter, all the different things—it was the loss of my mother, it was going through a breakup, it was an intestinal disease. I was talking about all of those things, and it was through stand-up.

Judd: People would not have enjoyed it if it wasn't riotously funny.

Tig: I felt very lucky that I had been doing stand-up for as long as I had at that point, that I was presented to the world at the time that I was, because I felt prepared. In the long run, I wasn't prepared. I was on such a roller coaster, to be getting all of that attention when I was going through what I was going through. I had to get through another year or so before I could really shake the trauma of that time, and I think I still have some PTSD around it. But I wasn't quite ready for everything right after it happened. I would say, once I caught my breath, I was off and running. So, it felt oddly timely in that way, where I was ready to go.

Judd: Did all the positive reaction help you as you went into all of your cancer treatments? Did it give you strength, or was it like, *I wish I didn't have to be distracted by job offers and new love.*

Tig: It was probably all of it. It was very nice to get the support from strangers and the comedy community and my friends and family, but I still had to go and have my quiet moments each day and night. I didn't know where my health was. I didn't know who I was as a comedian anymore. I didn't know who my real friends were. I just didn't know my head—I can't tell you how much my head was spinning. And I felt uncomfortable with my body for a long time, because I was in a lot of pain. I had new scars. I had sharp pains that would interrupt my speech. I didn't know what I had to offer of myself for the world or my comedy. It was to get the support but also, in the quiet moments, *What is happening? What just happened?*

Judd: Did you find your strength? Because there are plenty of people [for whom] all of that would put them in a room with the lights out for a year.

Tig: I got through it in that I swam to a boat that was bobbing around in the middle of the ocean. I was like, *I'm safe, but I'm still in the middle of the ocean, and I got to get this boat up and running and I got to get back to shore.* So, when I was resurfacing in the world, I was still just crawling back onto a boat. And I remember I went on *Conan* so quickly. I had incisions across my chest that it was painful to pull my shirt over, because the stitches are sticking out, and when you touch stitches it hurts the incision. It took everything to get that shirt on, because I wanted so desperately to go on *Conan* and tell the world I'm fine. Because I was so uncomfortable with the attention I was getting. Of course I liked it, and of course I appreciated it, but I was also so terribly uncomfortable. I remember my walk out to Conan, to sit on the couch—I was so newly out of the hospital, I was still having to clean blood from my body regularly. But I just wanted everyone to be able to just back off a little bit. Not in a bad way, but I was uncomfortable.

Judd: People want to know you, where before it was a different kind of relationship.

Tig: I kept saying to people, "I feel like I have to go to a deserted island when this comes out, because I really don't know if I can stomach this." I thought the reviews were gonna be like, "I guess you had to be there, but we wish her the best." I thought, at most, it was gonna sell ten thousand copies. There's not a fiber in me that thought it would sell more than ten thousand copies, or get any sort of critical acclaim. Nothing, nothing. I really thought, *I'll donate a portion to charity and for the people it does resonate with; there will be that.* But I couldn't believe I was about to put myself through that, and when the opposite happened and it just kept coming, I remember I called my manager, and I said, "When do you think this will all stop? Like in a couple of days?" And he said, "Oh, I don't think this is going away." I remember being like, "What are they getting out of this?" I was so confused.

Judd: Looking back, what do you think they're getting out of it? Now you must have your sense of what people took from it and why. I think it's not just people who are sick or have friends who are sick. It is about how we hope we would handle it. Probably, at some point, I'm going to have a moment in my life—maybe it'll be the end of my life, maybe in the middle of my life—where I have to see what I'm made of. There's something about that aspect that makes it so universal.

Tig: I'm sure it's a little bit of all of that, but it's so far from what I thought was coming.

Judd: It's also interesting, because in the beginning of your career, you don't have expectations for yourself, you don't really have goals for yourself. Then, suddenly, the world chooses you in a very organic way. It's not *How do I get them to like me?* You're not working from that place, which is how most people are working.

Tig: Of course, I hope people like me. I like being liked. But I also haven't ever lived or died by it. My mother, whenever there was a problem at school or with friends, if people didn't like how I dressed, she was just like, "Tell him to go to hell. Tell everyone to go to hell if they don't like you. You look adorable. You're the coolest person I know." And I was like, *All right.* Obviously, I still had to show up to school and have my hard moments, but having that in my head really informed me and helped me in those moments when I've taken these bigger risks. Speaking out at times when it's not safe and taking leaps—I think that's all very much tied to my mother.

Judd: The thing that I like about comedy is you can make the worst thing have a value. I think most people don't have that ability when bad things happen. They just feel fucking awful. And in our business, we see the best of people, and we also see the worst of people. Comedy feels like it got divided in the last few years, starting with all the Louis C.K. stuff. This idea, that I can say anything I want to say no matter how hurtful it is because it's just a joke. There's a real division in comedy with how people are dealing with the ideas of freedom of speech, or how jokes hurt people. That's been pretty heartbreaking to watch, too.

Tig: I have not made friends through speaking out. I mean, I've made new friends, and I've strengthened certain relationships, but there's certainly a feeling I get from people just being absolutely baffled that I would speak out against somebody, not just in the comedy community, but somebody that elevated me. That's, again, that moment where I'm happy to shake loose from you. And I am somebody that believes in redemption. I just am not somebody that believes that these people's redemption rates higher than the support of victims. I will always go back to that. Why is this the conversation, and why are *they* not the conversation? I can't get beyond that. I don't understand how people are left in the dust as they are as victims. But I feel the divide.

Judd: I remember, I went to a benefit at the rape treatment center, and all the victims of Bill Cosby were there. The courage it took for all those people to speak up and the damage to their psyche to be called liars for so long, to not have their experiences validated.

Tig: Or to be told, "Why did you go over there? Why didn't you leave the room? Why didn't you hang up the phone? Why? Why? Why? Why? Why?" I really don't understand. And I don't want to understand. When I say I'm happy to lose friends or fans over it, it's not that I'm happy to lose friends, it's just that it's such a divide, where I can be friendly and I can be cordial, but it's a hard line for me.

Judd: I got upset with Louis's Parkland jokes and spoke out a bunch about it. It just seemed like the weirdest target. And the number of comedians who are furious at me for saying "That's really fucked up." I'm not saying, "He should never work again; let's boycott this." But you're allowed to tell people their jokes are fucked up.

Tig: Your opinion is just as much free speech as his. It does feel like the comedy community is a microcosm of the country.

Judd: We didn't realize that, right? We didn't think that, at a comedy club, it would be the exact same divide.

Tig: I have a person that is an old friend in the comedy world, one of the closest people I've ever been to in my life, who said he is not in support of the Black Lives Matter movement. He was like, “My brother’s a cop, and somebody threw tomatoes at my brother,” and I’m like, “Oh. Okay. Somebody threw tomatoes at your brother.” I just don’t have time for it. I’m still working. I still have friends. I still have a family. I’m healthy. I’m thriving.

WHITNEY CUMMINGS

September 2019

Judd: What was your family situation like growing up? I feel like you're like me, in that you dealt with family stress by becoming a hyper-achiever.

Whitney: Yes. Do you have siblings?

Judd: I have an older brother and a younger sister.

Whitney: I was the youngest. For me, I definitely knew at a very early age that I was a mistake. And I instinctively had some kind of Darwinian survival instinct of *You better earn your place, because no one wanted you.*

Judd: Did your parents have money?

Whitney: No, but I thought we had money. You know how you always think everything is perfect until you go to another house? I remember going to a friend's house for the first time and opening the fridge and being like, *Oh! What's all this stuff? This looks like a grocery store.*

Judd: Twinkies?!

Whitney: Totally. It was very "keeping up with the Joneses" in my family. We had nice stuff. We had nice cars.

Judd: But no food.

Whitney: No food, and the electric bill wasn't paid.

Judd: My mom was like that. She would ask me for money, and then she would go lease a Mercedes. I would say, "Why don't you lease a Camry, and then you'd have money to eat?"

Whitney: Or go to the doctor.

Judd: Or go to the doctor! And she'd say, "Because I'm not an animal." So, where did you grow up?

Whitney: Born and raised in DC. I think I also was born into an alcoholic home.

Judd: Both of your parents?

Whitney: No. My dad was not. There's alcoholics, and then there's codependents. There was a lot of "Let's pretend everything is fine when it's not." Which, until very recently, was what I thought comedy was.

Judd: You thought that was the definition of comedy?

Whitney: Like, we alchemize very painful things and put them in pretty presents and make them digestible. My definition of what funny is has changed, but that is definitely a version of comedy—where, if we don't laugh, we're going to cry. In my family, I always had a hard time discerning when people were laughing or arguing because it would seamlessly go from one to the other. Our parents would be fighting and screaming, and then, two seconds later they would be laughing. And I don't know if that's alcoholism or maybe some mental illness that I will never understand, but I just remember learning at an early age that anger and laughter are very close. They're a millimeter away from each other. Maybe the same neurological response. The pendulum always swung, and it was like the angrier people were, the more they were laughing. I remember sitting at the Thanksgiving table as a kid, and everybody hated each other. You could feel the tension, but nobody was just, say, like "Hey, you owe me fifty dollars, man. Pay me back." It was always these passive aggressive roast jokes, like, "Well, maybe if Marcy didn't get *divorced* six times, we wouldn't have that problem!" And then everyone would laugh. It's how we communicated.

Judd: What did your dad do?

Whitney: I still don't know. It was high-risk venture capital. I just remember he would come home with a nice car, and then, three days later, it was gone.

Judd: What do you think it really was?

Whitney: I don't know, but he taught me that if you are funny and charming, you can get away with anything.

Judd: So, he was a salesman of some kind?

Whitney: High-risk loans. People that couldn't get loans from banks would go to him. As a kid, I had people come to our door saying, "Where's Bill? Where's Bill?" I'm like, "Bill? Who's Bill? No, he doesn't live here." They were looking for my dad. His name was not Bill. So, I would just charm them and try to make them laugh, and they would go away.

Judd: It's fascinating that you grew up and you still don't know. Usually there's a moment when you crack the code on what was really happening.

Whitney: He just passed. We had to move the funeral last minute, because people were showing up, trying to take pictures of me, which I was very flattered by, but we didn't have a priest, and my uncle had to improvise. So, we were already laughing at a funeral—that's magic. If someone pitched it to you as a story, you'd say it was too broad. It would never happen. My uncle's improvising a funeral, like, "Hear ye, hear ye." We have no idea what we're doing. Basically, it turned into "Everyone just go around and tell a story about him." And everyone's telling stories, like, "When he was like in the navy . . ." And I'm like, "He wasn't in the navy." He apparently told a different story to everyone. No one could corroborate what the truth was. I remember, as a kid, there'd be some Armenian men's store in DC, and he'd tell me, "Go in there; get whatever you want." And the manager would say, "Whatever you want!" And I'd think, "I don't need any men's suits." Like, how . . . ?

Judd: Did it feel like mobster stuff?

Whitney: It definitely felt under the table.

Judd: Were they "associates"?

Whitney: There would be guys living in our house for a couple of months. As I grew up, everything felt weird to me. Parties felt weird, college felt weird. And then I walked into the Comedy Store—it was like a bunch of weird degenerates—and I thought, *This feels right. I feel at home.*

Judd: And what about your mom?

Whitney: She worked in fashion. She worked in public relations for Bloomingdale's. She would bring me to work, and it was all about what you're wearing and your makeup and your lip color. My mother could put makeup on without looking in a mirror, while she was talking to you.

Judd: But she had a normal job.

Whitney: Yeah. She worked incredibly hard. She was funny, but by accident. She was always like, "Where are my glasses?" and her glasses would be on her head. She was a flaky, funny, hot mess. But also ambitious. I don't love the word *strong* because sometimes it implies suffering through things needlessly. But she was very engaging, very social. She needed to laugh. I could feel it was a need. You know when people laugh just a little too hard at something that's not that funny?

Judd: What were their parents like? What led your parents to be like they are?

Whitney: That's a great question. I've been on that quest, getting to the forgiveness of what we didn't get as kids. To be able to go, "Well, our parents didn't get what they needed, either." And that's really helped me have compassion. My dad's mother died young. It can do a number on people, to not have a maternal figure all of a sudden, especially in the 1940s and '50s, when that role was so important. Right now, parents can be women or men. But back then, mothers were their only source of permission to be vulnerable. My grandfather was in the war. He was very stern and all about work. He injured himself all the time and didn't tell anyone. Very stoic. Vulnerability is not in our vernacular. I think my dad definitely inherited that.

Judd: And your mom's parents?

Whitney: I don't know that much about them. She's from Texas, and her dad died young, and her mother had, like, a cantaloupe farm or something but was very enigmatic. There was an absence of expressing love, though I'm sure there was love there. My dad used to hug me sideways. There wasn't a lot of eye contact, so I think, as a result, I developed this deep need to be seen and loved.

Judd: You don't hear many comedians say, "My parents were solid as a rock."

Whitney: Exactly. We're all in therapy. But my therapist did tell me I probably had something called infant-maternal disruption, which is when you don't get enough eye contact from your mother in the first couple years of your life.

Judd: I do a bit about that.

Whitney: No way.

Judd: I was dating Leslie, and I was maybe twenty-six. And she goes, "When I talk, where are you looking?" And I go, "At your mouth." And she's like "Why?" And I go, "So, I can understand you and hear you." And she's like, "You know you're supposed to look people *in the eye.*" And I said, "I've never heard that before."

Whitney: Wow. I used to look at the side of someone's ear. I had to relearn eye contact as an adult.

Judd: My mom was always looking around, a nervous person, and I think that just wires you to feel anxiety for the rest of your life.

Whitney: Human beings would rather suffer physical abuse than neglect, because at least with physical abuse, you're acknowledging that they exist. For the first year, children don't know that they're separate from their mother yet. So, when they're not being looked at, they don't feel they exist. And I think a lot of stand-up is *I exist, right?*

Judd: When I do stand-up, I have a very strong desire to never do it again.

Whitney: Is it shame?

Judd: It's *Shut up. No one cares.*

Whitney: *No one cares. You're a phony. Why do you think you deserve to be looked at?* Even though you're doing a service to people. You're healing people.

Judd: I didn't do stand-up from the time I met my wife, in 1995, until a couple of years ago.

Whitney: You wanted her to stay with you.

Judd: Exactly. So, she didn't know me as a stand-up comedian. When I said I wanted to do it again, she wanted to know why. She asked me, "Is it something people do because they're insecure or—?"

Whitney: Too secure?

Judd: Yeah. Is it a positive thing or a negative thing?

Whitney: It's interesting. Whenever I get in that mode of *You needy, desperate narcissist. Who do you think you are?* I remind myself that it's only five thousand people. There are six billion in the world. I'm not really taking up that many people's time.

Judd: I thought you were going to say, *Five thousand people paid to come here to see me. Why do I doubt them?*

Whitney: *Now I'm insulting them instead of myself.* But yes, that inner monologue starts at a very early age. I also think I developed an adrenaline addiction, which I had never really heard anyone talk about. In the womb, epigenetic imprinting apparently occurs if your mother produced a lot of cortisol and adrenaline because of stress. My parents fought when my mom was pregnant, for sure. It's like a baby being addicted to drugs when they're born. I think I was addicted to adrenaline at a very young age.

Judd: I think I need to go to your therapist.

Whitney: From a very early age, I was always creating dramatic situations—like putting glasses on top of each other and going, "Are they going to fall?" Or hiding things and shoplifting and keeping secrets and engaging with dangerous people. I think stand-up sort of fit that bill for me. It's scary, I'm terrified, I'm producing adrenaline. I'm going to small towns with weird drunk men. This is perfect. I think it checked all the boxes in terms of my various addictions and wounds. And then, creating that shame cycle of *I don't belong here, I don't* *deserve to be here*, which goes back, I think, to how I felt as a child who believed she was born by accident.

Judd: And a daily, or nightly, chance to prove you do belong there.

Whitney: I'm fascinated by comics that keep doing it, because there's so many reasons to quit. You are bad for the first couple years, legitimately bad. The only way to get good is to suck publicly.

Judd: It's the only job where you have to do it for people when you're bad, and they have to pay to watch it.

Whitney: It's like paying to watch someone go to the gym to get in shape.

Judd: Do you think it ultimately has been a positive for you, doing stand-up?

Whitney: I started doing stand-up when Myspace was happening. That's how I first started hustling for spots. It was around 2004, and I was hustling, hustling, hustling. And it was working until Twitter. Then came all that feedback.

Judd: You'd start reading what people said about you.

Whitney: It was like, *This was working until I found a way to hurt myself with it.* It was just weapons out there.

Judd: Just knowing that, at any moment, if you want to hear someone say something negative about you, it's there.

Whitney: I can corroborate my inner monologue. I've had to work incredibly hard at EMDR [eye movement desensitization and reprocessing] and trauma therapy. I'm trying everything, so I can understand that the kind of person that needs to call someone the N-word, or call me a cunt, or say I am a hag, or whatever—they're in pain. The same reason I go onstage to get attention from strangers, *they* have to try to get that from *me*. They're getting their adrenaline fix.

It's interesting. When you asked me "Did stand-up work for you?" I guess it did work, because I started to monetize my pain and my failure. I started getting rewards and started paying my bills because of my mistakes and all the bad things that have happened to me. I remember, after the first special I did, I got a car. I had never had my own car before. I was renting a Kia and hustling. Anyway, I got a hybrid Lexus, and it was the first nice thing I ever bought for myself. I needed a good car, because I was always driving to open mics like, *Am I going to make it?* One day, I filled it up with diesel fuel. The hybrid. I just jammed the nozzle in. I literally thought the green nozzle meant, like, it's green! Good for the environment! Hybrid, green nozzle! It was like a seven-thousand-dollar mistake. I totally trashed my car. Then I wrote a bit about it, and people laughed. So, now I have this muscle that whenever something bad happens, I'm like, *Oh, I'm going to get a good bit out of this.* This is how I survive.

Judd: What was the trigger to go into comedy?

Whitney: The first time I understood comedy, I was, like, twelve. I was alone a lot as a kid, and I had to keep myself busy, so I was always creating. I was so bored, I would write out interviews and then answer questions in different characters. I was very lonely as a kid, but I did watch a lot of TV. I watched *Roseanne*, and I remember thinking, *This is healing me somehow. I feel better for this half hour every week.* They're poor and they're talking about being poor, and we're not allowed to talk about that. It was almost like a boy looking at *Playboy*. *Oh my God, they're saying they eat out of cans whereas we pretend like we don't,* you know. But when I was twelve, I was at a yard sale, and I picked up a book by Paul Reiser called *Couplehood*. I remember reading it and just being like, *Oh my God. That's how* I *think. I see the negative in everything, too!* He was complaining about mundane things. As a kid, really benign things would drive me crazy. I remember a doily somewhere and being so annoyed that it didn't fit right. I would obsess over it. I will obsess over the packaging of something being inefficient for too long. Anyway, after *Couplehood,* I read a book called *The Beauty Myth,* by Naomi Wolf. There's a lot of people who have debunked it since, but she was pointing out how the standard of beauty oppresses women. And this just broke my world open. The idea of rejecting a social construct: I was hooked on that idea. For a while, I thought journalism was the solution.

Judd: *I'm going to write a story about this.*

Whitney: *And then everyone's going to listen! Statistics, boring statistics—that's how you get people to wake up!* I interned at a local NBC station, and, actually, local news is probably accidentally funnier than anything we could ever script.

Judd: That's *Anchorman.*

Whitney: Exactly. And so, one day, they let me read at the anchor desk to make a tape, when audition reels were a thing. I got up there, and I was reading the news. And local news, as you know, is so sensational and just upsetting. There was a kid who had been kidnapped. They showed a picture of him. When something's too dark, I have to make a joke. That's how I cope. So, they showed a picture of the kid, and I made a joke; I couldn't help it. I was like, "Who would want to kidnap him?" And I just found myself making jokes. Not good ones. But I realized, serious is just too painful. I was making jokes in a news station about a child who might have been dead.

Judd: It's like George Carlin saying, "I root for disasters. I root for churches to burn down. I watch the Indy 500, and I want the cars in the stands."

Whitney: In hockey, I want the fight.

Judd: So, when were you aware of stand-up as an option?

Whitney: People always told me I was funny. I wasn't trying to be funny, but when I would tell stories, I would think, *Why is everyone laughing? Why won't anyone take me seriously?* And then I did that show *Punk'd* on MTV.

Judd: How'd you end up on *Punk'd*?

Whitney: I auditioned after the first season. There must have been like four hundred people there. It was one of those cattle calls, and my parking meter was about to run out, and I literally couldn't afford to get a ticket; I had that little money. So, I was like, *I have to get out of here,* and I think one of the producers saw me leaving, and he was like, "Where are you going?" And I was like, "I can't wait for this." There was something about me not wanting it that was attractive—which I don't know when I'm going to learn that lesson for real—and he called me in, and he said, "I'm just going to insult you for as long as I can." I had seen people coming out of this audition crying. I was just like, "Oh, I grew up in a verbally abusive household. Let's do this."

Judd: But why was that the premise?

Whitney: I think the premise was: Let's see how much emotional fortitude you have, because the pranks are so long and stressful, and you can't crack.

Judd: And is he just insulting you, or is he making you pretend you're someone else and he's someone else?

Whitney: It was me. I just remember being in there for a couple hours, and at the end of it, they asked me to do *Punk'd,* which was not a comedy show. The whole point was: Do not approach it like a comedy, because as soon as you try to be funny, the celebrities are going to know that something is up. You can't have empathy. You have to just let these famous people cry. I mean, it was awful.

Judd: Did you do it as long as they wanted you to? Or, at some point, were you like, *I can't do this anymore.*

Whitney: I needed health care so badly that I didn't care.

Judd: So, by that time, you don't think you're going to do journalism anymore, right? You're kind of drifting to some sort of hosting role?

Whitney: I studied theater in college. I did *A Doll's House* in college. I thought I was going to be a serious actress, and I guess thought I was going to do that when I came out here. Hosting was like my waitressing. I was just trying to make money.

Judd: But you thought you were going to act at that point?

Whitney: It was acting, journalism, hosting.

Judd: Did you think, *I don't know which one of these is going to hit, so I'm just going to spread some bets on the table*?

Whitney: Yes. I needed money. After *Punk'd*, I did a show called *Best Week Ever*, on VH1. It was a bunch of comedians. It's how every respectable comic starts: insulting talented people who have made it. Completely innocent celebrities who are just doing the best they can. It was Paul Scheer and Jessi Klein and Michael Ian Black.

Judd: Killers.

Whitney: Killers! And we were all making two hundred dollars to make fun of celebrities. All of a sudden, they started using me a lot, and I would write jokes, and the jokes were pretty good. And then other comics started asking me to write jokes for them.

Judd: Who did you write for?

Whitney: I can't tell. If they tell, fine, but I promised them. I want to tell so bad, because some of them still owe me money.

Judd: How much did you get paid per joke?

Whitney: I got fifty dollars a page.

Judd: A *page*?

Whitney: That was before I understood how much jokes were worth.

Judd: You got ripped off.

Whitney: Yes, very. Four or five years later, I was probably charging four hundred dollars a page. But then I wouldn't get paid that money. If you charge fifty dollars a page, you actually get paid. You charge four hundred, you're never getting paid.

Judd: When you heard about stand-up, were you scared to make that leap?

Whitney: This might be clinical narcissism, this might be God, this might be metaphysical, this might be me lying to myself, but when someone said, "You know, you should really do stand-up," I was like, "Oh, yeah. I'm a stand-up. That's what I am." It was like I found something I had been looking for. I had found my keys. The Sundance Channel did this thing called the *Festival Dailies,* which was coverage of the film festival, and I had gotten a correspondent gig on that. Jay Mohr was hosting it, and Jay is Jay: He likes to poke people's weaknesses. It's not my favorite quality in a person, but he finds what you're insecure about and just goes after it. It's actually kind of a gift, and I was able to come back at him, and he told [producer] Barry Katz, "I've never seen a girl be able to do that. Normally they just cry." And I think I did cry later, but it was a delayed response. But then Barry Katz took a meeting with me, and I was like, "I'm a stand-up, and I would like you to represent me." He goes, "Do you have a tape?" And I was like, "No, I haven't even done it yet." He said to me, "After you kill ten times in a row, let's talk." And so, I had my goal. I actually did well for my first time ever. I was like, this is my drug. I knew it right away. And then I bombed for, like, two years. First night was great, and then I spent two years chasing that first time.

Judd: I started in L.A., too. I moved here to go to college in '85, and I would just do weird one-nighters at, like, Temecula. And then I started booking Sammy Shore's comedy club in Marina del Rey. It was a comedy club in a fish restaurant. It had a little room in the back, and I would book it, and in return for booking it, the owner would let me do a spot.

Whitney: I remember there was one gig in Lucky Strike, the bowling alley on Highland. And then Sportsmen's Lodge was my other spot. On Friday and Saturday nights, the show would start at five. It's still light out. You're doing stand-up to the waiters while cars are zooming by. You would have to yell over the cars.

Judd: And then you got in at the Store, or was it at the Improv?

Whitney: The Comedy Store. I couldn't get a spot at the Improv, because it was always booked. I went every Sunday and Monday, when there was an open mic. You had to go sign up as early as three. You'd wait in line with homeless people. I remember, there was a guy who wore a dollhouse on his head.

Judd: Was [the owner] still Mitzi [Shore then]?

Whitney: It was Mitzi. I did that for about a year and a half. You'd wait and then come back, and they'd tell you if you got three minutes or not. And then you'd wait for three hours to bomb for three minutes. Something happens to your fight-or-flight response when you're up there on that stage. The way it's lit—and I know Mitzi lit it this way on purpose—you see David Letterman's name, and something would just power down in me. Something froze inside me up there, and I would just go bomb, bomb, bomb, bomb. I'd wait in the hallway and try to get comics to like me, which doesn't work, by the way. The harder you try with comics, the more they hate you. It's the best spot in the world to get better, but I didn't understand that at the time.

And then, one night, Mitzi happened to show up without my knowing she was there.

Judd: That's the best audition.

Whitney: I was bombing so hard, but I didn't know she was there, so I was at least having fun bombing. When I came offstage, she was like, "You remind me of Roseanne," and I was like, *I* think *that's a good thing?*

Judd: What year was that?

Whitney: It must have been 2005.

Judd: That's right when [Mitzi] got sick.

Whitney: She was sick already. There was just something so amazing about watching all these caustic, larger-than-life comedians that I look up to, and then she comes in, and they're all just kissing the ring. She is a prophet. The people that she has handpicked—there was something magical about it. The Comedy Store used to be where you go to bomb. It was like the gym. Lifting paint cans and working out the kinks and getting to the truth of who you are. I remember the night that I broke onstage. I would sometimes get the one A.M. spot, which ends up being a two A.M. spot, where you follow Don Barris. You're just cleaning up a mess. You're performing, and the lights are on, and everyone's looking for their stuff, and you're just bombing. I remember I got cheated on, and I went down to the Comedy Store, and did my spot, and I was just bombing. I started crying. There was this woman in the audience, and I started talking to her. I was like, "I don't know if I should text him back." I just had a meltdown. I started telling the truth, and people started responding and laughing, and I was like, *Oh, they don't want you to pretend to be funny. They just want to hear your vulnerabilities.* I thought doing stand-up was about going up and pretending you're really strong and put together and sharp.

Judd: It's like a eureka moment. Garry Shandling used to always say, "You're trying to get to your core."

Whitney: The armor came off. Something happened when I stopped caring what they thought. That's when they started liking it. It's like how Chris Rock says, "If you're bombing, slow down." Don't speed up, don't try harder. That's the worst thing you can do.

Judd: Steve Carell—the first time he did Jimmy Kimmel, promoting *40-Year-Old Virgin,* he was sweating more than Albert Brooks on *Broadcast News.* But he didn't acknowledge it, and the place was getting more and more tense. And then, finally, he made some joke about how much he was sweating, and the place laughed so hard, and Jimmy Kimmel said, "Thank God you mentioned it." And then the whole thing worked. So, after all that, you did roasts for a little bit?

Whitney: The first one was Joan Rivers, my idol. I had a joke that was like, "Joan, I loved you in *The Wrestler.*" It was rough. "Joan, you're so old, your vagina has a separate entrance for Black dicks." I was like, "By the way, I love you so much. I'm so sorry about this." It was such a conflict of interest, and I realized [that] comedy, even the meanest jokes, is how we show love to each other. I'm not saying it's healthy.

Judd: And she enjoyed it?

Whitney: She enjoyed it.

Judd: I never want to be roasted. I don't want to know what the joke of me is.

Whitney: I'm curious. There's something liberating about it.

Judd: The idea of everyone telling me the joke that I'm worried about when I leave a room. I don't want to know what that is. Ever.

Whitney: It hurts, it definitely hurts. I remember the one with Carrot Top. He got emotional because he's sort of sequestered. When you're around comics a lot, you're more used to it.

Judd: He's just with his friends in Vegas.

Whitney: All of a sudden, they're making plastic surgery jokes about his face, and I don't think anyone does that on a regular basis, so it was heartbreaking to watch. Roasts were a tricky balance for me. After a while, I was like, *This hurts too much. I can't do this anymore.*

Judd: Do you think it's different for women, the experience of opening up onstage?

Whitney: I still don't have a good answer about women in comedy and sexism. There's a comic, Kevin Christy, who I take on the road with me whenever I can. One night, someone charged the stage at me. I did some joke about—it's a generalization, obviously—how all guys have a jar of coins. It's a dumb observation. I said it, and people laughed; I guess it resonated. And one guy just snapped. He goes, "That's so we can pay for your shit!" I obviously stepped on a land mine, and Kevin said something to me later. He was like, "I think something happens with you, and I think it's probably just a female thing in general, where for men, you become their wife, their mother that didn't breast-feed." It's funny until forty-five minutes in, when they decide, *A woman is just yelling at me at this point.*

Judd: A woman who's strong and who might be wittier and smarter than me, who I don't want to make me feel bad about myself.

Whitney: Is it emasculating?

Judd: There's something about exposing yourself or being comfortable showing your flaws.

Whitney: It's triggering, showing your humanity. Being comfortable with yourself sexually or your body. How dare you not have shame? There's a tribalism when someone is not acquiescing to the norms of the tribe. There's something frustrating about a nonconformist, you know? We [humans] seek sameness on a very deep, tribal level. If that person is similar to me, they will protect me.

Judd: And people want to find a way to make certain people be quiet.

Whitney: Yes. "You're disrupting the status quo." Stop. And "I want to fuck you and I can't."

Judd: Well, that's a whole different part of the problem.

Whitney: Honestly, I was way more scared of women at the beginning than I was of men. I was such a jealous, scared person who saw a lot of cheating growing up, and I wouldn't even make eye contact with men. I just wanted the women to like me. I would talk about dating stuff, and I remember couples would get in fights in the audience. Because I'd be like, "And this guy cheated on me, and this is how he lied, and he sent this text," and I would see the girl [look at her boyfriend and] be like, "*You've* done that." I would have guys come up to me all the time and be like "What the fuck? Why did you do that?"

Judd: "Why did you give away my secret?"

Whitney: Totally! "I was just trying to take this girl on a date, and now we're fucking arguing!" It would happen all the time. Maybe it's just the areas I'm walking around in. But I think it's that when people don't have shame, it's very triggering to people who do, because shame is what keeps tribes controlled.

Judd: Amy Schumer has a funny line, where she is talking about being famous, and she understands why people turn on you a little bit when you get famous. She goes, "I have to admit, I have mixed feelings about Taylor Swift." In some way, it's as simple as that.

Whitney: Comedy is an extension of schadenfreude. *Watch me suffer for your enjoyment.* That's really what it is. Our job is to go into these areas people are uncomfortable talking about: money, race, sex. We're talking about really incendiary ideas that piss people off and [that] they have been avoiding for a reason. The worst set I've ever had was in Vegas. It was one of the scariest moments I've experienced as an adult. I go back to my hotel, and I'm about to go to sleep, when—*bang bang bang!*—on my door. Five guys yelling, "You know what you need? Some dick!"

Judd: How did they know where your room is?

Whitney: I had walked back to my room. I was with security, but they followed me back. And I was terrified. It was a tribe of drunk men telling me that, because I was successful, I needed to get fucked or humbled. So, that was a very interesting reaction. This is a huge generalization, but men, at least these men, they don't like the idea of not being needed.

Judd: Or [of] the other person being stronger.

Whitney: Or having money. Money, to me, is the newest taboo, if you want to make someone uncomfortable. If I say to you, "Hey, how many times a week do you have sex?" it's like, meh. But if I say, "How much money do you have?"

Judd: Wait, it's supposed to be "a week"?

Whitney: I have sex with my money twice a week.

Judd: Do you want to do another TV show?

Whitney: I do. I just want to do it right, if there's such a thing. I've been such a paralyzing perfectionist the last couple of years, and I have so much fear about what happened with my first show. I get that there are worse things than having your own TV show, but that trap of having your name on something and it not being good enough—it's your identity.

Judd: So, it paralyzes you about doing the next one?

Whitney: I think it did. I'm working on my next special, because stand-up doesn't hurt you like TV.

Judd: It takes so much energy to just get into the fucking business, where you're hustling and happy to do prank shows and be a host. But then, when things go well, it's so easy to get paralyzed, because now you've created some idea of what it is to be successful.

Whitney: I have an insecurity in that I want everyone to know that I'm turning stuff down, because I don't want them to think I'm not being asked. It's literally the high school playground.

Judd: You want to feel like you're still in the game and for them to *know* you're still in the game. Shandling always talked about how it's okay to not work. Like, you exist when you're not on TV, and you have to have something to say, or you shouldn't be saying it.

Whitney: "You exist when you're not on TV" is the most heartbreaking concept. We're all five, you know? My dad passed away, and I just was like, *Okay, the person whose approval I wanted is gone. Can I stop now?*

WHOOPI GOLDBERG

September 2020

Whoopi: When I think of all the things that I had planned to do in 2020, I see that they all went to hell in a handbasket.

Judd: It's a little bit like we're all having this pause to go, *What is my life? What's the value of it?*

Whoopi: That's kind of why everything is happening, isn't it? Now that people are paying attention, the little stuff that used to roll off your back now becomes a boulder. You notice things. And I think it's exciting to see people having to really stand up and take stock of where they're at. Many of my friends would call me in the early days of the Black Lives Matter protests and marches and would ask me if I thought they were privileged, and if I was resentful of them. I would usually respond by telling them, "Listen, you're a pretty decent person, but I'm not with you when you treat people poorly. You may treat me well, but if you think you've acted poorly toward other people, then you need to make a change." When my granddaughter and I had a big talk about these things, she said, "I'm so glad you're woke, Granny." I said to her, "What do you mean 'woke'? I've never been asleep. You just woke up, but when you're a kid who comes through the sixties and seventies and eighties, you fought for the vote, you fought for the right to decide what you do with your body. Those rights weren't a given. So, you had to be awake for all of it, to make sure that you weren't losing sight of the fight." When I said that to her, she said, "I never thought of it that way." And I thought, *Ah, to be in my twenties again, as opposed to my mid-sixties.*

Judd: You were born in '55. That's almost the perfect starting point to see what was achieved in each decade, and what was forgotten. Some of us are only realizing these things now, because of our privilege. I notice that when we try to hire diverse directors or writers, that the pipeline isn't even there. No one's been giving them the *smaller* break to get to the place where you can give them this *bigger* break. The pipeline hasn't been working.

Whoopi: Because there's no Rolodex for that. There's a dearth of diversity that's been everywhere for a very long time. So, you have to go person by person, incident by incident, to figure out what you need, until we get to the place where it's just people. Because, at some point, people are going to have to deal with the fact that there is no blueprint for this. If you want to fix the "OscarsSoWhite" problem, you've got to get to the casting directors, you've got to get to the people who are writing the movies. There is more to it than just, *Oh, there are no Black people.* There's a whole bunch more of us than there were, say, between the years of 1940, when Hattie McDaniel got her Oscar, to the time that Sidney Poitier got his Oscar, in 1964. That's a whole empty space of people who could have been here. It's empty of the Anna May Wongs, who *were* there acting and trying to do their thing. Meanwhile, people were painting white people up and saying, "Well, here's Mickey Rooney."

Judd: Playing an Asian man.

Whoopi: It's not that I'm mad that you're playing the Asian guy. It's not that I'm mad that you're playing the Black guy. But there *are* Black people. There *are* Asian people. They're here. So, give them a shot. Maybe you might find a couple that can act, or design clothes, or do hair, or create things, or make the space more interesting. But all of these things seem to be changing. It's slow, but I hear a shift coming. And I like it.

Judd: The first time I was around you, I was working at the Comic Relief charity event. I was probably seventeen years old. I'd heard about the event, and as a comedy fan, I just said, "Is there anything I can do to help you? I'd work for free." My job was to put together benefits at comedy clubs, but I was able to watch those rehearsals for the main shows, and part of my job was to get everybody to sign the poster for the show, so I got to walk up to every legend in the world to say, "Can you sign these fifty posters?" And I would get like eight minutes with each person, which, as a seventeen-year-old, was life-changing. When you look back at all of that, what was the Comic Relief experience like for you? How did you get involved?

Whoopi: I got a phone call from my agent, and they said, "Chris Albrecht wants to know if you want to be part of this telethon that they're doing. It's for the homeless, and it's with Billy Crystal and Robin Williams." Now, I'd known Robin for quite some time. He used to come down to San Diego, where I was living and performing years before, and worked at the Comedy Store. But I was crazy about Billy Crystal and really wanted to meet him. I said, "Whatever you want. I'm there." And, suddenly, I was among these legends, and I thought, *What the fuck am I doing here? I'm not a stand-up comedian. I tell ridiculously long stories that are funny at times. I don't fit here.* And one day, Billy sat me down and said, "I've seen your shows; you do fit here. And the three of us are going to go out, and we're going to find a way to help the homeless." And then, of course, Robin's like, "You feel Mr. Happy? He loves you, too." So, Billy and Robin became my big brothers, and from that moment on, they would call and check on me. They both talked me up to [producer] Gilbert Cates, and that's how I got to do the Academy Awards. I can't even describe how much I love them. I was a bit of an anomaly when I got there. Nobody really knew what to do with me. They were like, "You're Black, right?" And I go, "Yeah, I've been Black the whole time." Richard Pryor once said to me, "Listen, they don't get it. They're not going to get you, just know that. You look different. You don't look like you're trying to be anything but what you are. But as long as you are you, you'll be fine."

Judd: You're such a quintessential New Yorker. How did you end up in San Diego?

Whoopi: I grew up in Chelsea in New York, and we had the Hudson Guild Theater, where my mom was the theater manager. I'd go and hang out and help her and talk to these acting troupes that came through. And one of the guys says, "I'm getting ready to go home to California; my wife just had a baby. We have a four-year-old, and I'm gonna need a nanny." I had a one-year-old at the time, and I said, "I'll be the nanny." And my mother said, "What are you doing?" I said, "Well, I've always wanted to go to California. We don't have any money. So, I'm going to see what this is. And I'm taking my daughter, Alex, with me." That's how I got to San Diego, where we stayed for eight or nine years.

Judd: Did you know that you were trying to get to California to ultimately be a part of entertainment and performing? Did you have that dream?

Whoopi: I always was a performer. My mother was like, "You can do this if you want to. But you should remember that it's going to be a little harder for you, because you don't look like other people." But I always thought, *I have a different kind of thing I want to do.* So, when I got to San Diego and ended up at the San Diego Rep, I got to do lots of different things. We created a theater. I joined a troupe of people who were doing improv, which is really my joy. Years later, I met a guy who lived in San Francisco, and I thought, *What do you think, kids? Should we try San Francisco?* Later, my daughter and I are driving around San Francisco to buy shoes—she's around eight or nine—and we're listening to Alice Walker read *The Color Purple* on NPR in our van, and we pull over because we're so mesmerized by the story. So, we're sitting in the van at the Bay of Oakland, listening to her read these chapters. And because I'm a visualist, I can see everything she's reading. Afterward, I write a letter to her, via her publisher, saying, "My name is Whoopi Goldberg, and I'm a performer. And if they make a movie of your book, I will play the dirt on the floor." I give her my address in New York, which is my mother's address, and when I finally get to New York to do a monologue festival, my mother says, "Oh, a letter came for you about two weeks ago." I look at it, and the return address says "Alice Walker." I open it, and she says, basically, "Dear Whoopi, I live in Oakland. I've seen your shows. I know exactly what you do. Quincy Jones and several other people are trying to put this together to make the movie. I've already sent your paperwork. I already sent everything I know about you."

Judd: Wow.

Whoopi: Then I go to the festival, which no one had been coming to those first couple of days, and suddenly, Bette Midler is one of the twelve people in the audience. Then a couple of days later, there's forty-five people in the audience. And a couple of days later, there's a hundred people in the audience, and then a critic for *The* [*New York*] *Times* came, Mel Gussow, and if I had been his girlfriend, I could not have gotten a better review.

Judd: Were you doing a full night of monologues in San Francisco, and you brought a full night to New York? Or do you have to assemble it for New York?

Whoopi: I always had fifteen that I could choose from, because I wrote them all myself. I used each piece as an audition piece. I thought, *I'm going to just write some monologues and see if anybody knows that these aren't written by somebody else.*

Judd: When did you realize you could perform the monologues and not just audition with them? Where did you go?

Whoopi: There's a place in Berkeley, California, called the Cellar. There was also a little theater called the Rose Café in San Francisco. You could go and do shows at the Fillmore occasionally. I learned a lot of stuff because I was around a lot of dancers and a lot of performance artists. And then AIDS hit and cleaned out a whole bunch of folks, and that started a long fight to just get respect for our friends, whose roommates would sometimes kick them out and leave them in the streets in their dementia. It was a wild and scary time, because you didn't know how you got it.

Judd: Did that influence the types of monologues you were writing? It seems like, in the beginning, you're writing them just to showcase your talent. Did you become more aware of what you were trying to say and the purpose of it?

Whoopi: One of my friends at the time said, "Can you write a piece about somebody like me?" And I said, "I don't know." And he said, "But you can do anything. You're an actor. Why won't you do this?" At the same time, I had just come back from Amsterdam, where I visited the Anne Frank House. It was such a life-changing experience, I wanted to tell somebody what happened to me and how it felt. So, I thought, *Well, fuck, maybe I can just write something.* So, I wrote it through the eyes of a junkie, because I knew that life quite well. And once I wrote that, I thought, *Maybe I can do something else.* So, I wrote a piece about a girl who is physically different, but in her dreams, she thinks of herself as completely straight, and she moves onstage like a dancer. Suddenly, those two stories joined with my outrage at people who were throwing their children out because they got pregnant, which led me to write a piece about this surfer girl who gets pregnant. She goes to the church to confess, and the priest throws her out. So, she goes home to tell her mother, and her mother throws her out. So, she basically lives at the beach, and she took a hanger and did what she needed to do. But onstage, I would untwist the hanger. I made people very uncomfortable. And then she talks about the fact that she can't have children now, but she's still a great surfer. So, that became the sort of shows that I did, and that became *The Spook Show* that I did on Broadway.

Judd: It's always interesting to look at that early stage of a person's career, when you have no sense of what you should not be able to pull off. It's almost like you're delusional when you're young.

Whoopi: I got very lucky. And I continue to have the luckiest career on the planet. Because there's no way, looking like I did and sounding like I did, that anything should have gone in the direction that it did. I just am who I am.

Judd: I think of the idea of representation, that people see you up there and go, *Oh, there's a way to do this.* Mindy Kaling said she just never had the mindset that she *wouldn't* be accepted. Did you feel that way?

Whoopi: When I was in my early teens, my best friend, Rosie, and I were going to go see *Romeo and Juliet.* I was a bit of a freak back then. I had big Afro puffs and bell bottoms and was just a hippie girl. When Rosie came to get me, she looked at me and she said, "Are you gonna change?" And I was like, "No, why?" And she said, "Because you just look dirty." I said, "But I'm not dirty. Smell me. I'm clean." She said, "If you don't change your clothes, I'm not going with you," and I said, "Well, I'm not changing my clothes," so she left. And I said to my mother, "Am I wrong?" And my mother said, "Do you think you're wrong?" I said, "No, I don't think it's fair that I should change. I didn't ask her to change." And my mother said, "Well, that's a sign of independent thinking. And if you're comfortable the way you are, then you're fine. If you are not comfortable, then maybe you have to change." I said, "I'm comfortable." And she said, "Well, that's the answer to the question." And that cemented the idea that I could make decisions for myself, and sometimes they're right, and sometimes they're wrong, but they're mine.

Judd: Your mom just sounds like such an incredible person.

Whoopi: She was.

Judd: What do you think was the secret to her being such a great parent?

Whoopi: My mother thought she was a freak, too. So, she raised us like she was raised: as freaky kids.

Judd: Proudly.

Whoopi: She was different from folks in the neighborhood. Her interests were different, and she was interested in the greater experience of the world. We were raised so we should know what foreign cuisines taste like, in case we got to go to Ireland or to China. So, she fed us bok choy and things because it was inexpensive. She created stuff with nothing. And I loved what my mother did for us for Christmas. Eight days out from Christmas, we would wake up, and on our windows there were stencils of Santa's face and snowmen and all kinds of stuff. And we didn't know who did it. Every night, something would happen. The tree would show up. And then the next night, half of the tree was done. And then the night after, the other half of the tree was done. So, that took us up to Christmas Eve, and there was nothing under the tree. My brother and I would look everywhere for the presents, and there was nothing. But on Christmas morning, there would be a bicycle, there'd be a Lionel train set for me, there'd be board games like Sorry and Candy Land. My mother just made it magical.

Judd: It sounds like she worked really hard for you guys.

Whoopi: She worked her ass off, and she paid bills and did all that stuff that parents are supposed to do. And she did it with an eye to making us understand that when you're a kid, things are supposed to be magical. But when I turned twelve or thirteen, she had a nervous breakdown. She was gone for about two years, at Bellevue. Later, when I was an adult, and my mother was talking about that time, she said, "I didn't know who you kids were, and I did not want to go back. I just went along with whatever you all were telling me, and I learned about who you are." In those days, if you got put away, your husband could decide what treatments you got. So, they did all kinds of electroshock shit on her, and her thing was, "I will never go to another doctor in my life." She died when she was eighty-five and never went back to another doctor.

Judd: What was her diagnosis?

Whoopi: I don't know. I just came home from school one day, and she was crazy. But she was present enough to tell me to go get help from one of the neighbors, which I did, and the neighbor got hold of the hospital. But I'll never forget them taking her down into the elevator, the elevator stopping on different floors, people getting in the elevator and looking at us, and then watching them take her down the stairs into the ambulance. In those days, your kids couldn't go to the hospital with you. So, she went into the ambulance, and she was gone.

Judd: You didn't see her for years?

Whoopi: For about two years.

Judd: And what about your dad?

Whoopi: My dad and cousins came and took care of us so we didn't have to move. But it's very crazy when your dad comes out of the blue, and you don't really know him, and you don't know if you like him.

Judd: What did your dad do?

Whoopi: My dad was part of the Jewel Box Revue for a while. It was a group of male performers who dressed as women and would imitate people. They would get booked at bar mitzvahs and all kinds of great things. So, he did that for a while. He worked in the Diamond District for a while. He was a preacher. He was just really interesting. And I believe he was a very happy gay man.

Judd: So, he wasn't really around until that moment? Did you get closer with him after he returned?

Whoopi: He was there, but he didn't really want to be there. He knew that there wasn't a lot of choice. But you know, when I got famous, Bob, [my father,] told the *National Enquirer* that I wasn't paying enough attention to him.

Judd: That always helps.

Whoopi: Always. And then he passed away, and the *Enquirer* went down to take pictures of him in his coffin and to talk about the fact that I wasn't down there to bury my own father. My brother was. So, yeah, I have had a very interesting life.

Judd: I'm interested in Mike Nichols stepping into your life. To have this man from another generation step into your work process and somehow understand it. What did he have to tell you at that moment?

Whoopi: It will probably make more sense if I tell you how it happened. It was back when I was doing *The Spook Show,* where I do all my characters, and Mike was in town and came to see me perform. I think I started with Fontaine, who is the junkie who talks about traveling on the plane to Amsterdam and then going to the Anne Frank House. And Mike had been on the very last ship out of Germany, before the Nazis just shut everything down. So, the Anne Frank story took him and twisted him up. When I get offstage, my mother is sitting backstage, and she says, "I have to tell you something, Mike Nichols is here. He came to see the show." I said, "I can't believe it, fuck fuck fuck. Oh my God, are you sure?" And then there's a knock on the door, and it's him. He's standing right there. And his eyes are wet. He comes in and says, "I have to tell you, that story about being at the Anne Frank House just knocked me out. Do you have plans, would you consider doing Broadway?" And I said, "Yeah, okay." He said, "Are you not sure?" I said, "No, no, I'm sure, Mr. Nichols, but I don't want to suck. And then you get a bad mark because I was no good." He said, "Miss Goldberg, if you suck, I'll be there to unsuck you." So, I went back to Berkeley, and about a month later, the phone rings, and it was Mike. He said, "Do you remember when I asked you if you would be interested in doing Broadway? Well, I found a theater for us." So, we made the plan, and once I'm in New York, he goes, "Do you want to go to lunch with some friends of mine?" So, we walk into this restaurant, and as I'm walking, I'm thinking, *Is that Paul Simon? Is that Steve Martin? Oh, my God. Carl Reiner, oh my God.* I'm walking very coolly, but inside, I'm dying. And that's what he would do to me.

Judd: Was he desensitizing you to it? To get you comfortable with being part of Broadway and that pressure?

Whoopi: Yes, and what he thought was coming. Remember, I've had this amazing review from Mel Gussow, and Mike uses that as part of the advertising for the show, so we're sold out. We hadn't even started yet. And on opening night, Ruth Gordon is there. Garson Kanin and Diana Ross—all these people. I'm like, *What the fuck? What is happening here?* And they like it. They like the show. So, it was kind of spectacular.

Judd: Were you able to tune in and be present and enjoy the moment? It can be hard when you're trying to focus on the work and not melt down.

Whoopi: At the opening night party, my mother was all teeth. We were both standing there with these big smiles. And Paul Simon was at the party and came over, and he said, "I want you to enjoy everything that's coming, because Artie and I didn't know we were supposed to enjoy it. We missed a lot. Have the best time and know that people are going to try to take it from you." He said, "Do what you know you want to do and try not to smoke too much more weed."

Judd: How did you get from there to doing *The Color Purple*?

Whoopi: I met up with Steven Spielberg after the Broadway run, because he was getting ready to set up *The Color Purple*. He wanted me to bring my show to Amblin Studios, where he had a little theater, because he wasn't able to get to New York. By then, of course, I had a manager and an agent. And both of them say to me, "Look, we love your story. We love you. But when you do this thing for Steven, you cannot do Bleed T. You cannot."

Judd: Wait, what's Bleed T?

Whoopi: Bleed T is a piece that I wrote about what would happen if E.T. actually landed in the projects. And he can't find his way home because the phones don't work. He starts running the streets with Elliott, who works for a pimp. He then gets a Jheri curl—remember those? And he starts dressing like a pimp. He's got the shoes, because he's very short, and he's running chicks. Then, as his people come back to get him, he pulls out two machine guns and he machine-guns his people, because when you assimilate too much, you lose the spirit of who you are. That was the piece they didn't want me to do. So, I do the show for Spielberg, *without* that piece, and everyone is loving it. I'm looking out the curtain before I come out, and it's Michael Jackson, it's Ashford and Simpson, and Quincy Jones.

Judd: A low-pressure show.

Whoopi: Now I'm thinking, *Fuck fuck fuck*. So, I do the show. And they say, "More!" I said, "I can't really do more." And Steven says, "Why not?" I said, "Because my agent told me I shouldn't do this piece for you, because it would upset you." He said, "What is it? You can tell me." So, I tell him, and he says, "I want to see it." So, I did it, the whole piece. And as I'm doing it, I hear laughter. I'm afraid to look at anybody in the moment, of course. And then it ends where I explain that, you know, E.T. assimilated and forgot who he was and where he came from. *That* stopped the laughter. Then I went over to do my bow, and you know how you see those movies where people just stand up and start clapping? That's what it turned into. And Spielberg said, "I never would have thought that was the direction that it would go in, that you bring it all the way back around and talk about assimilation." I said, "Well, I always hear people talking about how you should learn how to speak English, you have to learn how to do this and that. I grew up in a neighborhood where the first generation never spoke English, and that helped us learn smatterings of different languages from our friends." He said, "That is a great way to learn. Would you like to do *The Color Purple*?" I was like, "Yes, I would." He said, "I want you to be Celie." I said, "I think I need something smaller, because I don't know anything about making movies." He said, "Leave that to me."

Judd: It's remarkable to get those mentors and collaborators. You had Mike Nichols for theater, which is the best you can do. And then, immediately, you work with Quincy Jones and Steven Spielberg. It's a real run of the exact right people to take you to the next level, who are at the top of their game.

Whoopi: As it turns out, years later, someone said to me, "You were such a disappointment. We all thought you would be the female Eddie Murphy." I was like, "Wait, I was the female Whoopi Goldberg." I didn't know I was supposed to try to be Eddie Murphy. But I got to do the things that I thought were fun, like *Fatal Beauty*, which was not a deep movie, but I love those movies. And I got to do *Sister Act* and *Clara's Heart* and all kinds of stuff. People kept saying, "You're always playing a housekeeper." I said, "Yeah, man. God bless those women. Most of you guys would not have a life without the fucking housekeeper." It doesn't seem degrading to me. I would meet up with directors and producers, and there was this one guy who was explaining their movie to me, and he put his hands in my hair and said, "What do we do with this shit?" I said, "You mean the shit on my head? Well, we can put it in a wig. Or we can keep it like that. How would you like this shit to be?" I thought, *I can either flip the fuck out or I can just recognize that you don't know any better.* It wasn't a good match. And then, suddenly, it was good matches. I ended up with [producer] Jerry Zucker and [director] Emile Ardolino.

Judd: It feels like show business was very different at that time, where you had megastars and big personalities. That seems to have gone away somewhat.

Whoopi: Or we've moved to the next rung, and it's not your turn anymore; it's *their* turn. So you have to keep moving. I got in trouble, too, because I was talking shit about the president. I didn't work for five years. All my endorsements disappeared.

Judd: This was in what year?

Whoopi: This was the first four years of Kid Bush, during the run-up to the second four years. I'd done a fundraiser for [John] Kerry and John Edwards, and I said, "You know, I love bush, but someone's been giving bush a bad name. And I think it's time that we keep bush where it should be and get your ass out there and vote." That was the extent of it. And people said that I had been vulgar. Like, really, disgustingly vulgar. By the time I got home, all my endorsements were gone. Everything was gone. Five years of trying to understand what the problem was, because it was a fundraiser where other people were *actually* saying some really rough shit. The DNC had the video, and all they had to do was play the video and say, "She didn't actually say anything like this." But they didn't share the video, because they wanted to protect Meryl Streep and Paul Newman. They didn't want to put them in jeopardy. So, I took that. I ended up spending everything I had saved to keep my family afloat. And then, three years later, Barbara Walters asked me if I would join *The View*, and I say, "You understand I'm persona non grata?" And she said, "Oh, yes." But then she hired Rosie O'Donnell, and then a year went by, and Rosie just imploded. And [Barbara] calls me back and is like, "Okay, really, will you come and do it?" And that's how I got to *The View*.

Judd: Does it feel good to do something like that—to become successful, in a gigantic way, for the same exact bold style that slowed you down?

Whoopi: I just desperately needed a job. Desperately, desperately needed a fucking job. You know, if they said, "You've got to go be Bozo with a red nose on your head and dance in front of the stereo store," that's where I would have been. It was a tough time. But then *The View* turned into something that was more than just a women's talk show.

Judd: Every time I go there, that set feels like it crackles with tension. It feels like there's a lot happening in that building, and even if the people change, it's still that same tension. It must be stressful to know you're going into some verbal warfare?

Whoopi: Well, the whole idea is to try to keep the verbal warfare on a scale where we can still have the conversation. We can be testy about it, but we can't be nasty. We have to be talking about the thing we're talking about and not personally zinging each other. For me, that's the thing. Sometimes people come, and they're ready to fight. It's like, I'm not fighting with you. I just want to know why you feel like that. Where did it come from? In my mind, I have to try to help people if they're feeling like they don't know why something's messed up. For instance, I once had a discussion with a woman who was upset that her pastor said, "Fuck America." She was like, "I can't believe he would say such a thing." I said, "Maybe it's because he fought in World War Two. He came home and had to get off the sidewalk to make way for white people to walk." And she said, "What are you talking about?" I said, "Well, the Black fighters who came back home to America after fighting to liberate other countries were not free to vote in their country." And she said, "I don't know anything about that." I said, "Because it doesn't have anything to do with you. That's why you don't know." So, she came back two, three days later, and she said, "I started reading about all that stuff you were talking about. I had no idea." I said, "I know. That's okay. But now you know." She and I have been friends from then on.

WILL FERRELL

April 2020

Judd: As you know, I went to the University of Southern California. I was there from 1985 to '87. Then I ran out of money and dropped out.

Will: We were there roughly at the same time.

Judd: But I went to cinema school, and you went to the University of Southern California and studied sports information—I still don't know what that means.

Will: I was going to be a sportscaster. That was the dream. But they only offered the major for five years, I think, and then they stopped doing it because it was too hard.

Judd: They got rid of the major. I remember seeing those kids at USC. You would see them walk around campus dressed up and looking like Bob Costas and Marv Albert.

Will: It'd be those kids, and then the rest of the class would be athletes. I thought I was going to be on *SportsCenter.* But when I saw that you had to start out in places like Yuma, Arizona, and you work your way through the system, I decided, *Well, I also want to try comedy, which seems equally as hard but more fun.* It was probably harder to break through, but I still thought, *I'm not going to try the broadcasting thing. I'm going to try this comedy thing.*

Judd: And you hadn't done any comedy up until then?

Will: No comedy, other than entertaining my fraternity brothers on occasion. I had gone and seen a show the spring semester of senior year at the Groundlings Theatre on Melrose, in Hollywood, which is kind of the jumping-off place for everyone from Phil Hartman to Lisa Kudrow, to Jon Lovitz, to Laraine Newman from the original *Saturday Night Live* cast, to Conan O'Brien. Tons of actors and writers have come through their school. I watched one of their shows and saw in the lobby afterward that they had a school that you could audition for, and I thought, *Oh, that looks like that would be fun.*

Judd: And how long after Groundlings did you get the job at *SNL*?

Will: From the time I took my first class until *SNL*, it was three years.

Judd: That's crazy.

Will: It's pretty quick.

Judd: Why weren't you terrified? Where did your confidence as a performer come from if you were still relatively new to this?

Will: I had the best conversation with my dad, who's a lifelong musician. He had an incredible career without "making it" and yet still was a working musician, which is so hard to do. He played with the Righteous Brothers on and off for twenty years, and he played in Vegas, and he'd had his own bands and this and that. He'd seen enough of the big time, so to speak, and we went to lunch one day, and I said to him, "I think I'm going to try this comedy thing. I think I'm going to give it a shot. Do you have any advice for me?" And his big gut talk to me was, "You know what? I think you have the skill, but it takes a lot of luck. If you don't make it, don't worry about it. You can just try something else." Like, don't worry if you fail, because it's a crapshoot anyway. And so, from that point, I was like, *Oh, I'm just playing the lottery here so I might as well just go have fun.* And at the same time, I was trying to do everything from the Groundlings to those crazy Largo shows and just any stand-up comedy that became available. I tried to throw as many darts against the dartboard as I could.

Judd: So, you weren't freaked out about not making it.

Will: I was like, *This is probably not going to happen. But I can always be a substitute school teacher.*

Judd: That took the pressure off of you, to not want it that much?

Will: Exactly. In a weird way, it made it feel like a game. But then—cut to the most nervous moment I ever had, to the point of nearly shitting my pants: the night of the first episode of *SNL* for our grand cast, and I got to say the first lines. That was the moment where I was like, *Oh, shoot. This is the thing you'd always dreamed about doing and you're about to do it. Your mom is in the audience, she's brought her friends, everyone back at your old theater is watching . . .* And the moment hit me, and, sure enough, I flubbed. The first thing I ever say on the show, I flub.

Judd: I want to talk a bit about your path to *SNL*. You had a sketch at the Groundlings, which was you yelling at a child, who we don't see, to get off the shed. You did that as your audition for Lorne, and then they put it on the first episode.

Will: Right.

Judd: So, at least you got to scream in your first sketch. That helped, I would assume.

Will: That helped. Because I was part of the cold open, and that's where I flubbed the line, and then the first sketch up was the BBQ dad yelling at his kids to get off the shed. So, I was able to really let loose. It's basically just a benign backyard barbecue, with suburban people talking about everything from their jobs to playing golf. And I just keep looking off-camera and saying, "*Hey, get off the shed. Okay? You do that for me?* Anyway, I don't know if you talked to Mr. Bilson at the office. I heard he threw his back out. *Hey, buddy. I need you to get off the shed. Please!* So, yeah, he said he was sidelined for about three weeks. *GET OFF THE SHED!*"

Judd: It's amazing that this very simple premise is what launched everything for you.

Will: I became known during the audition as the "Get Off the Shed Guy." There were two people singled out in our first show that year, Cheri Oteri and myself. And Cheri was singled out because she had a phenomenal first show. She was the breakout star. And then I was the second cast member mentioned by name because I was obnoxious and too loud.

Judd: Little did they know that America would fall in love with that.

Will: I clipped it out, and I put it in my office as a reminder that, *Oh, people already hate you.*

Judd: How do you keep the takedowns from getting to you? You don't seem like the kind of person who would read a negative comment and ruminate over it.

Will: I'm definitely not impervious to it, by any means. But especially in that case, I was like, *I'm sorry, I know that's funny. You're just wrong.*

Judd: But people always have enjoyed you losing your composure. Is that something that you understood as being funny about you, even in high school?

Will: I think it was the way I made my friends laugh. We'd go out into public looking like the normal guy next door. I would behave oddly and do strange things and get the best reaction. I knew it was cracking them up, and that registered with me as something I could go to. I don't know why it was fun to get that reaction from people that way, but it was.

Judd: There's a genre of Will Ferrell comedy that's the weird stuff. Right? Some of it is less weird. How do you divide, in your own mind, the type of comedy that really amuses you?

Will: I think, especially as it pertains to *Saturday Night Live*, that there were sketches that were classified as a ten-to-one sketch, which meant that at ten minutes to one o'clock, it's basically the last sketch of the night. The weirder stuff was usually saved until the end of the show, and I always relished trying to write those ten-to-one sketches. As much fun as I had doing the Spartan cheerleaders and the poppier things, I've always had weird thoughts pop into my head. Even just the notion of driving along and listening to "(Don't Fear) The Reaper," by Blue Oyster Cult and hearing a faint sound of a cowbell. I don't know how I had that idea. I remember, the first time I heard that song, for some reason I focused on the cowbell, and I immediately thought, *What's that guy's life like? Does he ever get to hang out?* The sad weirdo who's trying to be a part of the group really appeals to me.

Judd: [Your] James Lipton [imitation] was one I find endlessly hilarious.

Will: What's crazy about James Lipton is I'd been watching *Inside the Actors Studio*, and I was a fan of the show. I was thinking this would be a fun character to play, but I hadn't written anything as of yet, and we were rehearsing, and one of the NBC pages at the show said, "Bill Murray's on the phone for you." So, I ran to the page desk, which is right outside Studio 8H, and it's really Bill Murray. And he goes, "Hey, how ya doing?" I was like, "Uh, good. How are you, Bill?" I think we'd only talked two other times prior to that, and he was like, "You know who you should play? That host of *Inside the Actors Stu-*

dio. You should play James Lipton." I go, "That's so weird to say. I was literally thinking that myself," and he's like, "Yeah right. Take it easy." *Click.* So, I was like, *Oh, I have to write the sketch because Bill Murray told me I've got to write it.* And that led to this funny relationship with James Lipton.

Judd: It's got to be a strange experience, to create this demented interpretation of someone and then actually meet that person. Who else did you meet that you had impersonated, that you then had to deal with face-to-face?

Will: Well, that would be President Bush. I actually met him. But this is when he was still governor. It was during his presidential campaign, and he was at the show. They'd gotten both Al Gore and him to pretape an opening piece for a political sketch package show, where we showed all the political sketches over the years. And they called me and said, "Governor Bush is a huge fan. He'd love to meet you." I walk in the studio, and it's massive press, like a hundred photographers and everything. No one from *Saturday Night Live* is making the introduction. Someone just pushes me and goes, "Go in there. Say hi." And I walked in, and I startled him, and I think I literally had a weird beard on, from another sketch we were rehearsing, and I can tell he doesn't know. It was just awkward.

Judd: Then you did the Broadway show that you wrote, and you were George Bush for months.

Will: I really enjoyed getting a second chance to live in the character, doing eight shows a week, even though that's one of the scariest things I've ever done. It was an amazing experience to get to do a satirical commentary on his presidency. And our opening night of previews was Inauguration Day, so it was still visceral for the New York crowd, in terms of their reaction to what I would say. There were moments when they would just yell things out at me, because they wanted to have a conversation with him. And I would end up improvising with the audience, which sometimes didn't really go anywhere, and other times it was kind of amazing. Overall, it was fun to hear his thoughts and have him wax poetic about the fictitious upbringing I wrote for him. We wove in the real facts with some made-up stuff. And every night, I would stand backstage going, *Why did I agree to do this?* It was terrifying. But by the end of the night, I was so happy. I would be like, *Oh, it's so much fun.*

Judd: Did politicians or celebrities come to see the show and say hi afterward?

Will: A few. It was a cross section there. We would always end the last chunk of the show with an improvised moment. Bush was famous for giving nicknames to everyone, so we'd bring the house lights up, and I would say, "Okay, raise your hand and tell me what you do, your name, your profession . . . I'll give you a nickname." So, I'd go through the entire crowd and give names, and I would look out into the house, and it was just amazing. Once, I saw a guy sitting there and [I] was like, *God, do I call on that guy? He looks exactly like Sting in a fisherman's sweater with a beard. I don't know if it's him, I'll skip over it.* And sure enough, that was Sting. It was always surreal, the whole thing.

Judd: When you look back at your time at *SNL*, what are the first things that pop into your head that make you thrilled that they happened?

Will: It's hard to sum it all up, because there are so many of those moments. I just remember thinking to myself, *This will be the hardest and yet most fun job you'll ever have.* Because you basically live there, and these dumb little ideas you may have on a Tuesday actually have a chance to be on national television by Saturday. I was always amazed at the fact that it's a live show, where you have a hundred people running around, changing sets and wardrobe. It never grew old to me.

Judd: *Anchorman* was the first movie that you wrote, and for a lot of your movies, you seem to be playing, let's say, ignorant people who think they're smart. What is it about a Ron Burgundy type that attracts you?

Will: I've always been fascinated by the cocky American as a character. Growing up at the height of the 1980 Olympics and the Miracle on Ice—"USA's Number One!"—I was the kid who asked, "Wait, *are* we number one?" It's always been fascinating to knock those people down a peg just because we can do it. It's what's great about this country at the same time.

ACKNOWLEDGMENTS

I'd like to thank Keith Staskiewicz, Howie E. Kremer, Deena Rosenblatt, and Wayne Federman for their invaluable work putting this collection together. In addition, the team at Random House: Andy Ward, Marie Pantojan, Kelly Chian, Tom Perry, Karen Fink, Maria Braeckel, Ayelet Durantt, Barbara Fillon, and Paolo Pepe.

Mark Flanagan and everyone at Largo, the Comedy Cellar, the Improv, and the Comedy Store for all your support.

I'd also like to thank my representative, Jimmy Miller (since Comic Relief '87), David Kramer, Bryan Wolf, Sam Fischer, Andrew Wylie, and Dave Eggers, who is always an inspiration.

ABOUT THE AUTHOR

Judd Apatow is one of the most sought-after comedic minds in the industry—having directed, produced, and written many of the biggest comedy films and hit TV shows of the last two decades. Apatow's most recent films include the Netflix comedy *The Bubble*, which he directed, produced, and co-wrote; the two-part George Carlin documentary for HBO, which he co-directed and produced; and Universal's romantic comedy *Bros*, which he produced. Off-screen, Apatow gathered journal entries, photographs, and essays for an intimate portrait of Garry Shandling to create *It's Garry Shandling's Book*, a testament to the lasting impact Shandling had on Apatow personally and on the world. Published in 2019, the book expands on Apatow's Emmy Award–winning HBO documentary *The Zen Diaries of Garry Shandling*. Apatow also authored the *New York Times* bestseller *Sick in the Head* and edited the collection *I Found This Funny*. Previous director credits include *The 40-Year-Old Virgin*, *Knocked Up*, *Funny People*, *This Is 40*, *Trainwreck*, *May It Last: A Portrait of the Avett Brothers* (co-directed with Mike Bonfiglio), and *The King of Staten Island*. He produced the Academy Award–nominated *The Big Sick* and *Bridesmaids*, as well as *Superbad*, *Pineapple Express*, *Anchorman*, *Step Brothers*, *Talladega Nights*, *Forgetting Sarah Marshall*, and *Popstar*. For television, he executive produced *Crashing* (HBO), *Girls*, *Freaks and Geeks*, and *Undeclared*, and co-created *The Ben Stiller Show* and *Love* (Netflix). His Netflix comedy special, *Judd Apatow: The Return*, marked his comeback to the stage after a twenty-five-year hiatus.

Twitter: @JuddApatow
Instagram: @JuddApatow

Author's net proceeds are being donated to 826 National—a nonprofit organization dedicated to supporting students ages 6 to 18 with their writing skills by providing free tutoring and literacy programs. For more information, go to 826national.org.

ABOUT THE TYPE

This book was set in Electra, a typeface designed for Linotype by W. A. Dwiggins, the renowned type designer (1880–1956). Electra is a fluid typeface, avoiding the contrasts of thick and thin strokes that are prevalent in most modern typefaces.